Register Now for Online Access to Your Book!

SPRINGER PUBLISHING COMPANY
CONNECT™

D1592896

Your print purchase of *Counseling Women Across the Life Span,* **includes online access to the contents of your book**—increasing accessibility, portability, and searchability!

Access today at:

**http://connect.springerpub.com/content/book/978-0-8261-2917-8
or scan the QR code at the right with your smartphone
and enter the access code below.**

0GD26MWV

*Scan here for
quick access.*

LS

SPRINGER PUBLISHING COMPANY

View all our products at springerpub.com

Praise for This Edition

Jill Schwarz's book, *Counseling Women Across the Life Span: Empowerment, Advocacy, and Intervention,* will be an excellent addition to any gender library, or a course in gender. It is a solid and innovative text.—**Catherine B. Roland, EdD, LPC, NCC,** President, American Counseling Association (2016–2017)

Counseling Women Across the Life Span: Empowerment, Advocacy, and Intervention is very timely and fills a much-needed gap in the literature. One of the unique features of this book is that it is multidisciplinary and can be useful to anyone studying gender in the social sciences, as well as practical applications for counselors. This book can also stand alone as a self-help empowerment book for women and male allies to empower women of all ages. I applaud Dr. Schwarz for the organization and scaffolding to provide a distinct lens that is sure to advocate for all women!—**Kara P. Ieva, PhD, NCC, NCSC,** Rowan University

As a clinical social worker who has worked many years in outpatient mental health and most extensively in the field of violence against women, I am pleased to share my reaction to *Counseling Women Across the Life Span.* Many excellent publications contain modalities, strategies, and techniques in counseling theory. What this book does very effectively is to juxtapose counseling theory with the socialization and power imbalance inherent in the lives of women and girls in our society. Of important note is the final chapter that discusses our male allies. Dispelling the myth that men are the enemies of feminist theory is critical in bringing theorists and clinicians together in this work that is so important and has such potential to impact sustaining change. I found *Counseling Women Across the Life Span* to be a very well developed and organized book that can provide an important tool for all of us who work with women and girls in our practice and understand how important it is to consider every nuance that impacts our clients' lives.—**Patricia M. Hart, MSW, LCSW,** Executive Director of Womanspace, Inc.

Counseling Women Across the Life Span is an ideal text for any course in counseling girls and women. It fully examines the societal, environmental, and developmental factors impacting girls and women during each stage of life and offers concrete and effective counseling strategies and resources. Instructors and students alike will value this text due to its readability, connection to the latest research in the field, suggestions for personal reflection and advocacy, and thorough coverage of many effective counseling interventions.—**Marion Cavallaro, PhD, LPC,** The College of New Jersey

This book provides a comprehensive understanding of women's development and explains how to apply a positive, feminist empowerment model to address the major issues and challenges women experience across the life span. It will be well suited for use as a textbook in courses in Women's and Gender Studies and specialized courses on counseling women. I am confident that it will also [appeal] to a wide audience of practitioners from the mental health professions who work with girls and women.—**Mark S. Kiselica, PhD, HSPP, NCC, LPC,** Dean of the School of Humanities and Social Sciences, Cabrini University; Past-President, Division 51 of the APA

Dr. Schwarz and contributors provide a comprehensive picture of key issues experienced by girls and women across ages and cultures. This is an easy-to-read book, full of case examples and practical suggestions based on current research as well as the authors' clinical and teaching experiences. The focus on empowerment, prevention, and intervention strategies along with the inclusion of real-life experiences related to each chapter's topics, reflection and discussion questions, and practical suggestions for ways in which readers can engage in advocacy efforts to create social change makes this book an invaluable resource for students and seasoned professionals alike.—**Harriet L. Glosoff, PhD,** American Counseling Association Fellow, Professor, Counseling Program, Montclair State University

Jill E. Schwarz, PhD, NCC, has been teaching at the collegiate level for over a decade. Currently, she is a core faculty member at The College of New Jersey (TCNJ) in the CACREP-accredited Counseling Master's Degree Program and teaches students in the School; Clinical Mental Health; and Marriage, Couple, and Family Counseling and Therapy tracks. Dr. Schwarz also teaches internationally for off-site graduate programs and has worked with graduate students in Portugal, Mallorca, Taiwan, and Thailand. She developed and has taught a Counseling Women and Girls course for the past decade and serves as a research consultant for a counseling agency that provides services to survivors of sexual assault and domestic violence.

In addition to being a National Certified Counselor (NCC), Dr. Schwarz is certified as a school counselor, director of school counseling services, and elementary educator in New Jersey. She has extensive experience as a professional school counselor, during which time she established and implemented an adolescent girls' empowerment and leadership program. Dr. Schwarz regularly serves as an invited presenter and has provided numerous professional development workshops and presentations related to counseling women and girls. Her scholarly pursuits include publications, as well as international, national, and regional presentations, focused on counselor preparation and practice as well as spirituality and gender issues in counseling.

Counseling Women Across the Life Span

Empowerment, Advocacy, and Intervention

Jill E. Schwarz, PhD, NCC

Editor

SPRINGER PUBLISHING COMPANY

NEW YORK

Springer Publishing Company, LLC
11 West 42nd Street
New York, NY 10036
www.springerpub.com

Acquisitions Editor: Sheri W. Sussman
Compositor: Westchester Publishing Services

ISBN: 9780826129161
e-book ISBN: 9780826129178

Instructors' Materials: Qualified instructors may request supplements by e-mailing textbook@springerpub.com
Sample Course Calendar and Syllabus ISBN: 9780826129659

17 18 19 20 21 / 5 4 3 2 1

The author and the publisher of this Work have made every effort to use sources believed to be reliable to provide information that is accurate and compatible with the standards generally accepted at the time of publication. The author and publisher shall not be liable for any special, consequential, or exemplary damages resulting, in whole or in part, from the readers' use of, or reliance on, the information contained in this book. The publisher has no responsibility for the persistence or accuracy of URLs for external or third-party Internet websites referred to in this publication and does not guarantee that any content on such websites is, or will remain, accurate or appropriate.

Library of Congress Cataloging-in-Publication Data

Names: Schwarz, Jill E., editor.
Title: Counseling women across the life span : empowerment, advocacy, and intervention / [edited by] Jill E. Schwarz, PhD, NCC.
Description: New York : Springer Publishing Company, LLC, [2017] | Includes index.
Identifiers: LCCN 2016055479 (print) | LCCN 2017001956 (ebook) | ISBN 9780826129161 (hard copy : alk. paper) | ISBN 9780826129178 (ebook)
Subjects: LCSH: Women—Counseling of. | Women—Psychology. | Teenage girls—Counseling of.
Classification: LCC HQ1206 .C7238 2017 (print) | LCC HQ1206 (ebook) | DDC 305.42—dc23
LC record available at https://lccn.loc.gov/2016055479

Contact us to receive discount rates on bulk purchases.
We can also customize our books to meet your needs.
For more information please contact: sales@springerpub.com

Printed in the United States of America by Gasch Printing.

Contents

Contributors

Eva Barnewitz, MSc   Konstanz, Germany

Suzanne Degges-White, PhD   Professor and Chair, Counseling, Adult and Higher Education, Northern Illinois University, DeKalb, Illinois

Megan E. Delaney, PhD, LAC   Assistant Professor, Monmouth University, West Long Branch, New Jersey

Connie S. Ducaine, MA, LPC, LCADC, ACS, BCPC, NCC   Director, Clinical Account Management, Vital Decisions, Edison, New Jersey

Cheryl L. Fulton, PhD, MBA, LPC   Assistant Professor, Texas State University, San Marcos, Texas

Christopher Kilmartin, PhD   Professor Emeritus of Psychological Science, University of Mary Washington, Fredericksburg, Virginia

Dana Heller Levitt, PhD, LAC, NCC   Professor of Counseling and Educational Leadership, Montclair State University, Montclair, New Jersey

Lucy Charlene Parker, MA, NCC   Northern Illinois University, DeKalb, Illinois

Alyson M. Pompeo-Fargnoli, PhD, LPC, SAC, NCC   Assistant Professor, School of Education, Monmouth University, West Long Branch, New Jersey

Jennifer E. Randall, MA   Adjunct Instructor, West Virginia University, Bridgeport, West Virginia

Christine J. Schimmel, EdD, NCC, LPC   Associate Professor, West Virginia University, Morgantown, West Virginia

Jill E. Schwarz, PhD, NCC   Assistant Professor, The College of New Jersey, Ewing, New Jersey

Atsuko Seto, PhD, LPC, NCC, ACS   Associate Professor, The College of New Jersey, Ewing, New Jersey

Sarah I. Springer, PhD, LPC, ACS   Assistant Professor, Monmouth University, West Long Branch, New Jersey

Rebecca Vazquez, MA, LAC, NCC Doctoral Candidate, Regent University, Vineland, New Jersey

Alina S. Wong, PhD Associate Dean for Student Life, Barnard College, New York, New York

Amy D. Zavadil Associate Dean for Equity, Title IX Coordinator, Barnard College, New York, New York

Preface

Although it is challenging to capture the entirety of the female experience in a single book, this text incorporates an inclusive representation of women and girls across ages and cultures by examining the intersection of their identities and integrating experiences of women and girls around the world. The overarching themes of this book include an examination of the contextual elements that affect the female experience and a focus on prevention and intervention strategies to support the empowerment of women and girls throughout their life spans. The primary objectives are for readers to gain an enhanced understanding of the socialization and environmental factors that affect female experiences, to obtain greater utility in advocating for equality for women and girls through preventive efforts, and to implement empowering intervention strategies when counseling girls and women of all ages. Instead of pathologizing females as they survive and thrive through challenging life circumstances, this book will help readers in conceptualizing the issues females face through the context of the oppressive structures within which they live. The text integrates information, resources, and concrete strategies necessary for counselors to understand issues within the societal context, develop as advocates, and intervene as agents of social change.

The book was developed with the input of many students, professors, and practitioners and was also informed by my years of experience teaching about and counseling women and girls. It is designed to raise awareness, increase knowledge, emphasize prevention, and offer practical suggestions in a thought-provoking and digestible format. The three sections of the book provide readers with a framework of focus and also help instructors structure their courses. The first section provides a foundation for the book and offers a context for understanding gender socialization and the female experience. This section includes chapters introducing empowerment feminist therapy, gender socialization, intersectionality, and relational-cultural theory. The second section offers detailed information on developmental issues and counseling interventions for women and girls throughout their life spans. Chapters focusing on gender identity development, childhood, adolescence and young adulthood, and middle and older adulthood are included in this section. The third section provides an in-depth look at specific issues affecting women and girls and includes relevant background information and practical application for counselors. In this concluding section, readers will learn about violence against women and girls, educational and work environments, females and their bodies, and engaging men as allies.

A sample course calendar and syllabus are available to instructors to aid in course development. **Qualified instructors can request this ancillary by e-mail: textbook@springerpub.com**.

KEY FEATURES OF THE CHAPTERS

Worell (2001) identified five levels of feminist intervention: prevention, education, remediation, empowerment, and community change. These themes are integrated throughout this text. Each chapter includes helpful resources to further educate yourself and others, as well as practical suggestions for advocacy efforts that can help create social change. Prevention and empowerment are key themes and foci of the text, and counseling implications and interventions are offered for each area of concentration.

Each chapter of this textbook includes several key features designed to guide your learning, make the material more relatable, and enhance your reflection and practice. At the beginning of each chapter you will find **Learning Objectives**, which are designed to provide context for your reading and to highlight key concepts that are the focus of the chapter. Throughout the chapters you will also find quotations—voices from the frontlines—that are actual words from girls and women (and, in some cases, men) describing their perspectives and experiences related to the content of the chapter. As you consider these "real life" voices, the relevance of material in the chapter should become even more evident.

Advocacy is an important part of the role of counselors and other mental health professionals. Consequently, in addition to suggestions for practical application for counseling practice, each chapter contains a **Call to Action** section that focuses specifically on guidance regarding advocacy efforts recommended for the area(s) addressed. We know that self-reflection and critical dialogue are crucial in our personal and professional development as counselors. Consequently, each chapter includes **Reflection and Discussion Questions** designed to personalize your learning, help you engage critically with the material, and assist in connecting you in discussion with your classmates and colleagues. Finally, at the end of each chapter, **Helpful Resources** are also offered to assist in these learning and advocacy endeavors. The books, documentaries, websites, organizations, and other sources listed in this section serve as a supplement to the scholarly resources provided in the References section and offer multiple avenues through which students and counselors can gain more information. Many of the resources will also be helpful to share with clients, students, and families.

REFERENCE

Worell, J. (2001). Feminist interventions: Accountability beyond symptom reduction. *Psychology of Women Quarterly, 25*(4), 335–343. doi:10.1111/1471-6402.00033

Acknowledgments

I would like to acknowledge all of the women and girls who have supported me in my journey and have honored me by inviting me to be a part of their journeys as well. The hundreds of students I have taught and counseled over the years, especially my middle school girls' group members and the graduate students in my Counseling Women and Girls classes, are my inspiration for this work. I would especially like to recognize my graduate student readers who shared their perspectives and feedback throughout the development of this text: Joanna Kessling, Carolynne Lewis-Arevalo, Anna Nase, Nicole Ottmer, Margaret Plantes, and Kellie Sutterlin.

CHAPTER 1

Counseling Women and Girls: Introduction to Empowerment Feminist Therapy

Jill E. Schwarz

LEARNING OBJECTIVES

After reading this chapter, you will be able to:

1. Understand the need for a specific focus on counseling women and girls.
2. Identify systemic influences that affect the well-being and experiences of females.
3. Articulate the fundamental tenets of empowerment feminist therapy (EFT).
4. Apply feminist techniques when counseling women and girls.

Why counseling women and girls? Why not just counseling people? Why the need for a specific focus on this half of the population? There are many answers to these questions, beginning with the reality that, although males and females inhabit the same world, they have markedly different experiences in it. As a global society, we are invested in gender. One of the first questions expectant parents are asked is, "What are you having?" Some jokingly say, "a baby," but we all know what the question implies: "Is it a girl or a boy?" The question I pose for you to consider is, "Why do we ask this question so universally and consistently?" A potential answer is so that we know how to behave toward and treat babies based on their gender, even before they are born (Brown, 2010; Crawford & Unger, 2004). Gender-appropriate colors, clothes, toys, and even words are chosen based on this one socially constructed category of identity. As Brown (2010) explains:

> Assignment to gendered behavioral categories based on sex occurs at such an early stage in life that by the time people attain the capacity for language and self-consciousness, gendered constructions are already so deeply embedded that they are phenomenologically experienced as hard-wired, linked biologically to sex. (p. 53)

Sex is biological and explains some physical and reproductive differences between human beings, but cannot solely explain almost any other characteristic (Worell & Remer, 2003). On the other hand, gender is a social or cultural construct regarding what it means to be male or female and greatly influences how one is treated in the world. You will read more about gender socialization in Chapter 2.

Gender and gender differences are not inherently problematic; however, issues arise when they become markers for which individuals are esteemed or devalued. In the vast majority of cultures around the world, males and masculine-typed characteristics are valued and associated with power (Brown, 2010). The preference for males becomes alarmingly apparent when considering the following statistic: "60 million girls are 'missing' due to selective abortion of female fetuses and the mistreatment and neglect of female children" ("Half the Sky Movement," n.d.). We are often inundated with statistics, and sometimes it is easier to gloss over them than to truly consider what they represent. I urge you, as you read through the statistics and research in the following pages and chapters, to challenge yourself to pause and picture just one human being (e.g., in the previous statistic, one of the 60 million girls) who has experienced or is experiencing what you are reading.

OVERVIEW OF ISSUES AFFECTING WOMEN AND GIRLS

In modern-day society, there are questions as to whether females are a group that continue to experience oppression. Although there have been positive changes, there is still vast inequality for females in the United States and around the world. Violence against women and girls, inequity in pay, unequal access to education, and overrepresentation of men in positions of power are just some examples of the disparities that exist (Crawford & Unger, 2004). Evans, Kincade, and Seem (2011) explain that the "oppression of women/girls transcends culture" (p. 91) and offer the following examples of how females experience oppression in the United States alone: large numbers of women and girls experiencing sexual assault and harassment; lower wages in predominantly female fields (e.g., teaching or nursing); disproportionally fewer females in positions of political and business leadership; more responsibility in the home even if both partners work; and bias in education and mental health toward women. Despite some advancements, sexism is still evident in almost every aspect of society today (Bruns, 2011). In fact, just being female makes one more vulnerable to violence, poverty, and violations of one's human rights (Chant, 2016).

"Many of the oppressors and prejudices women face daily had slipped under my radar because of how subtly they are ingrained into our society. Despite the fact that I myself am a woman, I had never before been prompted to critically think about these obstacles or the confusing messages we are sent from a very young age about how to look, act, or even think. Now that I've become more aware of these factors, I feel I will be more effective in helping arm the women I meet as a counselor with the information they need to identify these sources of negativity, remain resilient when faced with them, and ultimately support them in feeling empowered enough to advocate for the changes needed to improve the lives of all women."—A 23-year-old female counseling student

Females' Physical and Mental Well-Being

Violence against women is a serious public health issue in every country in the world. According to the World Health Organization (WHO, 2013), more than one third of the world's women are victims of sexual or physical assault. Over 120 million girls worldwide have been subjected to forced sexual acts, and one third of adolescent females aged 15 to 19 years have experienced some form of physical, emotional, or sexual violence (UNICEF, 2014). Many of these assaults come at the hand of an intimate partner, or someone known to the victim, and can lead to mental and physical health issues including death, depression, substance use, and unwanted pregnancies. More than 100 countries around the world have no legal provisions specifically prohibiting domestic violence (DV), and in over 50 countries, marital rape is allowed ("Half the Sky Movement," n.d.). The prevalence and continuation of these practices, along with accepted power differentials between genders and pervasive messages about women's worth, often lead to internalized oppression. This is exemplified in females' beliefs about their value and what they think they deserve. UNICEF's (2014) study of 190 countries revealed that half of adolescent girls worldwide think that a male partner is sometimes justified in physically assaulting his wife.

Violence against women and girls takes many forms, some of which are accepted cultural practices that have severe negative repercussions for females' physical and psychological well-being. Child marriage and female genital mutilation are two of these cultural practices. According to the International Center for Research on Women (2015), in the developing world, one in three girls is married before the age of 18 years and one in nine is married before the age of 15 years. Oftentimes, girls as young as 7 or 8 years are forced to marry much older adult men. In addition to psychological and educational repercussions, girls married as children are more likely to contract HIV and to experience DV, sexual abuse, trauma, and teenage pregnancy. Worldwide, pregnancy is one of the leading causes of death among girls aged 15 to 19 years (International Center for Research on Women, 2015). There are also adverse physical, psychological, and sexual implications for more than 100 million girls and women who undergo female genital mutilation (Feldman-Jacobs & Clifton, 2014). Despite the human rights violations that a plethora of females experience around the world, less than 1% of U.S. foreign aid is specifically allocated for women and girls ("Half the Sky Movement," n.d.).

Women who immigrate are at particular risk for sexual assault and violence and describe their experiences of immigration to the United States in distinctly gendered terms (Yakushko & Morgan-Consoli, 2014). Oftentimes for immigrant women, the power differential in their partnerships is heightened as their husbands may "hold the right to request their wives' legal status" (Díaz-Lázaro, Verdinelli, & Cohen, 2012, p. 88). Chapter 9 offers a continued, focused discussion on violence against women and implications for mental health professionals regarding prevention and treatment.

Due in part to trauma, oppression, and gender-role expectations, women and adolescent girls experience the highest rates of anxiety, depression, and posttraumatic stress disorder (PTSD; WHO, 2016). In fact, women experience depression at approximately twice the rate of men and are the largest single group of people impacted by PTSD (Mental Health America, n.d.). According to the WHO (2016), "Gender-specific risk factors for common mental disorders that disproportionately affect women include gender based violence, socioeconomic disadvantage, low income and income inequality, low or subordinate social status and rank, and unremitting responsibility for the care of others." In addition to the violence described in the previous section, women also experience these other risk factors at overwhelmingly disproportionate rates.

Socioeconomic, Educational, and Leadership Disparities

In regard to socioeconomic disadvantage and income inequality, females represent more than 70% of people living in poverty and make less than 10% of the world's wages, despite working more than two thirds of the world's working hours ("Half the Sky Movement," n.d.). In the United States, women who work full-time still make only 78 cents to every dollar men are paid, which has lifelong implications for earning power (Whitehouse.gov, 2016). Unequal division of labor in the home also affects women's career and economic advancement (Croft, Schmader, Block, & Baron, 2014). This is sometimes referred to as the "second shift" and not only impacts adult women, but also children in the house who are observing. Parents' beliefs and behaviors around domestic gender roles influence their daughters' own beliefs and career aspirations (Croft et al., 2014).

Education contributes to the economic, physical, and psychological well-being of women and their families and communities, yet girls around the world continue to have restricted access to education. UNESCO's "2015 EFA Gender Report" revealed that girls who are poor face the greatest challenges in accessing even primary education, and that women account for two thirds of adults who are illiterate. These statistics have remained virtually unchanged in the past 15 years. In the United States, girls are underrepresented in science, technology, mathematics, and engineering fields of study and careers (National Research Council, 2012).

Despite the fact that communities benefit from women in leadership, there is an overwhelming lack of women as political leaders around the world. In fact, more than 90% of countries are led by a male head of state (UN Women, 2016). As of the writing of this text in 2016, there has never been a female president in the United States. In some countries, women are not even afforded the right to vote or participate in the political process. The lack of women in positions of power and leadership has implications for many of the issues discussed in this chapter and book. As purported by the WHO (n.d.), "gains in gender development that improve women's status are likely to bring with them improvements in women's mental health." These issues are integrated and need to be considered as intersecting parts of a whole in order for systemic change to occur.

Mental Health Treatment

As highlighted earlier, systemic inequities are pervasive and impact all people and societal structures, including the mental health field. Research has found that diagnostic criteria in the *Diagnostic and Statistical Manual of Mental Disorders (DSM)*, which is widely used by mental health professionals, may be biased against women (as well as being classist and heterosexist), leading to overdiagnosis for women and those in other oppressed groups (Evans et al., 2011). Women are, in fact, diagnosed with mental illness at higher rates than men and are prescribed a disproportionate amount of psychoactive drugs (Worell & Remer, 2003). Furthermore, women of color and lesbian women experience multiple levels of discrimination and bias in society and in mental health treatment (Holley, Tavassoli, & Stromwall, 2016).

Traditional or mainstream theories in psychiatry, psychology, and counseling have "ignored or trivialized important social, economic, and structural influences on people and retreated to theories that once again focus on individual development of disorders brought about through biological, neurological, and genetic factors, or problems with thoughts and behaviors" (Ballou, Hill, & West, 2008, p. xxi). The mental health field has a history of sexism. Conformity to conventional gender roles was viewed as optimal for mental health; however, male traits were viewed as "normal" and stereotypical feminine traits as deficient (Worell & Remer, 2003). Research revealed that practicing mental health professionals viewed "mentally healthy adult males" and "mentally healthy adults" as the same, both with socially desirable traits; whereas "mentally healthy adult women" were viewed as significantly different from both of these, rendering it virtually impossible to be both a "mentally healthy adult" and a "mentally healthy woman" (Broverman, Broverman, Clarkson, Rosenkrantz, & Vogel, 1970). Characteristics typically associated with women (e.g., nurturance) were viewed as less congruent with a "healthy adult" than traits typically associated with males (e.g., dominance). If women conformed to gender roles, they were often categorized as mentally ill, and if they resisted, they were pathologized (Worell, 2001). In response to societal inequities, feminism was developed to shine light on oppressive systems and create social change. Out of the feminist movement, and in response to the biases inherent in mental health treatment, feminist therapy came into existence.

RESPONSE TO INEQUITIES

Feminism

Sometimes progress or women's accomplishments are used as rationale for why there is no longer a need for feminism or a focus on gender equality (Walker,

2016). However, the entrenched power structures that disadvantage women are still in place, and now may operate even more covertly since there is denial of sexism and perpetuation of the idea that "we are beyond that." As Mary Pipher so aptly explained in her groundbreaking book, *Reviving Ophelia: Saving the Selves of Adolescent Girls*, "The lip service paid to equality makes the reality of discrimination even more confusing" (Pipher, 1995, p. 14). If girls are taught that sexism and oppression no longer exist, while simultaneously experiencing the previously mentioned inequities, then they are likely to internalize what is happening to them and devalue themselves and other women. Internalized oppression and "horizontal hostility" may manifest in relational aggression and distrust of and separation from other women, whereas feminist practice and principles can help reframe problematic relations between women and increase strong connections of women helping women (Brown, 2013). Women's relational connections are explored more in Chapter 4.

Feminism is defined as "the theory of the political, economic, and social equality of the sexes," or more simply, "the belief that men and women should have equal rights and opportunities" ("Feminism," n.d.). When presented with the statements included in this definition, most people would say that they agree; however, feminism is encumbered with a plethora of negative connotations. This is likely backlash to challenging the status quo and highlighting the power imbalances in society (Crawford & Unger, 2004; Pipher, 1995). The suffragettes experienced similar disparaging treatment when fighting for the right for women to vote.

One of the biggest misconceptions is that feminism is synonymous with man hating. In reality, feminists seek equality and freedom of individual expression for women *and men*, who are also limited and harmed by constricting gender roles and toxic masculinity. As Jackson Katz, author, educator, and antisexist advocate, explains in his *Ted Talk* (listed in the Helpful Resources section at the end of the chapter), gender is often synonymous with "female," with gender issues perceived as "women's issues." Women are then often the ones who are shouldered with the bulk of the responsibility for "fixing" or changing these societal issues, and men become increasingly distant, absent, or alienated from participation in change (Chant, 2016). In reality, these are humanity's issues and more specifically, "men's issues," as males are often the perpetrators or empowered bystanders with societal influence to enact change. Engaging men as allies is the focus of Chapter 12.

"While I always have considered myself a feminist, I learned the very important 'why' I am such. Using a feminist lens to understand my personal and professional experiences has enriched my life and enlivened my desire to be a better counselor. I encourage all women in clinical practice to engage feminist theory and practice. It will make a world of difference!"—A 60+ aged counseling graduate student

Feminist Therapy

Historical Foundation

Women faced similar bias, stereotyping, and invalidation in counseling and diagnosis that they did in society (Brown, 2010; Worell & Remer, 2003). Feminist therapy arose in part from the challenging of these harmful inequities and biased practice. Its roots are in the women's movements of the late 1800s and the 1960s (Crawford & Unger, 2004; Herlihy & Corey, 2013). First-wave feminism in the late 1800s included the Seneca Falls Declaration of 1848, which disputed the teaching that females were inferior to males. At the time, women were treated with "rest cures" where they were isolated and confined to a bed if they were diagnosed with a "nervous disorder" or some other mental health issue attributed to "defying their feminine nature" (Crawford & Unger, 2004).

Feminism reemerged with a second wave in the 1960s when gender disparities became a more widespread social concern and the field of psychology started to examine biases in mental health treatment as well (Crawford & Unger, 2004). Consciousness-raising groups provided space for women to gather together and discuss their shared experiences with misogyny, patriarchy, and sexism. In these spaces their voices were valued, rather than dismissed (Brown, 2010). Mental health professionals connected in these groups, gathered at conferences, and began to take steps toward making changes in the field. In August 1969, there was a feminist takeover of the American Psychological Association (APA) Council of Representatives meeting, which resulted in the formation of the Association for Women in Psychology (AWP; Brown, 2010). The APA assembled the "Task Force on Sex Bias and Sex Role Stereotyping in Psychotherapeutic Practice," which confirmed that there was sexism inherent in diagnosis, treatment, and perspectives of therapists. There was also a tendency for mental health professionals to relate to female clients as sex objects (Remer & Oh, 2013). From this report came recommendations to educate mental health professionals on information specific to the psychology of women and develop ethical standards to address sexism in the field (APA, 1975). Feminist therapy was first named as a therapeutic approach during this time frame in the late 1970s and early 1980s (Ballou et al., 2008).

Third-wave feminism began in the 1990s and was focused on being more culturally inclusive (Ballou et al., 2008). Feminism continues to grow and progress today. Postmodern feminism has become increasingly more focused on global injustice and the intersection of women's diverse identities (Bruns, 2011; Remer & Oh, 2013). Postmodern feminist therapy focuses on this intersectionality (detailed further in Chapter 3), or how all aspects of our identity are integrated and intersect with gender to inform our experiences in society and our social location in regard to power and oppression. The most recent iterations of feminism and feminist therapy emphasize the intersection of race, sexual orientation, ability, and socioeconomic status (SES) with gender (Herlihy & Corey, 2013). Postmodern feminism and feminist therapy are strongly influenced by multiculturalism and social justice movements (Brown, 2010).

Inadequacies of Traditional Approaches

The majority of counselors and clients are women, but almost all of the traditional counseling and developmental theories are androcentric—developed by White Western males and based on research with boys and men (Herlihy & Corey, 2013). The lens of the theorist impacts the approach, and the absence of female perspectives has implications for the relevance of those theoretical approaches for counseling with women and girls. Feminist therapy offered an alternative to psychoanalysis (which was inherently sexist and misogynistic) and the pre-scriptive behaviorism of the time. Carl Rogers's emphasis on person-centered counseling paved the path for theoretical approaches, such as feminist therapy (Brown, 2010).

Shifting Focus

The development of feminist theory moved away from approaches that patholo-gized women and girls toward a strength-based wellness model that focused on the impact of societal and environmental influences. Most theories focus on the individual, rather than on the individual in the context of culture and society as feminist theory does (Evans et al., 2011). This approach shifted the emphasis from "women's inadequacies" to the reality of the oppression and discrimina-tion females experienced in society and the mental health field (Brown, 2010). It shed light on how the impact and influence of oppression, discrimination, and stereotyping could result in responses or behaviors that previously may have been mischaracterized as pathology or disorders. For example, individual depres-sion could be reframed as a result of systemic oppression (Ballou et al., 2008). External forces were emphasized, rather than intrapsychic forces, which often pathologized the individual and contributed to victim blaming (Herlihy & Corey, 2013). Feminist counselors were at the forefront of bringing to light the realities of abuse and violence against women, and they worked to help survi-vors (Brown, 2010; Herlihy & Corey, 2013). Women's relational qualities (e.g., nur-turance and desire for connection) were valued and reframed as strengths.

For a feminist counselor, it is important to recognize that the goal of coun-seling is not to "fix" women, but to recognize that larger societal influences and environmental contexts contribute to many of the issues women experience. It is crucial to attend to how these influences affect women, as well as how we can intervene at a systemic level outside of the counseling office (Worell & Remer, 2003). This approach includes analyzing power and effects of prescribed gen-der roles, as well as acknowledging and considering how the impact of sexism contributes to women's presenting issues (Ballou et al., 2008). Instead of the goal being for women to acclimate to unhealthy environments, feminist ther-apy focuses on supporting clients in being empowered to challenge oppressive structures (Worell, 2001). Engaging in feminist practice includes acknowledg-ing social influences and power structures, advocating for equality, and valu-ing women's and girls' unique experiences and perspectives (Worell & Remer, 2003). Feminist therapy provides a space for women's voices to be heard, learned from, and valued.

Empowerment Feminist Therapy

> *"I will be using an empowerment feminist approach in counseling because it enables women and girls to understand themselves in the context of the sexist and hegemonic culture that so often produces fears and anxiety in women. For example, a feminist approach will recognize the disconnect between the ways in which the media tells women how they should be, and the reality of the many ways women actually are. Often, the best way to help women is to listen to who they are and give them the tools to better live out their authentic selves, despite the thousands of contradicting messages women receive."—A 25-year-old female, graduate counseling student*

According to Brown (2010), "A therapy may be feminist as long as it meets the criteria of supporting feminist practice—the creation of a feminist consciousness, the development of an egalitarian relationship, and the empowerment of the client" (p. 72). The collective voice valued in feminist therapy is evidenced in its many contributors, some of whom include Laura Brown, Phyllis Chesler, Carolyn Zerbe Enns, Olivia Espin, Carol Gilligan, Jean Baker Miller, Naomi Weisstein, and Judith Worell. As Brown implied in her statement, there are various approaches within the umbrella of feminist therapy. One approach, relational-cultural theory (RCT), is discussed in Chapter 4. In this chapter, I offer an introduction to empowerment feminist therapy (EFT), which incorporates multicultural and social justice perspectives (Remer & Oh, 2013).

Earlier feminist therapies were criticized for not being inclusive and focusing primarily on White middle- or upper-class women. More recent iterations reflect the work of examining biases and integrate more multicultural perspectives, therefore increasing applicability and effectiveness with diverse populations (Díaz-Lázaro et al., 2012). In EFT, all types of oppression are recognized and attention is given to women's diverse personal and social identities (Worell & Remer, 2003). The overarching goal is to change toxic and harmful societal systems and support clients in exercising influence over the interpersonal and institutional factors that affect their well-being (Worell & Remer, 2003). Client strengths and resilience in coping with past, current, and future trauma and stress are emphasized (Herlihy & Corey, 2013; Remember & Oh, 2013).

An empowerment feminist approach can be employed by both male and female counselors and used with clients of all ages and genders. An EFT approach can help men and boys express a fuller range of emotions and become more accepting of themselves and others. Men can be feminist therapists and make a meaningful impact, not only with their clients, but also in society. This can be accomplished if they are aware of and own their privilege and use their power to confront sexism and other forms of oppression (Herlihy & Corey, 2013).

EFT is not just for adults, but can be extremely effective with youth as well. Applying feminist principles with boys and girls from a young age can be valuable for prevention efforts and provide an empowering alternative for conceptualizing development (Lovell, 2016). It can be particularly beneficial for adolescents when combined with creative approaches to counseling (Otting & Prosek, 2016). Overall, EFT is an effective approach to employ with a wide range of populations and issues. Some examples include: with older adults and caregivers to combat depression and increase quality of life (Stripling, 2016); with men who have abused women (Herlihy & Corey, 2013); with diverse women who have experienced poverty, trauma, and oppression (East & Roll, 2015); with immigrant women (Díaz-Lázaro et al., 2012); in career counseling to increase women's career self-efficacy (Juntunen, 1996); in conceptualizing the etiology, prevention, and treatment of eating disorders (Pollack, 2003); integrated in sex education curriculum (Askew, 2007); combined with mindfulness to contribute to increased self-compassion and the healing of survivors of intimate partner violence (Crowder, 2016); in preventing and combating relational aggression (Brown, 2013); and in counseling adolescents and conceptualizing their development (Otting & Prosek, 2016).

Tenets

EFT is focused on gender, social location, and power (Brown, 2010), with the overarching goals of empowerment and social transformation (Enns, 2004; Herlihy & Corey, 2013). Throughout the therapeutic process, the impact of the socialization and power dynamics in clients' lives is examined (Díaz-Lázaro et al., 2012). EFT counselors make connections between the internal and external, individual and society, and experiences and environment. In this approach, the impact of culture and environment is examined on a number of contextual levels: global (e.g., worldview), institutional (e.g., educational system), relational (e.g., family dynamics), and individual identities (e.g., biological, spiritual; Ballou et al., 2008, p. 44). A client's relationships at each of these levels, as well the power structures inherent in each of these systems, should be considered. The ecological model of human development further conceptualizes levels of influences (e.g., microsystem, exosystem, macrosystem) and is detailed in Chapter 7.

Essential principles of an empowerment feminist approach include (a) critical consciousness and commitment to social change, (b) an egalitarian relationship between client and counselor, and (c) a focus on strengths and reframing of psychological distress (Brown, 2010; Enns, 2004; Evans et al., 2011; Herlihy & Corey, 2013; Remer & Oh, 2013; Worrell & Remer, 2003). At the heart of feminist therapy is the concept that the personal is political; there is a reciprocal effect between our personal lives and beliefs, political systems, and societal values (Evans et al., 2011). Empowerment feminist therapists believe that how clients view themselves, and how others treat them, are influenced by their social locations (Remer & Oh, 2013). They honor each woman's unique experience based on the intersection of her diverse identities (Remer & Oh, 2013). The client is considered the expert of her own life and EFT counselors are intentional about attending to and sharing power in the therapeutic relationship. A primary goal of EFT is to raise clients' awareness and consciousness that suffering and distress are not due to personal weakness, but rather to systemic inequities and devaluing of women (Crowder, 2016). This approach aims to increase clients' self-awareness, self-knowledge, and self-validation (Evans et al., 2011), so that they can be empowered to address external factors that are oppressive and navigate their life circumstances healthily and successfully (Worell & Remer, 2003).

Techniques

EFT is a "theory in action," or an example of translating philosophy into practice (Evans et al., 2011). It is an integrative approach that is more about a theoretical lens than a specific set of techniques; however, there are therapeutic interventions that have been developed, incorporated, and used within feminist therapy (Crowder, 2016). The successful implementation of these techniques requires that the counselor is self-reflective and aware of his or her own biases, intentional about customizing his or her approach to meet the needs of the client, and actively working to create a safe space for transformation throughout the counseling process (Crowder, 2016; Evans et al., 2011).

One of the techniques developed by feminists and used often in feminist therapy is *cultural analysis*, which includes *gender-role analysis* and *power analysis*. *Gender-role analysis* involves the client working with the counselor to (a) identify the messages she has internalized about gender and related roles; (b) examine the impact of those messages and beliefs on an emotional, cognitive, and behavioral level; (c) consciously decide which messages she wants to keep and which she wants to discard; and (d) make a plan to implement change (Worell & Remer, 2003). The primary goal of this intervention is to bring unseen messages into conscious awareness (Remer & Oh, 2013). The counselor can assist the client in this process by asking reflective questions, such as: "What messages did you receive when you were growing up and how do they impact you now?"; "Where did those messages come from (e.g., parents, teachers, media)?"; "What gendered expectations are you measuring yourself against and possibly trying to live up to?"; "What are the potential negative or positive effects of this?"; "Which messages do you want to keep and which do you want to change?"; and "How will you do it?" (Evans et al., 2011; Remer & Oh, 2013). Engaging in this exercise helps clients become aware of internalized messages and intentional about what they believe (Evans et al., 2011). This can help to free them from constricting gender-typed roles and allow them to live and express their authentic selves.

Attention to power is essential in feminist therapy and crucial to understanding the context of the client's life, experiences, and presenting issues (Remer & Oh, 2013). There is unequal access to power in society, which impacts women's lives and experiences of distress (Ballou et al., 2008). In *power analysis*, the counselor explores with clients the imbalance of power that exists in society between dominant and oppressive groups (e.g., men and women) and how it affects access to resources and self-confidence (Herlihy & Corey, 2013). Discussion and education about sexism, racism, and other forms of discrimination are incorporated throughout the process (Remer & Oh, 2013). Similar to gender analysis, it is important for the client to examine her own personal circumstances and the influence of power on her relationships and other aspects of her life (e.g., career/workplace; Evans et al., 2011). It is critical for the counselor to validate the client's reality, while also helping her overcome barriers and gain more access to power. When the client decides how she might like to exercise her power, the counselor and client explore the benefits and risks of enacting different power strategies.

These *cultural analyses* can be used across all counseling settings (e.g., school, clinical mental health agencies) and modes (e.g., individual, group, psychoeducational workshops). This intervention can help clients gain social awareness, so they can intentionally decide what to accept and reject, rather than being unconsciously controlled and influenced by underlying and pervasive societal messages. In cultural analyses, it is also important to examine cultural conflicts, such as the gender-role expectations for immigrant women in their home culture compared to host culture (Díaz-Lázaro et al., 2012). The counselor can ask questions regarding how the client's presenting problem (e.g., experiencing trauma after being raped) is defined and influenced by the perspectives and messages of the dominant culture and community. For example, victim-blaming tendencies inherent in rape culture may be influencing the client's feelings of guilt and shame after being assaulted (Remer & Oh, 2013). Sometimes oppressive messages become so internalized that they are mistaken for one's own voice (Brown, 2010); this technique helps to combat that.

Gender-role intervention is a technique that involves framing issues in the context of societal messages and expectations. *Reframing*, an important technique in EFT, involves a shift from an internal focus to a societal focus in relation to presenting issues (Díaz-Lázaro et al., 2012). Considering the external factors that are contributing to a problem can be beneficial in clients' healing, growth, and esteem (Herlihy & Corey, 2013). It can also help bring to light clients' self-defeating behaviors and connect them to larger societal issues rather than individual weaknesses (Evans et al., 2011). Symptoms are reframed as coping strategies or responses to the environment (Evans et al., 2011). For example, teenage girls are often stereotyped as vain and focused too much on looks. In reality, girls are bombarded with messages that what is most important about them is how they look. Their appearance is commented on more than anything else from the time that they are born, and the value of a girl's looks only escalates as she enters adolescence. Instead of blaming teenage girls and labeling them as vain, this issue can be more accurately represented as a natural response to what is constantly reinforced as their most valuable asset. This may still be problematic, but the source of the "problem" is reconceptualized. Lookism is explored in more depth in Chapter 11.

Relabeling, a technique originally developed for use in family therapy, has become a primary technique in an empowerment feminist approach to counseling (Remer & Oh, 2013). It involves shifting focus from negative to positive, and alters the label that has previously been applied to describe a client's characteristic or behavior (Herlihy & Corey, 2013; Worell & Remer, 2003). For example, a woman who has been criticized for being "too sensitive" relabels this as having awareness of her own and others' feelings, which is a valuable trait in relating and connecting with others and expressing oneself.

Strength-based assessment and exercises can also assist clients in recognizing their positive traits and resilience. One of my favorite exercises is to ask students or clients to reflect on a challenging circumstance in their past. Then instead of recounting the details of the incident, I ask them to focus on strengths that enabled them to survive and even thrive through and after that challenge (Remer & Oh, 2013). Finally, they speak their identified strengths aloud and we process what it was like to reconceptualize the experience in that way. These types of strength-based exercises can highlight resilience and help women recognize and own their power and strength.

Other techniques often employed with this approach include *assertiveness training, advocacy, group work,* and *bibliotherapy*. Oftentimes, women and girls are discouraged from being assertive or using their voices to challenge the status quo. In EFT, girls and women are encouraged to learn assertive communication skills and use them in their lives. *Assertiveness training* involves psychoeducation around the differences among assertive, aggressive, and passive behaviors. Role-playing and conflict resolution can be used in session to practice these skills. *Advocacy* is a hallmark of feminist therapy, and clients as well as counselors are encouraged to engage in advocacy efforts. Connecting to the tenet that the personal is political, it makes sense that part of a person's change as an individual would be accomplished through political or social action or change (Evans et al., 2011). In EFT, clients are empowered to exercise their assertiveness and advocacy skills in becoming change agents in ways that are meaningful to them (Enns, 2004). Having a safe space to examine and deconstruct messages and be empowered to advocate for self and others is essential in developing critical consciousness (Clonan-Roy, Jacobs, & Nakkula, 2016). As discussed previously in this chapter, consciousness-raising groups were impactful in the feminist movement. *Group work* is particularly powerful in EFT, as it fosters connection and provides rich opportunities for women to share and empower one another (Herlihy & Corey, 2013). Finally, *bibliotherapy* is a useful practice that helps clients educate themselves and others. Counselors can recommend books, blogs, websites, and documentaries for clients to learn more about certain topics or issues. The Helpful Resources included at the end of each chapter in this text will assist you in developing a reservoir of sources to share with clients, students, and colleagues. When bibliotherapy is included in the counseling process, clients report more satisfaction with counseling (Herlihy & Corey, 2013).

Clinical Implications

Counselors interested in implementing feminist therapeutic philosophy and techniques in their practice can consider adopting EFT as their main approach or integrate it within their current approach. Focusing on awareness, empowerment, identity exploration, and examination of how the client has internalized social and cultural messages that are contributing to the difficulties or pain she is experiencing can be beneficial when working with any client (Worrell & Remer, 2003). In EFT, issues are framed as coping strategies or methods of survival, not pathology (Herlihy & Corey, 2013; Worell & Remer, 2003). Feminist therapists avoid diagnosing (unless it is absolutely necessary), as it can dehumanize the client, place the focus on individual issues, and minimize social factors. If diagnosis is unavoidable, the counselor should involve the client in the process and be cognizant of not contributing to victim blaming or reinforcing stereotypes (Herlihy & Corey, 2013). It is important to look beyond the client's symptoms to understand how she is operating within her environment (Ballou et al., 2008). For example, women who have been victims of trauma and abuse may often be labeled with personality disorders when perhaps PTSD would be more appropriate given their experiences (Herlihy & Corey, 2013).

An egalitarian relationship is essential in EFT and should be intentionally established and maintained throughout the counseling process. The feminist therapist should share power and responsibility with the client, while acknowledging that there is inherently an imbalance of power (Brown, 2010; Worell & Remer, 2003). Openness to feedback and demystifying the therapeutic process can help to minimize the power differential and build trust. The counselor should avoid abusing power by acting as the "expert" and dispensing advice (Herlihy & Corey, 2013). Instead, collaboration is essential at each stage of the therapeutic process, including conceptualization, goal setting, treatment planning, and so forth. Appropriate self-disclosure around the counselor's experiences with gender and oppression can help to normalize women's experiences and contribute to an egalitarian relationship; however, self-disclosure should be used only if the counselor believes it will directly benefit the client and not detract from the process (Herlihy & Corey, 2013). Feminist counselors are continuously self-reflective and cognizant of not imposing their own values. Instead, they provide an environment where clients can safely explore their options and feel empowered to choose for themselves (Herlihy & Corey, 2013).

THE NEED FOR EDUCATION SPECIFIC TO COUNSELING WOMEN AND GIRLS

Let us now revisit the questions posed at the beginning of the chapter: "Why counseling women and girls?" and "Why the need for a specific focus on this half of the population?" After reading this chapter, how would you answer those questions? Several counseling graduate students explained the value they found in participating in a course specific to counseling women and girls.

"Being a woman, I went into the course Counseling Women and Girls interested in the subject, but thinking I didn't have too much to learn because, of course, counseling my own gender would come naturally. Instead, I found this class to be one of the most insightful and impactful classes I have had yet. I have no doubt that learning how to empower my female clients, learning how to help them counteract the negative aspects of sexism they likely encounter daily, and even learning how to empower boys and men to embrace the strengths of feminism will help to make me a much more effective therapist and allow me to help my clients make powerful changes in their lives."
—A 48-year-old marriage and family therapy graduate student

"Women and girls—who make up half the world population—have particular concerns that require a safe space to openly discuss these concerns, without being perceived as being 'anti-male' or 'overly-sensitive.' The freedom and

(continued)

(continued)

camaraderie I experienced as a student in a Counseling Women and Girls course helped me to overcome the shame I carried from experiences of oppression in my own life, which then made it possible for me, as a counselor, to educate my clients about the impact of oppression in their own life stories. Sometimes, inclusion in a supportive, nonjudgmental community is all we need to allow us to step beyond our self-created limitations and assume new, exciting roles as world-changers."—A 55-year-old mental health counselor and recent graduate

"Taking the Counseling Women and Girls course was beneficial for me because it opened my eyes to harmful, demeaning messages towards women within common media outlets that I would have otherwise ignored. After taking this course, I have become a critical consumer of the media and an active advocate for addressing, and ultimately disengaging from, media outlets that do not promote healthy, beneficial campaigns for women and girls. I am so grateful I took this course because it made me realize that this is not an issue solely for women or for men; this is an issue for humanity."—A 24-year-old female counseling student

In addition to counseling hundreds of adolescent girls, teaching a Counseling Women and Girls course for the past decade and consistently seeing the valuable impact it had on counselors-in-training was my impetus for developing this textbook. My hope is that you too will grow personally and professionally as you engage with this text.

CALL TO ACTION

Once we begin to become aware of the injustices inherent in society, we can feel overwhelmed and possibly experience a sense of helplessness. One way we can combat that perceived sense of powerlessness is to engage in advocacy, or an "act or process of supporting a cause or proposal" (By permission. From Merriam-Webster's Collegiate® Dictionary, 11th Edition ©2016 by Merriam-Webster, Inc. [www.Merriam-Webster.com]). If some of what you read in this book or hear in the news upsets or angers you, channel that emotion into action. If the idea of changing the world seems implausible, consider your own circle of influence. One of the most effective ways to advocate and create change is through small acts of challenging oppression in your everyday life. For example, most of us are exposed to countless messages that objectify women through music, media, pornography, and everyday dialogue. This is dangerous, as the first step toward abusing someone is dehumanizing her. You can participate in the process of change by not laughing at "jokes" that are demeaning toward

(continued)

CALL TO ACTION (*continued*)

women and pointing out to others the danger in their words. Opportunities like this are endless and present themselves each day.

Pay attention to language and examine the meaning and potential implications of commonly used sentiments such as "Boys will be boys." Consider how this and similar messages encourage a lack of accountability simply based on someone's being male. Think about the underlying meaning when someone describes a woman's dress as "provocative," which by definition means "serving to provoke." Provoke what? Often the underlying message is provoking men to sexual acts or assaults. These are examples of messages inherent in rape culture. Challenge yourself and others to be more aware of the power of language. Instead of dismissing poor behavior as "boys will be boys" (which is also insulting to boys and men, as it underestimates their ability to behave decently toward others), teach our boys that they are capable and responsible for controlling their own actions. Instead of engaging in victim blaming and perpetuating the idea that girls are responsible for the abuse inflicted on them, educate others that sexual assault is based on power, control, and entitlement of the perpetrator, not about what a victim is wearing.

Spreading awareness and educating others are essential to advocacy. Contemplate something you have learned from this chapter that you could share with others in your circle of influence (e.g., family members, friends, coworkers, social media contacts). Consider interrupting or exiting the conversation when someone is making sexist or other discriminatory remarks. These everyday acts of advocacy are the foundation for change and often have ripple effects of influence.

REFLECTION AND DISCUSSION QUESTIONS

1. What did you notice about your reactions as you read through this chapter? Did you feel surprised, upset, angry, empowered, resistant, _____? Note your reactions and share with a classmate or colleague. Continue to notice what comes up for you as you read through the textbook.

2. Many injustices were highlighted in this chapter, and many more exist in society. If you could change one of the inequities, which would it be? Did something immediately come to mind, or did you have to think for a while? Why did you choose what you did?

3. Consider the thing that came to mind when you answered question 2. Review what you read in the Call to Action section. What is one thing you could do this week to contribute to the change you wish to see in

(*continued*)

REFLECTION AND DISCUSSION QUESTIONS (*continued*)

the world? Tell someone what you are planning to do and then follow up after you have done it.

4. How likely do you think you are to incorporate feminist therapeutic principles in your counseling practice? What techniques or aspects of the approach resonated most with you?

5. Choose one organization, website, YouTube video, documentary, or book from the Helpful Resources list and explore it. What did you learn? Consider sharing with someone else or on social media.

HELPFUL RESOURCES

Books, Videos, and Documentaries

- Brown, C. S. (2014). *Parenting beyond pink & blue: How to raise your kids free of gender stereotypes.* New York, NY: Ten Speed Press.—book for parents
- "Dress Code Sexism" (www.youtube.com/watch?v=41J4XBjgOrw)—Laci Green (YouTube video)
- *Half the Sky: Turning Oppression Into Opportunity for Women Worldwide* (www .halftheskymovement.org)—documentary, book, and website with resources
- *The Hunting Ground* (www.thehuntinggroundfilm.com)—documentary highlighting the issue of sexual assault on college campuses
- "Violence Against Women: It's a Men's Issue"—Jackson Katz (www.ted.com/ talks/jackson_katz_violence_against_women_it_s_a_men_s_issue?language =en)—Ted Talk
- "We Should All Be Feminists"—Chimamanda Ngozi Adichie (www.youtube .com/watch?v=hg3umXU_qWc)—Essay and Ted Talk

Professional Websites and Organizations

- American Counseling Association (ACA) Women's Interest Network (www .counseling.org/aca-community/aca-groups/interest-networks#Women)
- American Psychological Association's (APA) Guidelines for Psychological Practice with Girls and Women (www.apa.org/practice/guidelines/girls-and -women.aspx)
- Association for Women in Psychology (www.awpsych.org)
- Girls Inc. (www.girlsinc.org)—"Inspiring girls to be smart, strong, and bold" (helpful website for youth)
- National Sexual Violence Resource Center (www.nsvrc.org)

REFERENCES

American Psychological Association. (1975). Report of the task force on sex bias and sex-role stereotyping in psychotherapeutic practice. *American Psychologist, 30,* 1169–1175.

Askew, J. (2007). Breaking the taboo: An exploration of female university students' experiences of attending a feminist-informed sex education course. *Sex Education: Sexuality, Society and Learning, 7*(3), 251–264. doi:10.1080/14681810701448051

Ballou, M., Hill, M., & West, C. (2008). *Feminist therapy theory and practice: A contemporary perspective.* New York, NY: Springer Publishing Company.

Broverman, I. K., Broverman, D. M., Clarkson, F., Rosenkrantz, P., & Vogel, S. (1970). Sex role stereotyping and clinical judgments of mental health. *Journal of Consulting and Clinical Psychology, 45,* 250–256.

Brown, L. S. (2010). *Feminist therapy.* Washington, DC: American Psychological Association.

Brown, L. S. (2013). Feminist therapy as a path to friendship with women. *Women and Therapy, 36*(1–2), 11–22. doi:10.1080/02703149.2012.720556

Bruns, C. M. (2011). Feminism and feminist therapy across generations. *Women and Therapy, 34*(1–2), 19–37. doi:10.1080/02703149.2011.532436

Chant, S. (2016). Women, girls and world poverty: Empowerment, equality or essentialism? *International Development Planning Review, 38*(1), 1–25. doi:10.3828/idpr.2016.1

Clonan-Roy, K., Jacobs, C. E., & Nakkula, M. J. (2016). Towards a model of positive youth development specific to girls of color: Perspectives on development, resilience, and empowerment. *Gender Issues, 33*(2), 96–121. doi:10.1007/s12147-016-9156-7

Crawford, M., & Unger, R. (2004). *Women and gender: A feminist psychology* (4th ed.). New York, NY: McGraw-Hill.

Croft, A., Schmader, T., Block, K., & Baron, A. S. (2014). The second shift reflected in the second generation: Do parents' gender roles at home predict children's aspirations? *Psychological Science, 25*(7), 1418–1428. doi:10.1177/0956797614533968

Crowder, R. (2016). Mindfulness based feminist therapy: The intermingling edges of self-compassion and social justice. *Journal of Religion and Spirituality in Social Work: Social Thought, 35*(1–2), 24–40. doi:10.1080/15426432.2015.1080605

Díaz-Lázaro, C. M., Verdinelli, S., & Cohen, B. B. (2012). Empowerment feminist therapy with Latina immigrants: Honoring the complexity and socio-cultural contexts of clients' lives. *Women and Therapy, 35*(1–2), 80–92. doi:10.1080/02703149.2012.634730

East, J. F., & Roll, S. J. (2015). Women, poverty, and trauma: An empowerment practice approach. *Social Work, 60*(4), 279–286. doi:10.1093/sw/swv030

Enns, C. Z. (2004). *Feminist theories and feminist psychotherapies: Origins, themes, and diversity* (2nd ed.). New York, NY: Haworth.

Evans, K. M., Kincade, E. A., & Seem, S. R. (2011). *Introduction to feminist therapy: Strategies for social and individual change.* Los Angeles, CA: Sage.

Feldman-Jacobs, C., & Clifton, D. (2014). Female genital mutilation/cutting: Data and trends: Update 2014. Retrieved from http://www.prb.org/pdf14/fgm-wallchart2014.pdf

Feminism. (n.d.). In *Merriam-Webster's online dictionary*. Retrieved from http://www.mer riam-webster.com/dictionary/feminism

Half the Sky Movement. (n.d.). *Half the Sky: Turning oppression into opportunity for women worldwide* (Action Packet). Retrieved from http://www.halftheskymovement.org/ page/-/high-contrast-action-guide.pdf

Herlihy, B., & Corey, G. (2013). Feminist therapy. In G. Corey (Ed.), *Theory and practice of counseling and psychotherapy* (9th ed., pp. 360–394). Belmont, CA: Brooks/Cole, Cengage Learning.

Holley, L. C., Tavassoli, K. Y., & Stromwall, L. K. (2016). Mental illness discrimination in mental health treatment programs: Intersections of race, ethnicity, and sexual orien- tation. *Community Mental Health Journal, 52*(3), 311–322.

International Center for Research on Women. (2015). Child marriage facts and figures. Retrieved from http://www.icrw.org/child-marriage-facts-and-figures

Juntunen, C. (1996). Relationship between a feminist approach to career counseling and career self-efficacy beliefs. *Journal of Employment Counseling, 33*(3), 130–143. doi:10.1002/j .2161-1920.1996.tb00445.x

Lovell, K. (2016). Girls are equal too: Education, body politics, and the making of teenage feminism. *Gender Issues, 33*(2), 71–95. doi:10.1007/s12147-016-9155-8

Mental Health America. (n.d.). Depression in women. Retrieved from http://www.men talhealthamerica.net/conditions/depression-women

National Research Council. (2012). *A framework for K–12 science education: Practices, cross- cutting concepts, and core ideas*. Washington, DC: National Academies Press.

Otting, T. L., & Prosek, E. A. (2016). Integrating feminist therapy and expressive arts with adolescent clients. *Journal of Creativity in Mental Health, 11*(1), 78–89. doi:10.1080/15401 383.2015.1019167

Pipher, M. (1995). *Reviving Ophelia: Saving the selves of adolescent girls*. New York, NY: Penguin Group.

Pollack, D. (2003). Pro-eating disorder websites: What should be the feminist response? *Feminism and Psychology, 13*(2), 246–251. doi:10.1177/0959353503013002008

Remer, P. A., & Oh, K. H. (2013). Feminist therapy in counseling psychology. In C. Z. Enns, E. N. Williams, C. Z. Enns, & E. N. Williams (Eds.), *The Oxford handbook of feminist multicultural counseling psychology* (pp. 304–321). New York, NY: Oxford University Press.

Stripling, A. M. (2016). The healthy aging group: A proposed treatment model for societal & individual aging empowerment. *Women and Therapy, 39*(1–2), 124–140. doi:10.1080/ 02703149.2016.1116324

UNICEF. (2014). Hidden in plain sight: A statistical analysis of violence against children. Retrieved from http://www.unicef.org/publications/files/Hidden_in_plain_sight_ statistical_analysis_Summary_EN_2_Sept_2014.pdf

UN Women. (2016). Fact and figures: Leadership and political participation. Retrieved from http://www.unwomen.org/en/what-we-do/leadership-and-political-participa tion/facts-and-figures#notes

Walker, M. (2016). What's a feminist therapist to do? Engaging the relational paradox in a post-feminist culture. *Women and Therapy, 34*(1–2), 38–58. doi:10.1080/02703149.2011. 532689

Whitehouse.gov. (2016). Your right to equal pay. Retrieved from https://obamawhitehouse .archives.gov/issues/equal-pay/rights

Worell, J. (2001). Feminist interventions: Accountability beyond symptom reduction. *Psychology of Women Quarterly, 25*(4), 335–343. doi:10.1111/1471-6402.00033

Worell, J., & Remer, P. (2003). *Feminist perspectives in therapy: Empowering diverse women* (2nd ed.). Hoboken, NJ: John Wiley.

World Health Organization. (n.d.). Gender disparities in mental health. Retrieved from http://www.who.int/mental_health/media/en/242.pdf?ua=1

World Health Organization. (2013). Violence against women: A 'global health problem of epidemic proportions.' Retrieved from http://www.who.int/mediacentre/news/ releases/2013/violence_against_women_20130620/en

World Health Organization. (2016). Gender and women's mental health. Retrieved from http://www.who.int/mental_health/prevention/genderwomen/en

Yakushko, O., & Morgan-Consoli, M. L. (2014). Gendered stories of adaptation and resistance: A feminist multiple case study of immigrant women. *International Journal for the Advancement of Counselling, 36*(1), 70–83. doi:10.1007/s10447-013-9191-y

CHAPTER 2

Gender Socialization

Cheryl L. Fulton

LEARNING OBJECTIVES

After reading this chapter, you will be able to:

1. Define key terms related to gender and gender socialization.
2. Understand agents and processes of gender socialization.
3. Gain awareness of one's own gender socialization experience.
4. Identify individual and societal consequences of gender norms and stereotypes.

Three little words that mean so much: "It's a girl!" or "It's a boy!"

As mentioned in Chapter 1, these seemingly innocent words can evoke a vast array of emotions and expectations and are imbued with personal and social meaning, all of which have important consequences. Gender can differentially impact "susceptibility and exposure to mental health risks and mental health outcomes" and "deepen disparities associated with important socioeconomic determinants such as income, employment, and social position" (World Health Organization, n. d., p. 2). These disparities are rooted in a binary system of gender (i.e., male and female), where being male is associated with greater power and privilege than being female in most societies around the world (Basow, 2006; Ryle, 2015).

The existence of such gender disparities raises questions regarding their origin. Are there inherent differences between males and females (e.g., aggressive vs. nurturing) such that gender discrepancies are inevitable? Does society play a role in defining "male" and "female" in a way that creates and maintains a hierarchical gender order? If society dictates gender roles, then how do individuals learn and adopt their respective gender roles such that the status quo is maintained? Although gender may seem obvious, inherent, and unchanging on the surface, these questions reflect that the origin of gender roles is a complex, debated, personal, and political topic.

Central to this debate is the question of whether gendered traits and behaviors are the result of nature (biology) or nurture (culture and society). Although there are many theories for explaining gender differences, there are two broad views: essentialist and sociocultural. The *essentialist view* is that observed differences in traits and behavior among males and females are largely rooted in biological determinants (Brannon, 2008), such as hormones, anatomy, and chromosomes. The essentialist view is reflected in the large body of neuroscientific studies focused on identifying differences in the male and female brain (Fine, 2010; Rippon, Jordan-Young, Kaiser, & Fine, 2014). When gender differences are deemed biologically determined, then gender is depicted as inherent and invariant.

In contrast, the *sociocultural view* is that gender and gender roles largely occur as a result of socialization. In the famous words of Simone de Beauvoir, "One is not born, but rather becomes, a woman" (de Beauvoir, 1973, p. 301). The way we "become our gender," or adopt our gender role, is through *gender socialization.* This is the process through which individuals learn the social expectations associated with their respective gender and come to develop their gender identity (Ryle, 2015). In other words, through gender socialization we learn *gender roles,* or how we are supposed to perform our gender, in accordance with our biological sex. Gender roles are informed by *gender norms* or "sets of rules for what is socially accepted masculine and feminine behavior in a given culture" (Ryle, 2015, p. 110). Therefore, gender roles are more related to the traits and behaviors expected of each gender, whereas *gender identity* involves coming to identify and accept one's self as male or female (Brannon, 2008). Based on the sociocultural view, the term *sex* typically refers to a biological designation whereas *gender* refers to the social meaning of that designation (i.e., male and female), which includes roles, expectations, and stereotypes. These roles, expectations, and stereotypes are transmitted primarily through agents of socialization, such as family, peers, education, and media (Leaper & Friedman, 2007).

Although the nature–nurture debate continues, it is widely accepted among social scientists that socialization is a significant factor in gender differences (Bussey & Bandura, 1999; Carter, 2014). Through the lens of socialization, gender roles are malleable because societal expectations, although deeply entrenched and seemingly fixed, can be changed. Barnes (2015) pointed out that in the United States, although change has been slow and inconsistent, there is evidence of increased gender parity in areas such as work and family life, including domestic labor. Changes in gender roles are also evident in the increasing number of women entering careers historically reserved for men (e.g., doctors, military leaders) and, likewise, the increasing number of men engaging in careers historically in the domain of women (e.g., nurse, homemaker). These shifts in gender roles debunk essentialist ideas that women cannot excel in math and science or that woman, but not men, are hardwired for nurturing.

Despite these changes, a hierarchical gender order and limiting gender roles persist such that there are inequities that adversely impact the wellness and potential of girls and women (Choate, 2008; Ram, Strohschein, & Gaur, 2014). Specifically, prescribed gender roles impact girls' and women's interpersonal relationships (Brannon, 2008; Hyde, 2005), career opportunities and choices, economic circumstances (Andersen, Ertac, Gneezy, List, & Maximiano, 2013; Hyde, 2005), leadership opportunities (Eagly & Carli, 2007), division of household labor (Leaper, 2014), and mental health and wellness (Choate, 2008; Ram et al., 2014). Knowledge and appreciation of gender socialization is important to counseling work as gender is a vital aspect of one's cultural identity (Sue & Sue, 2013). Furthermore, counselors will be better advocates and more effective in using preventive efforts and intervention strategies that empower women and girls if they are well versed in gender socialization and its consequences.

GENDER CATEGORIES AND GENDER ORDER

Because sex and gender are generally described in binary terms (i.e., male or female), theories and study of gender socialization have been largely based on these gender categories. However, binary gender categories are problematic in a number of ways. First, although most individuals are born with physical characteristics that make assigning gender straightforward, some individuals (nearly 2% of the population) are born *intersexed,* meaning they do not readily align with binary sex categories of male and female (Fausto-Sterling, 2000). An intersex infant may be born with ambiguous genitalia and/or conflicting gonads or genetics such that choosing a sex to assign is perplexing. Intersexuals challenge our notion of binary gender categories and point to the complexity of gender as biology. Fausto-Sterling (2000) stated that because "intersexuals quite literally embody both sexes, they weaken claims about sexual difference" (p. 8). Regardless, doctors and parents will agree to surgically alter an intersex infant to conform to a single sex even when such a choice may be problematic later in life (Walker, 2004). This conveys the extreme social significance placed on ensuring every individual conforms to *two and only two* socially sanctioned gender categories.

Basow (2006) noted that when we account for the myriad of gender factors such as biological sex, gender, gender identity, and sexual orientation, we have at least 36 sex/gender/sexual orientation combinations. This results in a much more complex picture of gender than "boys" and "girls." Fausto-Sterling (2000) argued that from a biological standpoint alone, there are at least five sexes (i.e., male, female, and three variations of intersexuals). Recently, several countries (e.g., Nepal, India, and Germany) legally sanctioned a third gender (i.e., transgender); however, the United States and most countries have not (Khaleeli, 2014). Most theories of gender socialization originated at a time when gender was viewed more traditionally, and, therefore, may have certain limitations in a more gender-complex world.

Second, when only two examples are presented (e.g., male and female), individuals will have the tendency to think of the two categories as being in opposition to one another (Fausto-Sterling, 2000). This can result in the tendency to exaggerate differences while ignoring similarities. Thus, boys and girls will be socialized into two *opposing* gender categories, even if they are more alike than dissimilar to the other gender. This is limiting to girls and women since most females do not fit the Western female stereotype (Basow, 2006). Furthermore, binary categorization tends to yield the use of one category as the norm and the other as deviant (Brannon, 2008). The traits and roles that are attributed to males are regarded as more desirable and higher status (Bussey & Bandura, 1999). Thus, gender categories elevate males (norm) and subordinate females (nonnormative).

Last, the binary categorization of gender has yielded an enormous body of social and neuroscientific research in which scholars essentially created, or at least reinforced, differences by virtue of seeking them (Hyde, 2005, 2014; Ribbon et al., 2014). Based on meta-analytic studies of gender differences in psychological variables, it seems there are little to no inherent gender differences (Hyde, 2005, 2014; Zell, Krizan, & Teeter, 2015). In sum, binary gender categories limit individual expression, create a gender hierarchy that privileges males, exaggerate gender differences, and carry gender stereotypes that may disadvantage women.

GENDER NORMS, ROLES, AND STEREOTYPES

Despite the complex nature of gender, expectations for gender roles are often based on stereotypes, or generalized assumptions about attitudes, traits, or behavior patterns of men and women (Brannon, 2008). For example, because of differences in reproductive capabilities and physical strength (biology), in many cultures throughout the world being female is stereotypically equated with *communal* traits, such as being nurturing and expressive, whereas being male is stereotypically equated with *agentic* traits, such as being competitive and rational (Brannon, 2008). It is not surprising, then, that women more commonly enter careers in which communal traits are valued (e.g., homemaker, nurse), whereas men pursue careers in which agentic traits are desirable (e.g., doctor, manager). Traits associated with stereotypes are not inherently good or bad, but stereotypes misrepresent reality and can be used to reinforce gender inequities.

> *"Growing up in the post-depression era the family mentality was that I was going to get a job as a secretary. College was never mentioned nor was there encouragement of my interests or talents. I viewed school as social days. Like most women, I got married and became a stay-at-home mom. When I was 40, I decided to go to college to become a dental hygienist. Later I opened a successful business and finally satisfied my drive as an entrepreneur. In retrospect, with a formal college education I probably would have taken things further. Women today have many more opportunities than 50 years ago."*—A 78-year-old retiree

Girls tend to be more flexible than boys in terms of the traits and behaviors they engage in, despite stereotypes. This may be because they have lower status, and, therefore, less to lose (Basow, 2006; Brannon, 2008). For example, in many countries girls wear pants; however, most boys would not wear a dress. Flexible gender roles are related to better mental health outcomes, such as greater self-esteem, self-confidence, and decreased depression, because gender-flexible individuals possess both agentic and communal traits, which increase the array of qualities they bring to life's challenges (Worell, 2006). It is important to note that gender fluidity may be more difficult in certain cultures and subcultures where religiosity or traditional values exert pressure to maintain rigid gender roles (Choate, 2008). Furthermore, the intersection of gender and other identities (e.g., race, class, and sexuality) can bring about different stereotypes from those that exist for a singular identity. In other words, a White, heterosexual, female stereotype is not necessarily the same as an African American female or lesbian female stereotype (Worell, 2006).

Additionally, gender roles can be impacted by cultural context (Ryle, 2015). For example, in many countries, it is socially acceptable for women to engage in most activities that men engage in, including working in diverse careers, participating in sports, and running for public office (although there are disparities in all these areas); whereas in a country such as Saudi Arabia, social norms (some enacted as laws) prohibit women from driving, showing skin (even a hand) in public, and freely participating in sports (*The Week*, 2015). Furthermore, although many cultures value agentic traits such as independence or assertiveness, they are not valued equivalently across cultures. For example, for both men and women in Japan, agentic traits are inconsistent with broader cultural norms of obedience and conformity (Brannon, 2008). Cultural differences in gender norms can also be found within facets of a culture. For example, among U.S. women, a trait such as assertiveness is less likely to be associated with femininity among European Americans and older generations than for younger women and African Americans (Basow, 2006). The nature of femininity and masculinity and gender norms are highly dependent on cultural and historical context.

Adherence to gender norms is often rewarded with benefits such as greater likeability, whereas gender nonconformity is often viewed less favorably (Sanchez, Crocker, & Boike, 2005). Nonconforming children may even encounter rejection or harassment (Lee & Troop-Gordon, 2011). In some countries, gender noncompliance, deeply entrenched in societal norms and religious practices (e.g., strict adherence to Islamic Sharia law), can result in harsh punishment or even death (Curtis, 2014). Thus, gender nonconformity may bring significant social and physical consequences.

THEORIES OF GENDER SOCIALIZATION

There are numerous perspectives regarding how the process of gender socialization occurs and each theory contributes to the overall understanding of the development of gender roles. As mentioned previously, biological theories focus on the determinant nature of biological factors, such as hormones. There are a number of classic psychological and sociological theories, however, that are prominent in discussions of gender socialization, and they each contribute to our understanding of how socialization occurs. These theories include psychoanalytic theory (Freud, 1949), social learning theory (Bandura, 1971), cognitive developmental theory (Kohlberg, 1966), and gender schema theory (Bem, 1983).

Briefly, based on psychoanalytic theory, gender socialization occurs via processes leading to a child's identification with the same-sex parent (Freud, 1949). Social learning theorists describe socialization as a result of rewards and punishment for gender-appropriate behavior and vicarious learning through observation and modeling (Bussey & Bandura, 1999). Cognitive developmental theorists emphasize a child's active role in socialization once the child develops the cognitive ability to understand her or his gender. Finally, gender schema theory, which builds on both cognitive developmental and social learning theories, involves the development of gender schemas or mental models that enable children to organize knowledge and process social information relevant to gender categories. These theories are discussed in more detail in Chapter 5 as they provide important context for how agents of socialization operate.

Agents and Processes of Gender Socialization

The way in which gender is experienced and performed is something we learn and renegotiate throughout our lives (Ryle, 2015). We learn our gender through both primary and secondary socialization and various agents of socialization. Gender norms and roles may vary based on many factors, such as nationality, racial/ethnic group, family, peers, and media exposure.

"Growing up in Vietnam, I was taught how women should talk, walk, eat, and my duties and roles to my family and society. I learned the Confucian teaching (tam tòng, tứ Đức) that a woman must obey the men in her life (father, husband, and son) along with her duties to maintain the home, her appearance, and her skills. I witnessed my mother being beaten while everyone stood by. When I moved to the United States, I did not see a major change in my gender role or societal expectations. However, I witnessed an instance of domestic violence on the metro platform in Houston. People were angry, some called the police, while others intervened. It was surprising to me as instances of domestic violence usually went unnoticed as bystanders are not willing to get involved in Vietnam. This changed the way I see the relationship of a woman and her family members and society. This instance gave me hope that society can change to positively promote the well-being of everyone, including women."—A 26-year-old female student

Primary and Secondary Socialization

Primary socialization, occurring in infancy and childhood, is the initial process of learning the ways of a society or group and is transmitted through the primary groups to which we belong. Primary groups are characterized by intimate, enduring relationships among small groups who generally spend a great deal of time together (Cooley, 1909 as cited in Ryle, 2015). A person's family members or closest friends are examples of proximal agents of primary socialization.

Due to the fact that learning gender is a lifelong process, gender socialization is also impacted by our association with various groups that, throughout our lives, have subtle or direct effects on our view of gender (secondary groups). As compared with primary groups, secondary groups are larger, more temporary, less personal, and more specialized (Ryle, 2015). For example, a counseling program might be a secondary group with its own ideas about gender that are directly or indirectly conveyed to its members. As people are exposed to different groups, they may adopt different ideas about their gender. Varying roles throughout life (e.g., partner, parent, and worker) will also impact gender roles over time (Ryle, 2015).

Agents of Socialization

Because gender roles are communicated in many ways, such as through family, peers, teachers, clothing, toys, advertisements, and television, it is nearly impossible to develop in a gender-neutral manner. Four of the most studied agents of socialization include family, peers, education, and media, as these are pervasive in an individual's life.

Family

The role of the family in gender socialization has been widely studied and is regarded as perhaps the strongest influence in shaping gender attitudes (Brannon, 2008). Infants and young children are capable of absorbing gender knowledge (Brannon, 2008), and, according to Kohlberg (1966), gender constancy, by age 6. Thus, it is not surprising that researchers have focused on family members, as they are the agents who are most proximal during early development. Family members are significant to the socialization process as they are the first to expose individuals to gender norms (Leaper, 2014). Given the varied nature of contemporary families, Carter (2014) noted that a family can be understood as "any primary group of people who share an obligatory relationship with one another" (p. 243), rather than defined in terms of the traditional conception of family (i.e., heterosexual, married couples with children).

Studies of family influence on gender roles have been largely focused on parental influence. Parental influence may occur through modeling and differential treatment, such as type of activities encouraged (e.g., type of toys, household chores). Parents also convey gender-typed expectations for personality traits (e.g., girls are emotional) and abilities (e.g., boys are proficient in math; Leaper, 2014), which can influence the type of activities children pursue. Parents, consciously or unconsciously, impose expectations on children in an effort to shape their behavior to align with social norms and increase social adaptability (Peterson & Hann, 1999).

Modeling
Children may observe primary caregivers modeling gender-role expectations through activities such as household chores and career participation (Leaper, 2014). Children raised by same-gender parents will be less likely to endorse gender stereotypes with respect to household labor and careers except when parents choose to divide homemaking and career along traditional lines (Leaper, 2014). Transmission of parental views of masculinity and femininity may also vary depending on family composition (presence/absence of father/mother) and racial/ethnic affiliation (Brannon, 2008).

Differential Treatment

Differential treatment of sons and daughters is more likely observed among financially disadvantaged families in poorer countries than in wealthier countries (Leaper, 2014); however, it occurs in many societies. The most common difference in the treatment of boys and girls in Western countries is with respect to the encouragement of gender-stereotyped activities (Leaper, 2014). For example, based on studies of adult interaction with infants (e.g., Seavey, Katz, & Zalk, 1975; Smith & Lloyd, 1978) where the infant was not necessarily dressed or named according to gender, researchers found evidence for differential gender-based treatment from the way adults played and interacted with the infant (e.g., more motor activity with perceived boys) to the types of toys offered, such as dolls for girls and toy hammers for boys. Interestingly, studies of parental attitudes toward play (largely conducted in Western cultures) revealed that parents will hold more flexible attitudes about play for girls (e.g., they can play with dolls and do sports) than for boys (e.g., playing with dolls would be discouraged; Leaper, 2014). Biases in play may be important as the type of play activities a child engages in can impact his or her cognitive development and skill acquisition (Lee & Troop-Gordon, 2011).

As part of shaping gender roles and perpetuating gender stereotypes, parents and other family members have the tendency to use gender-biased language, such as speaking about the physical characteristics of boys (e.g., strength), while focusing on the expressivity or fragility of girls (Carter, 2014). Parents also use verbalizations, even inadvertently, that are essentialist in nature, such as "boys like sports" and "girls like dolls," but rarely offer counter-gender statements, such as "girls can play sports" (Leaper, 2014). Parents may also show implicit sexist attitudes about children's academic abilities, such as a belief that boys are more competent in math. This can impact girls' math attitude and aptitude, as well as influence what activities and areas of study are encouraged among girls (Leaper & Brown, 2014). Based on meta-analytic studies, girls have achieved parity with boys on math ability (Hyde, 2014). Thus, even when gender differences are unsubstantiated, sexist parental messages can reinforce old, enduring stereotypes that may eliminate potentially rewarding experiences for girls.

Furthermore, the nature of communication between parents and children varies by the child's gender. For instance, mothers will talk more to daughters, use more supportive speech, and encourage them when they make supportive remarks to others, but avoid discussing anger. In contrast, mothers will encourage independence in their sons and frequently discuss and attribute emotional states to anger (Bussey & Bandura, 1999). Although girls and boys equally express anger overtly with physical aggression in early childhood, by preschool age girls learn that this is not acceptable for them, and they are less likely than boys to express anger overtly (Choate, 2008).

Researchers have largely focused on unilateral parent-to-child socialization effects, yet socialization can occur in a number of other ways. For example, children can socialize parents (i.e., change their attitudes about work and family roles); children and parents can reciprocally socialize one another; and all family members can be socialized within the larger social system (Carter, 2014). Although parental influence is relevant to gender socialization, Leaper (2011) relayed it may be less important than originally thought, as other relationships, such as peers, are also influential.

Peers

Although parents are important agents of socialization in early childhood, there is a shift toward peer influence as children enter middle childhood and early adolescence, when they become more concerned with adhering to the social norms of their peer group (Tenenbaum & Leaper, 2002). Starting around age 3, and increasingly over subsequent years, children demonstrate a preference for same-gender peer interactions (Brannon, 2008). The onset of puberty (age 11 or 12) marks a period of gender-role intensification, whereas adolescence into early adulthood marks a transition to greater gender-role flexibility (Choate, 2008). Both girls and women allow greater gender flexibility within their own group and are more tolerant of it among boys and men, whereas boys will tend to be more restrictive, focusing on same-gender play groups and gender normative activities (Brannon, 2008).

Similar to parents, peers model gender attributes, encouraging others to adopt and conform to gender normative behavior (Bussey & Bandura, 1999); and children report feeling pressure to conform to these norms (Lee & Troop-Gordon, 2011). Gender conformity is viewed more positively by adults and peers, whereas nonconforming children may be viewed as unpopular among peers (Sroufe, Bennett, Englund, Urban, & Shulman, 1993). McGuffey and Rich (1999) studied camp attendees in middle childhood and found that both boys and girls played an active role in gender socialization. They found the status of boys was higher than girls, and that boys policed gender nonconformity across groups, whereas girls had less power to police because they were lower status and played in smaller, less centralized groups. Gender nonconforming boys were strongly rejected by other boys, whereas nonconforming girls (e.g., being a strong athlete) and boys (e.g., showing emotion) were both supported by the girls. Nonconforming girls could enter the boys' social arena only if they were deemed masculine enough (McGuffey & Rich, 1999).

Children may react to peers' gender nonconformity through resistance to befriending them or even marginalizing or harassing them (Lee & Troop-Gordon, 2011). Peers may react with *overt aggression*, such as hitting or verbal insults, or with *relational aggression*, which involves manipulating social relationships via social exclusion, spreading rumors, and/or threatening friendship status (Lee & Troop-Gordon, 2011). Girls are more likely to engage in relational aggression (perhaps because overt aggression is gender nonconforming for girls), which is associated with anxiety, depression, and loneliness (Choate, 2008). Thus, counselors must be aware of the pressure children may feel regarding gender-role conformity and the consequences of nonconformity and victimization.

Education

Based on recent research, it seems that teachers are making an effort to be egalitarian in their approach to and expectations of students (Leaper & Brown, 2014); however, teachers, the curriculum, school environment, and peer dynamics have all been found to impact gender socialization (Stromquist, 2007). Peer influences, as previously discussed, can take place in the school environment where children spend much of their day. Teachers also model gender-related attitudes and behaviors. For example, math anxiety among female teachers was associated with greater likelihood that girls would endorse the stereotype that boys are good at math and girls are good at reading (Beilock, Gunderson, Ramirez, & Levine, 2010). Teachers also socialize gender differences through bias in their treatment and expectations of boys and girls (e.g., calling on boys more in class). Gender bias in teacher expectations is problematic as teacher expectations about students' ability can be self-fulfilling (Leaper & Brown, 2014). For example, if teachers believe girls are not as interested and capable as boys in science, they may inadvertently convey lower expectations of girls on science projects and provide less encouragement and tutoring; and teacher expectations can impact performance. Furthermore, perpetuation of stereotypes that girls are unable to succeed in math, despite all evidence to the contrary, can undermine girls' confidence, particularly when parents and teachers maintain these beliefs (Hyde, 2005). When girls internalize such gender stereotypes, it can adversely impact their interest and achievement in STEM subjects (science, technology, engineering, and math), which are important to obtaining the growing number of STEM jobs (Leaper & Brown, 2014). Thus, school counselors have a crucial role in advocating for girls by educating teachers about gender discrepancies in the classroom so that girls' interest in diverse subjects, including STEM subjects, are fostered and supported.

Media

Media is a pervasive and a well-identified agent of gender socialization (Leaper & Friedman, 2007). Advertisements in media "sell values, images, and ideals of love, sexuality, success, and normalcy" (Hodgson, 2011, p. 5). Many popular television shows commonly watched by most children are potent means for conveying sexism as they reinforce gender stereotypes (Leaper & Friedman, 2007). Based on social learning theory, persons/characters in the media serve as models of appropriate gender behavior (Bussey & Bandura, 1999).

> *"When I watch TV shows it always seems like the girls are dressed up in fancy clothing and wear lots of make-up. The girls always seem to be out shopping or getting a manicure while the boys get to go on all the adventures. I think this makes girls my age feel pressure to dress up and abandon their natural selves. That's why I like strong girl characters like Nancy Drew who get to be smart and be the center of all the action."—An 11-year-old girl*

For example, the Disney Princess line, targeted at young girls internationally through many films and more than 25,000 marketable products, reached $4 billion in sales by 2008 and is considered a powerful media source related to gender socialization (England, Descartes, & Collier-Meek, 2011). Disney films have been found to portray females in stereotypical and racist fashion with regard to appearance (e.g., emphasis on light skin, full breasts, and small waists) and women's primary functions, which are focused on their sexuality and domestic work (England et al., 2011). Furthermore, analysis of popular television shows for children tend to portray boys as more knowledgeable, directive, and innovative than girls, and these stereotypes are reinforced by teachers' differential treatment of boys (Leaper & Brown, 2014), such as allowing boys to be more assertive and expecting girls to be cooperative. Thus, it is evident that agents of socialization (education and media) can reinforce one another.

Media messages can be particularly impactful in shaping expectations for beauty (Hefner et al., 2014). Media transmission of ideal body expectations and internalization of these ideals are well-known factors for body dissatisfaction and disordered eating among women (Smolak & Chun-Kennedy, 2013). They also encourage the use of cosmetic surgery among women (Pike, Dunne, & Addai, 2013). "Aging beauty" media (i.e., actresses older than 40 who appear younger, thinner, and sexier than average) also was found to be associated with greater disordered eating and body dissatisfaction among older women (Hefner et al., 2014).

Teaching media literacy, which can mitigate the adverse impact of media, involves teaching critical thinking skills and working through four steps: identifying harmful cultural images; exploring and deconstructing their underlying meaning; resisting the message; and actively working to change the message (Choate, 2008). Teaching children, parents, and teachers media literacy is a way that counselors can help protect against negative consequences such as body dissatisfaction and disordered eating as well as mitigate reinforcement of stereotypes related to division of labor and career opportunity.

IMPLICATIONS OF GENDER SOCIALIZATION

In the broadest sense, gender roles limit all individuals, as they place boundaries on experience. However, the subordinate status of women's gender role has implications for many areas, such as leadership, violence, career, household labor, and even counseling. Understanding these consequences is important in advocating for and empowering girls and women.

Leadership

Gender roles and stereotypes adversely impact women's ability to achieve equal representation in some of the more influential leadership positions in society. For example, women make up half the U.S. population, but only represent 18% of Congress. Women also account for 44% of master's degrees in business and management, but only represent 14.6% of the top five leadership positions and less than 5% of chief executive officers (CEOs) at Fortune 500 companies (Warner, 2014). Eagly and Carli (2007) suggested that a labyrinth, rather than a glass ceiling, is a better metaphor for the complex leadership journey women must take and emphasized that leadership disparities stem from gender roles and stereotypes. They stated that traits associated with traditional leadership align with societal views of male traits rather than female traits. Even though women leaders may be evaluated as positively as men leaders, if they appear uncaring or overly authoritative, they are judged more harshly than men portraying the same traits (Hyde, 2005). This is one of many examples related to how nonconformity to gender-stereotyped traits and behaviors affects women in leadership. In sum, stereotypes, cultural norms, and expectations reduce opportunities for women to hold leadership positions in which they could influence public policy, legislation, and business.

Violence

Violence against women takes many forms including intimate partner violence, sexual assault, and sex trafficking. Societal definitions of masculinity (i.e., strong and aggressive) and femininity (i.e., weak and submissive) set the stage for violence against women. As such, a patriarchal society engenders violence against women and is a determinant of rape culture whereby rape is a "logical and psychological extension of a dominant-submissive, competitive, sex-role stereotyped culture" (Burt, 1980, p. 229). In this regard, the ways in which gender is socialized has serious implications for both women and men. Women, however, have greater exposure to mental health risks because they face a significantly greater threat of sexual violence over their lifetime than men (Choate, 2008).

Career

Women largely occupy careers in health care and education, which are professional roles that align with cultural ideals of femininity, but have lower prestige and pay (Swanson & Fouad, 2010). Compared with females, males are socialized to be competitive and therefore are more likely to self-select into competitive work environments. This may be one reason why men earn more money than women in most societies (Andersen et al., 2013). Additionally, gender stereotypes such as "girls are better caregivers" and "sports are for boys" affect girls academically and physically, resulting in limited engagement with STEM courses, which are important in the job market, and lessen athletic participation (Leaper & Brown, 2014), which fosters physical, emotional, and behavioral skills (Worell, 2006).

Women continue to be at a disadvantage in terms of career achievements due to gender-biased family roles, which still position women as primarily responsible for caregiving roles (Swanson & Fouad, 2010). Eagly and Carli (2007) noted that marriage and parenthood was associated with higher wages for men than for women because of the assumed lack of greater career stability. Thus, the ways in which a given culture defines gender roles can limit academic and career achievement, income, and career satisfaction, all of which are important to well-being (Worell, 2006). Women who violate the stereotype of being nurturing and nice and show agentic traits are less likely to be hired than males showing those same traits (Hyde, 2005). Thus, women face a double bind in the hiring process: They must come across as confident and capable without violating norms for stereotypical femininity.

Household Labor

The division of household labor is a clear example of the feminist tenet that the personal is political, as choices about the amount and type of household labor one engages in may seem like a personal choice. However, gender roles influence the division of household labor (Leaper, 2014; Nakamura & Akiyoshi, 2015). Attitudes regarding household labor and careers can be highly varied among families, but overall they have become more egalitarian in Western societies (Leaper, 2014). Despite this, Nakamura and Akiyoshi (2015) found that across 10 diverse countries, including the United States, women still perform more of the housework. Likewise, although same-sex couples tend to be more egalitarian with regard to household labor, if they choose to organize their family along traditional gender roles, they may experience similar disparities (Leaper, 2014). Because women are socialized to be relational, they may feel strongly about meeting the needs of family members while also balancing their careers (Swanson & Fouad, 2010). This may leave them susceptible to *role strain*, which often leads to feelings of confusion and guilt (Choate, 2008). Counselors can advocate for women and men by encouraging more equitable division of household labor and childcare among couples, as this has been associated with greater satisfaction and intimacy among Westerners (Worell, 2006). This may be harder to achieve with couples from countries such as Japan where the gender gap for division of labor is highly disparate and gender norms and cultural institutions reinforce this gap (Nakamura & Akiyoshi, 2015).

GENDER SOCIALIZATION AND COUNSELING

Counselors may bring biases based on gender stereotypes to the counseling process because they are subject to gender socialization as well (Swanson & Fouad, 2010). Gender bias may appear in a plethora of ways, including using theories based on the "male normal," which may pathologize women (Sue & Sue, 2013); evaluating traits of women and minorities less favorably; stereotyping in diagnosis; and attributing stress to intrapsychic versus sociocultural causes (Worell & Johnson, 2001). The gender role of the counselor may also interact with the client's gender (Swanson & Fouad, 2010). For example, a male counselor might be more directive with female clients because he adheres to a stereotype of female passivity. Similarly, a female counselor may overlook subtle expressions of emotion in a male client because she learned the stereotype of male stoicism. Career counselors must also be aware of how gender socialization may impact career choices, as women may be more likely to choose certain careers because these careers seem more accessible or acceptable (Swanson & Fouad, 2010). Feminist approaches to counseling may be a means to overcome such biases in counseling. Counseling can be a corrective experience that empowers girls and women rather than reinforces stereotypes and inequities. A feminist approach invites the counselor to advocate for change at the client, community, and societal level, thereby empowering women and girls, as opposed to colluding to pathologize them and support their adaptation to oppressive and discriminatory environments (Evans, Kincade, Marbley, & Seem, 2005).

In conclusion, gender roles and stereotypes are transmitted through family, peers, education, and media as well as secondary groups. Gender roles create and impact gender disparities that disadvantage women and girls throughout the world. Educating parents, teachers, children, and adults regarding gender roles, teaching media literacy, and supporting gender-role flexibility may help empower girls and women. Counselors must be aware of gender socialization in the counseling process and, through advocacy, seek to challenge gender roles and empower women and girls so that they may experience dignity and wellness.

CALL TO ACTION

Counselors can use the questions and resources that follow as a starting point for advocacy in addressing gender socialization, bias, and stereotyping.

- *Use the Reflection Questions in this chapter to examine your own gender socialization so that you can prevent the unintentional perpetuation of gender stereotypes in your personal and professional interactions.*
- *Teach media literacy to children, teens, college students, and parents so they learn to critically view social expectations regarding male and female as they are portrayed and reinforced in the media (see* Miss Representation *or* Killing Us Softly 4 *documentaries, in the Helpful Resources list for this chapter).*
- *Involve boys and men in the movement toward gender equity (see HeForShe campaign, in the Helpful Resources list for this chapter).*

REFLECTION AND DISCUSSION QUESTIONS

1. What is one of the most vivid memories from your childhood regarding what you learned about how members of your gender are supposed to behave?
2. In what way(s) do you conform to or resist the gender norms of your culture? How does this impact how others respond to you?
3. Describe a time when you felt you were being treated in accordance with a gender stereotype. How did that impact you? How did you react?
4. Describe how gender socialization may impact how you interact with a client (male and female), such as how you might reinforce gender stereotypes within the counseling process.

HELPFUL RESOURCES

Books and Documentaries

- Butler, J. (2004). *Undoing gender.* New York, NY: Routledge.—This is a seminal work that furthers Butler's thinking regarding gender performativity discussed in her earlier work, *Gender Trouble.*

- *Killing us softly 4: Advertising's image of women.* (Available from Media Education Foundation, 60 Masonic Street, Northampton, MA 01060)—This documentary is designed to help students think critically about how women and girls are portrayed in media/advertising and how this relates to sexism, eating disorders, gender violence, and contemporary politics.
- *Miss Representation*—This documentary offers insight regarding how the portrayal of women and girls in the media influences their power and ability to obtain leadership roles in society.

Advocacy Websites

- Geena Davis Institute on Gender in Media (www.seejane.org)
- HeForShe Campaign and Action Kit (www.heforshe.org)
- The American Association of University Women (AAUW) (www.aauw.org)
- UN Women (www.unwomen.org/en)

REFERENCES

Andersen, S., Ertac, S., Gneezy, U., List, J. A., & Maximiano, S. (2013). Gender, competitiveness, and socialization at a young age: Evidence from a matrilineal and a patriarchal society. *The Review of Economics and Statistics, 95*(4), 1438–1443. doi:10.1162/REST_a_00312

Bandura, A. (1971). *Social learning.* New York, NY: General Learning Press.

Barnes, M. W. (2015). Anticipatory socialization of pregnant women: Learning fetal sex and gender interactions. *Sociological Perspectives, 58*(2), 187–203. doi:10.1177/0731121414564883

Basow, S. A. (2006). Gender role and gender identity development. In J. Worell & C. Goodheart (Eds.), *Handbook of girls' and women's psychological health* (pp. 242–251). New York, NY: Oxford University Press.

Beilock, S. L., Gunderson, E. A., Ramirez, G., & Levine, S. C. (2010). Female teachers' math anxiety affects girls' math achievement. *Proceedings of the National Academy of Sciences of the United States of America, 107*(5), 1860–1863. doi:10.1073/pnas.0910967107

Bem, S. L. (1983). Gender schema theory and its implications for child development: Raising gender-aschematic children in a gender-schematic society. *Signs: Journal of Women in Culture and Society, 8*(4), 598–616. doi:10.1086/493998

Brannon, L. (2008). *Gender: Psychological perspectives* (5th ed.). Boston, MA: Pearson.

Burt, M. R. (1980). Cultural myths and supports for rape. *Journal of Personality and Social Psychology, 38*(2), 217–230. doi:10.1037/0022-3514.38.2.217

Bussey, K., & Bandura, A. (1999). Social cognitive theory of gender development and differentiation. *Psychological Review, 106*, 676–713. doi:10.1037/0033-295x.106.4.676

Carter, M. J. (2014). Gender socialization and identity theory. *Social Sciences, 3,* 242–263.

Choate, L. H. (2008). *Girls and women's wellness: Contemporary counseling issues and interventions.* Alexandria, VA: American Counseling Association.

Curtis, M. (2014). An end to discrimination against women in the Middle East. Retrieved from http://www.americanthinker.com/articles/2014/01/an_end_to_discrimination_against_women_in_the_middle_east.html

de Beauvoir, S. (1973). *The second sex.* New York, NY: Vintage Books.

Eagly, A., & Carli, L. (2007). Women and the labyrinth of leadership. *Harvard Business Review, 85*(9), 62–71.

England, D. E., Descartes, L., & Collier-Meek, M. A. (2011). Gender role portrayal and the Disney princesses. *Sex Roles, 64,* 555–567. doi:10.1007/s11199-011-9930-7

Evans, K. M., Kincade, E. A., Marbley, A. F., & Seem, S. R. (2005). Feminism and feminist therapy: Lessons from the past and hopes for the future. *Journal of Counseling and Development, 83*(3), 269–277. doi:10.1002/j.1556-6678.2005.tb00342.x

Fausto-Sterling, A. (2000). *Sexing the body: Gender politics and the construction of sexuality.* New York, NY: Basic Books. doi:10.1086/374142

Fine, C. (2010). *Delusions of gender: How our minds, society, and neurosexism create difference.* New York, NY: W. W. Norton. doi:10.1007/s12115-011-9527-3

Freud, S. (1949). *An outline of psychoanalysis.* New York, NY: W. W. Norton.

Hefner, V., Woodward, K., Figge, L., Bevan, J. L., Santora, N., & Baloch, S. (2014). The influence of television and film viewing on midlife women's body image, disordered eating, and food choice. *Media Psychology, 17*(2), 185–207. doi:10.1080/15213269.2013.838903

Hodgson, K. (2011). Killing us softly 4: Advertising's image of women. *Media Education Foundation Study Guide.* Retrieved from https://www.mediaed.org/assets/products/241/studyguide_241.pdf

Hyde, J. S. (2005). The gender similarities hypothesis. *American Psychologist, 60,* 581–592. doi:10.1037/0003-066x.60.6.581

Hyde, J. S. (2014). Gender similarities and differences. *Annual Review of Psychology, 65,* 373–398. doi:10.1146/annurev-psych-010213-115057

Khaleeli, H. (2014, April 16). Hijra: India's third gender claims its place in law. *The Guardian.* Retrieved from http://www.theguardian.com/society/2014/apr/16/india-third-gender-claims-place-in-law

Kohlberg, L. (1966). A cognitive-developmental analysis of children's sex-role concept and attitudes. In E. Maccoby (Ed.), *The development of sex differences* (pp. 82–123). Stanford, CA: Stanford University Press.

Leaper, C. (2011). Research in developmental psychology on gender and relationships: Reflections on the past and looking into the future. *British Journal of Developmental Psychology, 29,* 347–356.

Leaper, C. (2014). Parents' socialization of gender in children. C. L. Martin (Topic Ed.) In R. E. Tremblay, M. Boivin, & R. DeV. Peters (Eds.), *Encyclopedia on early childhood development* (pp. 1–5). Montreal, QC, Canada: Centre of Excellence for Early Childhood Development and Strategic Knowledge Cluster on Early Child Development. Retrieved from http://www.child-encyclopedia.com/documents/LeaperANGxp1.pdf

Leaper, C., & Brown, C. (2014). Sexism in schools. *Advances in Child Development and Behavior, 47,* 189–223. doi:10.1016/bs.acdb.2014.04.001

Leaper, C., & Friedman, C. K. (2007). The socialization of gender. In J. E. Grusec & P. D. Hastings (Eds.), *Handbook of socialization: Theory and research* (pp. 561–587). New York, NY: Guilford Press.

Lee, E. E., & Troop-Gordon, W. (2011). Peer socialization of masculinity and femininity: Differential effects of overt and relational forms of peer victimization. *British Journal of Developmental Psychology, 29,* 197–213. doi:10.1111/j.2044-835x.2010.02022.x

McGuffey, C. S., & Rich, B. L. (1999). Playing in the gender transgression zone. *Gender and Society, 13*(5), 608–627. doi:10.1177/089124399013005003

Nakamura, M., & Akiyoshi, M. (2015). What determines the perception of fairness regarding household division of labor between spouses? *PLOS ONE, 10*(7), 1–17. doi:10.1371/journal.pone.0132608

Peterson, G. W., & Hann, D. (1999). Socializing children and parents in families. In M. B. Sussman, S. K. Steinments, & G. W. Peterson (Eds.), *Handbook of marriage and the family* (pp. 327–370). New York, NY: Springer Science and Business Media. doi:10.1007/978-1-4757-5367-7_14

Pike, K., Dunne, P., & Addai, E. (2013). Expanding the boundaries: Reconfiguring the demographics of the "typical" eating disordered patient. *Current Psychiatry Reports, 15*(11), 411–418. doi:10.1007/s11920-013-0411-2

Ram, U., Strohschein, L., & Gaur, K. (2014). Gender socialization: Differences between male and female youth in India and associations with mental health. *International Journal of Population Research, 2014,* 1–11. doi:10.1155/2014/357145

Rippon, G., Jordan-Young, R., Kaiser, A., & Fine, C. (2014). Recommendations for sex/gender neuroimaging research: Key principles and implications for research design, analysis, and interpretation. *Frontiers in Human Neuroscience, 8,* 1–11. doi:10.3389/fnhum.2014.00650

Ryle, R. (2015). *Questioning gender: A sociological exploration* (2nd ed.). Thousand Oaks, CA: Sage.

Sanchez, D., Crocker, J., & Boike, K. (2005). Doing gender in the bedroom: Investing in gender norms and the sexual experience. *Personality and Social Psychology Bulletin, 31*(10), 1445–1455. doi:10.1177/0146167205277333

Seavey, C. A., Katz, P. A., & Zalk, S. R. (1975). Baby X: The effect of gender labels on adult responses to infants. *Sex Roles, 1*(2), 103–109. doi:10.1007/bf00288004

Smith, C., & Lloyd, B. (1978). Maternal behavior and perceived sex of infant: Revisited. *Child Development, 49,* 1263–1265. doi:10.1111/j.1467-8624.1978.tb04104.x

Smolak, L., & Chun-Kennedy, C. (2013). Sociocultural influences on the development of eating disorders and obesity. In L. H. Choate (Ed.), *Eating disorders and obesity: A counselor's guide to prevention and treatment* (pp. 3–20). Alexandria, VA: American Counseling Association.

Sroufe, L. A., Bennett, C., Englund, M., Urban, J., & Shulman, S. (1993). The significance of gender boundaries in preadolescence: Contemporary correlates and antecedents of boundary violation and maintenance. *Child Development, 64*(2), 455–466. doi:10.2307/1131262

Stromquist, N. P. (2007). The gender socialization process in schools: A cross-national comparison. Paper commissioned for the EFA Global Monitoring Report 2008, Education for All by 2015: Will we make it? New York, NY: UNESCO. Retrieved from http://unesdoc.unesco.org/images/0015/001555/155587e.pdf

Sue, D. W., & Sue, D. (2013). *Counseling the culturally diverse: Theory and practice* (6th ed.). New York, NY: Wiley Interscience.

Swanson, J. L., & Fouad, N. A. (2010). *Career theory and practice: Learning through case studies* (2nd ed.). Thousand Oaks, CA: Sage.

Tenenbaum, H. R., & Leaper, C. (2002). Are parents' gender schemas related to their children's gender-related cognitions? A meta-analysis. *Developmental Psychology, 38*(4), 615–630. doi:10.1037/0012-1649.38.4.615

The Week. (2015). Twelve things women in Saudi Arabia cannot do. Retrieved from http://www.theweek.co.uk/60339/twelve-things-women-in-saudi-arabia-cant-do

Walker, J. (2004). The death of David Reimer: A tale of sex, science, and abuse. Retrieved from http://reason.com/archives/2004/05/24/the-death-of-david-reimer

Warner, J. (2014). Fact sheet: The women's leadership gap. Retrieved from https://www.americanprogress.org/issues/women/report/2014/03/07/85457/fact-sheet-the-womens-leadership-gap

Worell, J. (2006). Pathways to healthy development: Sources of strength and empowerment. In J. Worrell & C. D. Goodheart (Eds.), *Handbook of girls' and women's psychological health* (pp. 25–35). New York, NY: Oxford University Press. doi:10.1017/s0033291706218075

Worell, J., & Johnson, D. (2001). Therapy with women: Feminist frameworks. In R. K. Unger (Ed.), *Handbook of the psychology of women and gender* (pp. 317–329). Hoboken, NJ: Wiley.

World Health Organization. (n.d.). Gender disparities in mental health. Retrieved from http://www.who.int/mental_health/media/en/242.pdf

Zell, E., Krizan, Z., & Teeter, S. R. (2015). Evaluating gender similarities and differences using metasynthesis. *American Psychologist, 70*(1), 10–20. doi:10.1037/a0038208

Intersectionality: Understanding Power, Privilege, and the Intersecting Identities of Women

Alina S. Wong

LEARNING OBJECTIVES

After reading this chapter, you will be able to:

1. Recognize the ways that social identities intersect and inform each other.
2. Develop an understanding of intersectionality as a lens to identify systems of oppression and their impact on women and girls.
3. Understand the impact of oppression and discrimination on mental health and well-being.
4. Gain insight into the application of intersectionality in counseling practice.

Gender identity has a significant impact on how an individual navigates and experiences the world. Hence, girls and women are centered in this volume, offering insight to counselors for providing effective support and treatment to clients who identify as women and girls. In this chapter, I use *gender identity* to refer to an individual's self-authored sense of self around gender identity and expression, which may be distinct from one's sex assigned at birth. *Women and girls* include all people who identify as girls or women or were socialized as girls in the most inclusive sense. Women and girls may include cisgender girls and women; trans girls/women; nonbinary/gender fluid/gender queer girls/women/people; and trans feminine people. Of course, gender is not the only social identity that humans inhabit. It is important to recognize that race, class, ability, religion, gender expression, spirituality, ethnicity, citizenship, and sexuality intersect with gender identity and mutually shape each other (Abes, Jones, & McEwen, 2007; Bowleg, 2008; Jones & McEwen, 2000; Torres, Jones, & Renn, 2009).

In order to provide effective therapeutic strategies for working with women and girls, it is necessary to examine the contexts, relationships, and politics within which an individual constructs meaning around social identities. Sexism, misogyny, and patriarchy are pervasive and impact how girls and women develop a sense of their gender identity and gender expression, as well as how they navigate relationships, institutions, and social systems (Berg, 2006; Swim, Hyers, Cohen, & Ferguson, 2001). Women and girls with multiple marginalized identities must contend with many systems of oppression and discrimination. These place women and girls in a vulnerable position as they are impacted by several systems of oppression simultaneously. Intersectionality (Crenshaw, 1991; Dill & Zambrana, 2009b) is an analytic lens to acknowledge the interlocking and interdependent systems of oppression (e.g., racism, sexism, classism, heterosexism, transphobia, ableism), which allow for individual and group discrimination. Intersectionality scholars argue that that these systems of oppression are mutually reinforcing mechanisms of control and discrimination. They have a direct and profound impact on our identities in terms of how we are defined (or categorized) as people, as well as how we live, express, and enact our identities.

In this chapter, I provide a brief overview of the intersections of social identities, offer an introduction to intersectionality, explore the impact of systems of oppression on mental health and well-being, and suggest strategies for incorporating principles of intersectionality and identity construction into counseling practice. The recently revised multicultural and social justice competencies for counselors approved by the American Counseling Association (ACA; Ratts, Singh, Nassar-McMillan, Butler, & McCullough, 2015, 2016) emphasize the need for counselors to develop awareness of their own social identities and to incorporate an analysis of systemic oppression and direct social change action into their practice.

I hope that the discussion presented will provide a foundation for understanding and applying intersectionality in counseling practice and aid in developing a strength-based approach to support women and girls of all marginalized identities in building resiliency, empowerment, and agency in and over their own lives. By using intersectionality as a lens to understand their clients' experiences, counselors may also implement more effective strategies for supporting their clients' development of an empowered and positive sense of self.

INTERSECTIONALITY AND INTERSECTING IDENTITIES

Psychological and Sociological Approaches to Understanding Identity Formation

Psychological approaches to understanding identity have emphasized development of an individual sense of self (i.e., Erikson, 1994) and define identity as "one's personally held beliefs about self in relation to social groups . . . and the ways that one expresses that relationship" (Torres et al., 2009, p. 577). Sociological approaches focus on the construction of group and collective identities (Omi & Winant, 1994) and an individual's identification with and interactions within a group (Torres et al., 2009). A sociological lens considers the impact of immediate and political contexts, noting that an individual holds multiple and simultaneous identities that intersect and interact. Thus, an individual cannot be summed up through a simplistic addition of multiple identities. Rather, a person's sense of self is a dynamic and shifting process of knowing, constructing, and making meaning of one's identities and experiences (Abes et al., 2007; Bowleg, 2008; Collins, 1990; Crenshaw, 1991; Torres et al., 2009; Weber, 1998). Bringing these two approaches together, social psychologists and identity theorists contend that gender, race, sexuality, ability, and spirituality are not fixed identities of self that one comes to realize, nor are they external categories that are imposed upon individuals and groups of people. Instead, social identities have different meanings dependent upon an individual's intersecting identities, family history, and immediate surroundings (Abes et al., 2007; Bowleg, 2008; Jones & McEwen, 2000; Shin, 2015; Weber, 1998).

Put another way, the meaning of being a "girl" or "woman" will be different for someone who identifies as White and heterosexual than for someone who identifies as Asian American and queer. Locating individual identity within sociopolitical contexts and recognizing the mutually constitutive interplay of social identities cause a significant shift in how identities are experienced, studied, and treated within counseling relationships and educational contexts (Goodman, 2015; Hernández & McDowell, 2010; McDowell & Hernández, 2010; Ratts et al., 2015, 2016; Shin, 2015; Sue et al., 2007; Torres et al., 2009). Previous approaches suggested that counselors should support students and clients to move through a series of stages to arrive at a final, predetermined, and fixed idea of self (i.e., what it means to be a Black, Christian, lesbian) based on mainstream scripts and generalizations. Practitioners now approach their work with clients and students as a means to support them in developing a critical consciousness around the specific experiences and contexts that inform their worldviews and perspectives, including how they understand and see themselves (Abes et al., 2007; Almeida, Parker, & Dolan-Del Vecchio, 2008; Hernández & McDowell, 2010; Shin, 2015; Sue et al., 2007; Watts-Jones, 2010).

More importantly, counselors and educators recognize that the counseling relationship itself is a location for enacting social change and that counselors have a responsibility to engage in systemic change work as well (Cheshire, 2013; Goodman & Gorski, 2015; McDowell & Hernández, 2010; Ratts et al., 2015, 2016; Shin, 2015; Sue et al. 2007; Watts-Jones, 2010; Wong, 2015).

Many practitioners now ground their work in social justice principles, recognizing that power, privilege, oppression, and discrimination impact sense of self as well as life experiences and expectations. Thus, counselors must develop knowledge and awareness in this area in order to provide effective interventions, particularly in working with people of marginalized identities (e.g., women and girls, people of color, LGBTQIA [lesbian, gay, bisexual, transgender, queer, intersex, and asexual] communities, people with disabilities, and so forth).

It is particularly noteworthy that the ACA has reframed the former "Multicultural Counseling Competencies" to the "Multicultural and Social Justice Counseling Competencies—MSJCC" (Ratts et al., 2015, 2016), which include competencies in awareness, knowledge, skills, and action. It is not enough to learn about inequities and discrimination; counselors are expected to build knowledge over a lifetime in order to take action to dismantle systems of power and oppression. In order to do so, Hernández and McDowell (2010) contend that counselors should analyze power, privilege, and oppression within their own lives and practices in order to recognize their impact on intersecting identities and the mental health of individual people and larger communities.

Intersectionality is useful in this work because it points to the structural and systemic processes by which power and privilege are distributed through the categorization and construction of social identities. Interlocking systems of power (bureaucratic, institutional, interpersonal, and intrapersonal) were created with the intention of privileging some while oppressing others (Bowleg, 2008; Crenshaw, 1991; Delgado & Stefancic, 2001). Control was maintained by establishing the inferiority of specific identities (i.e., women, people of color, LGBTQIA communities, people with disabilities, religious minorities, non-Western civilizations) through colonization, slavery, and legal systems. One of the more sinister means of domination was through hegemony, causing an internationalization of inferiority by those dispossessed of power (Collins, 1990; Delgado & Stefancic, 2001; Freire, 1970/2003; Omi & Winant, 1994). By locating the source of misfortune within the individual, the marginalized could be held responsible for their own misfortunes. As an example, women and girls were socialized around gender norms and roles that reinforced their subjugation to men. Intersectionality disrupts this very notion.

Intersectionality

Intersectionality as a specific phenomenon was conceptualized by Kimberley Crenshaw (1991), a legal scholar and activist, who used intersectionality as a way to describe and examine the multiple layers of discrimination that poor women of color must navigate through the criminal justice system and social services. However, intersectionality has deeper roots in the Combahee River Collective, Black feminist thought, critical race feminism (CRF), and critical race theory (CRT; Cole, 2009; Dill & Zambrana, 2009b). In 1977, the Combahee River Collective published a manifesto that is one of the earliest publications about intersectionality. It expressed the notion that oppression due to race, class, and sex cannot be separated (Cole, 2009). Dissatisfied with the ways that male voices were prioritized in the Civil Rights movement and White voices were prioritized in early feminist movements, Black feminist activists and scholars such as Patricia Hill Collins (1990), Angela Davis (1981), and many others argued that being Black and being a woman were not separate and exclusive identities, but rather were intricately linked and interdependent. Audre Lorde (1980, 2007) furthered this work by insisting on her identities as a Black lesbian woman, adding sexuality to discussions of feminism and racial identity. Building on Black feminism, Gloria Anzaldúa (1987/2012) and Chandra Mohanty (2003) brought global perspectives to the forefront by considering the ways that borders and borderlands both divide and unite communities of women around the world. These feminist scholars argued for the necessary inclusion of race, class, nationality, sexuality, and gender in social justice and social action, noting that dismissal or subjugation of any one identity would limit the scope and depth of revolution and change.

Critical Race Theory and Critical Race Feminism

Derrick Bell is credited with founding the movement known as CRT (Crenshaw, Gotanda, Peller, & Thomas, 1995; Delgado & Stefancic, 2001; Matsuda, 1996). Founded in legal studies, CRT explores the ways that race and racism were codified and defended in legal practice. Although a detailed discussion of CRT is beyond the scope of this chapter, it is important to note some of the central tenets of CRT that are foundational to intersectionality. First and foremost, CRT contends that racism is pervasive, normal, and institutionalized so much so that it is often unnoticed and unremarkable. Overt forms of racism are addressed; however, the subtler and more insidious forms of racism are allowed to pass because Whiteness is normed. CRT also considers race a social construction created as a tool for White supremacy, noting that different identities (i.e., Black, Latina, Asian American, Native) were racialized differently to best serve the purposes of White communities. For example, Asian Americans (specifically Chinese Americans and Japanese Americans) were praised as "model minorities" in 1968 to create discord between Asian American and other communities of color, suggesting that if Asian Americans could "overcome" racism, then so could Black and Latin Americans (Chan, 1991). Specifically related to intersectionality, CRT prioritizes the lived experiences of communities of color, citing narrative and storytelling as legitimate forms of knowledge. CRT also argues for antiessentialist approaches, maintaining that there is no one racial identity that is shared by all members of a community. Each person has his or her unique identity, informed by his or her specific contexts and multiple social identities. In fact, the only commonality experienced by all people of color is racism (Crenshaw et al., 1995; Delgado & Stefancic, 2001; Wong, 2013).

CRF (Crenshaw, 1991; Crenshaw et al., 1995) both deepens and broadens CRT's vision by considering the intersections of race and class in focusing on the experiences of women of color in legal settings. Holding the same central tenets as CRT, CRF explores the ubiquity of racism *and* sexism together, as interlocking systems of power and oppression. CRF holds the experiences of women of color as the center and foundation for analysis. The criminalization of poor Black mothers (Crenshaw, 1991), the regulation of women's reproductive rights (Roberts, 1995), and the relationship between gender and property (Matsuda, 1996) are examples of research conducted by CRF scholars.

Intersectionality as an Analytic Lens

Intersectionality has been deepened and broadened by scholars in education, counseling, sociology, psychology, cultural studies, history, queer theory, feminist studies, ethnic studies, and many other fields. Much of the early research that employed intersectionality examined the experiences of women of color (sometimes also poor, sometimes also queer) navigating various institutions and social structures (e.g., courtrooms, social services, education). This scholarship contributed new and valuable perspectives to recognize the ways women's social identities cannot be isolated or separated from each other. Dill and Zambrana (2009a) outline four theoretical interventions that are at the core of intersectionality as an analytic lens: (a) using the experiences of people of color and marginalized communities as a starting point for developing theory and practice; (b) exploring both individual and group identities; (c) examining the connections between systems of power that perpetuate inequality and oppression; and (d) connecting research and practice toward social justice.

First, rather than centering majority experiences that reinforce dominant perspectives as universal and normative, intersectionality argues that research and practice must recognize the differential experiences of marginalized populations in order to ensure that their narratives are visible and valued. This shifts the focus from privileged to marginalized identities (i.e., women and girls; people of color; LGBTQIA communities) and underscores how the status quo negatively impacts some communities.

Second, intersectionality leads to understanding individual experiences in collective spaces. There are no monolithic identities or one-size-fits-all descriptors. At the same time, consideration is given for the ways that cultures are formed through shared practice, language, rituals, physical spaces, and stories. Intersectionality suggests that cultures and identities are created by individuals, making them fluid and dynamic, infused with multiple meanings, histories, and knowledge. There is no monolithic identity or essential core that is imposed upon a community.

Third, scholarship and practice must also take into account the impact of inequity, discrimination, and systems of power and oppression, with an emphasis on understanding how these systems are connected and mutually reinforcing. For example, Crenshaw (1991) outlined the compounding systems of racism, sexism, and classism that not only neglected the needs of poor, Black, single mothers, but also punished them for their circumstances.

And finally, intersectionality seeks to bridge the gap between theory and practice by insisting that scholars conduct research on inequity and social dilemmas and that practitioners contribute lived experience as knowledge. Integral to projects that engage intersectionality as an analytic lens is a conversation about power and the mechanisms through which power is gained, held, distributed, and deployed. In order to understand the lived experiences of marginalized and oppressed populations, it is necessary to make power explicit and known, to name it as visible, real, and valid. Doing so is one part of doing social justice, which seeks to dismantle systems of power and inequality.

Collins (1990) discussed four domains through which power and inequality are organized: structural power, disciplinary power, hegemonic power, and interpersonal power. Through various means and mechanisms, each domain regulates individual behavior, as well as the distribution of and access to resources.

Structural power employs institutional structures, such as government, the criminal justice system, and education, to organize and reproduce hierarchies intended to subjugate specific communities. Historical and current examples include access to health care and medical procedures, housing segregation, marriage rights, mandatory sentencing, and immigration policies.

Disciplinary power refers to the bureaucratic procedures used to implement the policies dictated by institutions. Structures (e.g., social welfare, criminal justice) have been internally stratified to further perpetuate inequity and discrimination. For example, determination of which social benefits would be distributed via federal or state organizations allowed for continued discrimination, since state structures gave more space for individual bias and political influence (Dill & Zambrana, 2009b). In the criminal justice system, drug offenses that occurred more frequently in Black communities were given harsher penalties than those in White communities (Alexander, 2010).

Hegemonic power and interpersonal power are most relevant to this chapter's discussion, as they focus on the interactional and discursive practices that influence individual and collective norms and experiences. They also undergird the existing status quo by helping to defend the policies and practices of structural and disciplinary power. The ideologies reinforced by hegemonic power also inform and affirm the stereotyped depictions of social groups, which in turn sets expectations for behaviors, consequences, and outcomes. More specifically, hegemonic power describes the ideologies, perspectives, and portrayals that form personal and group consciousness. For example, teachers may reward boys for speaking up in school but reward girls for their "good" behavior. Both girls and boys may interpret this as signifying that girls should be quiet and their learning or intelligence is not as important as their behavior. Girls will then regulate their own behavior in the classroom so as to be a "good" girl (Scantlebury, 2009; Silva, Langhout, Kohfeldt, & Gurrola, 2015). Layering gender with race, scholars have found that teachers respond differently to Black girls depending upon their behavior. A Black girl who is "loud" in the classroom is read as disruptive or disrespectful and her learning may also be deprioritized (Evans-Winters, 2014; Silva et al., 2015). Internalization of socialization messages and negative images can cause self-regulation and self-imposed restrictions, such that individuals and communities contribute to their own marginalization, both consciously and unconsciously. This is also understood as internalized oppression. Hegemonic power informs perceptions of oppressed communities so that both dominant and subordinate groups enforce dominant beliefs. Structural and disciplinary power can be used to dampen resistance to hegemonic norms.

Interpersonal power refers to the daily, commonplace, and subliminal actions, behaviors, and language that reify dominant norms and beliefs. Interpersonal power includes microaggressions, traditional gender roles, and belief in the truthfulness of stereotypes. Microaggressions refer to the commonplace, unintentional speech, actions, or behaviors that are enacted upon people of marginalized identities as forms of discrimination. Examples include asking someone "Where are you from, originally?" or being surprised by someone's intelligence or ability to speak clearly (Smith, Allen, & Danley, 2007; Sue et al., 2007). Interpersonal power also defines which behaviors and language are accepted as universal norms. For example, heterosexuality is accepted as "normal," whereas queer identities are deviant. Thus, during puberty, peer pressure around dating expects girls to be attracted to boys and sex education in schools focuses on heterosexual intercourse only. Lesbian, bi/pansexual, and queer women receive messages that they are deviant, abnormal, or wrong and must repress or hide their sexuality.

What is most damaging about the exercise of interpersonal power is that it is enacted by and between individuals, and is often unnamed or unnoticed.

Intersectionality as Lived Experience

Common stereotypes about feminine beauty, or that girls are not good at math and science, can do more to regulate and limit behavior and ambitions than social institutions or overt discrimination. Girls receive both direct and indirect messages about gender norms, including appropriate behavior, expectations, and specific roles to play. Messaging comes from multiple locations, all of which operate within systems of patriarchy and sexism intertwined with and complicated by racism, classism, and other forms of discrimination. In a qualitative study I conducted, Mary, a Filipina American student, talked about her struggle to speak up in meetings and advocate for herself and her community. Both race and gender impacted her ability to utilize her own agency and power. Although she was a student leader on campus and confident in many ways, she had a difficult time speaking up in meetings with administrators and internalized the pain of those interactions.

> "It was really amplified 'cause you have to deal with administrators, too. . . . A lot of them are White males, elderly, tall, like, those are the epitome of power in this country and, look at me as this short Brown woman . . . I'd literally be facing the White boy in these meetings and I'd choke up and I'd come out of the meeting, like, so mad at myself, like, should've spoke up more."—Mary, a Filipina American student

Because of hegemonic narratives that blamed women for their own situations and positioned them as less than men, Mary did not recognize the ways that she had been socialized not to challenge authority or to speak against White men.

Rather than accept the status quo as simply "how things are," intersectionality makes these domains (structural, disciplinary, hegemonic, and interpersonal) visible in order to demonstrate how they create systems of power and oppression, and regulate and intrude upon daily behaviors, attitudes, and experiences, as well as identities. As Dill and Zambrana (2009a) stated, "Intersectional analyses, as knowledge generated from and about oppressed groups, unveil these domains of power and reveal how oppression is constructed and maintained through multiple aspects of identity simultaneously" (p. 7).

THE IMPACT OF OPPRESSION ON MENTAL HEALTH AND WELL-BEING

The four domains of power—structural, disciplinary, hegemonic, and interpersonal—significantly impact individuals' understanding, expression, and behavior. This is particularly poignant for people of marginalized identities because there are multiple systems and domains working congruently to maintain the status quo. Britzman, Santiago-Válles, Jiménez-Múñox, and Lamash (1993) noted, "The cost of identity entails reformulating the self with imperatives that, even while resisting the various forms of oppression, may still contradictorily veil and coincidentally assert how culture is lived as a relation of domination and subordination" (p. 190). Put more plainly, systems of oppression and discrimination have a negative impact on marginalized communities in terms of access to resources and opportunities (i.e., structural and disciplinary power). The "cost of identity" is paid in emotional well-being and psychological health (i.e., intrapersonal power). Multiple studies have recorded the detrimental effects of discrimination, including higher rates of depression, anxiety, self-harm and risk behaviors, posttraumatic stress, suicide, low self-esteem, obesity, heart disease, hostility, and loneliness among women, communities of color, LGBTQIA communities, and other marginalized communities (Berg, 2006; Bryant-Davis & Ocampo, 2005; Leary, 2005; Lee & Turney, 2012; Lewis & Neville, 2015; Lowe, Okubo, & Reilly, 2012; Monk, Winslade, & Sinclair, 2008; Pascoe & Richman, 2009; Ratts et al., 2016; Smith et al., 2007; Sue et al., 2007; Swim et al., 2001; Watts-Jones, 2010; Wilkin & Hillock, 2014).

Oppression and discrimination occur in both overt and covert forms, within institutions and structures (i.e., structural and disciplinary power), between people (i.e., interpersonal power), and may also be internalized (i.e., hegemonic power). Lee and Turney (2010) found that "everyday discrimination" had a stronger impact on women than men with regard to mental health. Furthermore, research has shown that the cumulative impact and frequency of microaggressions and everyday forms of discrimination have a stronger effect than overt incidents (Berg, 2006; Smith et al., 2007; Sue et al., 2007; Swim et al., 2001). Berg (2006) noted that rates of posttraumatic stress in women were twice that in men, even after controlling for types of events.

Everyday forms of discrimination and oppression have deep and long-lasting impact on women and girls, with especially devastating effects on those who hold multiple marginalized identities. Not only must oppressed communities contend with discriminatory systems and institutions, they are also impacted by interpersonal and intrapersonal domains of power. In Berg's 2006 study, 100% of the participants (all women) reported experiencing some type of sexist behavior in their lifetime and within the past year. An astounding 98% of participants reported hearing sexist jokes in their lifetime; 94% had experienced sexual harassment; and 92% felt they were disrespected because they were women. A majority of participants reported experiencing everyday sexist behaviors at work (particularly in the helping professions and education) and within their families (Berg, 2006).

Intersectionality reminds us that such experiences occur around race, sexuality, class, ability, spirituality, and all social identities (Crenshaw, 1991; D. J. Davis, Brunn-Bevel, & Olive, 2015; Dill & Zambrana, 2009b; Lee & Turney, 2012; Pascoe & Richman, 2009; Sue et al., 2007). These everyday forms of discrimination can include sexist or racist language; homophobic jokes; being ignored in the workplace; derogatory slurs/vandalism; demeaning behaviors; sexual objectification;

assumptions/stereotypes of sexuality, age, race, gender, and religion; being overly burdened for the emotional care of family members and colleagues; and being underestimated (Berg, 2006; Lee & Turney, 2012; Lewis & Neville, 2015; Lowe et al., 2012; Pascoe & Richman, 2009; Smith et al., 2007; Sue et al., 2007; Swim et al., 2001). What makes these small acts of discrimination and oppression even more hurtful is that they can manifest themselves in multiple ways, resulting in psychiatric disorders and mental health conditions, posttraumatic stress, hostility toward others, stress in relationships, and self-doubt, to name but a few. Clients and students may seek counseling to address these conditions, yet these are only symptoms of a problem. Additionally, because inequity and oppression are systemized and socialized, clients and counselors may not immediately recognize the cause of such conditions (Berg, 2006; Smith et al., 2007; Sue et al., 2007). Clients with multiple marginalized identities will be confronted with various and simultaneous forms of discrimination as well and may not know how to best address the situations they face. Discrimination based on the more invisible identities (e.g., ability, religion, sexuality) may go unnoticed or untreated because these acts seem less obvious, although they are just as harmful.

Emotional and physiological pain are only part of the "cost of identity" that Britzman et al. (1993) discuss. People of marginalized identities engage many strategies for addressing microaggressions, resisting stereotypes and assumptions, and building resilience and agency. These strategies may include help-seeking behaviors. Intersectionality points to the ways that one's identities are formed within these systems of oppression. As such, they permeate the ways that individuals make meaning of their identities, and whether these conform to or resist stereotypes and generalizations.

As examples, Abes et al. (2007) use narratives to illustrate the meaning-making filters that influence how three lesbian women constructed a sense of self. In their study, they noted that one participant, Amy, was still subject to dominant assumptions about lesbians even as she sought to resist them. "Even though Amy did not construct her identity in a manner consistent with stereotypes, stereotypes still dictated how she perceived her identity. Amy defined herself through who she is not, rather than through who she is" (p. 8). In my study on Asian American identities, Rory navigated her identities—as Chinese American, an immigrant, and a woman, in addition to a difficult relationship with her father in the United States and a mother who remained in Taiwan—by resisting people's assumptions of who she should be. She talked more explicitly about the interplay between her internal sense of self and dominant norms.

> *"I do cultural things, but my identity . . . like identity I think, is constructed largely on how people see you. And then you internalize it."*—Rory, a Chinese American immigrant woman

As such, Rory played against the model minority stereotype and sexist trope of submissive Asian woman.

"I'm very extroverted and very assertive. I feel like people didn't give me an identity . . . When I was growing up, I was always called white washed."—Rory

Although this allowed Rory to feel a sense of empowerment and agency to express herself as she wished, she also had a difficult time finding community. Racism did not allow her to fit in with White peers, although it also isolated her from Asian and Asian American peers. She struggled with knowing what being Asian American meant to her and feeling accepted for it.

"So I kind of internalized that a little and I felt like I wasn't a very Asian person."—Rory

As discussed in the ACA's MSJCC (Ratts et al., 2015, 2016), counselors must first develop an awareness of the negative impact of oppression on clients' mental health and their ability to develop a positive sense of self. A woman/girl who holds multiple marginalized identities will experience even greater debilitating effects. For example, Abes et al. (2007) described Carmen, a Puerto Rican-Caucasian, Christian woman who tried to make sense of her identity as a lesbian within a politically and religiously conservative family. Although she understood God to be accepting of her identity as a lesbian, she was unsure of how to keep her family support and still express who she is. Counselors can play an important role in creating supportive spaces for clients and students who are exploring their identities and navigating these systems of power. Most importantly, counselors must be careful not to replicate modes of discrimination within the counseling relationship itself.

INTERSECTIONALITY IN COUNSELING PRACTICE

The MSJCC (Ratts et al., 2015) outline four domains and multiple layers of engagement for counselors to develop competencies over a lifetime of personal and professional learning. The domains include "counselor self-awareness, client worldview, counseling relationship, and counseling and advocacy interventions" (p. 3). Competencies include awareness, knowledge, skills, and action within each domain. Counselors are encouraged to view their work as a mode and medium for social justice. As previously discussed, the revised competencies reflect a shift from a simplistic multicultural worldview (i.e., everyone is different and all differences are the same) to a social justice perspective (i.e., systems of power, privilege, oppression create hierarchies and differential impact, access, and opportunities for privileged and marginalized communities). This new approach resonates with the four tenets of intersectionality by suggesting that the experiences of oppressed people be centered in developing core competencies in the field, honoring both personal and social identities, explicitly acknowledging multiple systems of oppression, and connecting research and counseling practice (Dill & Zambrana, 2009a).

I will not summarize the competencies here; however, what is noteworthy are the ways that counseling and advocacy interventions are organized into six areas (intrapersonal, interpersonal, institutional, community, public policy, and international/global affairs) that correlate with Collins's domains of power (1990): intrapersonal, interpersonal, disciplinary, and structural. What Ratts et al. (2015) suggest are ways that counselors and counseling can disrupt the domains of power used to perpetuate oppression and discrimination. Within the intrapersonal and interpersonal, multicultural and social justice competent counselors are expected to support clients' exploration of internalized privileged and/or oppression; to develop a critical consciousness about the impact of systems of power on their lives; and to explore relationships and family dynamics that might reflect systems of power and oppression. Making space within counseling sessions to name microaggressions and everyday forms of discrimination can affirm clients' experiences around their multiple identities. Thus, the lived experiences of marginalized individuals are central. Racism, sexism, homophobia, classism, ableism, and other forms of discrimination are labeled as pervasive and oppressive (Cole, 2009; Crenshaw, 1991; Delgado & Stefancic, 2001; Dill & Zambrana, 2009b; Sue et al., 2007; Watts-Jones, 2010).

In consideration of structural and disciplinary domains (i.e., institutional, community, public policy, and international/global affairs in the MSJCC), counselors should help their clients understand the broader structures and systems that impact them. Intersectionality contends that interventions must identify systemic rather than individual causes and responsibilities. Pointing out the structures of power and oppression and exploring socialization messages that create expectations of behavior, prescribed roles and responsibilities, and narrow opportunities may help clients name and interrupt these external forces and prevent the internalization of such damaging messages. By recognizing women's and girls' power and choice to decide who they are and what being a girl or woman means to them, counselors support girls and women to develop whole, confident, and dynamic identities. Locating the problem outside of women and girls creates opportunities for them to realize they have the power to choose which issues they wish to address and which messages they choose to believe. Understanding that there are barriers to their liberation, and even people who disagree with them, will help clients understand the context in which their choices are made, and how they can work on long-term strategies to remove those barriers. Supporting women and girls, particularly those with intersecting marginalized identities, to develop a whole and healthy sense of self, will not only improve their lives but will also address systemic injustice and potentially transform the world.

Counselors must do their own work to develop a self-awareness and understanding of their perspectives and biases (Sue et al., 2007; Watts-Jones, 2010). The counseling relationship already inhabits a hierarchical power structure wherein the counselor has authority. Differences between the social identities of the counselor and the client, particularly around political or social power, will also affect the counseling relationship (McDowell & Hernández, 2010; Ratts et al., 2015, 2016; Shin, 2015; Sue et al., 2007; Watts-Jones, 2010).

Intersectionality and CRF argue against using generalities and assumptions in any field, since using the experiences of a few to treat the many would be ineffective at best and cause harm at worst. Within counseling relationships, it is important to focus on each person's voice and narrative and the impact of systems of power and oppression upon his or her own life (Shin, 2015). Counselors can best support their clients by guiding them to express their own experiences and frustrations and to locate their own sources of healing, resistance, and empowerment. Helping girls and women focus on their own lives can contribute to a more confident sense of self. Following the tenets of intersectionality and CRF, clients produce their own knowledge and identities and have the right to exercise their agency in self-determination. Counselors can help them recognize the possible costs and consequences of their choices and, in doing so, may also help them make healthy decisions for both the short and long term. Counselors should be thoughtful using multiple methods of exploration with clients, such as individual and group counseling, mindfulness and meditation, journaling, attending programs and events, taking classes, or joining community spaces.

CALL TO ACTION

The MSJCC recommend that counselors engage in their immediate and local communities, both in their home and work contexts. Counselors must understand their work environment in schools, hospitals, social services, or private practice. Who are their students and clients? Who has access to counseling in these communities? What are systemic and individual barriers to seeking counseling (e.g., cost, stigma, time)? Counselors should be actively involved in initiatives outside their counseling practice to participate in social movements more broadly. They should build an awareness of social issues that affect their local, national, and global communities and explore ways to address the issues that most resonate with them. In doing so, counselors will develop their own sense of self and agency. They may also become better attuned to the injustice that surrounds all of us.

Counselors have a responsibility for building their own self-awareness and critical reflexive practice to best support their clients, particularly those most vulnerable and targeted by oppression and discrimination. By bringing intersectionality as an analytic lens into their work, counselors can create space for honoring clients' multiple identities as complex, holistic, and valued. This is not only ethical practice; it is necessary practice. As Lorde (1980) asked, "because I am woman, because I am Black, because I am lesbian, because I am myself, a Black woman warrior poet doing my work, come to ask you, are you doing yours?" (p. 21).

REFLECTION AND DISCUSSION QUESTIONS

1. What are your intersecting identities? What privileged and what oppressed identities do you hold?

2. What socialization messages have you received about your social identities—race, gender, class, ability, sexuality, spirituality, and so forth? Which behaviors were rewarded? Discouraged? What are ways that you have observed or experienced the four domains of power? How do you participate or perpetuate them?

3. How have you experienced symptoms of oppression and discrimination? How have your privileged identities shielded you from experiencing these symptoms?

4. How have you observed symptoms of oppression and discrimination in girls and women? With girls and women of multiple marginalized identities?

5. Which identities should you discuss with clients in efforts to name power within the counseling relationship, and affirm your ability to provide supportive, caring, and effective spaces for treatment?

HELPFUL RESOURCES

- Audre Lorde Project (www.alp.org)
- Black Girl Dangerous blog (www.blackgirldangerous.org)
- Center for Assessment and Policy Development—Racial Equity and White Privilege (www.capd.org/white-privilege)
- Center for Nonviolence and Social Justice (www.nonviolenceandsocialjustice.org)
- Multicultural and Social Justice Counseling Competencies (www.counseling.org/docs/default-source/competencies/multicultural-and-social-justice-counseling-competencies.pdf?sfvrsn=20)
- Peacock Rebellion (www.peacockrebellion.org)
- Social Justice Training Institute (www.sjti.org)
- Sylvia Rivera Law Project (www.srlp.org)
- Undoing Racism: The People's Institute for Survival and Beyond (www.pisab.org)
- Vanissar Tarakali Blog (www.vanissar.com/blog)

REFERENCES

Abes, E. S., Jones, S. R., & McEwen, M. K. (2007). Reconceptualizing the model of multiple dimensions of identity: The role of meaning-making capacity in the construction of multiple identities. *Journal of College Student Development, 48*(1), 1–22. doi:10.1353/csd.2007.0000

Alexander, M. (2010). *The new Jim Crow: Mass incarceration in the age of colorblindness.* Berkeley, CA: The New Press.

Almeida, R. V., Parker, L., & Dolan-Del Vecchio, K. (2008). Critical consciousness: Recognizing the social and political context of daily life. In *Transformative family therapy: Just families in a just society* (pp. 22–54). Boston, MA: Allyn & Bacon/Longman.

Anzaldúa, G. (2012). *Borderlands: La frontera.* San Francisco, CA: Aunt Lute Books. (Original work published 1987)

Berg, S. H. (2006). Everyday sexism and posttraumatic stress disorder in women: A correlational study. *Violence Against Women, 12*(10), 970–988. doi:10.1177/1077801206293082

Bowleg, L. (2008). When Black + lesbian + woman ≠ Black lesbian woman: The methodological challenges of qualitative and quantitative intersectionality research. *Sex Roles, 59,* 312–325. doi:10.1007/s11199-008-9400-z

Britzman, D. P., Santiago-Válles, K., Jiménez-Múñox, G., & Lamash, L. M. (1993). Slips that show and tell: Fashioning multiculture as a problem of representation. In C. McCarthy & W. Crichlow (Eds.), *Race, identity and representation in education* (pp. 188–200). New York, NY: Routledge.

Bryant-Davis, T., & Ocampo, C. (2005). The trauma of racism: Implications for counseling, research and education. *The Counseling Psychologist, 33*(4), 574–578. doi:10.1177/0011000005276581

Chan, S. (1991). *Asian Americans: An interpretive history.* New York, NY: Twayne.

Cheshire, L. C. (2013). Reconsidering sexual identities: Intersectionality theory and the implications for educating counselors. *Canadian Journal of Counseling and Psychotherapy, 47*(1), 4–13. Retrieved from http://cjc-rcc.ucalgary.ca/cjc/index.php/rcc/article/view/2659

Cole, E. R. (2009). Intersectionality and research in psychology. *American Psychologist, 64*(3), 170–180. doi:10.1037/a0014564

Collins, P. H. (1990). *Black feminist thought: Knowledge, consciousness, and the politics of empowerment.* New York, NY: Routledge.

Crenshaw, K. (1991). Mapping the margins: Intersectionality, identity politics, and violence against women of color. *Stanford Law Review, 43,* 1241–1299. http://www.jstor.org/stable/1229039

Crenshaw, K., Gotanda, N., Peller, G., & Thomas, K. (Eds.). (1995). *Critical race theory: The key writings that formed the movement.* New York, NY: The New Press.

Davis, A. Y. (1981). *Women, race, and class.* New York, NY: Random House.

Davis, D. J., Brunn-Bevel, R. J., & Olive, J. L. (Eds.). (2015). *Intersectionality in educational research.* Sterling, VA: Stylus.

Delgado, R., & Stefancic, J. (2001). *Critical race theory: An introduction.* New York, NY: New York University Press.

Dill, B. T., & Zambrana, R. E. (2009a). Critical thinking about inequality: An emerging lens. In B. T. Dill & R. E. Zambrana (Eds.), *Emerging intersections: Race, class, and gender in theory, policy, and practice* (pp. 1–21). New Brunswick, NJ: Rutgers University Press.

Dill, B. T., & Zambrana, R. E. (Eds.). (2009b). *Emerging intersections: Race, class, and gender in theory, policy, and practice.* New Brunswick, NJ: Rutgers University Press.

Erikson, E. (1994). *Identity and the life cycle.* New York, NY: W. W. Norton.

Evans-Winters, V. E. (2014). Are Black girls not gifted? Race, gender, and resilience. *Interdisciplinary Journal of Teaching and Learning, 4*(1), 22–30. http://www.subr.edu/index.cfm/subhome/36

Freire, P. (2003). *Pedagogy of the oppressed.* New York, NY: The Continuum International. (Original work published 1970)

Goodman, R. D. (2015). A liberatory approach to trauma counseling: Decolonizing our trauma-informed practices. In R. D. Goodman & P. C. Gorski (Eds.), *Decolonizing "multicultural" counseling through social justice* (pp. 55–72). New York, NY: Springer-Verlag.

Goodman, R. D., & Gorski, P. C. (Eds.). (2015). *Decolonizing "multicultural" counseling through social justice.* New York, NY: Springer-Verlag.

Hernández, P., & McDowell, T. (2010). Intersectionality, power, and relational safety in context: Key concepts in clinical supervision. *Training and Education in Professional Psychology, 4*(1), 29–35. doi:10.1037/a0017064

Jones, S. T., & McEwen, M. (2000). A conceptual model of multiple dimensions of identity. *Journal of College Student Development, 41*(4), 405–414. Retrieved from http://multipleidentitieslgbtq.wiki.westga.edu/file/view/Jones%26McEwen_2000.pdf

Leary, J. D. (2005). *Posttraumatic slave syndrome: America's legacy of enduring injury and healing.* Portland, OR: Uptone Press.

Lee, H., & Turney, K. (2010). Investigating the relationship between perceived discrimination, social status, and mental health. *Society and Mental Health, 2*(1), 1–20. doi:10.1177/2156869311433067

Lewis, J. A., & Neville, H. A. (2015). Construction and initial validation of the gendered racial micro aggressions: Scale for Black women. *Journal of Counseling Psychology, 62*(2), 289–302. doi:10.1037/cou0000062

Lorde, A. (1980). *The cancer journals.* San Francisco, CA: Aunt Lute Books.

Lorde, A. (2007). *Sister outsider.* Berkeley, CA: The Crossing Press.

Lowe, S. M., Okubo, Y., & Reilly, M. F. (2012). A qualitative inquiry into racism, trauma, and coping: Implications for supporting victims of racism. *Professional Psychology: Research and Practice, 43*(3), 190–198. doi:10.1037/a0026501

Matsuda, M. J. (1996). *Where is your body? And other essays on race, gender, and the law.* Boston, MA: Beacon Press.

McDowell, T., & Hernández, P. (2010). Decolonizing academia: Intersectionality, participation, and accountability in family therapy and counseling. *Journal of Feminist Family Therapy, 22*(2), 93–111. doi:10.1080/08952831003787834

Mohanty, C. (2003). *Feminism without borders: Decolonizing theory, practicing solidarity.* Durham, NC: Duke University Press.

Monk, G., Winslade, J., & Sinclair, S. (2008). *New horizons in multicultural counseling.* Los Angeles, CA: Sage.

Omi, M., & Winant, H. (1994). *Racial formation in the United States: From the 1960s to the 1990s.* New York, NY: Routledge.

Pascoe, E. A., & Richman L. S. (2009). Perceived discrimination and health: A meta-analytic review. *Psychology Bulletin, 135*(4), 531–554. doi:10.1037/a0016059

Ratts, M. J., Singh, A., Nassar-McMillan, S., Butler, S. K., & McCullough, J. R. (2015). *Multicultural and Social Justice Counseling Competencies.* Retrieved from http://www.counsel ing.org/docs/default-source/competencies/multicultural-and-social-justice-counsel ing-competencies.pdf?sfvrsn=20

Ratts, M. J., Singh, A., Nassar-McMillan, S., Butler, S. K., & McCullough, J. R. (2016). Multicultural and Social Justice Counseling Competencies: Guidelines for the counseling profession. *Journal of Multicultural Counseling and Development, 44,* 28–48. doi:10.1002/jmcd.12035

Scantlebury, K. (2009). *Gender bias in teaching.* Retrieved from http://www.education.com/reference/article/gender-bias-in-teaching

Shin, R. Q. (2015). The application of critical consciousness and intersectionality as tools for decolonizing racial/ethnic identity development models in the fields of counseling and psychology. In R. D. Goodman & P. C. Gorski (Eds.), *Decolonizing "multicultural" counseling through social justice* (pp. 11–22). New York, NY: Springer-Verlag.

Silva, J. M., Langhout, R. D., Kohfeldt, D., & Gurrola, E. (2015). "Good" and "bad" kids? A race and gender analysis of effective behavioral support in an elementary school. *Urban Education, 50*(7), 787–811. doi:10.1177/0042085914534859

Smith, W. A., Allen, W. R., & Danley, L. L. (2007). "Assume the position . . . you fit the description": Psychosocial experiences and racial battle fatigue among African American male college students. *American Behavioral Scientist, 51*(4), 551–578. doi:10.1177/000 2764207307742

Sue, D. W., Capodilupo, C. M., Torino, G. C., Bucceri, J. M., Holder, A. M. B., Nadal, K. L., & Esquilin, M. (2007). Racial microaggressions in everyday life: Implications for clinical practice. *American Psychologist, 62*(4), 271–286. doi:10.1037/0003-066X.62.4.271

Swim, J. K., Hyers, L. L., Cohen, L. L., & Ferguson, M J. (2001). Everyday sexism: Evidence for its incidence, nature, and psychological impact from three daily diary studies. *Journal of Social Issues, 57*(1), 31–53. doi:10.1111/0022-4537.00200

Torres, V., Jones, S. R., & Renn, K. (2009). Identity development theories in student affairs: Origins, current statuses, and new approaches. *Journal of College Student Development, 50*(6), 577–596. doi:10.1353/csd.0.0102

Watts-Jones, T. D. (2010). Location of self: Opening the door to dialogue on intersectionality in the therapy process. *Family Process, 49*(3), 405–420. doi:10.1111/j.1545-5300.2010 .01330.x

Weber, L. (1998). A conceptual framework for understanding race, class, gender, and sexuality. *Psychology of Women Quarterly, 22,* 13–32. doi:10.1111/j.1471-6402.1998 .tb00139.x

Wilkin, L., & Hillock, S. (2014). Enhancing MSW students' efficacy in working with trauma, violence, and oppression: An integrated feminist-trauma framework for social work. *Feminist Teacher, 24*(3), 184–206. doi:10.5406/femteacher.24.3.0184

Wong, A. (2013). Racial identity construction among Chinese American and Filipino American undergraduates. In S. Museums, D. Miramba, & R. Teranishi (Eds.), *The misrepresented minority: New insights on Asian Americans and Pacific Islanders, and the implications for higher education* (pp. 86–105). Sterling, VA: Stylus.

Wong, A. (2015). In and of race: Identity construction re/considered. In D. J. Davis, R. Brunn-Bevel, & J. Olive (Eds.), *Intersectionality in educational research* (pp. 153–171). Sterling, VA: Stylus.

CHAPTER 4

Women and Relationships: Introduction to Relational-Cultural Theory

Alyson M. Pompeo-Fargnoli

LEARNING OBJECTIVES

After reading this chapter, you will be able to:

1. Critically analyze societal stereotypes about women's relationships with each other.
2. Recognize the importance of connection in women's lives in both non-romantic and romantic relationships.
3. Understand and apply tenets of relational-cultural theory (RCT) in clinical practice with diverse populations.

There is a widely held belief that women generally dislike each other. Women and girls are often portrayed as being "catty" or negative toward one another in relationships. This chapter helps to debunk those myths by highlighting how strong and unique female friendships are and by exploring the ways that women support one another around the world. Additionally, women's roles in romantic, family, and social relationships are explored. Relational-cultural theory (RCT) is explored, including an introduction to the theory. RCT is used as a way to conceptualize the need for connection that many women and girls feel in multiple areas of their lives. The chapter provides best practices for working in group and individual counseling settings, along with counselor implications.

SOCIETAL MESSAGES OF WOMEN EMOTIONALLY HARMING ONE ANOTHER

A few years ago, a popular media advertisement featured a beautiful woman sell-ing cosmetics with the tagline, "Don't hate me because I'm beautiful!" This prod-uct, which targeted women, also came loaded with preconceived notions and messages that women hate each other. Messages such as this teach women not only to mistrust one another, but also to participate in and proliferate the hurt. This message is also often transmitted throughout our larger society as well. It is used to fuel the myth that women are envious of one another and are catty to one another. This idea, constructed through the media, lends its way to a monetary gain through ratings and ticket sales for movies such as *Mean Girls* (Guinier et al., 2004) and *Carrie* (Misher & Peirce, 2013), which portray female relationships of jealousy, gossip, mistrust, cattiness, and bullying. Although there are instances where some of these factors do come into play, by and large and throughout his-tory, women have loved and supported each other. It is the relationships that women hold with one another that continue to sustain them. For every story of women's cattiness, distrust, or jealousy toward one another, there is countless research and anecdotal evidence to suggest the contrary.

"Yeah, sure I've had problems where girls have stabbed me in the back. But when it comes to having my back, and taking care of me, the only people I trust to do that are my girls!" —A female adolescent student

In addition to women supporting each other, there have been, and continue to be, activists highlighting and working on issues that impact women's lives. When we think back on all of the historical achievements and milestones for women, such as voting rights, reproductive health, and family leave, it is women who have been at the forefront of these movements, supporting, encouraging, and fighting alongside each other to make a better world for themselves and other women. For example, we can look back to August 28, 1917, when 10 women pick-eted the White House to bring awareness to President Wilson to grant women the right to vote. Throughout history, women have pushed forward for the rights of themselves and others, while connecting, bonding, and building friendships together.

Societal Resistance

Castaneda and Burns-Glover (2007) have noted that women's friendships can also serve as a form of resistance to oppression. In a patriarchal culture that values and centers men's experiences, the way women connect, bond, and create com-munity with one another can be seen as a form of resistance. Lewis (1990) calls this creating "vital arenas of political survival and cultural resistance" (p. 471). Although both men and women seek intimacy in their lives, research (Fehr, 2004) suggests that women engage in more intimate conversations in their friendships than men do. Hooks (2004) has argued that patriarchy's insistence that men subscribe to certain gender norms (e.g., emotional disconnectedness) robs them of the desire to form intimate friendships and connections.

> Patriarchy demands of all males that they engage in acts of psychic self-mutilation, that they kill off the emotional parts of themselves. If an individual is not successful in emotionally crippling himself, he can count on patriarchal men to enact rituals of power that will assault his self-esteem. (Hooks, 2004, p. 66)

It is important to understand that as men are demanded to reject certain emotional aspects of themselves, these qualities are the ones deemed weak within women. For instance, men are taught not to show tears or much affection. These are qualities expected instead of women and are seen as weak qualities. Rather than valuing all qualities, the dominant group continues to look down upon the qualities and attributes of the subordinate group, thus keeping both positions of power—and lack of power—intact.

Gender Socialization

In U.S. culture, which stresses individuation and values competition, girls and boys are socialized differently. Boys are socialized early on to emotionally and physically disconnect from parental ties and other forms of connections that may be seen as weak. They are instead conditioned to strive for independence and are encouraged to develop characteristics such as self-reliance. Girls, on the other hand, are encouraged to remain in connection, to stay close to the nest, and to pursue those activities that tend to be group oriented. As such, women and girls tend to view relationships as intrinsic to everything they do. Women are socialized to learn and practice empathy and mutual empathy (Miller, 1986). This gender socialization process in empathy development is essential to how men and women build and maintain friendships.

WOMEN IN FRIENDSHIPS

In the United States and many countries around the world, girls spend a great deal of time in the company of other girls. Their first friendships are often with other girls, paving the way to a lifetime of female friendships that are deeply intimate and rewarding (Jordan, 2001). A recent *New York Times* article entitled "What Women Find in Friends That They May Not Get From Love" (Traister, 2016) argued that women's friendships with one another are as fulfilling as their romantic relationships, if not more so. Traister (2016) goes on to suggest that because more and more women are choosing to forgo marriages, as compared with their peers in earlier times, the friendships that women have with one another tend to be the central relationships in their lives. These relationships are often intense, intimate, and satisfying; "As women live more of our adult lives unmarried, we become ourselves not necessarily in tandem with a man or within a traditional family structure, but instead alongside other women: our friends" (Traister, 2016, para. 4). In many ways, the friendships between women can far outreach casual friendships and may endure beyond other intimate and romantic relationships. Healthy and mutually empathic relationships between women can accomplish emotional needs that other relationships cannot (Jordan, 2001; Miller, 1976).

WOMEN IN ROMANTIC RELATIONSHIPS

When discussing women's relationships, it is also important to discuss their romantic relationships. In a study conducted with 82 Swiss women to gauge their relational abilities and satisfaction in the context of a romantic relationship, Meuwly, Feinstein, Davila, Nuñez, and Bodenmann (2013) found that women in romantic relationships with other women, as compared with those in heterosexual relationships, reported higher satisfaction in their relationships. The women reported feeling more supported and experiencing less conflict in their interactions with their partners. The results from the Swiss study were similar to previous studies conducted in the United States (Gottman et al., 2003; Roisman, Clausell, Holland, Fortuna, & Elieff, 2008). Also noteworthy in Meuwly et al.'s (2013) study was the way the couples reacted to conflicts in their relationships. Women in same-sex relationships reacted more positively when they received negative comments or criticisms from their partners than women in heterosexual relationships, or men in same-sex relationships. These findings suggest that women communicate better when interacting with their partners in same-sex relationships. Meuwly and colleagues (2013) also concluded that there is evidence that women are better at providing relational support than men.

In heterosexual relationships, women are generally more supportive and attentive to the emotional needs of their partner, particularly in times of stress (Mickelson, Claffey, & Williams, 2006). During stressful times when emotional support is most needed, women not only provide support, but also are more aware of this need. Women also tend to be more emotionally expressive and to request more emotional support from their partners in times of stress (Bodenmann & Cina, 2006; Pasch, Bradbury, & Davila, 1997, as cited by Meuwly et al., 2013).

WOMEN'S SUPPORT OF ONE ANOTHER GLOBALLY

The relationships that women form are essential to their sense of well-being and influence their daily lives. In this section, we highlight real-life examples of how women support each other globally.

Women's relationships with one another often consist of spending time together, sharing laughter, and engaging in fun activities. These are important aspects of women's relationships, but they are only one dimension of the myriads of ways that women connect and are present for each other. The love and connection that women have for one another is also shown in the way they support and advocate for one another. As noted previously, many of the advancements in the lives of women around the world are a result of the actions of women. This is not to diminish the role that men have played, and continue to play, as friends, partners, and allies. Rather, it is to highlight the ways in which women are a source of support and inspiration for one another. The following provides some examples of the unique ways that women work together to support, inspire, and uplift one another globally.

City of Joy

City of Joy is a community of women working together to support and empower female survivors of violence in the Democratic Republic of Congo. The community was founded by local women with the support of V-Day.org (a U.S.-based organization working to end violence against women and girls), UNICEF (United Nations Children's Fund), and Fondation Panzi (a local Congolese organization). City of Joy was conceived with the intention of creating a safe place for women where they could live, work, and heal. It is a place to turn pain into power and joy. The women receive leadership training, trauma counseling, computer literacy training, classes on knitting, and a host of other life skills to help them become independent. Led by 10 guiding principles, primary among them is the belief to: "Treat your sisters' lives as if they were your own" (V-Day.org, 2014).

Women of Liberia Mass Action for Peace

The peace-building efforts in the 14-year-long Liberian civil war were spearheaded by a collective group of women known as the Women of Liberia Mass Action for Peace. What started as a small group of Christian and Muslim women coming together to pray, sing, and support each other during a civil war, led to a mass movement of thousands of women using various forms of nonviolent protest. They demanded that the men, who were the perpetrators and leaders of the violence, bring an end to the war. Through their efforts, the women were able to help broker a peace deal among the warring factions, involve more women in the postconflict democracy process, and help elect the first female president in the history of modern day Africa. The Liberian women's story is chronicled in the award-winning documentary, "Pray the Devil Back to Hell." Additionally, Leymah Gbowee, the leader of the Women of Liberia Mass Action for Peace, along with Africa's first female president, Ellen Johnson Sirleaf, was awarded the 2011 Nobel Peace Prize for "their non-violent struggle for the safety of women and for women's rights to full participation in peace-building work" (Nobelprize.org, 2016). Gbowee also received the 2009 John F. Kennedy Profile in Courage Award.

A Village of Women

There is a popular phrase, "It takes a village," which implies that many must come together to bring about action and change. For the village of Umoja (meaning "unity" in Swahili) in Kenya, it took a village of women. In this village where only women live, men are allowed to visit, but they cannot stay overnight. The village was started in 1990 by 15 women who were survivors of sexual violence at the hands of British soldiers (Bindel, 2015). Their leader, Rebecca Lolosili, conceived the idea while in a hospital for injuries sustained from beatings by a group of men. She has been advocating for women's rights ever since (Bindel, 2015). Umoja has since become a sanctuary for women and girls escaping domestic violence (DV), forced marriage, female genital mutilation (FGM), and other gender-based violence. The women work together and share community resources equitably. Together they farm and raise livestock, as well as make jewelry and other crafts to sell as a source of income. All conflict and decisions are discussed by the women under a tree called "The Tree of Speech" (Bindel, 2015). As it can be seen from this example, women can come together to form healthy, safe, and successful communities with mutual respect and peace.

The examples noted are just a brief account of the countless ways in which women support each other globally. Although we have discussed practical ways that women support each other globally, it is also important to note specific theoretical underpinnings that highlight the way women form relationships. Practitioners and similar advocates for women seek ways to best support them and the following provides theoretical knowledge and practical implications with this purpose in mind.

RELATIONAL-CULTURAL THEORY

We cannot talk of women's relationships without a discussion on the theory that highlights the centrality of relationships in our lives. Relational-cultural theory (commonly referred to as RCT) has its roots in feminist philosophy and thought. Although a postmodern theory, it has gained widespread acceptance and respect since its formulation in the late 1970s.

Brief Historical Overview

The theory began its development in 1978 when Jean Baker Miller, a psychologist, wrote *Toward a New Psychology of Women* (1976). This was at the height of the second wave of the feminism movement as issues of gender and its impact on women's lives were being discussed. Influenced by the works of Betty Friedan's landmark *The Feminine Mystique*, Carol Gilligan's *In a Different Voice*, and Nancy Chodorow's *The Reproduction of Motherhood: Psychoanalysis and the Sociology of Gender*, Jean Baker Miller and three of her colleagues (Irene Stiver, Judith Jordan, and Janet Surrey) began meeting each month to discuss and write about the issues of their time. As psychologists, they also began to critique the way traditional psychotherapy misrepresented women's experiences. Their aim was to depathologize the many aspects of women's lives and to take those things that society sees as weaknesses and reframe them as strengths. This collaboration came to be known as the Stone Center Theory, which is located at Wellesley College for Women.

Known as the "Founding Scholars of RCT," these four women describe their experience of coming together to listen and reframe beliefs about relationships. Due to its focus on the importance of relationships in the lives of individuals, the theory came to be known as the self-in-relation theory. This approach was criticized for its lack of attention to intersectionality and eventually evolved to become RCT, which emphasizes the impact of oppression and other sociocultural influences on the lives of individuals (Jordan, 2001; Miller & Stiver, 1997; Walker, 2004).

Central Tenets of RCT

RCT posits that humans grow through and toward connection throughout the life span and that culture has a huge influence on that relationship. It examines the ways stratified institutions, marginalization, and dominance over others create hopelessness and isolation through systems such as sexism, racism, ableism, and homophobia, which cause chronic disconnections (Jordan, 2010). Isolation and disconnections are primary causes of human suffering. Therefore, the goal is to strive for connection. Taking an ecological approach, RCT acknowledges disconnection as occurring on individual, social, cultural, and systemic levels. RCT draws much of its work from social constructivist thinking, viewing gender differences as formed by stereotypes, power dynamics, and sex role standards that are imposed during child development. Additionally, unacknowledged privilege and the blatant use of power over others can create division, anger, disempowerment, and disconnection. From a therapeutic viewpoint, healing and growth occurs through the relationship between the counselor and the client (Jordan, 2010).

Core Concepts of RCT

RCT has many core principles to guide practitioners in their work with clients. The following concepts are a guide to understanding the way RCT is practiced and exhibit a philosophical stance in how RCT practitioners view the world and their clients.

Authenticity

Allowing yourself to be seen for who you really are is a key component to authenticity. This often necessitates risk, conflict, and expression of a full range of anger and other difficult emotions, along with a willingness to challenge old images. It is an ongoing challenge to feel genuine in one's emotional connectedness and at the same time purposeful in relationships (Walker & Rosen, 2004). Authenticity does not simply mean a lack of a filter between what we think and what we say. Rather, it is about being honest (including with our emotions), and realizing that our words impact our relationships (Jordan, 2010).

Empathy

Walker and Rosen (2004) assert that profound respect is the foundation of empathy. Empathy, as described by Jordan (2002), is an emotional and cognitively involved ability to join with another person in his or her experience. It is feeling connected, and, at the same time, appreciating your own separateness.

Mutuality

Mutuality means being open to the influence of others on us, having an impact on others, and seeing that our actions, feelings, and thoughts affect other people. Mutuality is often difficult to maintain in relationships where there are overt or covert power differentials, as it requires a respect for the experience of the other (Surrey, 1985). Mutuality, in the RCT context, should not be confused with reciprocity, which implies sameness. The intent is based on mutual understanding (Jordan, 2010). It is important to note that while mutuality is created in the counselor–client relationship, focus should still be on the client. Humanistic psychology encourages counselors to be empathic; whereas RCT encourages mutual empathy—a flow of empathy from the therapist to the client and vice versa. This means that the client is also well aware that the therapist has been affected by what the client has shared; however, healthy boundaries in line with ethical considerations should be maintained. Counselors can have an honest conversation with clients about the purpose of ethical boundaries and a client focus. Counselors also have the responsibility to establish, model, and maintain this delicate balance.

Growth-Fostering Relationships

Growth-fostering relationships allow everyone to contribute and grow. Development is not seen as a one-way street. Individuals are able to bring themselves most fully and authentically into connection with each other. This leads to what Miller calls the Five Good Things: increased sense of zest or energy (connection with another); feeling empowered to act beyond the relationship; increased clarity about one's self and others; greater sense of self-worth; and a desire for more connection (Miller & Stiver, 1997). Through better knowing others, one will better know one's self. Through healthy relationships, we grow and learn more about ourselves and how we can contribute to our relationships.

Disconnections

RCT acknowledges disconnection as a normal aspect of all relationships. Disconnections happen when individuals are misunderstood, humiliated, invalidated, excluded, or hurt. When addressed and worked on, disconnections are not always problematic and can, in fact, be a source of growth. When the less powerful person in the relationship is able to voice his or her sense of disconnection or pain to the more powerful, and is heard by the more powerful, the exchange can strengthen the relationship. If, on the other hand, the less powerful person is not heard or is discouraged from voicing his or her pain, he or she may learn to hide his or her suffering and, thus, begin to operate from a place of inauthenticity (Jordan, 2010). For some though, even if they are not heard, the actual act of voicing oneself and making a choice to disconnect from an unhealthy relationship can prove empowering in its own right.

Central Relational Paradox

The central relational paradox of our existence is that we develop strategies of disconnections in order to protect ourselves from pain and hurt, but paradoxically, those strategies contribute to our sense of isolation (Jordan, 2010). We do this out of the fear of authentically relating because we are often afraid that we may get rejected if we show our true selves. This is viewed as a defense mechanism in traditional psychotherapy, but in RCT it is seen as a way to recognize our need for relational connections.

Condemned Isolation

RCT sees isolation as the primary source of suffering. "Condemned isolation" is a phrase coined by Miller (1976) that captures the sense of isolation and aloneness that leaves us feeling like we are shut out of the human community. In this state, individual feels alone, paralyzed, and powerless to the forces impeding their connection. They often blame themselves for this disconnection. Condemned isolation is not to be mistaken with "being alone" or solitude, as it involves much more than that. Being alone is self-imposed and the individual can still feel connection to others, to nature, and to the community around them, whereas condemned isolation involves a loss of all connections.

Strategies of Disconnection

Strategies of disconnection are the strategies that people employ to stay out of relationships in order to keep from getting hurt. RCT's primary work in therapy is to bring people back into connection and to help replace past relational images (Miller, 1976). Relational images are the images we have come to expect from others in relationships due to our past experiences. Through past hurts, people may feel that future relationships will result in the same pain. As a result, they may avoid relationships; however, such avoidance will bring about its own pain and isolation. Such strategies of disconnection may only seem to avoid pain on the surface (Jordan, 2001).

Traumatic Disconnection

Banks (2008) describes traumatic disconnection as an "amygdala hijack." The amygdala is the brain organ responsible for the fight-or-flight response in times of trauma. Therefore, such an amygdala hijack is a disconnection that occurs from a traumatic event. Individuals suffering from posttraumatic stress disorder (PTSD) often find themselves in this state. The individual goes into a place of reactivity and becomes unable to repair relationships. The person struggles with forming healthy relationships with others due to a heightened sense of danger. Until safety can be reestablished, the therapist must respect the client's use of strategies of disconnection. Traumatic disconnections often happen when the individual feels vulnerable and may resort to strategies of disconnect as a means of protection.

Power in Relationships

RCT, like all forms of therapies practiced around the world, takes place within a context that is characterized by unequal distribution of power. Miller and Stiver (1997) defined power as the capacity to produce change, suggesting that power is a fundamental element of everyday living and not necessarily a negative thing. However, in a culture that overvalues separation and deterministic control, this power can easily transform into *power over* others. Miller (1976) defines a power-over culture as one where those with more power act in ways that maintain the power differential, undermining any movement that threatens the status quo. Those with power behave in ways that create conflict. The powerful therefore oppose movements toward shared power while hiding the function and intent of their actions (Walker & Rosen, 2004). Counselors practicing RTC must be mindful of and work with the client around the power differential. Although the session maintains a mutual empathy with healthy ethical boundaries, the counselor helps guide and support the client. Nonetheless, it should be communicated with the client that there is an equality of power.

RCT Versus Traditional Theoretical Approaches

In contrast to the traditional psychological theories that value independence, autonomy, self-interest, and competition as markers of maturity, RCT is built on the premise that throughout the life span, people grow through their connections with others. In discussing traditional psychotherapy, Jordan (2010) describes a valuing of individualism and competition among others. RCT espouses a break away from this traditional model, embracing the collectivistic and relational notion that we achieve our utmost potential in connecting, joining, and working together. This thinking is in line with many cultures around the world, and highlights an African saying by an unknown source: "If you want to go fast, go alone, but if you want to go far, go together."

Unlike other theories that propose step-by-step stages that determine growth and development, the fundamental principle of RCT is simple: Relationships are at the center of our growth and change comes from an increased understanding of who we are. Due to society's value on independence, RCT acknowledges the disconnecting experience women face as a result of societal power arrangements, such as sexism, racism, and class prejudice. Those in privileged positions have what RCT considers a power over others, which places people in categories: dominants and subordinates. People of the dominant culture appear more self-sufficient, mature, and worthy of privilege, therefore putting down the subordinate groups. The concern with this picture is that within the collectivistic culture, each person is encouraged to be an active contributing member of his or her community, promoting unity and selflessness specifically. This disconnection from societal and cultural expectations is at the heart and soul of RCT, which acknowledges the lived experiences of women and combats the stereotypes that influence their lives.

As Jordan (2010) discusses, the goal of RCT is to progress toward relational resilience, mutual empathy, and mutual empowerment, as opposed to separation from others. Ward (2000) supports this idea as she speaks to the importance of adolescent girls actively creating healthy resistance to the dominant narrative, which encourages young women to be silent and internalize oppression. She encourages young women to think critically about the dominant realities by naming them and opposing them. This awareness and push toward change mirrors the beliefs of RCT.

Research done on mentoring by Liang, Tracy, Taylor, and Williams (2002) found that using a relational approach with Asian women influenced the success of a mentoring program, evidenced by the women's reports of higher levels of self-esteem. Finally, Belgrave, Chase-Vaughn, Famebrdige, Addison, and Cherry (2000) looked to build resiliency (specifically focusing on self-esteem and a sense of culture) using a relational approach among young Black women. The women completed a month-long intervention program and the results indicated that these young women reported positive feelings about themselves and their cultures. Hence, RCT attends carefully to power dynamics, relationships, and understanding disconnections. These studies as well as other examples mentioned show the benefit of healthy relationships for growth, resiliency, and authenticity.

Choosing RCT

RCT's focus on relationships, connections, systemic structures such as sexism, racism, classism, homophobia, and other forms of oppression lends itself well to working with women from a collectivist culture and those that have experience with oppression and other forms of marginalization (Jordan, 2001). Many women come to counseling burdened by strategies for disconnections that may have served them well in navigating a patriarchal culture. Although RCT works well with women, it should be noted that RCT is effective with male clients as well. RCT is concerned with the imposition of structure in individuals' lives and maintains that while men do benefit from privileges bestowed upon them by the dominant culture, it comes at great detriment to their sense of connection and intimacy. Although there is not a specific stepwise process to practicing RCT, we will discuss later more specific examples of RCT application in counseling sessions.

Challenges to the Practice of RCT

RCT is a comprehensive theory that works well with various populations, including women, men, people of color, sexual and DV survivors, and individuals with other mental health issues. However, it has a number of challenges and may not work as well with certain populations. For example, the RCT concept of mutuality and viewing clients and therapists as equal partners in a therapeutic alliance may be uncomfortable for individuals from authoritative cultures or who view the therapist as an expert or authority figure in the relationship.

Another obstacle to practice is that it is not meant for brief therapy. Although there have been studies (Comstock, Duffey, & St. George, 2002) suggesting its effectiveness in short-term therapy, it does lend itself to long-term therapy. For example, RCT discourages termination and views the therapeutic relationship as a stop-and-go process where the client may accomplish a piece of work, decide not to meet for some time, and return if new issues arise. Through RCT, the relationship is maintained and the practice is continued. Although this method might be beneficial for a client's sense of security and continuity, it is particularly problematic for those with managed care. Insurance companies often require a beginning and end date of treatment along with a diagnosis and resolution of problems. On the other hand, RCT can be very effective for school counselors who can meet with students periodically over the course of an entire school year.

Practicing RCT can have the additional challenge that it is driven by theory and philosophy rather than techniques. There is not a step-by-step guide on how to practice RCT in a session. As a result, this may pose as a challenge for beginning practitioners and counselor educators. Careful supervision is recommended to give supervisees enough opportunity to discuss working around mutual empathy and authenticity with clients. It is important to note that RCT does not serve as a replacement for other theoretical orientations; rather, it is a worldview that enhances clinical practice and can be integrated with most approaches. For example, a counselor practicing cognitive behavioral therapy (CBT) can still incorporate RCT into his or her practice. Although most theories remain static over the years, RCT has evolved and grown, adjusting to the changing times and incorporating the voices of those who have been marginalized and left out of traditional psychotherapy.

RCT Summary

RCT posits that humans grow through and toward connection throughout the life span and that culture has a huge impact on that relationship. Simply put, RCT is based on the belief that human beings inherently desire to connect to one another through relationships. It looks at the ways stratified institutions and marginalization create hopelessness and isolation through racism, sexism, and homophobia, which lead to chronic disconnections (Jordan, 2010). This theory sees connections and disconnections as two sides of the same coin and seeks to overcome the challenges of disconnections as much as its goal is connection. Maintaining that isolation and disconnections are primary causes of human suffering, RCT is concerned with the impact of dominance and subordination on groups and individuals and focuses on a social justice agenda. Disconnections can occur at an individual, social, cultural, and systemic level.

Stratified systems around the world encourage power over others, discriminatory sociopolitical policies, prejudice, sexism, homophobia, and racism, all of which cause pain and disconnection. Unacknowledged privilege and blatant use of power over others create division, anger, disempowerment, and disconnection (Jordan, 2010). Healing and change occur through the relationship between the counselor and the client. RCT can be characterized as relationship-centered therapy in contrast with Rogers's client-centered therapy, which holds a focus only on the client. RCT emphasizes the bias inherent in traditional theories—a focus on self to the detriment of relationships. To that end, RCT is about the development of mutuality and factors of power dynamic in all relationship. Since chronic disconnection is the source of enormous suffering, healing a sense of isolation is RCT's central task.

RCT and Groups

The idea of women as a special population with unique growth and developmental needs leads naturally to the idea that women would then also have distinctive needs in a therapeutic environment. The relational-cultural belief that relationships are at the basis of development, combined with the idea of the group as a microcosm of other social groups in daily life, such as families, other relationships, and even society itself (Yalom, 2005), illustrates the relevance for RCT within a group context.

Just as when practicing RCT in the individual session, in the group setting the relationships formed can become a model of healing for clients to use outside of the therapeutic setting. The group facilitator understands this and helps foster such relationships in the group, while remembering and bringing member awareness to the cultural context.

> *"Being able to form relationships with the other women in the group, although some only came after some struggles, gave me the understanding and confidence to seek other healthy relationships in my own life."—A 21-year-old, at the end of her RCT group process*

RCT and Group Development

The widely recognized model of the stages of group therapy focuses on group movement through the stages of preaffiliation, power and control, intimacy, differentiation, and termination (Garland, Jones, & Kolodny, 1965, as cited by Schiller, 1997). Yet, findings suggest that not all groups, especially women's groups, travel through this model of group development (Schiller, 1995). Tied to the premise behind a relational-cultural model (Miller, 1976), the importance of connections and bonds between women is the focal point when considering alternate paths of growth for women's groups. Schiller (1995) has proposed a specific model for the stages of development of women's groups. This model is based around the premise that connections with others, feelings of safety in a group, and women's relationships with power and conflict are unique aspects to consider in the development of a women's group. In this model, the beginning and ending stages (preaffiliation and termination) remain universal, yet the middle three stages change to accommodate for the uniqueness of a women's group. The transformed three stages are establishing a relational base; mutuality and interpersonal empathy; and challenge and change. Schiller (2002) recounts the moment when she "suddenly had a flash" of thoughts and realized the need for an alternative developmental path for women's groups:

> There was an abundance of new scholarship about women's psychological growth and development, much of it stressing women's ability and need for connection as a hallmark of growth, but none of it had touched on this developmental variation for groups. (p. 160)

Schiller's (1995) theory of women's group development professes that a relational base must be established early on in the group's development before productive conflict may occur. This belief ties in with RCT, which also focuses heavily on a relational base as a necessity for growth. RCT focuses on the positives that occur when personal boundaries are viewed as a place of exchange rather than protection (Jordan, 2001). Instead of the focus being on developing the individual by keeping a distance from others and relationships, the theory has held that the interactions with others and those connections and relationships are necessary for growth and personal development.

Supporters of RCT believe that relationships are at the basis of development, and thus, finding one's self is not to come before relationships, but rather as a result of developing through relationships. Schiller's model for women's group development lines up with RCT because it too proposes that building relationships and having intimacy are a necessary precursor to group change. It seems a natural progression, as Schiller's model and RCT suggest, that women would first need to find group connections and relationships, and then grow to feel mutuality and empathy, and only then, as a result, would find safety to challenge power and produce productive conflict and group change.

Vulnerable Populations

Schiller's (1995) theory of the development of women's groups is also relevant when working with groups of vulnerable populations, such as women suffering from trauma, oppression, or loss (Schiller, 2007). It is likely that vulnerable populations may experience frequently intense emotional periods and a sense of disconnection from one's inner self and the people in their lives. As a result of this, these women may experience more feelings of hopelessness and depression (Schiller, 2007).

Also challenging for these vulnerable group members is the building of meaningful relationships and trust (Schiller, 2007). As Jordan (2001) pointed out, when feelings of disconnection are discussed and worked through in group relationships, then a positive outcome can be achieved as group members become more bonded. In addition, the group members can then apply the experience to other relationships, outside of the group. In doing so, they become comfortable with showing their genuine self in other relationships. This thought again falls in line with Yalom's (2005) idea that relationships developed in a therapeutic group have parallel applicability to other relationships in one's life. For group members who are struggling with relationship disconnects, Schiller's (1995) theory of women's group development is applicable, as it is focused on building relationships and feelings of trust and safety in the initial stages of the group.

Another vulnerable population is women with the diagnosis of an eating disorder. Practicing a relational-cultural approach in women's eating disorder groups has shown favorable results (Tantillo, 2006). In working with these groups, risk factors have been shown to include the disconnection between relationships, whereas protective factors involve the ability to work through disconnections toward mutual connections. Tantillo (2006) also discusses how relational patterns and disturbances, including those of the family, can reinforce an eating disorder. This idea relates to Yalom's (2005) curative factor of corrective recapitulation of the primary family. Work in the group can become a parallel substitute for the member's parental and family interactions. Having this simulation can help allow the group member to work out unresolved issues and help her begin to correct interpersonal relationships.

Interpersonal Learning

As Yalom (2005) points out, interpersonal learning is a major curative factor that can help lead to change. This idea parallels with RCT in that both highlight the importance of relationships and our basic human need for them. Yalom (2005) takes the idea of group therapy as a source of interpersonal learning by viewing the group as a place where members can learn to relate better to others and transfer these skills and new outlooks onto their everyday lives. Gaining these new perspectives in the group may even have the power to increase healthy relationships and thus, increase self-esteem and interpersonal functioning.

CLINICAL IMPLICATIONS

Group Facilitator Implications

A paramount quality of any group facilitator is to have a strong appreciation for and understanding of the many variables that affect group dynamics and the development of the group. It is this knowledge and understanding that will enable the facilitator to make the best choices for the group, including which theory and developmental sequencing is best for the group's optimal growth (Schiller, 2007).

When leading a women's group from a relational-cultural perspective, there are some specific ideas and interventions for the facilitator to keep in mind. These include keeping the idea of building connections and member intimacy at the forefront of the group; maintaining that a shared sense of safety between group members must be achieved prior to group risk taking; nurturing mutuality within the group, while recognizing differences and similarities between members; and practicing a nonhierarchical style of facilitation (Schiller, 1997). Ultimately, although the facilitators will be leading the group, they must remember that all members need to feel equally important and as in control as the facilitator. Building mutuality and respect among all members, as well as the facilitator, is key. Furthermore, the facilitator will support the group to work through disconnections, which will ultimately result in healing and growth.

RCT can be an effective model in counseling groups of women (Schiller, 1995, 1997), as well as with groups that experience oppression based on any aspect of their shared identity (Schiller, 2007). However, it is important to avoid assuming that all women will identify with a relational perspective. For example, counselors must be sensitive to cultural variations that may present specific needs that RCT might not include. As Schiller (2007) admits, "Feedback from some African American women imply that this model is not applicable to how they see themselves in groups; however, some Afro-Caribbean women have indicated that it does fit their perception of group development" (p. 17). Therefore, although RCT can be very useful, the counselor must first ensure its applicability to members' culture. In the group setting, this can be achieved through pregroup screening interviews. As the counselor interviews each potential group member, a better understanding of culture can be attained. The counselor can then decide if an RCT group will best fit the needs of the members.

Individual Counseling Clinical Implications

Counselors working from a relational-cultural approach will work with clients to help them gain a better understanding of themselves so that they may go on to have growth-fostering relationships. Considering client issues from a relational-cultural perspective allows the counselor to keep an open mind to the important role that relationships can play in the client's current situation. Furthermore, the therapeutic relationship often becomes a model for healthy relationships outside of the counseling setting.

One such way that counselors may help clients form better relationships is to help them have a healthier and more realistic view of their current relationships. Women can be especially affected by relationship problems and rejection from others can be very psychologically wounding for the individual (Jordan, 2001). As Mellin (2008) has noted, those who expect rejection from others, or have intense reactions to being rejected, are at an increased risk to develop depression. This idea illustrates the crucial role that relationships can play in psychological health. It is interesting to consider that an individual's expectation or perception may cause as much psychological harm as rejection itself. As a result, it is important for counselors working with women to assess for the presence of relationship rejection as well as client expectation or perception of rejection. After such assessment, the counselor will help the client come to such understanding and realizations about his or her expectations and perceptions of rejection in his or her relationships. In session, the counselor will work to identify times when the client exhibits these thoughts, and how he or she impacts and ultimately sabotages current relationships. Role plays may also occur in the session as a way for the client to safely explore alternative forms of relationship communication. Counselors may facilitate dialogues with clients about relational disconnections, by discussing reasons and causes for disconnections. Also, helping the client view the therapeutic relationship as an example for other relationships in his or her life will have value. In fact, an RCT framework posits that the best way to strengthen new ways of looking at relationship connections is through the therapeutic relationship (Jordan, 2000).

The therapeutic alliance allows an opportunity for the client to experience healthy connections and repair any relational distortions that she may have (West, 2005). Finally, as the client allows her true self to be seen and accepted in the therapeutic relationship, there will be an inclination toward a more genuine self in outside relationships.

When counseling through a model that considers individualization as a marker and goal of psychological health, the behaviors, goals, and experiences of groups that place focus on connections and relationships may be viewed as pathological (Frey, Beesley, & Miller, 2006). It is important that counselors appreciate the unique situation of their clients. Although symptoms of problems such as depression and anxiety may be seen, it is important to realize that the cause of these problems may be related to the client's situation, including peer support or lack thereof (Frey et al., 2006); loss of relationships and separation (Frey, Tobin, & Beesley, 2004); body dissatisfaction (Ackard, Croll, & Kearney-Cooke, 2002); and gender prejudice (Brinkman & Rickard, 2009). Even more so, gender (Frey et al., 2004) and relationships (Frey et al., 2006) may have a great impact on psychological health and recovery. Although it is important to be aware of how relationship issues may be a factor in the psychological distress of women, this knowledge is also important in helping the client improve her psychological health. The counselor holds a key role in helping clients have a safe place to identify and work toward fixing, maintaining, and building new relationships and connections with others. The first relationship of focus, however, is that of the client and counselor.

Finally, when working with clients from a relational-cultural perspective, mutual empathy within the therapeutic relationship is important. Counselors should be open to allowing themselves to be affected by their clients and the counseling process. While still maintaining healthy boundaries and ethical standards, counselors may share appropriate experiences with their clients. Clients will equally share their reactions to this. Participating in this give and take of emotions will help foster mutual empathy as opposed to one-way empathy.

CASE EXAMPLE

As has been discussed throughout this chapter, women often define themselves through their relationships (Miller, 1976). Furthermore, women seek out relationships and social connections in many different contexts. Although this can be a great strength, in some situations, these needs have the potential to contribute to poor decision making through peer pressure. The following is a case example of such an instance.

Samantha, an 18-year-old college woman, has been referred to counseling for alcohol abuse. It is revealed that Samantha started drinking when first going to college as a way to build relationships with her peers. She described having had difficulty adjusting to college because while being disconnected from her friends from home, she also had limited social support and connections on campus. Soon, Samantha was introduced to alcohol as part of the campus culture and began to use it as a way to cope with her social anxiety. She believed that each time she drank, she was more social and able to "make friends." She also perceived more acceptance from her male peers and was more likely to engage in sexual risk-taking behaviors. When explored in session, it became evident that these "friendships" and romantic encounters rarely lasted beyond one night. This left Samantha feeling emotionally wounded, depressed, and with low self-esteem. Without any healthy and lasting social supports, Samantha again turned to alcohol, but this time to numb her emotionally painful feelings. This became an unhealthy cycle.

During her time in counseling, Samantha identified which relationships in her life were unhealthy. She soon realized that her sexual risk taking was only causing her more hurt and confusion and was not a source of authentic social connectedness. Practicing from an RCT perspective, Samantha and her counselor discussed the different ways in which Samantha was losing power based on these unhealthy relationships. Her desire and need for relationships was validated and supported but together they explored how to accomplish this in a healthy and mutually empowering way. Samantha was able to address her feelings of low self-esteem and self-worth. She also began to evaluate her own issues of needing "instant" friends in large quantities, rather than establishing quality and growth-fostering friendships with mutuality that needed time to develop. Finally, alcohol education and prevention methods were employed in session, along with the development of new healthy coping skills.

Also, through Samantha's mutually empathetic relationship with her counselor, she learned that she was worthy of healthy relationships. The therapeutic relationship also served as an example to Samantha of how to enter into and maintain such growth-fostering relationships. As Samantha later commented, "Counseling has helped me so much. Before I didn't realize that I could be an equal in a relationship and be able to get my needs met too. I feel much more connected to myself and others now."

The importance of strong relationships can be seen through their connection to increased social support, feelings of connectedness, and psychological health. In fact, social connectedness has been identified as a main variable in the prevention of depression and low self-esteem (Williams & Galliher, 2006). This idea mimics the basis of RCT and the importance of relationships and feelings of connectedness, especially for women. During times of stress and transition, when relationship support is critical, relationship loss and separation may occur. When these relationships are lost, the woman's whole self can be simultaneously shaken. Through this, it can be seen how important it is to make new and healthy relationships.

CALL TO ACTION

Advocacy must be done from a culturally sensitive perspective that seeks to understand and utilize the inherent power that each woman has. It must speak to the strength and resiliency that women possess. It must believe in the power that each woman and girl possesses, understanding that while this power may be suppressed, subordinated, or ignored due to her circumstances, she nonetheless has it within herself to alter the course of her life. As advocates, counselors are not to give voice, but to amplify the voices of those who are oppressed, or marginalized. All women have a voice, but it is a matter if they choose to use it and are heard. The call to action then is to provide amplification or avenues for those voices that have been silenced; provide listening ears for those voices that are ignored and unheard; and create birthing spaces for those voices that are yet to be born.

As counselors, we have a responsibility to our clients as well as to society as a whole. We can be involved in speaking up and combating the stereotype of women and girls "being catty" and instead raise awareness of how to change this societal narrative to reflect the reality of how many women and girls

(continued)

CALL TO ACTION (*continued*)

provide invaluable support to one another. Through a call to action, counselors are asked to consider ways in which they can provide education, mentorship, and to lead by example to bring about social change.

REFLECTION AND DISCUSSION QUESTIONS

1. Reflect upon someone who contributed positively to your growth. How did he or she make a difference? Consider a time when you contributed positively to someone's growth. What did you do that made a difference?

2. Recall a time when you experienced a truly authentic relationship that was mutually beneficial. What were some of the things that worked in that relationship?

3. What can we do as a society to make sure that values such as connection, empathy, mutuality, and so forth are encouraged and not relegated?

4. Despite the strong evidence presented in this chapter and in our daily lives that women do love and support each other, the idea that women are catty and are envious of each other continues to permeate our society. Why might that be and what can we do to change that narrative?

HELPFUL RESOURCES

- All In Together (www.aitogether.org)—All In Together is a nonpartisan, collaboration driven campaign to empower women with the tools they need to drive meaningful change—amplifying their voices on the civic, social, and political issues that matter to them

- Empower Women (www.empowerwomen.org)—An organization that empowers women to achieve their full economic potential by inspiring both women and men to become advocates, change makers, and leaders in their community. They equip them with resources, opportunities, and a global platform that facilitates networking, learning, and sharing of experiences

- Equality Now (www.equalitynow.org)—Equality Now has become a standard for activism on the ground where women's needs are translated into national, regional and international law, policy, and practice

- Higher Heights for America (www.higherheightsforamerica.org)

- Ignite (www.igniteworldwide.org)

- Peace is Loud (www.peaceisloud.org)—Peace is Loud inspires action through media and live events that spotlight women leaders on the frontline of peace-building worldwide; an organization with a global movement mission to end violence against women and girls

- Women Empowered (www.women-empowered.com)—Women Empowered is an organization that connects, educates, and supports women of all ages and backgrounds, and inspires them to give back to their communities through mentorship, networking, and volunteerism

ACKNOWLEDGMENTS

We would like to acknowledge Sailume Walo-Roberts for her contributions to this chapter.

REFERENCES

Ackard, D. M., Croll, J. K., & Kearney-Cooke, A. (2002). Dieting frequency among college females: Association with disordered eating, body image, and related psychological problems. *Journal of Psychosomatic Research, 52*, 129–137. doi:10.1016/S0022-3999(01)00269-0

Belgrave, F. Z., Chase-Vaughn, G., Famebrdige, G., Addison, J., & Cherry, V. (2000). The effectiveness of a culture and gender-specific intervention for increasing resiliency among African American preadolescent females. *Journal of Black Psychology, 26*, 133–147.

Bindel, J. (2015). The village where men are banned. *The Guardian.* Retrieved from https://www.theguardian.com/global-development/2015/aug/16/village-where-men-are-banned-womens-rights-kenya

Brinkman, B. G., & Rickard, K. M. (2009). College students' descriptions of everyday gender prejudice. *Sex Roles, 61*, 461–475.

Castaneda, D., & Burns-Glover, A. (2007). Women's friendships and romantic relationships. In F. Denmark & M. Paludi (Eds.), *Psychology of women: A handbook of issues and theories* (pp. 332–345). Westport, CT: Praeger.

Chodorow, N. (1978). *The reproduction of motherhood: Psychoanalysis and the sociology of gender.* Los Angeles: University of California Press.

Comstock, D., Duffey, T., & St. George, H. (2002). The relational-cultural model: A framework for group processes. *Journal for Specialists in Group Work, 27*, 254–272. doi:10.1080/15401383.2012.660118

Fehr, B. (2004). Intimacy expectations in same-sex friendships: A prototype interaction-pattern model. *Journal of Personality and Social Psychology, 86*, 265–284.

Frey, L. L., Beesley, D., & Miller, M. R. (2006). Relational health, attachment, and psychological distress in college women and men. *Psychology of Women Quarterly, 30*, 303–311. doi:10.1111/j.1471-6402.2006.00298

Frey, L. L., Tobin, J., & Beesley, D. (2004). Relational predictors of psychological distress in women and men presenting for university counseling center services. *Journal of College Counseling, 7*, 129–139. doi:10.1002/j.2161-1882.2004.tb00244.x

Friedan, B. (1963). *The feminine mystique.* New York, NY: W. W. Norton.

Gilligan, C. (1982). *In a different voice.* Cambridge, MA: Harvard University Press.

Gottman, J. M., Levenson, R. W., Swanson, C., Swanson, K., Tyson, R., & Yoshimoto, D. (2003). Observing gay, lesbian and heterosexual couples' relationships: Mathematical modeling of conflict interaction. *Journal of Homosexuality, 45,* 65–91.

Guinier, J., Messick, J. S., Michaels, L., Rosner, L., & Shimkin, T. (Producers), & Waters, M. (Director). (2004). *Mean girls* [Motion picture]. United States: Paramount Pictures.

Hooks, B. (2004). *The will to change: Men, masculinity, and love.* New York, NY: Atria Books.

Jordan, J. V. (2000). The role of mutual empathy in relational-cultural therapy. *Journal of Clinical Psychology/In Session: Psychotherapy in Practice, 56*(80), 1005–1016. doi:10.1002/1097-4679

Jordan, J. V. (2001). A relational-cultural model: Healing through mutual empathy. *Bulletin of the Menninger Clinic, 65*(1), 92–104.

Jordan, J. V. (2002). A relational-cultural perspective in therapy. In F. Kaslow (Ed.), *Comprehensive handbook of psychotherapy* (Vol. 3, pp. 233–254). New York, NY: Wiley.

Jordan, J. V. (2010). *Relational-cultural therapy.* Washington, DC: American Psychological Association.

Lewis, M. (1990). Interrupting patriarchy: Politics, resistance, and transformation in the feminist classroom. *Harvard Educational Review, 60*(4), 467–489. doi:10.17763/haer.60.4.w1r67q5135585122

Liang, B., Tracy, A. J., Taylor, C. A., & Williams, L. M. (2002). Mentoring college-age women: A relational approach. *American Journal of Community Psychology, 30,* 271–288.

Mellin, E. A. (2008). Rejection sensitivity and college student depression: Finding and implications for counseling. *Journal of College Counseling, 11,* 32–41. doi:10.1002/j.2161-1882.2008.tb00022.x

Meuwly, N., Feinstein, B. A., Davila, J., Nuñez, D. G., & Bodenmann, G. (2013). Relationship quality among Swiss women in opposite-sex versus same-sex romantic relationships. *Swiss Journal of Psychology, 72*(4), 229–233. doi:10.1024/1421-0185/a000115

Mickelson, K. D., Claffey, S. T., & Williams, S. L. (2006). The moderating role of gender and gender role attitudes on the link between spousal support and marital quality. *Sex Roles, 55,* 73–82. doi:10.1007/s11199-006-9061-8

Miller, J. B. (1976). *Toward a new psychology of women.* Boston, MA: Beacon Press.

Miller, J. B. (1986). *What do we mean by relationships?* (Work in Progress Series no. 22). Stone Center for Developmental Studies, Wellesley College, Wellesley, MA.

Miller, J. B. (1991). Aren't you idealizing women? Aren't you idealizing relationships. In J. V. Jordan (Ed.), *Women's growth in diversity: More writings from the Stone Center* (pp. 25–49). New York, NY: Guilford Press.

Miller, J. B., & Stiver, I. P. (1997). *The healing connection: How women form relationships in therapy and in life.* Boston, MA: Beacon Press.

Misher, K. (Producer), & Peirce, K. (Director). (2013). *Carrie* [Motion picture]. United States: Misher Films.

Nobelprize.org. (2016). Nobel Peace Prize press release. Retrieved from http://www .nobelprize.org/nobel_prizes/peace/laureates/2011/index.html

Roisman, G. I., Clausell, E., Holland, A., Fortuna, K., & Elieff, C. (2008). Adult romantic relationships as contexts of human development: A multimethod comparison of same-sex couples with opposite-sex dating, engaged, and married dyads. *Developmental Psychology, 44*, 91–101. doi:10.1037/0012-1649.44.1.91

Schiller, L. Y. (1995). Stages of development in women's groups: A relational model. In R. Kurland & R. Salmon (Eds.), *Group work practice in a troubled society: Problems and opportunities* (pp. 117–138). New York, NY: The Hawthorn Press.

Schiller, L. Y. (1997). Rethinking stages of development in women's groups: Implications for practice. *Social Work with Groups, 20*, 3–19.

Schiller, L. Y. (2002). Process of an idea: How the relational model of group work developed. *Social Work with Groups, 25*, 159–166. doi:10.1300/J009v25n01_20

Schiller, L. Y. (2007). Not for women only: Applying the relational model of group development with vulnerable populations. *Social Work with Groups, 30*, 11–26. doi:10.1300/J009v30n02_03

Surrey, J. (1985, November 16). *Self-in-relation: A theory of women's development.* Paper presented at a Stone Center Colloquium.

Tantillo, M. (2006). A relational approach to eating disorders multifamily therapy group: Moving from difference and disconnection to mutual connection. *Families, Systems, and Health, 24*, 82–102. doi:10.1037/1091-7527.24.1.82

Traister, R. (2016, February 27). What women find in friends that they may not get from love. *New York Times.* Retrieved from https://www.nytimes.com/2016/02/28/opinion/sunday/what-women-find-in-friends-that-they-may-not-get-from-love.html?_r=0

V-Day.org. (2014). About City of Joy. Retrieved from http://drc.vday.org/about-city-of-joy

Walker, M. (2004). How relationships heal. In M. Walker & W. Rosen (Eds.), *How connections heal: Stories from relational-cultural therapy* (pp. 3–19). New York, NY: Guilford Press.

Walker, M., & Rosen, W. B. (2004). *How connections heal: Stories from relational-cultural therapy.* New York, NY: Guilford Press.

Ward, J. V. (2000). *The skin we're in: Teaching our children to be emotionally strong, socially smart, and spiritually connected.* New York, NY: Free Press.

West, C. K. (2005). The map of relational-cultural theory. *Women & Therapy, 28*(3–4), 93–110. doi:10.1300/J015v28n03_05

Williams, K. L., & Galliher, R. V. (2006). Predicting depression and self-esteem from social connectedness, support, and competence. *Journal of Social and Clinical Psychology, 25*, 855–874. doi:10.1521/jscp.2006.25.8.855

Yalom, I. D. (2005). *The theory and practice of group psychotherapy* (5th ed.). New York, NY: Basic Books.

CHAPTER 5

Gender Identity Development

Megan E. Delaney

LEARNING OBJECTIVES

After reading this chapter, you will be able to:

1. Understand meanings of terms, including gender, gender assigned at birth, and gender identity.
2. Explain early theories of gender identity development.
3. Understand how early influences (nature and nurture) influence gender identity development.
4. Identify situations in which gender and gender identity can influence mental health and how that impacts the work of counselors.

An individual's identity development, including his or her preferred gender identity, is a lifelong process, which starts with the earliest interactions with the world. The concepts of gender identity have been explored, studied, debated, and discussed for decades and are currently going through a resurgence of examination, especially in Western cultures. Society and different cultures have well-defined cultural norms for what it means to be a woman or a man, both physically and emotionally. Individuals in all cultures internalize these definitions from a very early age and look to understand themselves within these rules and regulations. Long-held beliefs and expectations of gender are being reconsidered and redefined. This has implications for counselors who work with individuals trying to navigate conflicts arising between societal expectations and their own thoughts and feelings.

This chapter provides an overview of gender identity development, beginning with an explanation of terms, followed by an exploration of theoretical perspectives and a historical account of the conceptualizations that create gender identity. Topics include current research and perspectives on how gender identity evolves in children and recent shifts in understanding atypical gender identities, including transgender, gender neutral, and gender fluid identification. Finally, implications and strategies for mental health professionals are discussed, especially related to counseling those who are experiencing conflict or distress surrounding issues of gender and gender identity.

DEFINITIONS AND TERMS

Sex and gender are often considered to be synonymous; however, these terms can have very different meanings to different people. Key definitions include the following:

Sex refers to a person's anatomy and physical characteristics, which are determined by chromosomes, internal and external genitalia, and hormones (Dragowski, Scharrón-del Río, & Sandigorsky, 2011). Most people are born with reproductive organs that differentiate male and female and, unless an individual receives sex-altering hormones or surgery, this differentiation remains throughout their lives. Intersex is an additional classification referring to individuals whose biological features are not clearly male or female, or are otherwise atypical (American Psychiatric Association [APA], 2013).

Gender refers to traits associated with masculinity and femininity, including preferred interests, careers, appearance, behaviors, and mannerisms (Bussey, 2011). Gender is a by-product of societal norms, values, and the associated behaviors that are expected in a culture.

Gender identity refers to a person's feelings toward his or her sense of gender and is influenced by culture, ethnicity, and religion (Dragowski et al., 2011). Behavior that is consistent with cultural expectations is referred to as gender normative; whereas behaviors that are seen as inconsistent are identified as gender nonconforming (APA, 2013).

Gender role is the outward way that people exhibit gender identity; it is the act of displaying societal norms or behaviors deemed typical for girls/women and boys/men (APA, 2013). When an individual's gender assignment at birth and gender identity are not congruent, he or she may identify as either transgender or another gender category (Nagoshi, Nagoshi, & Brzuzy, 2014).

Gender expression refers to the way in which a person behaves in order to communicate his or her gender identity within a given culture, such as ways of dressing, communicating, and particular likes and interests. Gender expression may not always be congruent with society's expectations of gender roles (APA, 2013).

Sexual/affectional orientation refers to how and with whom people express sexual affinity and intimacy (Dragowski et al., 2011). Categories of sexual orientation include heterosexual, or attraction to members of the opposite sex; gay men and lesbian women, or those attracted to members of the same sex; bisexual, or those attracted to males and females; and pansexual, those not limited in sexual attraction based on gender, gender assigned at birth, or gender identity (APA, 2013). The concepts of sexual orientation and gender identity are often intertwined in society, but they are actually distinct concepts, which may or may not be related (Dragowski et al., 2011).

Transgender is a term used to represent people whose gender identity differs from the sex assignment made by medical personnel on their birth certificate (Diamond, Pardo, & Butterworth, 2011; GLAAD, 2016; Nagoshi et al., 2014). These individuals may or may not wish to transform their physical appearance and often reject society's rigid dichotomy of male and female. Instead, they may subscribe to *gender fluidity* or the idea that the gender identity can be flexible and broad (Diamond et al., 2011). As GLAAD (2016) notes, people are born as babies and challenge the notion that a baby needs to be labeled as a girl or a boy.

Transsexual is an older term derived from medical and psychological models that is sometimes preferred by individuals who have had surgical or medical procedures to change aspects of their bodies to fit their gender identity. These individuals may be in different stages of transition using hormonal or surgical interventions (Nagoshi et al., 2014). According to GLAAD (2016), most individuals choose to use the term transgender although it is advised to ask individuals their preference.

EARLY THEORIES OF GENDER IDENTITY

Understanding how gender identity develops has long been of interest to psychologists, theorists, and social scientists. An early debate in scientific and theoretical perspectives of human development is the influence of nature and nurture. The impact of nature on development includes hereditary and genetic influences on personality and development (Eagly & Wood, 2013). These inherited properties passed down through the genetic makeup of biological parents influence a person's abilities and personality throughout the developmental process (Dragowski et al., 2011; Vignoles, Schwartz, & Luyckx, 2011). Nurture, on the other hand, is how the environment, such as cultural and societal interactions and conditions, affects the developmental learning process (Eagly & Wood, 2013). Thus, if nature was the only influence on development, a child's genetic makeup would prescribe his or her intellectual and physical capabilities; whereas if nurture was the only influence, a child's development would depend solely on environmental and cultural influences. Today, most researchers agree that human development is a complicated interaction of genetic and environmental influences (Eagly & Wood, 2013) and that a person's identity is not rigid but a fluid process influenced by multiple factors (Vignoles et al., 2011).

Psychoanalytic Theories

Most psychological and developmental perspectives of gender identity have been influenced by the work of Sigmund Freud's psychoanalysis theory. Freud postulated that the physical and anatomical features of females and males shaped their differences in personalities, but he was not under the assumption that one was born preprogrammed with these differences (Kimmel, 2000). Instead, he believed that gender identity, a critical part of personality development, was influenced by interactions with others, especially with parents (Ahlqvist, Halim, Greulich,

Lurye, & Ruble, 2013). Freud's complex theory linked gender identity with sexuality. He stated that a child identified with the parent of the same sex and sexual attraction was aimed toward the parent of the opposite sex. He also introduced the concept of *gender identity failure*, which he defined as failure to conform to sexual norms imposed by society (Kimmel, 2000). Although Freud's thoughts on gender development created interest and inspired future study, there is little empirical support for his theory of gender identity development (Ryle, 2011).

Erikson, an early scholar of development, emphasized the process of identity through psychosocial stages and crises (Erikson, 1968). He believed the way one learned to cope with each phase or crisis was important. Role commitment, which is specifically identifying as being male or female and embracing the prescribed societal characteristics of that gender, was a critical task in Erikson's theory. He believed that a strong gender identity was necessary for heterosexual intimacy. According to Erikson, for a functioning society, men and women should be compliant in assuming "proper roles" specific for their gender (Erikson, 1968; Kimmel, 2000). Although psychoanalytic theory remains an important influence on the roots of developmental theories of gender identity, the perspectives espoused are rooted in patriarchal and heterosexual beliefs and lack empirical evidence to support the tenets of the theory (Enns, 1997; Ryle, 2011). Recent theories, including cognitive theory, social learning theory, and gender schema theory, suggest that socialization is the theoretical underpinning for gender development.

Cognitive Developmental Theory

Building upon the cognitive developmental theory of Jean Piaget (1954), Lawrence Kohlberg (1969) proposed one of the first social cognitive theories for gender development. Cognitive theories focus on the perceptions and thoughts of the child. Kohlberg's theory stated that rather than being influenced by others in adopting gender-role identity, children first recognize that they are either girls or boys and then seek out same-sex examples on which to base their actions and behaviors. Kohlberg's theory suggested that development occurs in cognitive stages in which children gain understanding of gender, even before being influenced by others.

In this theory, rather than being passive recipients of gender ideals, children seek to understand gender on their own. If a child identifies herself as female, she begins to act and arrange her thoughts and actions to fit cultural norms for girls. Kohlberg suggested that by the age of 2 or 2½ years children acquire a basic understanding of gender and label themselves as girls or boys. After the age of 3 years, children have an understanding that boys become men and girls become women. Between the ages of 5 and 7 years, Kohlberg stated that children are thought to reach gender consistency, which is the understanding based on experience, societal messages, and cultural expectations that sex cannot be changed (Bussey, 2011; Kohlberg, 1969). For some children, this time of development may cause conflict and confusion if they are questioning their gender birth assignment and/or sexuality. Cognitive theories also emphasize that children are active participants in their own development, using *cognitive filters* to make interpretations and formulate opinions about gender (Halim et al., 2014). Kohlberg's work was very influential in the discussion of gender identity development, sparking further research and the expansion of other theories, including social cognitive and social learning theories (Martin, Ruble, & Szkrybalo, 2002).

Social Learning Theory

Expanding upon the concepts of cognitive theory, social learning theorists include the influence of social environments and how a child observes and imitates others (Bussey & Bandura, 1999). Development occurs within the context of personal, behavioral, and environmental influences. The *personal* refers to how an individual perceives his or her ability to successfully perform a behavior; *behavioral* refers to patterns that are developed, in this case, related to gender identity; and *environmental* regards the setting or social context that influences the behavior, thought, or action (Bandura, 1986). Social learning theorists believe that children learn concepts of masculinity and femininity, including specific behaviors associated with those identities, through observational learning and differential reinforcement (Bussey, 2011; Bussey & Bandura, 1999). For example, the traditional definition of masculinity includes traits typically assigned to boys and men, such as assertiveness, courage, strength, power, and drive. Feminine traits typically associated with women and girls include sensitivity, beauty, empathy, and nurturing.

Observational learning is the process by which a child learns and mimics the gender-specific behaviors of his or her same-sex parent or caregiver. These behaviors are reinforced through modeling as well as correction by the same-sex parent/guardian (Bussey, 2011). Social learning theory highlights the differences in treatment of both girls and boys by their parents, in school, with peers, and by the media. Children observe what toys, books, and objects are "for girls" and what are "for boys." They also observe the behaviors and patterns of the men and women in their lives, including their parents, teachers, and other adults. The concept of *differential reinforcement* involves the ways in which parents (or other caregivers) teach girls to be "girls" and boys to be "boys." By the time their children turn 2, parents are likely to start reinforcing sex-typed behaviors, including choosing or encouraging the types of toys the children interact with and the type of play encouraged (Lytton & Romney, 1991). Fathers are more likely than mothers to reinforce gender specification directly, such as telling a son not to cry or commenting on girl's appearance (Endendijk et al., 2013). The result of this reinforcement is that boys begin to understand that they should not look or act like girls, and girls understand that they should not look or act like boys (Blakemore, 2003).

Social learning theories also emphasize the influence of *self-regulation*, or the ability to act in your own best interests based on your personal values. As such, people develop their own standards and abilities for pursuing an activity (e.g., a sport or a particular job) within the *gender relatedness* of that activity. Furthermore, individuals also have expectations for either positive or negative outcomes for different activities based on their own gender (Bussey, 2011). For example, a woman might not pursue a high-level management position in a company because she might not think she is assertive or strong enough to be a leader. In contrast to other theories that state that gender identity, once formed, undergoes little variation, the social learning perspective posits that the process of understanding one's gender identity is ongoing throughout a person's life span. As such, individuals might adapt their understanding of gender through the maturation process as well as through changing societal messages about gender (Bussey, 2011). Criticisms of the theory include the lack of empirical evidence to support the claim that children will only model those of the same gender and are passive in their own gender identity development (Ryle, 2011).

Gender Schema Theory

First introduced by Sandra Bem (1981) as an expansion of cognitive theory, gender schema theory further explores how gender and sex-role expectations are culturally conveyed in society. Like cognitive theories, Bem's and also Martin and Halverson's (1981) gender schema theories emphasize that early on, children begin to learn and understand gender labels or stereotypical terms used to describe characteristics of girls and boys. Bem (1981) described an individual's ability "to encode and to organize information—including information about the self—in terms of cultural definition of maleness and femaleness that constitutes the society's gender schema" (p. 355). Similar to social learning theory, Bem postulates that children learn gender roles by being rewarded for some behaviors and punished for others, as well as by modeling behavior seen by others. Bem believed that although children learn gender norms through observation, they are not passive in this process but rather actively seek examples and models of behaviors and mannerisms.

Martin and Halverson added that gender identity formation and subsequent *self-socialization*, or the process by which we actively influence our own development and outcome, begin as early as 2 to 3 years of age. By using labels for gender, children develop *schemas*, or conceptual frameworks, that propel them to perform activities society deems typical of their gender (Bussey, 2011). Gender schemas allow for children to have culturally specific expectations of behavior based on their gender. With behaviors conforming to stereotypes for their own gender, children are able to gain cognitive consistency and process new information through their schemas and retain and even distort memories to fit within their understanding of gender (Bem, 1981; Martin & Halverson, 1983). A traditional gender schema for children at play may involve collaboration and socialization for girls and competition and physicality for boys.

Bem's contribution to the research and debate on gender identity is important, as she brought a female voice to a professional conversation previously dominated by male theorists. Her underlying belief emphasized the restrictiveness of prescribed gender roles on both individuals and society as a whole. This momentum was propelled and expanded upon by the feminist movement, pushing the boundaries of the dichotomous and rigid roles prescribed mostly by earlier White male theorists. Continued discussion around gender and recent changes in parental behavior in Western society have resulted in more gender flexibility in how children are raised (Bussey, 2011). This energy is also propelled by the LGBTQ (lesbian, gay, bisexual, transgender, queer) and transgender movement for a more egalitarian and fluid definition and understanding of gender identity (GLAAD, 2016).

Feminist Theory

As the field of psychology and human development progressed, feminist scholars began to push back against traditional theories of human development that portrayed stereotypical male characteristics as powerful, strong, and dominant and female characteristics as emotional, weak, or secondary (Worell & Remer, 2003). Early feminists such as Betty Friedan (1963) and Jean Baker Miller (1986) discussed the social, political, and psychological context of gender, including recognizing the ways feminine qualities and attributes were dismissed and identifying the inequalities of power in society (Worell & Remer, 2003). As catalysts for change, feminists and women scholars challenged societal messages and expectations for women and provided a new, female voice to the conversation (Enns, 1997; Miller, 1986). Bem (1981) challenged the notion that having prescribed feminine qualities as a woman or masculine qualities as a man is necessary for the psychological health and well-being of that individual.

Feminists confronted the gender biases in psychological theories that pathologized characteristics commonly attributed to femininity (Evans, Kincade, Marbley, & Seem, 2005). As evident in the earlier chapter on gender socialization, societal and cultural experiences, behaviors, and norms influence the construction of gender identity and gender roles. Furthermore, feminists argue that although Western society has come far in the equalization of rights and privileges for girls and women, a patriarchal culture still exists. Feminists advocate for reducing gender-role stereotyping and promoting change to a more gender-balanced society for the benefit of both men and women (Evans et al., 2005; Worell & Remer, 2003).

To summarize the theories presented in this chapter, psychoanalytic theories suggest that gender identity develops through association with those of the same gender and especially parents. Cognitive developmental theories suggest that children use socialization and observation to develop a cognitive understanding of their gender. Social learning theories state that the gender identity process is supported by rewards and punishments based on gender-specific behaviors. These behaviors are learned by proxy of observation and modeling of adults and peers. Gender schema theories state that children develop schemas, or patterns of behaviors, that are based on culture-specific expectations for their gender. Finally, feminist theories state assumptions about gender norms and expectations influence power and status differences. Feminists advocate for a balanced understanding and acceptance of all gender identities. As outlined in this section, theoretical perspectives provide conceptual frameworks for the formation and understanding of gender identity development. The remainder of this chapter includes how culture and diversity influences gender identity; how the classifications of gender are shifting with greater understanding and expression of gender; and how issues of gender may impact the work of counselors and other mental health professionals.

CULTURAL FACTORS IN GENDER IDENTITY

"The social institutions of our world—workplace, family, school, politics—are gendered institutions, sites where the dominant definitions are reinforced and reproduced, and where 'deviants' are disciplined. We become gendered selves in a gendered society" (Kimmel, 2000, p. 16).

Gender constructs and identity vary among different cultural groups and may deviate from norms typical of a dominant culture. For example, what it means to be a girl or woman, or how to define femininity, can be different for a Latina versus an African American (Hoffman, 2006; Singh, 2007). The statement "I am a woman" encompasses certain ideas of being female in society, whereas "I am an African American woman" carries additional connotations that include personal and cultural understandings of being a woman.

Many subcultures throughout the world still promote very rigid gender roles that carry behavioral expectations. These norms are often historically founded from long-held cultural and religious beliefs. For example, the "machismo" male in Latino culture is understood to represent manliness, or being strong and authoritative. Middle Eastern cultures, as well as some conservative religious sects, can carry expectations such as care-taking and child-rearing roles for women and provider roles for men. Furthermore, women in developing countries are often dependent upon men for survival and may live in cultures founded on long-held inequities for women (Singh, 2007).

Research on gender identity in Native American cultures provides additional perspective. The Navaho, for example, have three different gender classifications: masculine men, feminine women, and "nadle," a name given at birth to those not clearly identified as male or female (Kimmel, 2000). Nadles will interchangeably perform tasks that are typically done by women or men and often will change their style of dress to reflect the task being performed. To the Navaho, the label of nadle is seen as prestigious, possibly a result of women's elevated status in Navaho society (Kimmel, 2000). The Plains Indians also had a third gender type called "berdache," a term used to refer to a younger male in a same-sex relationship. Berdaches were more likely to do the work typically associated with women, wear a combination of male and female type clothing, and sometimes have relationships with men who were not berdache (Kimmel, 2000).

The Zuni, a Native American tribe in New Mexico, does not label a sex of a baby at birth and believe that sex/gender may change over time (Dragowski et al., 2011). In the Independent State of Samoa, there are individuals who identify as "fa'afafine," or men who follow feminine-typical behavior and are sexually interested in men. Although cultural norms for men in Samoan cultures include masculine-typical behaviors and roles, there are no heteronormative requirements for sexual relationships. Sexual relationships with other men or with fa'afafine fall within the boundaries of "normal" behavior (Dragowski et al., 2011). The cultures presented here offer an expanded understanding of gender identification and support the notion that the concept of gender could be understood as fluid rather than dichotomous.

TRANSFORMATION OF GENDER IDENTITY

> *"Because it took me a long time to come to terms with my gender identity, I am now fiercely protective of it. I'd always had femininity forced onto me because I was assigned female at birth and that always made me very uncomfortable. The moment I realized I was nonbinary was a revelation because I finally could put a word to what I had been confused about for years. I love telling people I get to know my gender identity because it is such a big part of who I am and I know it's also important to thousands of other trans individuals."—Fox, a 20-year-old*

Western society has long dichotomized the characteristics and social roles of males and females. As such, traditional definitions of masculine and feminine have mostly remained intact despite many years of feminist and LGBTQ advocacy and meaningful changes in the assignment of gender roles. Although the concept of gender fluidity is not new and has variations in other cultures (Dragowski et al., 2011), there is a movement within Western culture toward more egalitarian understanding and treatment of people who do not subscribe to cultural norms. The LGBTQ community is at the forefront of this movement and, with support from high-profile celebrities such as Caitlyn Jenner and Ruby Rose, is promoting a greater understanding of the development, experience, and understanding of the spectrum of gender identities. For example, gender terminology has expanded to include terms such as transgender, gender nonconforming, gender fluid, genderqueer, and intersex. Gender variance, gender diverse, and gender nonconforming have become umbrella terms for those who do not identify with the binary system of gender identity.

Children who begin to suspect that they do not fit within stereotypical gender roles may be particularly vulnerable to mental health issues and other challenges. Forcing children, directly or indirectly, to conform to gender stereotypical thoughts and behaviors can create long-term suffering and other negative consequences (Gray, Carter, & Levitt, 2012). Gray et al. (2012) state that a staggering 41% of transgender people in the United States have reported attempting suicide as compared to 1.8% of the general population. From their research on gender-variant children, Riley, Sitharthan, Clemson, and Diamond (2011) offer the acronym H-A-P-P-I-N-E-S-S to represent children's needs: "to be Heard; to be Accepted; to have Professional access and support; to have Peer contact; to have access to current Information; Not to be bullied, blamed, punished, or otherwise discriminated against; to have freedom of Expression; to feel Safe; and to have

Support" (p. 648). Parents, educators, and counselors best serve the interest of children by allowing them to explore and develop their own understanding of gender identity (Lev, 2010). Respecting a child's need to express his or her true selves, write his or her own narrative, (Lev, 2010), and feel adequate and included (Egan & Perry, 2001) are important factors in promoting healthy development as well as mental and physical well-being.

Proponents for a more fluid view of gender advocate for the flexibility it affords individuals to explore, describe, and express themselves (GLAAD, 2016). Someone might feel more feminine one day and masculine another or a mixture of both. In other words, neither term fully describes an individual's thoughts and interests. Furthermore, the term *genderqueer* is used to represent the change in rigidity that society imposes on gender identity and sexual orientation. Gender-queer represents individuals who are more fluid in gender expression and may identify not just as male or female, but as neither or a blend of the two. Gender-queer also is a more encompassing term in sexual orientation and removes the restrictions of declaring one's sexuality as heterosexual or gay (Nagoshi et al., 2014). Although the depth of the full movement is beyond the capacity of this chapter, there are excellent resources that include historical considerations, definitions, explanations, and ways to be involved in advocacy work including the GLAAD (www.glaad.org) and Gender Diversity (www.genderdiversity.org) websites and Nagoshi et al.'s (2014) text, *Gender and Sexual Identity: Transcending Feminist and Queer Theory.*

IMPLICATIONS FOR COUNSELORS

> *"It's true, women have made great strides in the past several decades to be recognized as more than domestic wives. However, in my work with teen girls, I see a continued struggle to fit in with the societal norm created by mass media and pop culture. This norm defines beauty as an impossible-to-attain standard of extreme thinness and an emphasis on sexuality. Most girls struggle with the internalization of the message that they are not beautiful enough, not sexy enough, and therefore not feminine enough. We must work on re-defining femininity and beauty for our girls so that they grow to be a generation of women empowered to express themselves honestly and proudly in all areas of their lives."*—A licensed professional counselor who specializes in gender issues

Counselors will inevitably work with clients struggling with their gender identity. The presenting issues will likely vary and could include the self-esteem of a girl who is comfortable wearing "boy" clothes and is being teased by other girls; an individual assigned female at birth who is struggling with gender conformity and societal expectation; or a Latina woman who is pursuing a graduate degree and postponing a family and is experiencing conflict both with cultural and societal expectations for marriage and motherhood. Some clients may be unaware of societal expectations, pressure, and oppression their assigned gender might have on their everyday experiences and their mental and physical health. Others, however, may have a deeper understanding of the impact of gender, and may have experienced discrimination or conflicts involving their assigned gender (Gray et al., 2012). Issues around gender are one of the many factors counselors need to consider in order to build effective therapeutic relationships and help clients find greater well-being (Anderson & Levitt, 2015).

A recent development in considering gender and the therapeutic process is the removal of childhood gender identity disorder from the latest edition of the *Diagnostic and Statistical Manual of Mental Disorders (DSM)*. This diagnosis had long been disputed and considered discriminatory, especially since most children who had received the diagnosis later identified as gay or lesbian (Dragowski et al., 2011). The current *DSM-5* diagnosis is gender dysphoria, a broader category that removes the word "disorder," which often holds a negative and stigmatizing connotation. In order to be diagnosed with gender dysphoria, a client must be significantly distressed and have ongoing (6 months or more) issues either at school, work, or at home (APA, 2013). The APA states that having this category in the *DSM-5* allows those individuals who feel incongruent with their assigned gender to access care and resources they may need.

Feminist therapists were first to challenge early theories that were based mostly on interactions and observations of White males. Feminists reject assumptions and beliefs that pathologize behaviors and characteristics typically ascribed to women (Enns, 1997; Worell & Remer, 2003). Placing gender at the forefront of the therapeutic process, feminist theorists challenge gender stereotypes and propose therapeutic processes to address issues of gender. Research has correlated strong feminist identity with higher gender orientation or positive feelings toward gender traits (Saunders & Kashubeck-West, 2006). These findings suggest that counselors may benefit from finding avenues to explore concepts of feminism and feminist therapy in practice.

Counselors' understanding of their own gender identity is also very important for the counseling relationship. Research on how much importance a counselor places on his or her own masculinity or femininity had a significant negative impact on the therapeutic relationship; in other words, it is not how a counselor labels himself or herself (as woman, man, transgender, and so forth), but how he or she understands and accepts his or her own gender identity that is important in building a strong therapeutic alliance (Anderson & Levitt, 2015). In addition, a counselor must be aware of his or her own limitations and or biases in terms of gender expression. This includes being up to date on current issues and knowing your client's preferred terminology. If a counselor lacks knowledge in this area, he or she must pursue educational avenues to increase his or her understanding and competency. To begin increasing competence, it would be helpful to become familiar with the Association for Lesbian, Gay, Bisexual, and Transgender Issues in Counseling (ALGBTIC)'s Competencies for Counseling Lesbian, Gay, Bisexual, Queer, Intersex, Questioning, and Ally (LGBQIQA) Individuals, as well as the American Counseling Association's Competencies for Counseling Transgender Clients (which can be found at www.counseling.org/knowledge -center/competencies).

CONCLUSION

"To be a girl means being strong and don't let anyone put you down."
—Sunny, age 13

"To be a girl means being powerful."—Eve, age 11

"To be a girl means that I could be anything, you can be a sports player, a horseback rider, a teacher. Being a girl is just being a girl."—Fiona, age 9

"Being a girl is cool!"—Maeve, age 6

Human development is a lifelong process that begins with a reciprocal relationship with a parent or caregiver. Through that relationship, and relationships with other influential adults and peers, children begin to build an understanding of who they are. In this chapter, we discovered that gender identity is a multifaceted construct that includes how someone understands, conceptualizes, and internalizes external and internal ideas of gender. Throughout history, different theorists have provided research and interpretations of gender identity development. These theorists include Freud and Erickson, who first explored gender identity development in terms of sex-role expectations and the consequences for individuals who did not conform to traditional expectations of gender roles. Cognitive and social learning theories expanded the concepts of gender identity development to include the way individuals think and understand gender through personal, behavioral, and environmental factors. Gender schema and feminist theories identified the social and cultural context of gender, including the imbalance in power and influence of male and female traits, attributes, and perceived abilities.

Cultural factors greatly influence the development of a person's gender identity. Children absorb concepts of gender (how to act, what to wear, which toys to play with, and with whom to play) as early as 18 to 24 months of age. The emerging movement of gender fluidity and gender expression challenges the traditional dichotomous definition of gender, expanding the understanding of how gender can be internalized, understood, and expressed. Children and adults are both vulnerable to biases and prejudices for "deviating" from societal norms of gender roles. It is important that counselors understand the influence of gender and gender identity on an individual's development and well-being and become knowledgeable about the competencies needed to work with LGBQIQA clients.

CALL TO ACTION

As counselors, we are charged with being advocates "at individual, group, institutional, and societal levels to address potential barriers and obstacles that

(continued)

CALL TO ACTION (*continued*)

inhibit access and/or the growth and development of clients" (ACA, 2014, p. 5). In regard to gender, the movement continues to support rights related to equal pay, education, treatment, voice, and the safety and sanctity of one's own body. Transgender and other gender-fluid individuals also need advocacy, support, understanding, and equality. Part of our role as counselors is to understand the societal and cultural influences on gender identity (Evans et al., 2005). Exploring gender identity within the therapeutic relationship allows the client a safe place to discover his or her own gender identity. As counselors, we can help our clients understand and process feelings as well as develop empowering thoughts and behaviors in regard to gender (Di Ceglie, 2009). Outside of the therapeutic relationship, counselors are called to act as advocates for causes of equality and the promotion of mental health. Getting involved in local LGBTQ chapters and causes that empower women and girls and using your vote and writing and petitioning your political representatives are examples of such advocacy. The ACA, as well as regional and local chapters, has active movements, some of which can be found at ACA Action Center (www.counseling.org/ government-affairs/actioncenter). In their everyday lives, counselors can speak up when they witness acts of discrimination or microaggressions. These interactions could help to educate a person on preferred language and terms or provide a broader understanding of the issues and struggles of those similar to and different from ours.

REFLECTION AND DISCUSSION QUESTIONS

1. Does your family, culture, religion, or ethnicity have gender-specific norms and expectations? If so, what are they?

2. Do you see any changes in societal norms for gender identity? If so, what do you think they are?

3. Does your preferred theoretical orientation specifically address gender identity? If so, in what way? If not, how might you integrate gender into this theory?

4. What is your understanding about gender variant, genderqueer, gender questioning, transgender, and others that identify outside the dichotomous classification of male and female? If a client presents an issue involving the questioning of his or her assigned gender, how would you work with this client? What type of additional research or reading (if any) would you need to do?

HELPFUL RESOURCES

- Amy Poehler's Smart Girls (www.amysmartgirls.com)—Founded by actor and writer Amy Poehler and producer Meredith Walker, the Smart Girls organization is dedicated to providing a healthy alternative to much that is being marketed to young people on the Internet. Their motto is: "Change the World by Being Yourself"
- GenderPac (www.gpac.org)—A national organization working to end discrimination and violence caused by gender stereotypes
- Gender Spectrum (www.genderspectrum.org)—An organization that helps to create gender-sensitive and inclusive environments for all children and teens
- GLAAD (www.glaad.org)—A leading organization for the LGBTQ community and serves as a communication and educational resource and advocacy center
- National Center for Transgender Equality (www.transequality.org)—A national social justice organization devoted to ending discrimination and violence against transgender people
- Trans Lifeline (877-565-8860)—A U.S. support hotline staffed by and for transgender people

REFERENCES

Ahlqvist, S., Halim, M. L., Greulich, F. K., Lurye, L. E., & Ruble, D. (2013). The potential benefits and risks of identifying as a tomboy: A social identity perspective. *Self and Identity, 12*(5), 563–581. doi:10.1080/15298868.2012.717709

American Counseling Association. (2014). *ACA code of ethics.* Alexandria, VA: Author.

American Psychiatric Association. (2013). Gender dysphoria fact sheet. Retrieved from http://www.dsm5.org/documents/gender%20dysphoria%20fact%20sheet.pdf

Anderson, R. S., & Levitt, D. H. (2015). Gender self-confidence and social influence: Impact on working alliance. *Journal of Counseling and Development, 93*, 280–288. doi:10.1002/jcad.12026

Bandura, A. (1986). *Social foundations of thought and action: A social cognitive theory.* Englewood Cliffs, NJ: Prentice-Hall.

Bem, S. L. (1981). Gender schema theory: A cognitive account of sex typing. *Psychological Review, 88*, 354–364. doi:10.1037/0033-295x.88.4.354

Blakemore, J. E. O. (2003). Children's beliefs about violating gender norms: Boys shouldn't look like girls and girls shouldn't act like boys. *Sex Roles, 49*, 411–420. doi:10.1007/s11199-005-7729-0

Bussey, K. (2011). Gender identity development. In S. J. Schwartz, K. Luyckx, & V. L. Vignoles (Eds.), *Handbook of identity theory and research* (pp. 600–628). New York, NY: Springer-Verlag.

Bussey, K., & Bandura, A. (1999). Social cognitive theory of gender development and differentiation. *Psychological Review, 106*(4), 676. doi:10.1037/0033-295x.106.4.676

Diamond, L. M., Pardo, S. T., & Butterworth, M. R. (2011). Transgender experience and identity. In S. J. Schwartz, K. Luyckx, & V. L. Vignoles (Eds.), *Handbook of identity theory and research* (pp. 629–647). New York, NY: Springer-Verlag.

Di Ceglie, D. (2009). Engaging young people with atypical gender identity development in therapeutic work: A developmental approach. *Journal of Child Psychotherapy, 35*(1), 3–12. doi:10.1080/00754170902764868

Dragowski, E. A., Scharrón-del Río, M. R., & Sandigorsky, A. L. (2011). Childhood gender identity . . . disorder? Developmental, cultural, and diagnostic concerns. *Journal of Counseling and Development, 89*(3), 360–366. doi:10.1002/j.1556-6678.2011.tb00100.x

Eagly, A. H., & Wood, W. (2013). The nature–nurture debates 25 years of challenges in understanding the psychology of gender. *Perspectives on Psychological Science, 8*(3), 340–357. doi:10.1177/1745691613484767

Egan, S. K., & Perry, D. G. (2001). Gender identity: A multidimensional analysis with implications for psychosocial adjustment. *Developmental Psychology, 37*(4), 451. doi:10.1037/0012-1649.37.4.451

Endendijk, J., Groeneveld, M., Berkel, S., Hallers-Haalboom, E., Mesman, J., & Bakermans-Kranenburg, M. (2013). Gender stereotypes in the family context: Mothers, fathers, and siblings. *Sex Roles, 68*(9/10), 577–590. doi:10.1007/s11199-013-0265-4

Enns, C. Z. (1997). *Feminist theories and feminist psychotherapies: Origins, themes and variations.* Binghamton, NY: The Hawthorn Press.

Erikson, E. (1968). *Identity, youth, and crisis.* New York, NY: W. W. Norton.

Evans, K. M., Kincade, E. A., Marbley, A. F., & Seem, S. R. (2005). Feminism and feminist therapy: Lessons from the past and hopes for the future. *Journal of Counseling and Development, 83*(3), 269–277. doi:10.1002/j.1556-6678.2005.tb00342.x

Friedan, B. (1963). *The feminine mystique.* New York: NY: W. W. Norton.

GLAAD. (2016). GLAAD media reference guide—Transgender issues. Retrieved from http://www.glaad.org/reference/transgender

Gray, S. A., Carter, A. S., & Levitt, H. (2012). A critical review of assumptions about gender variant children in psychological research. *Journal of Gay and Lesbian Mental Health, 16*(1), 4–30. doi:10.1080/19359705.2012.634719

Halim, M. L., Zosuls, K. M., Ruble, D. N., Tamis-LeMonda, C. S., Lurye, L. E., & Greulich, F. K. (2014). Pink frilly dresses and the avoidance of all things "girly": Children's appearance rigidity and cognitive theories of gender development. *Developmental Psychology, 50*(4), 1091–1101. doi:10.1037/a0034906

Hoffman, R. M. (2006). Gender self-definition and gender self-acceptance in women: Intersections with feminist, womanist, and ethnic identities. *Journal of Counseling and Development, 84*(3), 358–372. doi:0.1002/j.1556-6678.2006.tb00415.x

Kimmel, M. S. (2000). *The gendered society.* New York, NY: Oxford University Press.

Kohlberg, L. (1969). Stage and sequence: The cognitive developmental approach to socialization. In D. A. Goslin (Ed.), *Handbook of socialization theory and research* (pp. 347–480). Chicago, IL: Rand McNally.

Lev, A. I. (2010). How queer! The development of gender identity and sexual orientation in LGBTQ-headed families. *Family Process, 49*(3), 268–290. doi:10.1111/j.1545-5300.2010.01323.x

Lytton, H., & Romney, D. (1991). Parents' differential socialization of boys and girls: A meta-analysis. *Psychological Bulletin, 109,* 267–296.

Martin, C. L., & Halverson, C. F., Jr. (1981). A schematic processing model of sex typing and stereotyping in children. *Child Development, 52,* 1119–1134. doi:10.2307/1129498

Martin, C. L., & Halverson, C. F., Jr. (1983). The effects of sex-typing schemas on young children's memories. *Child Development, 54,* 563–574.

Martin, C. L., Ruble, D. N., & Szkrybalo, J. (2002). Cognitive theories of early gender development. *Psychological Bulletin, 128*(6), 903. doi:10.1037/0033-2909.128.6.903

Miller, J. B. (1986). *Toward a new psychology of women.* Boston, MA: Beacon Press.

Nagoshi, J. L., Nagoshi, C. T., & Brzuzy, S. (2014). *Gender and sexual identity: Transcending feminist and queer theory.* New York, NY: Springer-Verlag.

Riley, E. A., Sitharthan, G., Clemson, L., & Diamond, M. (2011). The needs of gender-variant children and their parents: A parent survey. *International Journal of Sexual Health, 23*(3), 644–659. doi:10.1080/19317611.2011.593932

Ryle, R. (2011). *Questioning gender: A sociological exploration.* Thousand Oaks, CA: Sage.

Saunders, K. J., & Kashubeck-West, S. (2006). The relations among feminist identity development, gender-role orientation, and psychological well-being in women. *Psychology of Women Quarterly, 30*(2), 199–211. doi:10.1111/j.1471-6402.2006.00282.x

Singh, S. (2007). Deconstructing "gender and development" for "identities of women." *International Journal of Social Welfare, 16*(2), 100–109. doi:10.1111/j.1468-2397.2006.00454.x

Vignoles, V. L., Schwartz, S. J., & Luyckx, K. (2011). Introduction: Toward an integrated view of identity. In S. J. Schwartz, K. Luyckx, & V. L. Vignoles (Eds.), *Handbook of identity theory and research* (pp. 1–27). New York, NY: Springer-Verlag.

Worell, J., & Remer P. (2003). *Feminist perspectives in therapy: Empowering diverse women* (2nd ed.). Hoboken, NJ: Wiley.

CHAPTER 6

Childhood

Sarah I. Springer

LEARNING OBJECTIVES

After reading this chapter, you will be able to:

1. Recognize the impact of gender-role socialization and stereotypes on the development of preadolescent girls.
2. Identify advocacy and prevention opportunities that empower young girls with the awareness and skills to navigate these challenges.
3. Support young girls and their caregivers with language and initiatives that recognize their strengths and foster their authentic interests and talents.

From a very early age, society influences girls' expectations of themselves, including perceptions of their bodies, competence, and career endeavors (Adler, Kless, & Adler, 1992; Emolu, 2014; Kerr, Vuyk, & Rea, 2012). From the pink diapers and strollers to the Barbie dolls that depict unrealistic body types, girls are flooded with overt and covert societal messages of "gender appropriateness" and synthetic views of "ideal beauty." The intersection of gender and other cultural factors (e.g., racial identity, ethnicity, socioeconomic status [SES], religion) can compound these societal messages (Letendre & Rozas, 2015; Qin, 2006). For instance, girls from immigrant families may struggle with intersecting cultural values with respect to gender expectations (McCarthy, 1998); perhaps a girl's home culture values caretaking responsibilities as a collective priority, whereas the surrounding culture advocates for individualism and a career-driven mind-set. Conflicting messages around role socialization can present a challenge for girls struggling to live authentically. These challenges manifest themselves in many ways as school-aged girls reach developmental milestones while navigating the social hierarchies that influence their identity development (Letendre & Rozas, 2015). Validating gendered experiences, while providing both intervention and prevention to girls at a young age, is critical. Mental health professionals are in an important position to help empower young girls with contextual awareness and the tools to value their own voices and strength. Recognizing these contextual factors is a first step in advocating for children's emotional needs. As you read through this chapter, you are encouraged to reflect on your own upbringing, values, and susceptibility to these messages.

MODELING AS CONTEXTUAL FOUNDATION

The socialization of humans arguably begins from the moment they are born (Emolu, 2014). From the congratulatory welcome cards to the first set of blankets, bibs, and onesies prepared for their arrivals, infants and their families are showered with gender-specific expectations. Reflect for a moment: If an expecting mother does not choose to announce the gender of the baby, can you hear the mumbling voices of friends and family as they uncomfortably attempt to purchase gifts for a baby shower? Can you think of times where you have heard someone say "She is so cute" only to find that the long-haired toddler of interest happens to be male? Or how about a time when a baby girl was dressed in blue and assumed to be a handsome little boy? From colors to toys, children are inundated with messages about how to dress, what to play, and, as they get older, how to play. These messages have a profound effect on the internalization of gender norms as well as the way developing children both experience and are experienced by the world (Adler et al., 1992; Benton, 2013; Emolu, 2014).

As we explore the sociocultural context of child development, it is important to begin by acknowledging that one of the most important ways in which children learn is through observing others (Bandura, 1986). Children learn vicariously in any number of ways, which may include direct discussion and/or adults' behavioral reactions, passive agreement, or even nonresponsiveness. Perhaps you have heard people say to girls: "You always look prettier when you smile" or "That's not a ladylike way to sit." Maybe you have given a woman a genuine compliment and heard, "Oh, stop, you're just being nice" or "You really think so?" Somehow, accepting a compliment has become "unladylike" and young girls are watching. They also hear us associate food and behaviors as "good" and "bad," such as "I shouldn't eat that piece of cake; I'm starting my diet on Monday. I should really go to the gym." These comments can be problematic for girls if they are not given a context with which to understand the messages; associated consequences include both physical and emotional disturbances. For instance, maternal discussions and behavior associated with weight control and weight-loss encouragement have been linked to disordered eating attitudes and behaviors in children (Evans & le Grange, 1995; Grosick, Talbert-Johnson, Myers, & Angelo, 2013; Hill & Franklin, 1998; Mussell, Binford, & Fulkerson, 2000; Rodgers & Charbrol, 2009; Wertheim, Martin, Prior, Sanson, & Smart, 2002). In these cases, without further discussions, girls may hear their role models chastising themselves or others in these ways and see commercials for weight-loss products and the latest gym equipment and be unable to differentiate themselves from the adult audience for which the messages were intended. Sadly, adults who may be unconsciously modeling such behaviors may be equally paralyzed by society's expectations. In many cases, support is necessary for both children and their caregivers.

MICROAGGRESSIONS

Although many stereotypical messages exist in overt forms, many others are so discreet that even adults are left with more questions than answers. Microaggressions, defined as "brief and commonplace daily verbal, behavioral, and environmental indignities whether intentional or unintentional that communicate hostile, derogatory or negative slights and insults" (Sue et al., 2007, p. 271), can impact any marginalized population, including females. A common example might include labeling a woman who expresses emotion as hysterical or a male sharing feelings as "girly." Regardless of the intent, such messages are detrimental to both genders and contribute to shaping the sociocultural context impacting individuals' identity development (Sue, Bucceri, Lin, Nadal, & Torino, 2009).

There are various forms of microaggressions, including microassaults, microinsults, and microinvalidations. Gender-based microassaults and microinsults represent more overt forms of discriminatory acts and language and are not the focus of this chapter. Microinvalidations, "characterized by communications that exclude, negate, or nullify the psychological thoughts, feelings, or experiential reality" (Sue et al. 2007, p. 274), can often be so subtle that the messages are internalized without our conscious awareness. For instance, imagine hearing a young girl who plays softball receive the following "so called" compliment: "Wow, you throw like a guy." This comment is likely aimed at her throwing mechanics but subtly implies that it is better to play like a male than a female. Many such messages are perpetuated daily through commercial advertisements, TV shows, and other media outlets and need to be discussed with young people and dissected for meaning and intent (Anuradha, 2012). Bringing the impact of this language to our conscious awareness may facilitate meaningful dialogue, which can ultimately lead to cultural shifts and advocacy for the healthy development of girls.

TRENDS AND THE MEDIA

The onset of puberty appears to be decreasing by 4 months each decade (Knez, Munjas, Petrovečki, Paučić-Kirinčić, & Peršić, 2006). Currently, research shows that many girls are beginning puberty as early as age 9 years, while they are likely still in elementary school (Cheng et al., 2012). This is particularly noteworthy given that children's physical development may no longer be in sync with the speed of their brain development with respect to decision making and emotional regulation. The media and fashion designers are noticing this trend and, in many ways, are capitalizing on these developmental shifts. Children whose physical bodies are changing but who may be in the earlier stages of emotional maturity could therefore be more susceptible to advertisements, trends, and messages that appeal to their physical development.

"I can't even find shorts long enough for me to wear to school in the spring."—A 9-year-old girl

Contextual Issues

Consider this girl's internal predicament: Do I adhere to the dress code policy by shopping for "appropriate school clothes" or do I "chance it," like many of my classmates, in order to fit in more comfortably with my peers? This common dialogue, as anecdotally shared by many young girls, can create challenges for children, parents, and school personnel. There is undoubtedly a reciprocal interaction among the clothing industry, designers, and the media, which together play a huge factor in gender-role socialization. Hypersexualization of young children can be seen on the screen, in music, and through various other avenues of communication (Thompson, 2010). In fact, marketers appear to be targeting girls with products that were once intended for adult women. As suggested in *Sexy Inc. Our Children Under Influence* (provided as a media resource in Helpful Resources at the end of this chapter), the birth of "transitional items" has made it even easier to capture the attention of young girls. For instance, advertisements for lipstick now may include lip gloss for teenagers and sparkly lip balm with characters from Disney's movie *Frozen* on the packaging that appeal more to younger girls. Clothing lines promote styles that are inappropriate for school and often reinforce stereotypical messages, such as a girl's t-shirt carrying the message: "Girls Just Wanna Have Fund$." Promoting messages that suggest that women and girls are attracted to money over other priorities only perpetuates assumptions about girls' motivations and intentions. Furthermore, the young consumer does not intellectually understand such implicit messages until she and her peers have likely internalized their meanings.

Additionally, marketers are aware that now, more than ever, children are using their own money to purchase merchandise. Developmentally, children want to fit in with their peers. As a result, they may not think anything of buying items that say "sexy," "bad girl," or "juicy"; after all, many of the dolls that these girls are playing with are dressed with this exact clothing. The results of Starr and Ferguson's (2012) findings provide empirical rationale for this phenomenon. In this study, 60 six- to nine-year-old girls were given dolls and asked to choose one that best represented their ideal popular selves. Overwhelmingly, these girls preferred the more sexualized figures. This suggests that many young girls may be internalizing hypersexualized appearances, which could result in them beginning to define their own popularity based primarily on their outward appearance.

Young boys are also internalizing these messages and likely formulating ideas about what girls are and are not. "I love shopping," "Better to be late than to be ugly," and "I am not a bitch, I'm THE bitch" can be seen on t-shirts and posters and can perpetuate stereotypes that impact the way boys interact with girls as they get older. Television shows, movies, and music videos may reinforce these messages by highlighting "girly habits" and scripting extreme characterizations of overly emotional or cold-hearted women.

"I was taken aback by a second grade girl at our school as she talked about and demonstrated twerking to her friends at last night's dance."—An elementary school teacher

Recognizable TV and movie figures conforming to gendered stereotypes may serve to further reinforce the objectification of girls (Jackson & Vares, 2015). Belly shirts, revealing dresses, and sexualized dance moves are portrayed in children's TV shows and highlighted in stores and on billboards. Girls can be heard belting out songs with suggestive lyrics, such as Tove Lo's *Talking Body* and Selena Gomez's *Good for You*. The frequency with which children are exposed to these audio and visual messages can create (for girls and boys) a desensitization to sexualized language and images. The following sections highlight key relational and developmental experiences impacting the world of young girls as they learn to communicate effectively and navigate the stressful process of academic and career decision making. Counseling issues and intervention and advocacy strategies are embedded within each section, followed by discussion questions and supplemental resources.

THE IMPACT OF GENDER-ROLE SOCIALIZATION IN CHILDHOOD

Play and Communication

Play is one of the most important avenues through which children begin communicating and understanding the world (Lin, 2010). Toys and games are often designated by gender and can reinforce the way children learn to interact with each other. Can you recall the last time you saw a children's kitchen set marketed in the boys' toy aisle? A boy who engages in what might be considered a cross-gender activity may receive disapproving messages from both peers and adults (Fagot, 1977). Likewise, girls who enjoy tools, cars, and certain sports may be referred to as tomboys. These examples suggest that nonconformity may brand even very young children with socially isolating labels.

Contextual Issues

Gender-typical messages surrounding boys and girls from infancy are often internalized, reinforced by the family context, and generalized to other areas in children's lives. According to Freeman (2007), children as young as 3 years are able to learn and apply gender stereotypes to activities. For example, in a Starbucks Coffee line, a 3-year-old boy was overheard saying, "Mommy, the movie *Cars* is only for boys." Minutes later, this same boy was observed being asked by his mother whether he wanted a brown or pink lollipop. The boy's answer was pink, and the mother smiled and said, "Great." The mother turned to the customer behind her in line and said, "You can tell the influences he gets from his father and me."

Freeman's (2007) findings also suggest that young children can predict their parents' assumptions about gender-typical play. For instance, although parents reported that they were gender neutral when it came to the types of toys and games they reinforced with their children, many of these children actually reported that their parents' expectations of them would conform to gender stereotypes. For example, children, associating skateboards and motorcycles with boys and dolls and tea sets with girls, reported that their parents would approve of these choices and disapprove of cross-gender selections. This suggests that they have already internalized their parents' (and society's) gender stereotypes.

Maintaining distinct gender expectations may also result from the fact that "our culture privileges and punishes certain gender roles" (Benton, 2013, p. 141). Adults who hear of boys physically expressing their aggression on the playground simply declare, "Boys will be boys." Reactions tend to be quite different if girls dare to express anger or extreme emotion in this manner. In children's media, boys are often portrayed in domineering leadership and "savior" roles, whereas girls are unassertive princesses or damsels in distress. Halloween costumes reinforce each year's crop of Disney male heroes and female villains. Girls internalize these messages and as they get older may hear women villainized as "bitches" for speaking out and asserting their opinions. These emotional expression norms, regularly tied into the characterizations of media figures, can also be implicitly reinforced by societal and familial messages.

Many children learn very early on that boys should be "tough" and not cry, whereas girls should be "sugar and spice and everything nice" and suppress overt expressions of anger.

"When I was sad about the way a friend was treating me, my dad told me to man up and stop crying."—An 8-year-old boy

For this 8-year-old boy, sadness likely became associated with a weaker "feminine" trait that must be suppressed. Although boys are not being taught to express sadness and disappointment in a healthy manner, girls are similarly provided with messages that include not being "overly emotional" or aggressive when they are frustrated. Both genders are likely left with emotional confusion and increased susceptibility to developing maladaptive means of coping with their emotions.

Furthermore, gendered messages can be even more confusing for children who experience clashes between the expectations of the dominant society and those of their home cultures. In school, for instance, girls may be supported in (and graded on) initiating conversations and asserting themselves, but in their homes, they may be taught not to speak unless spoken to. Navigating the emotional roller coasters of preadolescence can become increasingly more challenging as a result.

Counseling Issues

Many girls receive mixed messages about appropriate ways to communicate emotions. On the one hand, they recognize that it is okay to express sadness and concern in certain contexts, as long as they do not become "overly emotional." On the other hand, they may have learned that anger is a male expression of emotion and must be suppressed. This may result in more girls engaging in passive–aggressive communication and relational aggression, defined as "harming others through purposeful manipulation and damage of peer relationships" (Crick & Grotpeter, 1995)—often associated with "female" aggression. Crick and Grotpeter's (1995) initial study of relational aggression found that children who engaged in this covert form of communication had more social difficulties. These children (predominantly girls) reported greater feelings of loneliness, depression, and peer isolation.

Chaplin and Aldao's (2013) meta-analysis of gender differences and emotional expression likewise demonstrated that suppressing certain emotions may be linked with increased chances for psychopathology. For instance, boys may struggle more frequently with conduct and aggression. This can include outbursts of anger, an "umbrella" emotion, which can mask feelings of sadness, shame, and fear. Although many boys struggle to express these deeper emotions, their outward displays of anger are often considered acceptable forms of expression. On the other hand, girls (having been taught that displaying anger is inappropriate) may internalize their emotions, which could result in anxiety or depression later in life (Chaplin & Aldao, 2013). Research suggests that other associated psychological consequences appear to be connected to relational aggression as well, including peer rejection, isolation, and self-harm (Crick & Grotpeter, 1995; Keenan, Hipwell, Stepp, & Wroblewski, 2014). A recent study conducted by Keenan et al. (2014) examined the reported behaviors of early adolescent girls and found that relationally aggressive behavior over a period of time was a significant predictor of nonsuicidal self-injury (NSSI). Their findings also highlight the potential for adolescents engaging in NSSI behaviors to continue to participate in self-harm and even suicide attempts later in life. Society's gendered expectations may therefore have a hand in the development of unhealthy forms of emotional expression, resulting in future mental health concerns.

Counseling Application

Mental health professionals are in an important position to empower girls with the knowledge and skills to promote healthy emotional and relational growth. Within a relational-cultural framework, one way in which to accomplish this is through validating girls' experiences and exploring the impact of their current relationships on the development of their identities. This begins with the establishment of a meaningful therapeutic alliance founded on mutual empathy and authenticity. Counselors can take opportunities to coconstruct therapeutic goals and focus attention on connections that girls experience in relationships in and outside of the therapeutic setting. In doing so, counselors may work to expand girls' relational capacities. At a time where girls are beginning to seek more autonomy in decision making, they are also looking for connection from peers and outside adults outside of the home. The connection between counselors and clients may become a vehicle for counselors to use in processing and modeling healthy emotional expression and coping skills. With a trusting working alliance, counselors may also find opportunities to process disconnection in relationships.

Exploring contextual factors (e.g., power structures, gender-role socialization) and maladaptive coping strategies (e.g., relationally aggressive behavior) that may be contributing to disempowerment and relational struggles may help girls minimize self-blame and separate their worth from victimizing gender-based societal messages. Empowering young girls with this knowledge and the skills to find and use their voices assertively can result in healthier relational and psychological functioning.

Group Counseling
A group counseling modality may be an alternative way to validate girls' experiences and provide them with opportunities to develop healthy emotional expression skills. Relational-cultural theory (RCT) posits that people find growth through relationships. Counselors may choose to organize "friendship" psychoeducational groups that focus on assertiveness skills and emotional expression. This type of group has the potential to increase relational capacity by focusing on the power of therapeutic factors, such as universality and cohesion that lead to trust and the willingness to engage in healthy relational risk taking. Furthermore, negative relational images such as "I don't fit in because I don't wear make-up" often contribute to girls' feelings of isolation and can be explored through group member relationships. Group discussions can also serve to promote members' strengths as well as the resilience developed through the navigation of challenging experiences. This may be especially true of girls who struggle with competing gender-based bicultural values. Offering a safe place to process conflicting familial and societal expectations, the group setting may help individuals share their personal struggles and recognize their own resilience. At a developmental time where preadolescents may be feeling powerless, isolated, and disconnected, engaging in positive and empowering peer experiences through group process can help young girls develop both intrapersonally and interpersonally in productive ways.

Family Support
Mental health practitioners can also help families learn strategies in which to promote girls' healthy emotional expression. For instance, counselors could provide prevention-based community workshops and/or counseling groups that highlight ways to infuse cross-gender play and gender-inclusive language into the home environment. Providing information about potential health consequences of reinforcing gender stereotypes may also increase awareness of potential signs of pathology that would benefit from therapeutic intervention.

School-Based Intervention
Expanding these initiatives into the school environment may include leveraging the expertise of school counselors, who have a captive audience. School-based counselors may consider running joint parent/child groups to engage stakeholders in important dialogue around the development of healthy emotional expression. Several resources for the initiation of girls' and boys' groups can be found at the end of this chapter. Presentations can also be designed to help educators increase their understanding of their roles in creating an emotionally healthy school climate. Supporting families and educators with awareness of

their own behaviors and reactions to their children may further help to create an environment where young girls are praised for expressing themselves openly and engaging in play and communication congruent with their interests and personalities.

Career Aspirations: Decision Making

Career decision making is a process, which arguably begins during early childhood. According to some career theorists (e.g., Gottfredson, 1981), a person's career choice derives from both their social and psychological self-concept (Swanson & Fouad, 1999). Gender-role socialization can play an important part in the development of occupational stereotypes. The internalization of these stereotypes, such as categorizing careers based on perceived sex type, has the potential to limit career decision making. Circumscription is a process by which children determine what they perceive to be acceptable and unacceptable career options (Gottfredson, 2005). Accessibility, modeling, and gender stereotypes can each play a role in the way young girls consider and pursue career interests. One of the most recognizable consequences of gender stereotyping is the underrepresentation of women (particularly women of color) in STEM (science, technology, engineering, and math) careers (National Research Council, 2012). Archer et al. (2012) suggest that underrepresentation of women in science careers is a global problem. Thus, examining the way in which girls are supported in developing their strengths and career aspirations is particularly important.

According to the National Research Council (2012), girls and boys have similar interests in science throughout elementary school. The transition to middle school, however, is often marked by a decline in girls' interests in STEM careers. Many elementary-aged girls express an early interest in pursuing STEM careers but reject science as a career path. Using discourse analysis, Archer et al. (2012) discovered two types of girls endorsing careers in the sciences: those who self-identified as quiet and enjoyed focusing on academics, rather than socializing or "girly stuff" (e.g., talking about makeup and celebrities), and those who were able to "balance their clever science identities through performances of heterofemininity" (p. 975). Examples of heterofemininity included focusing on relationships and appearance. The majority of respondents in this three-phase study, however, considered science to be an "unthinkable identity due to its profound incongruence with key elements of popular femininity" (Archer et al., 2013, p. 187). This response reflects gender norms that are often internalized and reinforced in the home and in school settings. The influence of parents on girls' career development is profound, as evidenced by the testimony of one 8-year-old, struggling with a science project, who stated, "My mom said I'll never be a scientist, anyway."

Parents are especially influential in children's social learning (Bandura, 1977). Even as young as infancy, children tend to imitate their same-sex parent (García de Polavieja & Platt, 2014). Role socialization may further be influenced by parents' knowledge of resources and SES; in fact, according to García de Polavieja and Platt's findings, both access and SES affect parents' aspirations for their children's career endeavors. Other researchers (e.g., Kerr et al., 2012) also discuss how differences in parenting impact girls' access to career knowledge. For instance, some parents may not be aware of or expose girls to enrichment activities. These messages, communicated both overtly and covertly, about career choices can strongly influence career decision making of young girls.

Modeling from parents, an integral part of children's learning processes (Bandura, 1977), is especially influential in career development. Bandura's (1986) social cognitive theory (SCT) posits that both vicarious learning and verbal persuasion are strong predictors of self-efficacy, or individuals' beliefs about their abilities to be successful in future endeavors. This suggests that children who watch and/or receive feedback associated with a person's lived experience may be influenced to believe similar characteristics about themselves. Accordingly, these beliefs, gathered from a number of sources, can significantly impact a person's motivation to engage in particular tasks.

Research examining girls' career influences supports this notion. According to García de Polavieja and Platt (2014), parents' occupational choices and sex-role modeling impact the career options girls consider. Although boys have many opportunities to see same-sex role models engaging in traditional and nontraditional careers and in leadership positions, girls have considerably fewer role models in nontraditional careers (e.g., STEM) and in organizational leadership positions (Shapiro et al., 2015). This is compounded by the fact that starting from a young age, many of these girls have already internalized messages that math and science careers are considered masculine (Bamberger, 2014). According to Bamberger, this is likely to impact their beliefs about their capabilities to perform in such careers. This is particularly important, as García de Polavieja and Platt (2014) found that girls with higher motivation were more likely to aspire to higher positions on the occupational ladder. This becomes an inherently cyclical process, as fewer females are motivated to pursue nontraditional careers, leaving young girls with fewer role models. Female educators may thus represent another important and influential group of adults with whom children can relate to on a regular basis.

School Considerations

During the school year, children spend the majority of their days interacting with teachers and peers, developing knowledge and skills needed for a variety of careers. These interactions represent opportunities for school personnel to model career advocacy. In response to a national call for more STEM-trained graduates, schools are providing more hands-on learning in STEM. Still, however, gendered practices significantly influence the acquisition of knowledge and pursuit of further career exploration in young girls (Bianco, Harris, Garrison-Wade, & Leach, 2011). Bianco et al. suggest that educators may unknowingly provide different career encouragement, impose different career expectations, and assess the genders differently, based on their own assumptions of male and female roles. Studies have often shown that boys are given more attention during instruction and their voices praised more often in the classroom (e.g., Wellesley College Center for Research on Women, 1992). This may be especially true in male-dominated classes, such as math and science. These subtle microinvalidations represent the "intersecting cluster of social, cultural, and structural factors [operating] to dis-suade and pull girls and women away from science" (Archer et al., 2012, p. 968).

An examination of gifted programs reveals similar gendered invalidations. Bianco et al. (2011) highlight the impact of teacher bias on referrals of girls to gifted programs. Teachers provided with similar profiles of male and female applicants for a gifted program were much more apt to refer boys. Teachers often cited poor social skills as the reason why female applicants were not considered strong candidates. Teachers also suggested that girls' behavior was arrogant, bossy, and domineering; characteristics that were overlooked or even praised in males. Bianco's earlier (2005) study found similar trends in referrals of culturally and linguistically diverse students, suggesting that girls belonging to cultural minority groups may be even more susceptible to gendered practices. This is likely to be yet another contributor to the underrepresentation of women of color in math and science careers.

Access to Education

Although subtler forms of gender discrimination can affect career interest and access to education, overt forms of gender inequity, including human rights vio-lations, have also impeded educational access for women and girls within the United States and across the globe. As cited in Greenbaum (2014), human sex traf-ficking is estimated to affect 26 million people worldwide with a marked increase in cases specific to young girls. Not only does this impact the physical and psy-chological well-being of victims, but it compromises health care and economic opportunities as well (Mathur, Greene, & Malhotra, 2003).

Unfortunately, despite laws prohibiting marriage before the age of 18 years in some countries, many young girls across the world are secretly forced to wed and, thus, are deprived of childhood exposure to education, health, and child-hood socialization; these experiences clearly impact a girl's career trajectory (Mathur et al., 2003). For example, a notable "underground" practice in an area of rural north India includes the exploitation of a group of young girls known as the "Midnight Ceremony Brides." Silently, these girls suffer as they are secretly married away and deprived of their childhood as young as 5-years-old (Gorney, 2011). Mutyaba (2011) likewise discusses the prevalence of unlawful early mar-riages in four African countries and similarly articulates consequences for young girls that include health risks, lack of access to education, and "inhumane and cruel treatment" (p. 339).

Other cultural practices around the world reserve schooling, an expensive investment, for males only, creating gendered practices that take away educa-tional opportunities for women (Gorney, 2011). Even girls who are afforded access to educational opportunities may still be at risk for hostility. For example, the known terrorist group, *Boko Haram* (loosely translated into a message that sug-gests Western education is unclean) from northern Nigeria, has actively targeted and captured women from educational institutions and enslaved them into the world of human trafficking (Luscombe & Foroohar, 2014). Whether connected to overt brutality or covert microaggresive behaviors, these examples suggest that even those privileged enough to receive educational opportunities may still share childhood commonalities (e.g., vicarious trauma) that can contribute to a lack of safety and more severe future mental health concerns.

Counseling Issues

There are many potential consequences associated with the mixed messages and overt behaviors surrounding girls and their career aspirations. According to Bandura (1986), predictors of self-efficacy include mastery experiences, vicarious learning, and verbal persuasion. If girls are not given sufficient opportunities to participate in enrichment activities, their skills may not be as fully developed, which can contribute to underachievement in specific subject areas. Likewise, lack of female role models and/or encouragement to develop skills may negatively impact their motivation and cause circumscription of perceived career options. This may result in girls ruling out certain careers and potentially denying aspects of their identities in which they would find success and enjoyment. Enrichment activities are essential for girls in learning new skills, developing mastery, and benefiting from group learning opportunities.

Girls' abilities to navigate social hierarchies (often reflective of power structures borne out of privilege) may be another factor impacting their career decision making. Developmentally, childhood and preadolescence is a time where girls typically seek connection to their peers. Depending on the makeup of their groups, girls may seek out or dismiss careers based on their social attractiveness. In fact, Archer et al.'s (2012) study suggested that girls 10 to 14 years old who confidently discussed pursuing careers in science had either learned how to navigate the "brainy" world and the world of femininity or disregarded gendered norms altogether. Unfortunately, many of those who disregarded heterofemininity norms may not have found an encouraging peer group, resulting in further challenges. In Archer et al.'s (2012) study, parents reported that many of these girls experienced bullying and social isolation throughout their school years. "Slipping into geek identity," as suggested in this study, seemed to leave girls open to increased social vulnerability (p. 981). Given the association between bullying behaviors and academic decline (Espelage, Sung Hong, Rao, & Low, 2013; Juvonen, Yueyan, & Guadalupe, 2011), girls who openly express nonconforming academic interests and behaviors may find themselves struggling to manage more than social isolation. The potential to develop future mental health issues (e.g., anxiety, depression) is a realistic concern.

Practical Application

As counselors, we have a role in advocating for girls' career exploration. Counselors might consider organizing groups that bring young girls together in support of nontraditional career choices. LEGO® or robotics' groups for elementary-aged girls may be one way to unite young females through shared experiences. Using activities and group process, facilitators can provide a safe environment for girls to work on tasks together while discussing their interests and academic experiences. With the potential for young children to experience isolation when their interests and values do not coincide with societal expectations, these groups may serve as an opportunity for mutual empathy, validation, and the development of healthy coping strategies. Discussions may also afford opportunities for continued growth through relational connections. Accompanying parent/daughter groups might further expand conversations and support adults in learning language to validate girls' experiences and promote continued dialogue around conflicting societal messages specific to women and STEM careers.

Discussions involving career exposure, modeling, and encouragement can also come through the school environment. Practitioners may consider partnering with the schools to offer parent workshops across the K-12 school setting that highlight gendered language and practices that may inhibit girls' healthy career development. Parent book clubs may be a unique way to infuse group process into prevention-based advocacy efforts. These opportunities can afford families a forum in which to discuss how they can partner with the schools to create additional learning and career exposure for young girls. For instance, adding a mentoring component to the annual science fair might generate girls' interest in STEM careers and promote follow-up experiential projects. Buck, Cook, Quigley, Prince, and Lucas's (2014) study discussed the impact of experiential learning from a female mentor. Their results suggested that a hands-on experiential learning opportunity provided by a supportive female science educator was found to be highly effective for fostering motivation and self-efficacy for science in African American girls. Moreover, these researchers found that presenting and discussing realistic scenarios in an inquiry-based learning format encouraged girls to investigate their own questions, increasing their motivation and self-efficacy for science-related careers. Mental health professionals can advocate for such learning opportunities in and outside of the school settings.

CALL TO ACTION

Understanding children's early gender-role socialization must include examination of relational influence in their lives. Rather than solely addressing young girls who struggle socially due to relationally aggressive behaviors, it is important to consider and address the systemic reasons many of our young girls are choosing to engage in this behavior. As cited in Grossman and Porche (2014), "Systemic understanding of discrimination can protect youth from its worst effects and help prevent self-blame for these experiences" (p. 719). Providing girls with opportunities to learn healthy ways of expressing their emotions and asserting themselves appropriately is essential. To accomplish this may require shifts in adult expectations, as well as the ways in which we communicate with girls.

Over the years, many researchers (e.g., Bosacki, Woods, & Coplan, 2015; Chapman, 2016; Sandberg & Pramling-Samuelsson, 2005) have found that teachers tend to hold strong gender-role expectations, particularly in the areas of play and communication. This may result in consequences for girls that

(continued)

CALL TO ACTION (continued)

include underdeveloped leadership potential. For instance, expectations to conform to female-appropriate communication and play may limit opportunities for girls to practice leading and engaging in problem solving, especially if they are thrust into submissive roles during play. Girls with fewer opportunities to play with associated cross-gender toys (e.g., LEGO and other building toys) may likewise lose out on opportunities to develop fine and gross motor skills. It is therefore important to advocate for more marketing and support for enrichment groups, such as LEGO building, computer coding, and robotics to both genders equally.

Another way to address gender stereotyping and bias on a systemic level may be to increase awareness through educator in-service training and the preservice teacher education curricula. At the training level, professors may advocate for specific core courses (e.g., Counseling/Teaching Women and Girls) to be included in the program sequence or advocate for infusing materials and assessments into courses that equally highlight and address the unique needs and experiences of both genders. At the in-service level, school administrators may advocate for increased professional development that encourages self-reflective practice through professional learning communities (PLCs). Additionally, school administrators may continually evaluate school assessment tools used to identify struggling or gifted students and examine any patterns in the ways students are evaluated throughout the curriculum.

Promoting empowerment community-based organizations such as Girls on the Run may be another way to support the healthy development of young girls. Through similar groups, girls learn to value their own voices and support each other in setting and achieving short- and long-term goals. In doing so, girls have the opportunities to live more authentically, which not only benefits their physical, social, and emotional well-being but also enhances the overall productivity of society.

REFLECTION AND DISCUSSION QUESTIONS

1. Make a list of traditional careers that you associate with each gender. What assumptions come up for you when you hear of a man going into the field of nursing or a female interested in becoming a mechanic?

2. If you were to organize a professional development presentation for teachers to increase awareness of gendered practices in the schools, how might you design and assess the outcome of this presentation?

3. Can you identify gender stereotypes that you have internalized and that have impacted your social, emotional, academic, and career trajectories?

(continued)

REFLECTION AND DISCUSSION QUESTIONS (continued)

4. Given the underrepresentation of girls and minorities in gifted programs, consider the role of mental health practitioners in advocating for the validity of measures that are used to predict and assess giftedness.

HELPFUL RESOURCES

Books

- Belgrave, F. Z., Cherry, V. R., Butler, D. S., & Townsend, T. G. (2008). *Sister of Nia: An empowerment cultural curriculum for African American girls.* Champaign, IL: Research Press
- Lamb, S., & Brown, L. M. (2006). *Packaging girlhood: Rescuing our daughters from marketers' schemes.* New York, NY: St. Martin's Griffin
- Sandberg, S. (2014). *Lean in: For graduates.* New York, NY: Alfred A. Knopf
- Taylor, J. V. (2005). *Salvaging sisterhood.* Chapin, SC: Youthlight

Videos and Professional Websites

- "A Dove Film" (www.youtube.com/watch?v=hibyAJOSW8U)—Using editing tools to enhance women's features on advertisements
- Panel Patter (www.panelpatter.com/2015/02/princeless-pirate-princess-1.html)—Series of books that feature girls as heroes
- "Sexy Inc. Our Children Under Influence" (www.onf.ca/film/sexy_inc)—Countering youth hypersexualization video
- Women in Nontraditional Careers (www.nontraditionalcareers.com)—Resources that highlight women in nontraditional careers

REFERENCES

Adler, P. A., Kless, S. J., & Adler, P. (1992). Socialization to gender roles: Popularity among elementary school boys and girls. *Sociology of Education, 65*(3), 169–187.

Anuradha, M. (2012). Gender stereotyping in television commercials aimed at children in India. *Media Asia, 39*(4), 209–215.

Archer, L., DeWitt, J., Osborne, J., Dillon, J., Willis, B., & Wong, B. (2012). "Balancing acts": Elementary school girls' negotiations of femininity, achievement, and science. *Science Education, 96*(6), 967–989. doi:10.1002/sce.21031

Archer, L., DeWitt, J., Osborne, J., Dillon, J., Willis, B., & Wong, B. (2013). "Not girly, not sexy, not glamorous": Primary school girls' and parents' constructions of science aspirations. *Pedagogy, Culture and Society, 21*(1), 171–194. doi:10.1080/14681366.2012.748676

Bamberger, Y. (2014). Encouraging girls into science and technology with feminine role model: Does this work? *Journal of Science Education and Technology, 23*(4), 549–561. doi:10.1007/s10956-014-9487-7

Bandura, A. (1977). Self-efficacy: Toward a unifying theory of behavioral change. *Psychological Review, 84*(2), 191–215.

Bandura, A. (1986). *Social foundations of thoughts and action: A social cognitive theory.* Englewood, NJ: Prentice-Hall.

Benton, B. H. (2013). Gender, games, and toys: Role communication and socialization through play. *Communication Teacher, 27*(3), 141–145. doi:10.1080/17404622.2013.782416

Bianco, M. (2005). The effects of disability labels on special and general education teachers' referrals for gifted program. *Learning Disability Quarterly, 28*(4), 285–293.

Bianco, M., Harris, B., Garrison-Wade, D., & Leech, N. (2011). Gifted girls: Gender bias in gifted referrals. *Roeper Review, 33*(3), 170–181. doi:10.1080/02783193.2011.580500

Bosacki, S., Woods, H., & Coplan, R. (2015). Canadian female and male early childhood educators' perceptions of child aggression and rough-and-tumble play. *Early Child Development and Care, 185*(7), 1134–1147.

Buck, G. A., Cook, K. L., Quigley, C. F., Prince, P., & Lucas, Y. (2014). Seeking to improve African American girls' attitudes toward science. *Elementary School Journal, 114*(3), 431–453.

Chaplin, T. M., & Aldao, A. (2013). Gender differences in emotion expression in children: A meta-analytic review. *Psychological Bulletin, 139*(4), 735–765. doi:10.1037/a0030737

Chapman, R. (2016). A case study of gendered play in preschools: How early childhood educators' perceptions of gender influence children's play. *Early Child Development and Care, 186*(8), 1271–1284. doi:10.1080/03004430.2015.1089435

Cheng, G., Buyken, A. E., Shi, L., Karaolis-Danckert, N., Kroke, A., Wudy, S. A., . . . Remer, T. (2012). Beyond overweight: Nutrition as an important lifestyle factor influencing timing of puberty. *Nutrition Reviews, 70*(3), 133–152. doi:http://dx.doi.org/10.1111/j.1753-4887.2011.00461.x

Crick, N. R., & Grotpeter, J. K. (1995). Relational aggression, gender, and social-psychological adjustment. *Child Development, 66*(3), 710–722.

Emolu, E. (2014). Play, toys, and gender socialization. *Journal Plus Education/Educatia Plus, 11*(2), 22–30.

Espelage, D. L., Sung Hong, J., Rao, M. A., & Low, S. (2013). Associations between peer victimization and academic performance. *Theory into Practice, 52*(4), 233–240.

Evans, J., & le Grange, D. (1995). Body size and parenting in eating disorders: A comparative study of the attitudes of mothers toward their children. *International Journal of Eating Disorders, 18*(1), 39–48. doi:10.1002/1098-108X(199507)18:1<39::AID-EAT2260180105>3.0.CO;2-I

Fagot, B. I. (1977). Consequences of moderate cross-gender behavior in preschool children. *Child Development, 48*(3), 902–907.

Freeman, N. (2007). Preschoolers' perceptions of gender appropriate toys and their parents' beliefs about genderized behaviors: Miscommunication, mixed messages, or hidden truths? *Early Childhood Education Journal, 34*(5), 357–366. doi:10.1007/s10643-006-0123-x

García de Polavieja, J., & Platt, L. (2014). Nurse or mechanic? The role of parental socialization and children's personality in the formation of sex-typed occupational aspirations. *Social Forces, 93*(1), 31–61.

Gorney, C. (2011). Too young to wed. *National Geographic, 219*(6), 78–99.

Gottfredson, L. S. (1981). Circumscription and compromise: A developmental theory of occupational aspirations [Monograph]. *Journal of Counseling Psychology, 28*, 545–579.

Gottfredson, L. S. (2005). Applying Gottfredson's theory of circumscription and compromise in career guidance and counseling. In S. D. Brown & R. W. Lent (Eds.), *Career development and counseling: Putting theory and research to work* (pp. 71–100). Hoboken, NJ: Wiley.

Greenbaum, V. J. (2014). Commercial sexual exploitation and sex trafficking of children in the United States. *Current Problems in Pediatric and Adolescent Health Care, 44*, 245–269. doi:10.1016/j.cppeds.2014.07.001

Grosick, T. L., Talbert-Johnson, C., Myers, M. J., & Angelo, R. (2013). Assessing the landscape: Body image values and attitudes among middle school boys and girls. *American Journal of Health Education, 44*(1), 41–52. doi:10.1080/19325037.2012.749682

Grossman, J. M., & Porche, M. V. (2014). Perceived gender and racial/ethnic barriers to STEM success. *Urban Education, 49*(6), 698–727. doi:10.1177/0042085913481364

Hill, A. J., & Franklin, J. A. (1998). Mothers, daughters, and dieting: Investigating the transmission of weight control. *British Journal of Clinical Psychology, 37*, 3–13. doi:10.1111/j.2044-8260.1998.tb01275.x

Jackson, S., & Vares, T. (2015). "Too many bad role models for us girls": Girls, female pop celebrities and "sexualization." *Sexualities, 18*(4), 480–498. doi:10.1177/1363460714550905

Juvonen, J., Yueyan, W., & Guadalupe, E. (2011). Bullying experiences and compromised academic performance across middle school grades. *Journal of Early Adolescence, 31*(1), 152–173.

Keenan, K., Hipwell, A. E., Stepp, S. D., & Wroblewski, K. (2014). Testing an equifinality model of nonsuicidal self-injury among early adolescent girls. *Development and Psychopathology, 26*(3), 851–862. doi:10.1017/S0954579414000431

Kerr, B. A., Vuyk, M. A., & Rea, C. (2012). Gendered practices in the education of gifted girls and boys. *Psychology in the Schools, 49*(7), 647–655. doi:10.1002/pits.21627

Knez, R., Munjas, R., Petrovečki, M., Paučić-Kirinčić, E., & Peršić, M. (2006). Disordered eating attitudes among elementary school population. *Journal of Adolescent Health, 38*(5), 628–630. doi:10.1016/j.jadohealth.2005.04.011

Letendre, J., & Rozas, L. W. (2015). She can't fight 'cause she acts white: Identity and coping for girls of color in middle school. *Children and Schools, 37*(1), 46–53.

Lin, Y. (2010). Improving parent-child relationships through block play. *Education, 130*(3), 461–469.

Luscombe, B., & Foroohar, R. (2014). Bring back all girls. *Time, 183*(20), 30.

Mathur, S., Greene, M., & Malhotra, A. (2003). Too young to wed: The lives, rights and health of young married girls. Retrieved from http://www.icrw.org/publications/too-young-to-wed-2

McCarthy, K. (1998). *Adaptation of immigrant children to the United States: A review of the literature* (Working Paper No. 98–03). Princeton, NJ: Center for Research on Child Wellbeing.

Mussell, M. P., Binford, R. B., & Fulkerson, J. A. (2000). Eating disorders: Summary of risk factors, prevention programming, and prevention research. *The Counseling Psychologist, 28*(6), 764–796. doi:10.1177/0011000000286002

Mutyaba, R. (2011). Early marriage: A violation of girls' fundamental human rights in Africa. *International Journal of Children's Rights, 19*(2), 339–355. doi:10.1163/1571818 11X584514

National Research Council. (2012). *A framework for K–12 science education: Practices, cross-cutting concepts, and core ideas.* Washington, DC: National Academies Press.

Qin, D. B. (2006). The role of gender in immigrant children's educational adaptation. *Current Issues in Comparative Education, 9*(1), 8–19.

Rodgers, R., & Chabrol, H. (2009). Parental attitudes, body image disturbance and disordered eating amongst adolescents and young adults: A review. *European Eating Disorders Review, 17*(2), 137–151. doi:10.1002/erv.907

Sandberg, A., & Pramling-Samuelsson, I. (2005). An interview study of gender difference in preschool teachers' attitudes toward children's play. *Early Childhood Education Journal, 32*(5), 297–305. doi:10.1007/s10643-005-4400-x

Shapiro, M., Grossman, D., Carter, S., Martin, K., Deyton, P., & Hammer, D. (2015). Middle school girls and the "leaky pipeline" to leadership. *Middle School Journal, 46*(5), 3–13.

Starr, C. R., & Ferguson, G. M. (2012). Sexy dolls, sexy grade-schoolers? Media & maternal influences on young girls' self-sexualization. *Sex Roles, 67*(7), 463–476. doi:10.1007/s11199-012-0183-x

Sue, D. W., Bucceri, J., Lin, A. I., Nadal, K. L., & Torino, G. C. (2009). Racial microaggressions and the Asian American experience. *Asian American Journal of Psychology, S*(1), 88–101. doi:10.1037/1948-1985.s.1.88

Sue, D. W., Capodilupo, C. M., Torino, G. C., Bucceri, J. M., Holder, A. B., Nadal, K. L., & Esquilin, M. (2007). Racial microaggressions in everyday life: Implications for clinical practice. *American Psychologist, 62*(4), 271–286. doi:10.1037/0003-066X.62.4.271

Swanson, J. L., & Fouad, N. A. (1999). *Career theory and practice: Learning through case studies.* Thousand Oaks, CA: Sage.

Thompson, K. (2010). Because looks can be deceiving: Media alarm and the sexualisation of childhood—do we know what we mean? *Journal of Gender Studies, 19*(4), 395–400. doi:10.1080/09589236.2010.533492

Wellesley College Center for Research on Women. (1992). *How schools shortchange girls: A study of major findings on girls and education* (AAUW Report). Washington, DC: American Association of University Women Educational Foundation.

Wertheim, E. H., Martin, G., Prior, M., Sanson, A., & Smart, D. (2002). Parental influences in the transmission of eating and weight related values and behaviours. *Eating Disorders, 10*, 321–334. doi:10.1080/10640260214507

CHAPTER 7

Adolescence and Young Adulthood

Jennifer E. Randall, Christine J. Schimmel, and
Eva Barnewitz

LEARNING OBJECTIVES

After reading this chapter, you will be able to:

1. Understand adolescent and young adult development from a bioecological perspective.
2. Describe common issues with which adolescent girls and young adult women struggle.
3. Implement creative ideas and techniques to assist adolescent and young adult females in the counseling process.

FEMALE ADOLESCENT AND YOUNG ADULT DEVELOPMENT

Many developmental models view human growth from a space of lack or abundance, a perpetual fulcrum swinging from the word *survive* at one end to *thrive* at the other. On the survival end, unmet needs become developmental gaps that will need filling later in life for individuals to move toward the thriving end of the spectrum. On the thriving end are those who met all their developmental milestones at the appropriate ages with sufficient family support alongside environmental abundance. Our goal in proposing that counselors integrate the bioecological theory of human development is to give them a tool to effectively gauge whether or not developmental gaps are present and then determine an evidence-based approach to address those gaps within the families, cultures, and contexts that can either provide support or deter growth.

As authors, our goal is to instruct counselors on creative, empowering ways in which they can best work with adolescent and young adult women. Therefore, we chose Urie Bronfenbrenner's bioecological theory of human development (1977, 1979) to conceptualize female adolescent and young adult development. The contextual focus of this theory provides a global framework for counselors to view young women as individuals who both influence, and are influenced by, their surroundings. Note that we are drawing from the entire span of Bronfenbrenner's bioecological theory (2005), as he consistently reflected upon and revised his work during his life span (Bronfenbrenner & Morris, 2006). Emerging academics and researchers have further refined his ideas as well.

Foundational Systems and Concepts of the Bioecological Theory

Tudge, Mokrova, Hatfield, and Karnik (2009) outlined the initial foundation for Bronfenbrenner's developmental theory as concentric rings that showed the various ways in which individuals interact with their surrounding world. Bronfenbrenner used the terms *microsystem, mesosystem, exosystem, macrosystem,* and, much later, *chronosystem* to label those rings of mutual influence. The *microsystem* refers to the child's immediate surroundings, including family, peers, and school. The *mesosystem* refers to the way in which each important player in the microsystem interacts with one another. As an example of the mesosystem, consider the fact that many adolescents go through a period where they rely less on their parents' suggestions and instead start to lean more heavily on their friends' advice. The *exosystem* refers to systems that the individuals are not directly part of, yet still provide a critical role in their development. Extended family, the parent's workplace, and mass media are all examples of influences from the exosystem. The *macrosystem,* which refers primarily to the influence of the culture in which the child is raised, can be simultaneously enhanced and challenged by the interactions among systems. The final system, the *chronosystem* is an environmental concept of how time, and more specifically, changes across the life span, can impact future generations in waves of unforeseeable consequences. For example, although we largely accept that parental divorce can negatively impact children, rarely do we think forward to how the effects of that relational rupture will impact not only the children of divorce, but also the next generation who will be raised by the children of a divorced family system.

As an illustration of the pull and push between these systems, imagine a young girl who grows up in a rural part of the world, such as Appalachia in the eastern United States. There, a young woman could learn conservative, Christian, family-driven ideals. Since the Appalachian mountain range was historically geographically inaccessible, its natives have long been stereotyped for insular family systems. While this young girl might find strength in the way of life she is accustomed to living in this region, picture her coming into adolescence as the technological revolution brought Internet access to vast swaths of the world outside of urban city centers. Within the span of one decade, centuries of isolation are virtually wiped away as the entire world becomes available at the click of a button. This is an example of how the macrosystem and the influence of the culture in which the child is raised can be simultaneously enhanced and challenged by the interactions among systems.

Customs, beliefs, and the government all play a role in the development of children and adolescents. According to Bronfenbrenner (1979), any change or disruption in any of the systems can lead to upheaval in a young person's development. This is clearly relevant in the development of adolescents as we examine their progression through a notably difficult developmental stage.

Bronfenbrenner's ideology notably shifted toward the second half of his career. His later work (2005) demonstrated a more holistic inclusion of individuals alongside the environmental systems within which they find themselves. To link the following concepts, remember the example used earlier to illustrate two of the authors' experiences of having been faced with the challenge of integrating into a digital age amid traditional Appalachian values. Process, person, context, and time (PPCT) are the four key conceptual tools of Bronfenbrenner's most refined form of his theory (Rosa & Tudge, 2013; Tudge et al., 2009). It is from the intersection of the individual shaping and being shaped by his or her environmental and relational experiences (Farley & Kim-Spoon, 2014) that we begin our discussion of how adolescence and young adulthood are uniquely experienced (Bronfenbrenner, 1986) by females.

Process, Person, Context, and Time (PPCT)

Bronfenbrenner's early ideas on human development were introduced in his first book, entitled *The Ecology of Human Development* (1979). The second phase of his work included a movement toward the greater inclusion of individual characteristics and biological traits as they develop in relationship to the various environmental systems described earlier (i.e., the microsystem, mesosystem, exosystem, macrosystem, and chronosystem). These can be pictured as a set of concentric circles that radiate outward from the individual. The final phase of Bronfenbrenner's work until his death in 2005 was the inclusion of the proximal processes, which are described in further detail.

Process

Bronfenbrenner defined process as the "progressively more complex reciprocal interaction between an active evolving biopsychological human organism and the persons, objects, and symbols in its immediate environment" (Bronfenbrenner & Ceci, 1993, p. 317). Adolescence is a time of growth where the primary processes, or experiences through which we learn, are no longer entirely dictated by caregivers. Adolescence involves developing an individual identity, while simultaneously integrating into a peer system and experiencing hormonal and physical changes. Then, young adulthood expands a woman's world even further as she continues to have experiences with increasingly diverse groups and relationships. The developmental changes described earlier are exponential. For instance, a young woman's overall development is impacted more than just the previous two levels combined in each successive stage of life. She is engaged in a physically and socially transformative process throughout adolescence and early adulthood. This type of exponential learning is a good example of Bronfenbrenner's process concept.

Person

The individual and how his or her unique set of characteristics develop are referred to as *force, resource,* and *demand* characteristics by Bronfenbrenner. These undergo significant changes in early adolescence (Bronfenbrenner, 2005; Rosa & Tudge, 2013). *Force characteristics,* which can be generative or disruptive, are those that will impact a young woman's development most (e.g., motivation level; Rosa & Tudge, 2013). Generative forces are those positive personal characteristics that provide opportunities for a young woman to demonstrate (to herself and others) that she can be inquisitive or resilient in the face of a challenge. An example could be the curiosity a woman shows when she is faced with an opportunity to interact with new people. Disruptive force traits, on the other end of the force trait spectrum, are those characteristics that could deter a young woman from reaching her full potential. An example would be impulsivity, especially if that characteristic overrides common sense. *Resource characteristics,* as the term implies, are the inherent qualities we possess at birth. These characteristics can be enhanced in both positive and negative ways as we age and interact with others. Low birth weight could be a negative resource characteristic that becomes a positive resource trait as a child develops, since the developmental need presents a chance for additional interaction with trained medical professionals outside of the immediate family. If other birth defects are detected and treated early, as a result of the increased medical presence in that child's infancy, the negative resource produces a long-term gain. *Demand characteristics* are the traits that pull others toward an individual (such as a calm demeanor), or push them away (such as an agitated demeanor) when making a first impression (Rosa & Tudge, 2013).

Context

The microsystem, mesosystem, exosystem, macrosystem, and chronosystem are central to understanding Bronfenbrenner's concept of context (Bronfenbrenner, 1986). Context is the backstory that helps us, as counselors, understand what elements have been most crucial to an individual's development. For example, a young woman attends a counseling session for the first time (*microsystem*); the backstory gives us clues about all of the ways that this moment is particularly relevant for both the young woman and her counselor (*mesosystem*). A quick musical montage showed the young woman growing rapidly from childhood through adolescence and now into adulthood (*chronosystem*). We know that she has had her fair share of heartbreak and joy along the way as a young girl exploring the world with her adoptive parents. We also know that the sudden death of her mother has brought her to a counselor's office to finally address the reality of being an adopted child who did not know anything about her birth family until her 18th birthday (*exosystem*). Since she was born as an American and has access to a legal system that upholds an adult's right to personally relevant medical information, she now has the opportunity to learn more about her birth family (*macrosystem*). These are all contextual examples of her development in and across all five systems.

Time

Time refers to the historical period in which developmental changes occur across the life span. Although Bronfenbrenner did not expand much upon this final aspect of his PPCT model in his later writing (Rosa & Tudge, 2013), he did continue to include the chronosystem as an essential component in understanding bioecological development. For adolescent and young adult women in particular, this element of Bronfenbrenner's bioecological theory of human development is vital to understanding how the biological, psychological, social, and cultural components of puberty and menstruation in the early years of a woman's fertility cycle impact the course of her adult female life. Consider the following example of an African American teenager living in Mississippi in the late 1950s. Her young lover is a White teenage boy and neither of their families is aware of their relationship, nor would either support it, given the political climate at that time across the South. This young couple learns that she is pregnant. Regardless of the choices made regarding the pregnancy, there is no doubt that there would be ripples across the waves of both of their young lives for years to come.

CONSIDERATIONS FOR VARIOUS TREATMENT SITES

When young females overcome the stigma associated with mental health services (Chandra & Minkovitz, 2007; Merikangas et al., 2010), they typically seek treatment in one of two primary settings: community mental health centers and schools. Counselors working in clinical settings are uniquely poised to provide an additional layer, and perhaps objective perspective, for adolescent females among their family of origin, their school setting, and even their community interactions. Clinical settings are of vital importance when we also consider that the one in four adolescents (Merikangas et al., 2010) who suffer from a mental illness are in a higher risk group than their peers to develop alcohol- and drug-related problems later in life (Conway, Swendsen, Husky, He, & Merikangas, 2016). Additionally, we must not underestimate the impact that professional school counselors can have in working with young women. School counselors are in a unique position to observe, interact, and connect with young adolescent females almost daily. As such, there is a growing interest in the school counseling literature in assisting school counselors to become more culturally responsive to the needs of a diverse population (Holcomb-McCoy, 2010; Suárez-Orozco, Bang, & Kim, 2010). Professional school counselors can provide services to adolescents in individual counseling and group counseling, as well as large group guidance, to address universal issues that students face (Erford, 2015). Unfortunately, many young women across the United States, and even more in developing countries, do not have access to a well-trained professional school counselor. For example, in Turkey, where the relatively young profession of counseling began in school settings, there remains much confusion over the appropriate training and role of the school counselor (Stockton & Guneri, 2011).

COMMON PRESENTING ISSUES AND COUNSELING APPROACHES

Peer Relationships

"A lot of girls don't even have a full handful of 'true' friends. By true, I mean someone who will defend you, someone who will never judge you, no matter what mistakes or choices you've made, someone who was destined to be your sister."—A 15-year-old female high school student

Girls being mean to each other, or acting out in "relational aggression," is a growing issue. Counselors who work with female adolescents are increasingly called upon to help them resolve issues related to getting along with their peers. Relational aggression is expressed through activities such as cyber bullying, which is defined as any type of bullying, spreading rumors, or gossiping that occurs through the use of computers (Wang, Iannotti, & Nansel, 2009; Wiseman, 2009). Other types of relational aggression that have gained attention include social exclusion and threats to withdraw friendship (Werner & Nixon, 2005). Wiseman (2009) details how young adolescent girls often feel pressure to conform to the demands of their more dominant female adolescent counterparts to engage in these relational forms of aggression, thus succumbing to societal pressure to "fit in" socially with the "right" crowd. Submissive females will follow the lead of dominant females in order to be accepted into the social group. Relational aggression can impede a young woman's ability to successfully navigate her world without life disruption. It is important to note in this discussion of female relational aggression that recent peer-reviewed research (Juvonen, Wang, & Espinoza, 2013) has failed to definitively demonstrate this issue as a gender-specific concern. Adolescent boys tend to display their aggression more overtly, whereas young women tend to do so in the complex interplay of their interpersonal relationships. Both genders try to attain and maintain the ever-elusive status of being "cool" (Kiefer & Wang, 2016). Juvonen et al. (2013) first showed that boys are just as likely as girls to use spreading rumors to assert their social dominance. Kiefer and Wang (2016) later demonstrated that while boys tended to use more overt displays of aggression than girls, both groups were doing so in an attempt to be popular, show their dominance, or meet intimacy needs.

Prinstein, Boergers, and Vernberg (2001) found that victims of multiple forms of aggression are at significantly higher risk of adjustment difficulties than their peers who experience one or no forms of aggression. It should be noted that this type of aggression is not reserved for White, European, or American young women. French, Jansen, and Pidada (2002) found that the concept was present in their study of both U.S. and Indonesian children. They also report that previous studies have examined the phenomenon in Italian, Russian, and Chinese populations.

Although it is not fully understood how peer relations affect self-concept in the long term, research has shown that victimization is related to social psychological maladjustment (Blakely-McClure & Ostrov, 2016; Hawker & Boulton, 2000).

Blakely-McClure and Ostrov (2016) point out that, "Through the experience of victimization, children may come to internalize these experiences and judge themselves and their abilities in a negative light" (p. 377). It stands to reason then, when young women are impacted by relational aggression in adolescence, the effects will carry over into adulthood, in the form of continued low self-concept, a negative view of abilities and emotional difficulties, such as depression, loneliness, and anxiety (Prinstein et al., 2001). Undoubtedly, then, these issues carry over into adult love relationships and work and career settings, where positive self-concept and a positive view of one's abilities are important for functioning effectively.

Research has shown that social support from close friends helps mitigate the negative effects of relational aggression on adjustment issues (Prinstein et al., 2001). Counseling and positive mental health interventions such as group counseling can assist adolescent females in recognizing and validating such positive social supports. According to Enns (2004), "Women's positive connections to others validate their capacities as relations begin, provide the necessary foundation for personal beliefs about autonomy, competence, and self-esteem, and are central to helping women experience continuing growth and well-being" (p. 181).

Treatment Approaches and Creative Interventions

Mental health professionals are often trained in a variety of treatment approaches and counseling theories that are geared toward helping individual clients deal with both their thoughts and feelings. However, an emerging treatment approach that is gaining popularity among professionals who work with young women on relational issues, not yet broadly taught in counseling programs, is relational-cultural theory (RCT; Cannon, Hammer, Reicherzer, & Gilliam, 2012; Enns, 2004). RCT is an evolving feminist model of human development that views connection to others as essential to growth and disconnection as a major cause of disrupted functioning (Jordan, 2000; Jordan & Hartling, 2002). Historically used in work with people of color, gay, bisexual, transgender communities, and more recently prison populations, counseling from an RCT perspective focuses on moving clients away from detrimental relationships and toward those relationships that encourage strength and discourage dysfunction (Cannon et al., 2012; Jordan, 2004). Counselors who subscribe to an RCT approach help clients develop more connections to their peers and will commonly choose to conduct group counseling sessions using this approach. Relational practice groups (RPGs) attempt to help participants understand how they often hide or conceal parts of their true personality in order to be understood and accepted by peers. A goal of RPGs is often to assist girls in healing old relational wounds and improving relational competence among group members (Cannon et al., 2012).

Counselors who want to run group counseling sessions that assist adolescents in the development of positive peer relations do not have to reinvent the wheel in terms of resources. Group curricula such as Jordan and Dooley's (2001) *Relational Practice in Action: A Group Manual* and Taylor's (2005) *Salvaging Sisterhood: A Small Group Counseling and Classroom Curriculum for Relationally Aggressive Girls (Grades 5–12)* can provide the basis for working with this population.

Additional resources and curricula are provided in the Helpful Resources section of this chapter.

Body Image

> *"I cannot remember ever being in my grandmother's home without her commenting on my physical appearance. Because her own mother did so, this was typical in our household, too, growing up. I wonder if I would have the same body image issues that I do now if the women in my world that were most important to me had asked me what I thought instead of commenting on how I looked."*—A 19-year-old college student

Adolescence is a uniquely transitional period where rapid changes are taking place at almost every level (Bronfenbrenner, 1977, 1979, 1986, 2005). In the midst of this rapidly changing developmental process, adolescents and young females are suddenly inundated with images of the female body in today's media. Overexposure to these images, media-internalization, and social comparison of body types has resulted in more than 45% of early adolescent girls reporting dissatisfaction with body image (Rodgers, McLean, & Paxton, 2015). Positive body image refers to the "love, respect, acceptance, and appreciation held for one's body" (Van der Bink, Smeets, Hessen, & Woertman, 2015, p. 1217). When young women hold a negative view of their bodies, mental health concerns can arise. Issues such as disordered eating (Polivy & Herman, 2002) and depression (Stice, Hayward, Cameron, Killen, & Taylor, 2000) are two of the potential negative psychological effects. Additionally, there is believed to be a relationship between alcohol use disorders and poor body image (Holzhauer, Zenner, & Wulfurt, 2016).

Treatment Approaches and Creative Interventions

Although the research on effective treatments for body image treatment is limited, cognitive behavioral therapy (CBT) is the "gold standard" treatment for adults with body image issues that manifest themselves as disordered eating (Bhatnager, Wisniewski, Solomon, & Heinberg, 2013, p. 2). Bhatnager et al. found that their intervention, CBT for body image disorder, was successful in decreasing negative body image perceptions. Although this intervention was conducted primarily with adults, the sample of participants included a significant number of adolescents and, therefore, offers much promise and is deserving of further research on this intervention when geared toward adolescent and young adult females.

Much has been written regarding the potential impact and effectiveness of the use of creativity in counseling with adolescents (Jacobs & Schimmel, 2013; Lopez & Burt, 2013; Whitten & Burt, 2015). Experiential techniques involving props, chairs, movement, writing, drawing, and the use of expressive art are powerful tools for the clinician who works with adolescent females. The benefits of using creative interventions include making connections between the mind and body, increased level of engagement on the part of both the therapist and the client, better ability to stay focused on the goal of the therapy, and greater potential for insight into the issues at hand (Lopez & Burt, 2013).

Jacobs and Schimmel (2013) describe many creative techniques that can be used in working with clients around issues of body image and self-worth. One such technique is the use of a dollar bill. Counselors making use of this technique can simply hold the bill upright (vertical) and fold it lengthwise so that is appears very long and thin. The counselor then asks the client how much the bill is worth in this configuration. The client often responds that the bill is worth no more than it was when in its original, presented form where it was unfolded. The counselor can then engage the client in a conversation about the idea that worth does not change, even though the dollar bill is now technically "thinner."

Depression and Anxiety in Young Females

> "This (anxiety and depression) is something that teenagers suffer with a lot, more so girls than boys. I believe this has a lot to do with society. Most of us feel like we are in a competition trying to blend with everyone else, but we are scared and insecure. After a break-up, I am very sure I suffered from depression, I put so much time into a relationship that I forgot about my friends and my family."—An 18-year-old female recent high school graduate

Depression and anxiety symptoms are extremely prevalent in adolescents between the ages of 15 and 18 years (Malaquias, Crespo, & Francisco, 2015). Additionally, Mellin and Fang (2010) note that 13% of the female adolescent population (aged 13–17 years) meets the criteria for moderate to severe depression. Depression and anxiety, when left untreated, can lead to many issues, including substance abuse, suicide attempts, and low academic performance. Many adolescent females may also be misdiagnosed with a condition, the symptoms of which mirror depression, such as attention deficit disorder or oppositional defiant disorder (Millen & Fang, 2010).

When working with adolescent females to mitigate and treat depression and anxiety, counselors should consider promoting protective factors known to offset these issues. They can encourage clients to increase family cohesion, social supports outside of the family unit, and positive affiliations with peers. Counselors may also consider that positive qualities in friendships (i.e., feeling close to another person, participating in social groups, maintaining a perception of others as being friendly) and dating relationships have also been identified as protective factors against social anxiety and depression (Hjemdal, Vogel, Solem, Hagen, & Stiles, 2011; Malaquias et al., 2015).

Treatment Approaches and Creative Interventions

When helping young females deal with issues of depression and anxiety, many creative techniques can be beneficial. Mellin and Hang (2010) recommend that

counselors review examples of popular media with female adolescents who struggle with depression. The counselors can engage females in a discussion regarding how those images contribute to the internalization of self-defeating internal
dialogue and lead to risk-taking behaviors. Counselors may also find it useful to
employ this technique when working with clients on body image.

Sommers-Flanagan and Sommers-Flanagan (2016) also suggest the use of creative interventions when working with adolescents. One particular technique
called "What's good about you?" can help adolescents struggling with depression. This involves the counselor asking the client to number a piece of paper 1
to 10. Then, the therapist asks the client "What is good about you?" in a repeated
fashion, 10 times. Each time, the client is required to write a brief answer to the
question while only being permitted to respond with "I don't know" once. Each
time, the therapist is to respond with an acknowledgment of the response by
repeating it, out loud, and also saying "Thank you" to the client. The purpose of
"What's good about you?" is to attempt to mitigate strong, negative images and
perceptions that the client holds about herself.

Many clients dealing with depression and anxiety feel that it will never be
possible for them to feel better. Jacobs and Schimmel (2013) promote the use of
chairs in demonstrating to clients that change is possible. For example, two chairs
can be placed in the middle of the room with a span of about 6 feet between chairs
with one chair labeled "depressed" or "anxious." The other chair can be labeled
"feeling better" or "less depressed" or "less anxious." The counselor can then use
this scene to discuss with the young client how change and movement are possible. The counselor can say, "It IS possible for you to feel better; it IS possible for
you to sit in that chair where you are feeling better. I can help you get there if you
want to be there." Oftentimes, this can promote hope and the feeling of connection that is needed for young females to begin to heal. Additionally, it provides a
sense of empowerment to the client that she can be in control of her treatment
and her progress.

Suicidality

*"It is time to change our society's perception of suicide. Instead of identifying
affected individuals as weak, we need to reach out to them, make it okay to talk
about suicide, and take a closer look at its relation with mental health."*
—*A 24-year-old college student*

According to the Centers for Disease Control and Prevention (2015), suicide
is the second leading cause of death among girls aged 12 to 25 years in the United
States (webappa.cdc.gov). Although adolescent girls are four times more likely
than adolescent boys to attempt suicide, they are less likely to use lethal means.
Therefore, girls are more likely to survive suicide attempts (Park, 2015). McHolm,
MacMillan, and Jamieson (2003) speculate that the interaction between an individual's (lack of) resiliencies (e.g., predisposition to psychiatric disorders, age at
onset, probability to develop comorbid conditions) and her environmental context

during childhood and adolescence (e.g., childhood physical abuse and sociode-mographic variables) determine suicidality. Suicide prevention programs are widely spread (Cusimano & Sameem, 2011) but often have not proved to be effective in preventing suicide attempts (Brent & Brown, 2015; Wei, Kutcher, & LeBlanc, 2015).

Treatment Approaches and Creative Interventions

The phrase "Suicide is a permanent solution to a temporary problem" (Dovel, 2015) might be helpful to some. To others, it might stress that suicide is indeed a solution and possibly its permanence may be appealing to someone who is struggling. This is especially urgent when it comes to adolescents because they are experiencing not only a confusing phase in their biological development but are also facing the challenging task of identity formation (Erikson, 1968).

When an adolescent presents with suicidal ideation, it is important to assess the immediate risk for suicide. A helpful tool for counselors to do so is "PRISM-S" (Pictorial Representation of Illness Self Measure–Suicidality; Ring et al., 2014), shown in Figure 7.1. In addition to a survey section on suicidality, the Mini International Neuropsychiatric Interview (MINI; Lecrubier et al., 1997) is a multisensory and physical/experiential assessment tool. A white metal sheet represents the client's "life," a fixed round yellow plate (diameter 7 cm) in one of the corners represents her "I." The client is handed a round black plate (diameter 5 cm) depicting "the wish to end her life." She is then asked to place the black plate according to her current situation.

This tool offers numerous possibilities for counselors to work with suicidal clients, using questions such as, "What do you need to increase the distance

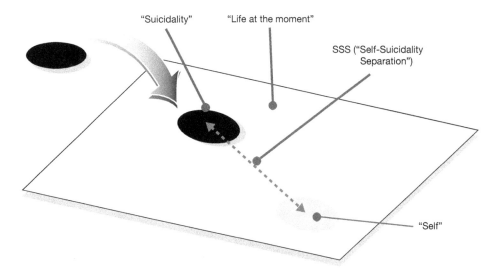

FIGURE 7.1 PRISM-S.

Reproduced with permission from *Crisis* 2013; Vol. 34(2):131–136 © 2012 Hogrefe Publishing www.hogrefe.com

between the yellow and the black plates?" or "Up until now, how have you managed to keep the black plate at this distance?" PRISM-S has been found to offer a brief and valid tool for the assessment of suicidal ideations in clients; furthermore, it is easy to administer and is well accepted by clients (Harbauer et al., 2013).

If there is imminent risk of suicide, the adolescent may need to be referred immediately to a hospital. If the risk is lower, however, the counselor can work directly with the adolescent to create a safety, or a positive action, plan. Such a plan should entail specific events that may trigger a crisis for the client and include specific plans for what the client can do if those triggers occur (Lewis, 2007). Such an agreement should be developed in collaboration with the adolescent and are time limited, meaning they should be revisited often. Both the counselor and the client should retain a copy of the plan (Myers & Range, 2002).

Many clients who are struggling with thoughts of suicide suffer from what Shneidman (1993) refers to as "psychache," a "free-floating, non-situation specific, chronic hurt, anguish, despair or, more generally, internal perturbation that causes individuals to seek permanent escape from it" (Troister, Davis, Lowndes, & Holden, 2013, p. 611). In this state, the client only feels there are two options for escape. Those options are either to go on feeling this level of pain and despair forever, or kill oneself and end the pain. This "psychache" is characterized by an inability to see any other options. Sommers-Flanagan and Sommers-Flanagan (2007) describe a technique that can be useful in getting adolescent, suicidal clients to consider other options. This technique involves working with the adolescent client to brainstorm a list of all possible alternatives to committing suicide, including suicide itself as an option. Nothing is off the table for this list; the counselor and client work together to list options that the client might not have thought of in the past. After a substantial list is generated, the counselor asks the client to rank order the options in order of desirability. Clients will typically list the option of suicide itself no higher than the third or fourth option (Sommers-Flanagan & Sommers-Flanagan, 2007). The therapist and client can then engage in a conversation about how options that were ranked higher may be put into action. The process of brainstorming is believed to help create/open neural pathways that have been stunted by the "psychache."

Devenish, Berk, and Lewis (2016) found evidence for the helpfulness of using psychosocial interventions such as CBT for depression in the treatment of suicidality in adolescents. Additionally, Alavi, Sharifi, Ghanizadeh, & Dehbozorgi (2013) found that adolescents who participated in a 12-session CBT intervention for suicidal ideation (where females were the majority of participants) were successful in decreasing the hopelessness and depression that often underlie suicidal ideation. The authors concluded that CBT is "an effective, appropriate and acceptable treatment modality for the adolescents with recent suicide attempts or current suicidal ideas" (Alavi et al., 2013, p. 471). Most CBT programs are based on Beck, Rush, Shaw, and Emery's (1979) cognitive theory of emotional disturbance that proposes that individuals' emotional and behavioral responses are the direct result of their cognitive interpretations (i.e., your thoughts cause your feelings and, in turn, your behaviors). In traditional CBT-based programs, clients are encouraged to recognize and monitor affect, physical awareness, and thoughts or cognitions in an attempt to gain greater self-awareness and opportunities to change their thinking (Macrodimitris, Hamilton, Backs-Dermott, & Mothersill, 2010).

Sharry, Darmody, and Madden (2002) argue for the use of solution-focused therapy (SFT) techniques in working with suicidal clients. SFT is a strength-based, collaborative approach to working with clients, which focuses on clients' strengths and assets as opposed to their problems. SFT helps the client move from problems to goals and to understand the more positive goals associated with the thoughts of suicide like living a life with no pain. A specific technique to help achieve this is known as the miracle question. The miracle question technique asks clients to speculate how their world would be different if they awoke tomorrow to find that their problems had disappeared. The goal of the miracle question is to focus on the client's resources and coping strategies while establishing individually meaningful goals that are worth reaching. The Suicide Prevention Resource Center (www.sprc.org) offers further valuable information and resources to both individuals and professionals on prevention and care of suicide.

CONCLUSION

In this chapter, we began by introducing a model of human development that we find useful as both counselor educators and mental health professionals. Bronfenbrenner's bioecological theory (1977, 1979, 1986, 2005) serves as a framework for counselors to holistically view female adolescent and young adult development. The underlying notion is that the individual is both influencing and influenced by his or her unique set of biological characteristics and environmental contexts (such as the political and cultural landscape in which the individual lives). We have further addressed some specific issues that are particularly relevant to female adolescents and young adults, such as peer relationships, body image, depression, anxiety, and suicidality. The treatment approaches and creative interventions we have provided for each of those issues are simply a starting point. Above all else, we implore you to get curious and ask your female clients what their experiences have been. As Pinkola Estés (1995) said, "It is a mistake for others to think that just because a woman is silent, it always means she approves of life as is" (p. 360).

CALL TO ACTION

Counselors can take the following actions in advocating for their female adolescent and young adult clients:

- *Research and explore the resources provided in the Helpful Resources section of this chapter to identify helpful programs that can be used to mitigate the effects of relational aggression in young females.*
- *Consider working with a local school or school district to assist in implementing a schoolwide program aimed at the prevention of relational aggression.*
- *Become engaged in local and state efforts to bring awareness to and introduce legislation that addresses the problem of adolescent suicide.*

(continued)

CALL TO ACTION (*continued*)

- *Expand your professional network by joining with providers in your area who are working within the lesbian, gay, bisexual, and transgender (LGBT) community to expand mental health services to adolescent and young adult female populations.*

REFLECTION AND DISCUSSION QUESTIONS

1. How might Bronfenbrenner's process, person, context, and time (PPCT) classifications inform how you conceptualize counseling adolescent females and young adults?

2. Describe a creative intervention you may choose to use with an adolescent female if she were struggling with relational aggression or issues of self-worth. Why did you choose that intervention or technique?

3. What mental health issues could arise for adolescent and young adult females who experience negative body image? How might you creatively address those issues in counseling?

4. How might you interweave creative, strength-based approaches into your future assessments and screenings for anxiety, depression, and suicidality when counseling female adolescents and young women?

HELPFUL RESOURCES

- National Institute of Mental Health (www.nimh.nih.gov/health/topics/suicide -prevention/index.shtml)—Web-based resource for information on common mental health issues including prevention of suicide
- National LGBTQ Task Force (www.thetaskforce.org)—National organization committed to advancing LGBTQ rights
- National Suicide Prevention Lifeline (www.suicidepreventionlifeline.org)— Suicide prevention resource
- "Preventing Relational Aggression in Schools Everyday (PRAISE) Program: A Preliminary Evaluation of Acceptability and Impact"—Curricular tool for dealing with relational aggression
- "Social Aggression Prevention Program" (childtrends.org/?programs=social -aggression-prevention-program-sapp)—Tool for addressing relational aggression
- "Steps to Respect" (www.cfchildren.org/steps-to-respect.aspx)—Curricular tool for dealing with relational aggression
- The Suicide Prevention Resource Center (www.sprc.org)—Web-based resource for suicide prevention

REFERENCES

Alavi, A., Sharifi, B., Ghanizadeh, A., & Dehbozorgi, G. (2013). Effectiveness of cognitive-behavioral therapy in decreasing suicidal ideation and hopelessness of the adolescents with previous suicidal attempts. *Iranian Journal of Pediatrics, 23*(4), 467–472.

Beck, A. T., Rush, A. J., Shaw, B. F., & Emery, G. (1979). *Cognitive therapy of depression.* New York, NY: Guilford Press.

Bhatnager, K. A. C., Wisniewski, L., Solomon, M., & Heinberg, L. (2013). Effectiveness and feasibility of a cognitive-behavioral group intervention for body image disturbance in women with eating disorders. *Journal of Clinical Psychology, 69*(1), 1–13. doi:10.1002/jclp.21909

Blakely-McClure, S. J., & Ostrov, J. M. (2016). Relational aggression, victimization and self-concept: Testing pathways from middle childhood to adolescence. *Journal of Youth and Adolescence, 45,* 376–390. doi:10.1007/s10964-015-0357-2

Brent, D. A., & Brown, C. H. (2015). Effectiveness of school-based suicide prevention programmes. *Lancet, 385*(9977), 1489–1491. doi:10.1016/S0140-6736(14)61586-5

Bronfenbrenner, U. (1977). Toward an experimental ecology of human development. *American Psychologist, 32,* 513–531.

Bronfenbrenner, U. (1979). *The ecology of human development: Experiments in nature and design.* Cambridge, MA: Harvard University Press.

Bronfenbrenner, U. (1986). Ecology of the family as context for human development: Research perspectives. *Developmental Psychology, 22,* 723–742. doi:10.1037/0012-1649.22.6.723

Bronfenbrenner, U. (2005). *Making human beings human: Bioecological perspectives on human development.* Thousand Oaks, CA: Sage.

Bronfenbrenner, U., & Ceci, S. J. (1993). Heredity, environment, and the question "how?" A first approximation. In N. J. Smelser & P. B. Baltes (Eds.), *Nature, nurture, and psychology* (pp. 313–323). Washington, DC: American Psychological Association.

Bronfenbrenner, U., & Morris, P. A. (2006). The bioecological model of human development. In W. Damon & R. M. Lerner (Eds.), *Handbook of child psychology, Vol. 1: Theoretical models of human development* (6th ed., pp. 793–828). New York, NY: Wiley.

Cannon, K. B., Hammer, T. R., Reicherzer, S., & Gilliam, B. J. (2012). Relational-cultural theory: A framework for relational competencies and movement in group work with female adolescents. *Journal for Creativity in Mental Health, 7,* 2–16. doi:10.1080/15401383.2012.660118

Chandra, A., & Minkovitz, C. S. (2007). Factors that influence mental health stigma among 8th grade adolescents. *Journal of Youth and Adolescence, 36,* 763–774. doi:10.1007/s10964-006-9091-0

Centers for Disease Control and Prevention, National Center for Injury Prevention and Control. (2015, September 19). Web-based injury statistics query and reporting system (WISQARS). Retrieved from http://webappa.cdc.gov/cgi-bin/broker.exe

Conway, K. P., Swendsen, J., Husky, M., He, J., & Merikangas, K. R. (2016). Association of lifetime mental disorders and subsequent alcohol and illicit drug use: Results from the National Comorbidity Survey-Adolescent Supplement (NCS-AS). *Journal of the*

American Academy of Child and Adolescent Psychiatry, 55(4), 280–288. doi:10.1016/j.jaac .2016.01.006

Cusimano, M. D., & Sameem, M. (2011). The effectiveness of middle and high school-based suicide prevention programmes for adolescents: A systematic review. *Injury Prevention, 17,* 43–49. doi:10.1136/ip.2009.025502

Devenish, B., Berk, L., & Lewis, A. J. (2016). The treatment of suicidality in adolescents by psychosocial interventions for depression: A systematic literature review. *Australian and New Zealand Journal of Psychiatry, 50*(8), 726–740. doi:10.1177/0004867415627374

Dovel, M. D. (2015). Suicide is a permanent solution to a temporary problem. *International Journal of Emergency Mental Health and Human Resilience, 17*(2), 546–547. Retrieved from http://www.omicsonline.com/open-access/suicide-is-a-permanent-solution-to-a -temporary-problem-1522-4821-1000e212.pdf

Enns, C. Z. (2004). *Feminist theories and feminist psychotherapies: Origins, themes, and diversity* (2nd ed.). New York, NY: Haworth.

Erford, B. T. (2015). *Transforming the school counseling profession* (4th ed.). Upper Saddle River, NJ: Pearson.

Erikson, E. H. (1968). *Identity: Youth and crisis.* New York, NY: W. W. Norton.

Farley, J. P., & Kim-Spoon, J. (2014). The development of adolescent self-regulation: Reviewing the role of parent, peer, friend, and romantic relationships. *Journal of Adolescence, 37*(4), 433–440. doi:10.1016/j.adolescence.2014.03.009

French, D. C., Jansen, E. A., & Pidada, S. (2002). United States and Indonesian children's and adolescents' reports of relational aggression by disliked peers. *Child Development, 73*(4), 1143–1150. doi:10.1111/1467-8624.00463

Harbauer, G., Ring, M., Schuetz, C., Andreae, A., & Haas, S. (2013). Suicidality assessment with PRISM-S—simple, fast, and visual: A brief nonverbal method to assess suicidality in adolescent and adult patients. Reproduced with permission from *Crisis, 34*(2), 131–136. © 2012 Hogrefe Publishing www.hogrefe.com. doi:10.1027/0227-5910/a000164

Hawker, D. J., & Boulton, M. J. (2000). Twenty years' research on peer victimization and psychosocial maladjustment: A meta-analytic review of cross-sectional studies. *Journal of Child Psychology and Psychiatry, 41,* 441–455. doi:10.1111/14697610.00629

Hjemdal, O., Vogel, P. A., Solem, S., Hagen, K., & Stiles, T. C. (2011). The relationship between resilience and levels of anxiety, depression, and obsessive-compulsive symptoms in adolescents. *Clinical Psychology and Psychotherapy, 18,* 314–321. doi:10.1002/cpp.719

Holcomb-McCoy, C. (2010). Involving low-income parents and parents of color in college readiness activities: An exploratory study. *Professional School Counseling, 14,* 115–124. doi:10.5330/prsc.14.1.e3044v7567570t04

Holzhauer, C. G., Zenner, A., & Wulfurt, E. (2016). Poor body image and alcohol use in women. *Psychology of Addictive Behavior, 30*(1), 122–127. doi:10.1037/adb0000115

Jacobs, E., & Schimmel, C. J. (2013). *Impact therapy: The courage to counsel.* Star City, WV: Impact Therapy Associates.

Jordan, J. V. (2000). The role of mutual empathy in relational/cultural therapy. *Journal of Clinical Psychology, 56,* 1005–1016. doi:10.1002/1097-4679(200008)

Jordan, J. V. (2004). Toward competence and connection. In J. Jordan, M. Walker, & L. Hartling (Eds.), *The complexity of connection* (pp. 11–25). New York, NY: Guilford Press.

Jordan, J. V., & Dooley, C. (2001). *Relational practice in action: A group manual* (Project Report, No. 6). Wellesley, MA: Stone Center.

Jordan, J. V., & Hartling, L. M. (2002). New developments in relational-cultural theory. In M. Bailou & L. S. Brown (Eds.), *Rethinking mental health and disorders: Feminist perspectives* (pp. 48–70). New York, NY: Guilford Press.

Juvonen, J., Wang, Y., & Espinoza, G. (2013). Physical aggression, spreading of rumors, and social prominence in early adolescence: Reciprocal effects supporting gender similarities? *Journal of Youth and Adolescence, 42,* 1801–1810. doi:10.1007/s10964-012-9894-0

Kiefer, S. M., & Wang, J. H. (2016). Associations of coolness and social goals with aggression and engagement during adolescence. *Journal of Applied Developmental Psychology, 44,* 52–62. doi:10.1016/j.appdev.2016.02.007

Lecrubier, Y., Sheehan, D. V., Weiller, E., Amorim, P., Bonora, I., Sheehan, K. H., . . . Dunbar, G. C. (1997). The Mini International Neuropsychiatric Interview (MINI): A short diagnostic structured interview: Reliability and validity according to the CIDI. *European Psychiatry, 12*(5), 224–231.

Lewis, L. M. (2007). No-harm contracts: A review of what we know. *Suicide and Life Threatening Behavior, 37*(1), 50–57. doi:10.1521/suli.2007.37.1.50

Lopez, A., & Burt, I. (2013). Counseling groups: A creative strategy increasing children of incarcerated parents' socio-relational interactions. *Journal of Creativity in Mental Health, 8,* 395–415. doi:10.1080/15401383.2013.844660

Macrodimitris, S. D., Hamilton, K. E., Backs-Dermott, B. J., & Mothersill, K. J. (2010). CBT basics: A group approach to teaching fundamental cognitive-behavioral skills. *Journal of Cognitive Psychotherapy: An International Quarterly, 24*(2), 132–146. doi:10.1891/0889-8391.24.2.132

Malaquias, S., Crespo, C., & Francisco, R. (2015). How do adolescents benefit from family rituals? Links to social connectedness, depression and anxiety. *Journal of Child and Family Studies, 24,* 3009–3017. doi:10.1007/s10826-014-0104-4

McHolm, A. E., MacMillan, H. L., & Jamieson, E. (2003). The relationship between childhood physical abuse and suicidality among depressed women: Results from a community sample. *American Journal of Psychiatry, 160*(5), 933–938. doi:10.1176/appi.ajp.160.5.933

Mellin, A. E., & Fang, H. N. (2010). Exploration of the pathways to delinquency for female adolescents with depression: Implications for cross-systems collaboration and counseling. *Journal of Addictions and Offender Counseling, 30,* 58–72. doi:10.1002/j.2161-1874.2010.tb00057.x

Merikangas, K. R., He, J., Burstein, M., Swanson, S. A., Avenevoli, S., Cui, L., & Swendsen, J. (2010). Lifetime prevalence of mental disorders in U.S. adolescents: Results from the National Comorbidity Study-Adolescent Supplement (NCS-A). *Journal of American Academy of Child and Adolescent Psychiatry, 49*(10), 980–989. doi:10.1016/j.jaac.2010.05.017

Myers, S. S., & Range, L. M. (2002). No-suicide agreements: High school students' perspectives. *Death Studies, 26*(10), 851–857. doi:10.1080/07481180290106616

Park, S. (2015). Brief report: Sex differences in suicide rates and suicide methods among adolescents in South Korea, Japan, Finland, and the US. *Journal of Adolescence, 40,* 74–77. doi:10.1016/j.adolescence.2015.01.007

Pinkola Estés, C. (1995). *Women who run with the wolves: Myths and stories of the wild woman archetype.* New York, NY: Ballantine Books.

Polivy, J., & Herman, C. P. (2002). Causes of eating disorders. *Annual Review of Psychology*, *53*, 187–213. doi:10.1146/annurev.psych.53.100901.135103

Prinstein, M. J., Boergers, J., & Vernberg, E. M. (2001). Overt and relational aggression in adolescents: Social-psychological adjustment of aggressors and victims. *Journal of Clinical Child and Adolescent Psychology*, *30*(4), 479–491. doi:10.1207/S15374424JCCP 3004_05

Ring, M., Harbauer, G., Haas, S., Schuetz, C., Andreae, A., Maercker, A., & Ajdacic-Gross, V. (2014). Validierung des Suizidalitätseinschätzungsinstrumentes PRISM-S (Pictorial Representation of Illness Self Measure–Suicidality). *Neuropsychiatrie*, *28*(4), 192–197. doi:10.1007/s40211-014-0123-9

Rodgers, R. F., McLean, S. A., & Paxton, S. J. (2015). Longitudinal relationships among internalization of the media ideal, peer social comparison, and body dissatisfaction: Implications for the tripartite influence model. *Developmental Psychology*, *51*(5), 706–713. doi:10.1037/dev0000013

Rosa, E. M., & Tudge, J. (2013). Urie Bronfenbrenner's theory of human development: Its evolution from ecology to bioecology. *Journal of Family Theory and Review*, *5*, 243–258. doi:10.1111/jftr.120222

Sharry, J., Darmody, M., & Madden, B. (2002). A solution-focused approach to working with clients who are suicidal. *British Journal of Guidance and Counselling*, *30*(4), 383–399. doi:10.1080/0306988021000025690

Shneidman, E. S. (1993). Suicide as psychache. *The Journal of Nervous and Mental Disease*, *181*, 145–147.

Sommers-Flanagan, J., & Sommers-Flanagan, R. (2007). *Tough kids, cool counseling: User-friendly approaches with challenging youth* (2nd ed.). Alexandria, VA: American Counseling Association.

Sommers-Flanagan, J., & Sommers-Flanagan, R. (2016). *Clinical interviewing* (6th ed.). Hoboken, NJ: Wiley.

Stice, E., Hayward, C., Cameron, R., Killen, J. D., & Taylor, C. B. (2000). Body-image and eating disturbances predict onset of depression among female adolescents: A longitudinal study. *Journal of Abnormal Psychology*, *109*, 438–444. doi:10.1037/0021-843X.109.3.438

Stockton, R., & Guneri, O. Y. (2011). Counseling in Turkey: An evolving field. *Journal of Counseling and Development*, *89*, 98–104. doi:10.1002/j.1556-6678.2011.tb00065.x

Suárez-Orozco, C., Bang, H. J., & Kim, H. Y. (2010). I felt like my heart was staying behind: Psychological implications of family separations & reunifications for immigrant youth. *Journal of Adolescent Research*, *26*, 222–257. doi:10.1177/0743558410376830

Taylor, J. V. (2005). *Salvaging sisterhood: A small group counseling and classroom curriculum for relationally aggressive girls (grades 5–12)*. Chapin, SC: Youthlight.

Troister, T., Davis, M. P., Lowndes, A., & Holden, R. R. (2013). A five-month longitudinal study of psychache and suicide ideation: Replication in general and high-risk university students. *Suicide and Life Threatening Behavior*, *43*(6), 611–620. doi:10.1111/sltb.12043

Tudge, J. R., Mokrova, I., Hatfield, B. E., & Karnik, R. B. (2009). Uses and misuses of Bronfenbrenner's bioecological theory of human development. *Journal of Family Theory and Review*, *1*, 198–210. doi:10.1111/j.1756-2589.2009.00026.x

Van der Bink, F., Smeets, M. A. M., Hessen, D. J., & Woertman, L. (2015). Positive body image and sexual functioning in Dutch female university students: The role of adult romantic attachment. *Archives of Sexual Behavior, 45*(5), 1217–1226. doi:10.1007/s10508 -015-0511-7

Wang, J., Iannotti, R. J., & Nansel, T. J. (2009). School bullying among adolescents in the United States: Physical, verbal, relational, and cyber. *Journal of Adolescent Health, 45*(4), 368–375. doi:10.1016/j.jadohealth.2009.03.021

Wei, Y., Kutcher, S., & LeBlanc, J. C. (2015). Hot idea or hot air: A systematic review of evidence for two widely marketed youth suicide prevention programs and recommendations for implementation. *Journal of the Canadian Academy of Child and Adolescent Psychiatry/Journal De L'académie Canadienne De Psychiatrie De L'enfant Et De L'adolescent, 24*(1), 5–16.

Werner, N. E., & Nixon, C. L. (2005). Normative beliefs and relational aggression: An investigation of the cognitive bases of adolescent aggressive behavior. *Journal of Youth and Adolescents, 34*(3), 229–243. doi:10.1007/s10964-005-4306-3

Whitten, K. M., & Burt, I. (2015). Utilizing creative expressive techniques and group counseling to improve adolescents of divorce social-relational capabilities. *Journal of Creativity in Mental Health, 10*(3), 363–375. doi:10.1080/15401383.2014.986594

Wiseman, R. (2009). *Queen bees and wannabees: Helping your daughter survive cliques, gossip, boyfriends, and the new realities of girl world.* New York, NY: Three Rivers Press.

CHAPTER 8

Middle and Older Adulthood

Lucy Charlene Parker and Suzanne Degges-White

LEARNING OBJECTIVES

After reading this chapter, you will be able to:

1. Understand the phenomenological realities, as well as the developmental and systemic experiences, of both middle and older adult women.
2. Identify societal influences that marginalize women of all types in their middle and older adulthood.
3. Conceptualize the experiences and challenges of middle and older adult women, taking into account the multiple and varied demographic and experiential factors (including ethnicity, sexual identity, cultural constraints, and so forth) that contribute to identity and shape a woman's emotional, mental, and physical experiences.

As recently as the final two decades of the 20th century, the period of midlife was only beginning to be explored and conceptualized as a discrete period of life (Quadagno, 2001). With longevity expectations for women now stretching toward 81 years of age (National Center for Health Statistics, 2015), it is apparent that the 40th birthday should no longer be considered as the gateway into "old age." Although it may be the statistical midpoint of the life span, there is still a lot of living left to be done in those remaining four or more decades. For the purposes of this chapter, the period of middle adulthood will include the years between the 40th and the 65th birthday. During this period, the normative changes for women typically include menopause and increasing self-introspection. Older adulthood is being used to describe the period from the 65th birthday onward. During this stage, women typically experience significant challenges and transitions in all spheres of their lives including social, professional, psychological, physiological, and cognitive sectors.

FRAMING MIDDLE AND OLDER ADULTHOOD THROUGH A NEW PERSPECTIVE

Most individuals have an inner set of expectations regarding the timing of the significant life events that mark their transition from one stage of life to another. These socially embedded and unspoken guidelines are termed *age norms* (Neugarten, Moore, & Lowe, 1965). As longevity and cultural expectations have shifted, the midlife period has blossomed from a period in which women traditionally undervalued themselves due to increased awareness of advancing age, into a time in which women are embracing new opportunities across multiple life sectors, from the professional to the social to the personal (Degges-White & Myers, 2006). Transitions that had once been relegated to earlier life stages now appear in middle adulthood years as well. First marriages, first pregnancies, and first jobs have moved into many women's midlife stories.

Is Midlife a Time, a Place, or a Feeling?

Mental health counselors may find women in middle and older adulthood to be especially motivated and growth oriented with a new sense of vitality activated by the diverse transitions they experience during this period (Neugarten, 1996). Transitions may occur within personal relationships, health and reproductive status, and social and professional roles. These transitions may be motivated or accompanied by increasing self-awareness, acceptance, and reflection. In fact, one study of midlife women found that more than 50% of the 224 participants, all aged 35 years and older, had experienced an increase in introspection (Degges-White & Myers, 2006).

Not only are middle adult women beginning to reflect on their lives and where they have been, but they also are increasingly aware of the balance between the finiteness of time and their future potential (Neugarten, 1996). Increased self-awareness may fuel a positive type of midlife crisis that provides the drive to explore aspects of dreams, goals, and self that may have been overlooked at earlier ages. The desire to "reinvent" herself, or investigate paths previously unexplored, can motivate a woman to pursue a career change or a return to school or work, if she had taken a break to raise a family. The increasing fluidity of adults' career journeys has contributed to the development of the construct of the boundaryless career, a significant component of the concept of a personalized careerscape (Arthur & Rousseau, 1996). This career construct provides a canvas on which women can create their own individual professional trajectories that incorporate parenthood, caregiving, and paid employment (Lewis, Harris, Morrison, & Ho, 2015). Regardless of a woman's menopause status, the fertility or "generativity" of her life should not be circumscribed by her reproductive capacity. Throughout this chapter, we move beyond the use of biological and reproductive markers as measures of a woman's worth. Instead, we explore the multiplicity of ways in which women holistically experience their lives and their many roles, as well as the ways in which clinicians can best meet the needs of an increasingly diverse midlife population.

As noted, beliefs about the experience and expectations for women at midlife were considerably different even a generation ago than they are today. Although an old adage "A woman's work is never done" has been true for centuries, the value of a woman's work to the larger world has been undervalued for just as long. In addition, a woman's very existence was circumscribed by her relationships and perceived obligations to others beyond herself. For many years, cultural expectations regarding motherhood, paid work, and educational opportunities shaped the life trajectories of women.

For centuries, women have self-advocated vigorously for their rights and for their voices to be heard. Women now fill a panoply of roles that include serving as appointed and elected politicians, teachers, inspirational advocates, and nurturing caregivers, among other traditionally and nontraditionally female-categorized roles. The freedom to pursue degendered careers is the result of battles waged against cultural and social pressures as well as firmly engrained preconceived traditions and norms. Throughout this chapter, we explore both the intrinsic and extrinsic factors that influence the interpersonal and intrapersonal experiences of both middle and older adult women. This includes an exploration of systemic factors that have obstructed, and those that have empowered, women around the globe to use their own resiliency and strength to thrive.

As we continue to explore women and their development, please consider these comments from a woman who has enjoyed the various roles she has held in her lifetime including nurse, mother, and friend. Her words provide insight into just one perspective on the aging process for contemporary women.

> "Well first, it is so scary turning older and you think about it a lot. You are unsure about your ability to be healthy, work, and be attractive. You wish for the earlier days when your children were younger, your spouse was new, and your connections were just beginning. In a way, it feels that with age . . . you have lost connection. In other ways, however, you stay true to your younger self. At this age, you feel great purpose at times, and closer to your God and/or your other forms of support."—A 60-year-old woman

This woman's comment encourages us to recognize that not only do women in midlife face multifaceted developmental shifts, identity shifts, and role shifts, but each of these areas is influenced by external constraints located within a woman's cultural milieu. Practitioners must recognize the various components of identity, such as age, gender, and ethnicity. With such recognition, we can assist women in exploring the ways in which their multiple intersecting identities function as a whole to shape their lived experiences.

GENDER DEFINES SOCIAL IDENTITY

Women's worth has long been measured by their attractiveness to others (Morgan & Kisley, 2014). Societal pressure to meet specific appearance guidelines is communicated through media messages on television, billboards, the Internet, and other sources. Unrealistic expectations often contribute to women's feelings of being valued solely on their physical appearance. In fact, media messages enforce what many psychologists and counselors call a double standard of aging for women. This double standard has a significant negative impact on women in their middle and older adulthood development (Matlin, 2008). As an illustration of this double standard, take a moment and imagine an older, distinguished, successful leader. Generally, we perceive the image of a mature, wise male as signifying earned respect, wisdom, expertise, and insight. Although maturing men typically gain respect as they age, the opposite is often true for aging women (Chrisler, Golden, & Rozee, 2008). Older women are commonly perceived as needy, fragile, and unfit. Additionally, both middle-aged and older women who act as leaders in politics, business, or other duties in the world of work may be perceived as brazenly rebelling against traditional gender norms. Fortunately, recent research has shown a decrease in society's habit of valuing women based solely on traditional expectations and roles (Brimrose, McMahon, & Watson, 2013); however, this is not a universal phenomenon. Some of the enduring external influences that impact both middle and older women include societal pressures such as ageism, sexism, and preconceived role expectations (Narayan, 2008).

As advocates, counselors should address these double standards and marginalization of women propagated by external factors and internalized stereotypes in our society (Chrisler et al., 2008). According to Matlin (2008) and Narayan (2008), middle and older adult women must regularly meet and work against societal pressures. Although a woman's privileges and place in society have historically been beneath that of men, it was only in the late 1960s that the term *ageism* was coined (Butler, 1969). This term describes the negative experiences faced by aging adults, especially women, who feel stereotyped, segregated, and discriminated against due to their age. Women may internalize the ageism that they experience from media and other societal pressures. Aging can take a heavy emotional toll. A widow in her 80s reflected on her own aging process and internalized shame by declaring, "I am not getting old. I am becoming fossilized!" When asked if she wished that she had more age mates in her social circle, she affirmed that she missed her friends but that she "wouldn't wish [her] age on anyone!"

Unsurprisingly, older women experience not only emotional damage from ageism and sexism, they also suffer health consequences due to the presence of age and gender bias within the health care system (Chrisler, Barney, & Palatino, 2016). Advocates in all sectors of the helping and caregiving professions can benefit from further understanding, researching, and focusing on the effects of various societal influences including ageism. Just as an individual's multiple intersecting identities should be taken into account to fully understand a person's story, the multiple intersecting *isms* that are faced by a middle or older adult woman must also be taken into consideration to fully understand her struggles. Although ageism crosses gender lines, Matlin (2008) found that older women reported experiencing more ageism than older men. Ageism may be supplanting sexism to a degree for older women who report decreases in outright sexism toward them; yet the desexualization of older women is perhaps a complex product resulting from an intersection of sexism and ageism for this age group. Regardless of their origins, it is unacceptable that any *isms* remain a fact of life for members of any cultural or identity group.

Who Defines Beauty?

American society's standard of beauty is virtually monolithic and is represented by young, thin, Caucasian women with flawless skin, long legs, and fashionable attire. Youth is another prerequisite for earning society's approval of one's appearance. Makeup ads are developed to target women who are insecure about their advancing age to buy products that promise the appearance of eternal youth. This promotes a cultural mind-set that age and maturity are the enemy (Koza, 2010; Matlin, 2008). A double standard of aging is also present in beliefs about the levels of sexual activity and interest of older adults, especially women (Lai & Hynie, 2011). Although "the little blue pill" is viewed as the fountain of youth and vigor for men, postmenopausal women's needs have yet to receive the research focus or airplay that maturing men's erectile dysfunction has received.

There are many macro- and microscale pressures such as ageism, sexism, and other *isms* that women of all types may face in their middle and older years. In order to better advocate and understand women of all ages, it is important for counselors to learn about each individual woman's phenomenological experience regarding her own experiences of societal pressures. Counselors are in an excellent position to increase awareness of these injustices and societal pressures by raising clients' awareness and modeling resistance to unrealistic cultural messages.

THE SHIFTING ROLES AND TRANSITIONS OF CONTEMPORARY MIDDLE AND OLDER ADULT WOMEN

Women's lives are often defined by their relationships. For instance, milestones in women's life trajectory often include "fiancée," "newlywed," "wife," "mother-to-be," "mother," "empty-nester," and so on. Although there are male variations on these terms, they are seldom used as frequently to describe men's life paths. External factors that shape middle and older women's development include family constellation changes; residential relocations; the empty nest experience; changes in or losses of roles; loss of loved ones; and career transitions (Brimrose et al., 2013, p. 594). As Degges-White and Myers (2006) noted, the number of transitions that women experience during their 40s is significant, and adjusting to these transitions may be more difficult for some women than for others. According to Schlossberg's (1984) transition theory, the effect of any given transition is influenced by context, timing, expectations, and the self-perceived impact of the transition. By exploring each of these four aspects with women seeking help at times of transition, clinicians can better understand the specific personal intensity of the challenges, as well as know how to best provide support.

Existential and Identity Development

Aging, in and of itself, can influence a woman's personal schema in unique and powerful ways. Women globally have been found to experience various existential issues around their changing identities and advancing age (Erikson, 1959).

One significant existential force that many older women may experience is death anxiety (Madnawat & Kachhawa, 2007). Death anxiety is defined as anxiety that arises as an older and more introspective woman considers her ultimate death. When loved ones pass away and children grow older, this anxiety may grow for women. This is an especially salient factor for women who live alone, either having been widowed, divorced, or never married. Older adulthood is a period of multiple losses (Gurung, Taylor, & Seeman, 2003) and identities once built on relationship to others may undergo unprecedented battering as women lose both significant others and the associated relationship roles in their lives.

The actions of a 70-year-old woman, Jane, provided an excellent example of how deep and unsettling this death anxiety can be for some individuals, as recounted in a story told by Jane's midlife daughter-in-law. After a family dinner, Jane was leafing through the day's mail and came upon a large envelope from her sister-in-law, an 80-year-old who was caring for her own centenarian mother. Jane opened the envelope with curiosity that quickly turned to fury. Inside the package were sample living wills, "Do Not Resuscitate" forms, and a planning guide for making end-of-life decisions. These were tasks that Jane was clearly not ready to complete. Her daughter-in-law was shocked as she watched Jane take the envelope and its contents and throw them angrily across the room. Jane exclaimed, "Damn her! She always oversteps her bounds!" Jane's adult children and children-in-law were aghast at this surprisingly vehement reaction. Despite their shock, this incident provided them with insight regarding their mother's current state of mind regarding death and aging.

Use of Erikson's Psychosocial Framework

Counselors can support older adult women and mitigate some of their anxiety by helping them develop a sense of holistic meaning that ties together their current and past experiences (Horton-Parker & Brown, 2002). Erik Erikson (1959) conceptualized middle adulthood as a stage of development in which we balance the tensions between generativity and stagnation. Considered one of many identity crises faced over the life span, this period is when individuals may feel driven to produce, create, and influence others, and to identify or solidify their purposes in life.

In the older adult years, Erikson proposed that the crisis of ego, integrity versus despair, is experienced. The focus of this period, which Erikson believed began around the 60th birthday, is finding a way to make sense of one's past experiences in a holistic manner. Examples of stage-related activities during this period include reminiscence and self-reflection on earlier choices. Ideally, an older adult is able to accept herself and her mistakes and imperfections with less self-judgment, while appreciating the aspects of her life of which she is proud. Those in this stage of development are also able to recognize and acknowledge the contributions they have made in life. As advocates and helpers, counselors can help women find their own meaning and purpose by facilitating a healthy reflection on the meaningful events and experiences they have accomplished in their lives.

The Influence of Motherhood on Identity

One of the most prominent traditional roles played by women is that of mother. Even as women's roles have expanded and grown increasingly complex in terms of professional identities, women still embrace and prioritize the role of mother (Donorfio & Kellett, 2006; Matlin, 2008). Other external factors that impact both middle and older women's development include such family changes as divorce, death of relatives, and the experience of the empty nest syndrome (Chrisler et al., 2008; Matlin, 2008). In fact, according to Matlin, many women of both middle and older ages may continue to find immense value in their identities as mothers.

According to both anecdotal stories and formal research on middle and older adult women, a woman's identity and sense of life's meaning is ever changing throughout her lifetime.

"As a mom, I tried to make sure I met my daughter's every need when she was a baby. I read the books, asked the pediatrician, did whatever I could to make sure I was being the best mother I could be. To answer your question about what motherhood means to me now, I have to say that even though I can't make decisions for my daughter anymore, or control her environment, or keep everything in her life clean and free from germs, I still think of my most important role as 'mother,' even now. My daughter changed my whole identity the day she was born and though I adore my husband and love him as much as ever, being a mother shapes me even more than being a wife does. But don't tell [my husband]!"—A woman in her mid-50s

Though we may emphasize motherhood in this chapter, we ask readers to remain aware that the media often excessively stereotypes and idealizes mothering. Although this role holds primary importance for many women, motherhood should not be considered the "holy grail" of female accomplishment. It should never be the sole identity for women and practitioners should be careful to never assume that a mature woman is also a mother or grandmother. As helpers, it is important to be aware of each woman's layers of identity and her roles and to encourage clients' discussion of the weight and value they place on these. Today, fewer women than ever before are making the choice to have children. Being sensitive to each woman's choice, circumstance, or desire is essential.

Motherhood can be especially significant to some women and it is important to understand how each client perceives motherhood throughout her development. Just as their children's identities develop, so too do mothers' identities change and grow. In fact, Matlin (2008) and Degges-White and Van Tieghem (2015) reference a phenomenon of what many call the *empty nest syndrome*. This experience is often marked by dissonance—being a "mother," yet having no children present to "mother"—and grief. These feelings typically arise when a mother's adult children leave the family home. Many mothers may experience changes to their motherhood identity prior to the "empty nest." In regard to changes in her identity as a mother of adult children, one woman stated,

"At first seeing my children grow was very sad because I felt as though with age, I had lost connection. However, now, I appreciate being able to be better friends with my adult children . . . and I also love seeing my grandchildren grow."—A 54-year-old woman

As evidenced in this anecdote, in conjunction with changes in identity many middle and older mothers may face, the middle and older adult period can also offer the opportunity for a woman's reformulation of new intrapersonal identities (Degges-White & Van Tieghem, 2015; Horton-Parker & Brown, 2002). Not all mothers experience sadness or grief when their adult children move away. As Matlin (2008) described, some women greatly enjoy revaluing their time and reclaiming pieces of their identity they once held prior to the arrival of their children. Thus, women transitioning into this period may experience enhanced intimacy in other interpersonal relationships including friendships and romantic relationships. According to Erikson (1959), a change in intrapersonal identity formation in both middle and older women may subsequently affect their interpersonal relationships. Thus, if motherhood and its associated transitions are salient to a woman with whom you are working, remember to consider this role in your work together (Newton & Stewart, 2010). For example, empathizing and reflecting about what mothers do and are expected to do may help counselors relate better to and further advocate for clients who are mothers.

There can be challenges inherent in role transitions as evidenced by a mother with whom we spoke. She described her own sense of loss as she and her partner tried to reinvent their lives, stating,

"With the last child finishing high school, my spouse and I decided it was a good time to make career changes as well. We both found new jobs in a new geographical location, sold our home, packed up the kids' childhoods, and moved 600 miles away. The excitement of the major change buoyed us through the first month or two, but the empty house, my partner's long hours, my less than ideal job, and loneliness sent me into a depression tailspin. It took two years to finally feel like I was getting my life back on track and figuring out who I was without being a full-time, round-the-clock neighborhood mom anymore."—Sandy, a professional counselor and mother of three adult children

This example reflects one woman's experience of her own change in identity and motherhood, from mothering children to being a mother of adult children. In fact, for many women such as Sandy, motherhood becomes the defining stage of their adult lives. As children grow and mature, however, it can often take a significant amount of time and effort for her own identity to be reshaped around a new family constellation in which she remains a mother but her children leave the home.

Building New Social Connections

According to Degges-White and Borzumato-Gainey (2013), many middle and older adult women may experience the revitalization or creation of brand new, later life friendships once their children leave home. During these later stages of development, middle and older adult women may form closer and even more intimate bonds with authentic, chosen friends, as they limit time spent with friends of convenience. A woman's relationships with her own adult children can develop into deeply satisfying and rewarding friendships as well (Degges-White & Borzumato-Gainey, 2013). Along with the potential for deeper, more intimate friendships, women also face potential loss of friends and family due to the natural process of aging and other happenstance factors (Madnawat & Kachhawa, 2007).

As women grow older, life events increasingly affect the size of their *friend-scapes* (Degges-White & Borzumato-Gainey, 2013), or friendship circles, as social networks tend to grow a little smaller as they age. Some of the factors that contribute to this decrease include relocation, decreased mobility, illness, death, and even finances. Friendship circles undergo the greatest amount of transition during this final third of a woman's life (Gurung et al., 2003). Fortunately, however, friendscape size is not the defining characteristic of a healthy support network. Whether women have just a single good friend or a much larger group of friends, positive relationships will positively influence health and welfare. Smaller friendship circles have been revealed to yield fewer opportunities for conflict or unsatisfactory relationships (Degges-White & Borzumato-Gainey, 2013). In addition, if a woman considers herself to have a best friend, then she reaps a little added natural protection against emotional depression and compromised well-being (Antonucci, Lansford, & Akiyama, 2001). Simply knowing that she is a part of a social support network can enhance a woman's level of self-esteem. For some women, the main source of their social support, as well as economic support, is realized through their career settings. These professional networks, however, are also subject to significant transition through this life period.

Professional Transitions

Another external factor affecting middle and older adult women includes their changing roles along their career paths. Generally, older women must come face to face with approaching retirement and other career transitions as they age (Vandewater & Stewart, 2006). Just as it does for men, the notion of retirement can elicit a diverse array of emotions for women. Although career shifts may include only a switch to more flexible hours, reduced duties, and more intrinsic engagement, women may experience stress related to reasons such as a decrease in full-time compensation and engagement (Chrisler et al., 2008; Vandewater & Stewart, 2006). According to the existing, but limited, career research on women in middle and late adulthood, factors such as transitions, intrapersonal influences, life-long learning, employment type, financial means, work, and social influences may affect a woman's attitudes before and after her retirement. Thus, a host of highly individualized factors affect a woman's transitional experiences during her middle and older adult years (Brimrose et al., 2013).

INTRAPERSONAL FACTORS INFLUENCING WOMEN

Now that we have briefly introduced various societal, environmental, and developmental factors affecting both middle and older aged women, we describe various supplementary and internal (e.g., intrapersonal and identity) factors that can affect women during their life stages.

Changes in Self-Esteem

Midlife women experience a variety of physical, mental, and emotional reactions to their changing bodies and roles. In a study of age and self-esteem, it was found that women in their 30s and 40s reported lower levels of self-esteem than women in their 20s, 50s, or 60s (Borzumato-Gainey, Kennedy, McCabe, & Degges-White, 2009). This finding may reflect the overwhelming collection of challenges to satisfy expectations placed on women during the very busy 30s and 40s. One relevant developmental construct that may be at play to counter this self-esteem sink during the fifth decade of life is the emergence of *healthy adult narcissism* (Horton-Parker & Brown, 2002; Kohut, 1977). Contrary to the common negative connotation of narcissism, Kohut (1977) noted that this form of narcissism reflects a newly developed sense of confidence and acceptance of oneself coupled with a realistic consideration of one's imperfections and life mistakes. *Healthy adult narcissism* is not based on grandiosity, but is built upon a more realistic self-evaluation and centered on gratitude for the experiences in one's life. In fact, healthy adult narcissism is also described as one form of resilience that allows women to successfully navigate through many of their lives' transitions. One woman described her own surprise at the unexpected and totally unbidden development of this narcissism as she revealed,

> "As a teenager, I always compared myself to the rail-thin, shiny blond haired cheerleaders. I knew that I would never fit that mold but it didn't keep me from feeling like a high school outsider and 'geek'—I guess the word would have been. However, in the last year or two, I have found myself looking into the mirror and finally, without warning, actually liking, no loving, what I see. I'm not trying to sound 'vain' or 'conceited' but I really do think that I'm even more beautiful than I ever could have imagined I would be at this age. Or at any age, really. But it's not that classic, symmetrical beauty. It's a comfort and sense of inner acceptance of who I am and how I got where I am today. Midlife is not the 'toxic wasteland' that I feared it would be, after all."—A woman in her early 50s

Midlife women's resiliency is addressed in Erikson's (1959) stage of generativity versus stagnation. As a reminder, this is the stage that accompanies women's entry into midlife. This stage of development describes the tension between desiring to give back to others (generativity) and the potential for giving in to self-centeredness and disengagement from others (stagnation). A woman's appreciation for all that she has achieved in her own life can spur her to find ways to give back to the community and others. Regretting her decisions or feeling that she is unappreciated by others can lead her to let go of unsatisfying or disappointing relationships or to narrow her life and her activities. Generativity is influenced by the accumulation of life experiences, as well as psychological and emotional development. Despite their hope for generativity, some women may give in to stagnation, in which their activities are self-isolating and reflect an unhealthy egocentric pattern. Practitioners may need to refocus their midlife clients through interventions that encourage them to acknowledge and appreciate their own inner beauty, strength, and resiliency. Through building their resiliency, midlife women will be better prepared to manage any subsequent critical incidents that may arise as they age.

Keeping Transitions From Becoming Insurmountable Obstacles

As middle adult women mature, other potential emotional and mental health challenges may arise. Changes in circumstances, expectations, and roles may exacerbate these concerns in middle and older adult women. The changes, as mentioned earlier, may elicit depression, generalized anxiety, or existential angst for these women (Matlin, 2008). However, with enhanced social support, productive introspection, and reinforced inner strength, women will be better situated to manage the next critical juncture as they move from midlife into older adulthood. Erikson (1959) described the developmental challenge associated with this transition as the ego integrity versus despair stage.

Clinicians working with women at this stage are reminded that transitions and the aging process are inherent to the human condition. Clinicians should encourage women to accept these processes as a natural part of maturity and to look for the opportunities these processes offer where possible. Women who are faring poorly during this period are not to be pitied, even though they may be experiencing shrinking roles, bereavement, or other losses. Counselors can offer support and encouragement to their clients to self-advocate and ask for as much or as little assistance as they feel they need. Making assumptions about what is "normal" or what is needed in terms of support can be deleterious to a client's progress. Due to the individuality of each woman's needs, helpers should explore the magnitude of a client's loss or transition, the instrumental and emotional support needed, and the specific ways they can be as effective as possible in helping their clients.

Physical Changes and Potential Psychological Ramifications

Many of the external factors described earlier may directly and indirectly generate emotional and psychological distress or disequilibrium for middle and older adult women. For example, according to Ferraro et al. (2008), society increasingly tends to judge women based on their appearance as they become older. For some women, body dissatisfaction can present as a major concern that affects them both physically and psychologically. As Gagne et al. (2007) discovered, eating disorders and body image concerns are not limited to adolescents or young adults; 13% of their sample of 50-and-older women disclosed some level of eating disorder.

Another common physical change that older middle and older women experience, which is often symbolic of women's aging process, is the onset of menopause (Degges-White, 2001; Matlin, 2008). Menopause brings a cessation of a woman's fertility, which can yield a variety of responses depending on each individual woman's perspective. This physical change is inherently developmental and affects a woman for the rest of her later life. With this change, some women may experience hot flashes, genital changes, headaches, and/or fatigue. As we have centralized this chapter on the most significant developmental changes affecting women, remember that each woman is different and distinct. This means that no single woman's experience of any event, even menopause, should be used as a model or template for another's.

Despite changes in both environment and physical composition, helping professionals may want to consciously acknowledge their clients for showing resilience during the transitions that occur as they move into middle and older adulthood. Many women often reframe this experience and emphasize their revelations about the benefits of growing older. For example, one postmenopausal woman with whom we spoke shared that having a pet helped her keep her mind off intrapersonal body changes and transitions. Another woman mentioned that although her body has changed due to menopause, she is now able to enjoy intimacy with her husband more freely without the worries of possible pregnancy. It is important for counselors to be aware that each woman's response to her own physiology will be framed within her own personal worldview.

EVIDENCE-BASED INTERVENTIONS FOR MIDDLE AND OLDER ADULT WOMEN

In this section, specific evidence-based approaches and techniques are presented in addition to the various considerations and approaches described earlier. One relevant approach that has consistently proved to be efficacious in counseling women of all ages is known as relational-cultural therapy (RCT; Jordan, 2010). The bedrock of RCT is the establishment of an honest connection and genuine understanding between the counselor and the client. Counselors must consider each woman's development in relation to her physical, psychological, and emotional well-being, in order to further assist clients and to develop counselors' own deeper understanding of each client's lived experience. Thus, instead of a set of "one size fits all" techniques, this section provides reinforcement of the foundational elements of RCT, which accentuates deep understanding and awareness of the context in which human connections occur. Practitioners should bear in mind that it is necessary to understand the inequalities and internalized expectations that affect women in order to know how to deeper and more mutually connect with them (Jordan, 2010; Matlin, 2008).

Relational-Cultural Therapy

Use of RCT as a theoretical basis for helping includes the incorporation of strength-based activities to promote authentic expression. Activities might include story-telling, journaling, drawing, and song selections. Many successful practitioners have recognized the benefits that arise from emphasizing various creative and narrative techniques into their work (Stuckey & Nobel, 2010).

These modalities are especially useful when working with women. Clinicians are more frequently researching and using holistic theories, such as RCT, to more accurately understand, facilitate, and meet the various needs of women. For example, many researchers (Duffey & Somody, 2011; Hammer, Crethar, & Cannon, 2016; Harper, 2010; Oakley et al., 2013) have noted that RCT is becoming more frequently used since this theoretical lens addresses individuals, holistically and with incorporations of the multilayered biopsychosocial model. In fact, RCT is seen as more efficacious than certain previous theories, because, according to RCT, clients are seen as "complex" and "context driven," rather than being facilitated or conceptualized without considerations of current context (Hammer et al., 2016). Furthermore, through their professional experience, these authors have found that expressive therapeutic activities often allow female clients to externalize their feelings, such as pain, grief, anger, and/or guilt in a safe way that is not usually acceptable in their everyday lives (Hammer et al., 2016). Cultural and relational constraints are frequently placed on women's roles and women are not encouraged to openly express their authentic feelings. Women are instead socialized to be the nurturers or the beauties in society and to exhibit predictably pleasant and tolerant dispositions (Matlin, 2008). As a caveat to counselors, it is important to consciously incorporate the core conditions of counseling including congruence, unconditional positive regard, and empathy (Rogers, 1951). By providing the most fundamental core conditions to your clients, you open the gateway for a facilitative relationship in which your work together can be most efficacious.

One intervention that is both effective and simple to implement involves the introduction of visual art through a client's drawing. Practitioners can offer paper and pens, pencils, markers, or pastels to their clients and invite clients to create a representation of what Jordan (2010) described as the client's inner experience. For instance, a woman seeking counseling to address unresolved grief would use her experience of grief as the inspiration for her art. As counselors introduce this type of intervention to their clients, they should stress that it is not the product but the process that is of significance. Creating a space in which women feel safe enough to still the voice of their inner critics is an important component of effective creative interventions.

RCT provides recognition of the power systems and societal factors that influence women and their psychological manifestations (Jordan, 2010). A theoretical perspective that is often coupled with RCT is feminist theory (FT; Jones-Smith, 2016). FT, like RCT, provides a lens through which external power systems that are embedded within culturally shaped beliefs can be viewed. Behaviors are concurrently acknowledged and considered within the counseling relationship and process. For example, the tenets of FT encourage a deconstruction and challenge of many of the latent implications that result from a gendered culture. In contrast to the concept of two immutable genders categories, FT asserts that gender is not binary and that gender is a socially created construct. FT also addresses the phenomenological reality of each individual.

Feminist Theory

Theoretically, FT has a significant place among theories as it addresses various liberal, cultural, social, and systemic influences on *all* members of society. Practically, FT is important as current research indicates that systemic influences affect all individuals, especially women (Jones-Smith, 2016). It is imperative that helpers implement theories and techniques that have been shown to be effective with women. Current feminist theorists address societal misrepresentations of the punitive gender binary, as well as specific limitations in the current mental health resources available for female clients.

Importantly, FT addresses various limitations of the *Diagnostic and Statistical Manual for Mental Disorders, 5th edition (DSM-5;* American Psychiatric Association [APA], 2013). This resource, if used with a mind-set of "one size fits all," may invalidate women from varying cultures and beliefs (Jones-Smith, 2016). For example, according to the *DSM-5* (APA, 2013), various behaviors, such as a high level of closeness within one's family, may be viewed as a diagnosable concern. Thus, when considering a woman's attachment within her family, extreme closeness may be categorized as "enmeshment" or as elevated signs of a "dependent personality" when using the *DSM-5*. However, this closeness may simply exemplify cultural norms or forms of identification for a female client in a culture other than the Western one that significantly drives much the *DSM-5*'s content. In this case, instead of providing a diagnosis of a possible dependency elevation, a feminist counselor may use FT to look at the various intersectionalities of the female client's culture to consider various contextual aspects. Please note FT is not dichotomous to medically based models, such as those described by and found in the *DSM-5* (APA, 2013). In fact, many feminists agree that with increased inclusion and holistic consideration, the *DSM-5* may be used effectively with other therapies (Crowder, 2016). However, FT and feminist theorists caution against the categorical or punitive use of any resource in the treatment of clients.

Cognitive Behavioral Theory Interventions Based in Feminist Theory

In addition to the RCT techniques addressed, FT also incorporates selected practical cognitive behavioral therapy (CBT) techniques. CBT is one of the most frequently utilized treatments due to its empirical support and easily measurable outcomes (Jones-Smith, 2016). CBT addresses a client's cognitions and behaviors, and views these as interdependent on one another. In fact, many CBT techniques are currently used for women today, including boundary creation, assertiveness training, exposure therapies, and feminist-based mindfulness (Crowder, 2016).

Boundary creation is a technique whereby a helper facilitates a client to reflect on her preferred-versus-perceived boundaries in her interpersonal relationships and roles. Assertiveness training is used when a helper teaches a client how to express herself and her needs in various social and interpersonal situations (e.g., asking one's boss for a well-deserved pay raise). Exposure therapy is a form of

CBT where clients are repeatedly encouraged to safely confront their fears so that they may be more successful in various sought behaviors (e.g., using learned assertiveness through role-play enactments where female clients "act out" an anticipated action). Feminist-based mindfulness practice incorporates an awareness of the fluidity of identity and of the self, while recognizing the need for self-compassion and the restructuring of one's sense of self. All of these techniques are beneficial for midlife and older adult clients who may have unknowingly accepted the constraints placed on them by external sources. Each of these interventions contributes to strengthened boundaries, empowerment, self-awareness, self-authorship, and self-advocacy throughout one's life.

Feminist Theory Interventions

FT techniques are also exceptionally well suited for women who are facing challenges that have roots intertwined with gender and/or age. As referenced earlier in this text, these interventions include *consciousness raising* (CR), social- and gender-role analysis, and resocialization (Jones-Smith, 2016). CR encourages clients to acknowledge the external factors that influence current difficulties and presenting issues. Similar to narrative therapy (White & Epston, 1990), CR facilitates the process of externalizing a woman's problem. CR is especially beneficial for middle and older adult women who exhibit a tendency toward self-blame or take responsibility for the choices of others. Self-compassion for past regrets and disappointments can be validated and reframed through CR, as counselors encourage women's empowerment versus shaming of themselves.

Social- and gender-role analysis is useful for women in middle to older adulthood as the self-expression generated through this technique encourages them to break down the cultural stereotypes and presumptive obligations by which they have enacted their lives. Client self-expression may be accomplished through oral story development, pictorial drawings (e.g., life maps and/or genogram creations), or written expressions at all ages of a woman's development. Women who take responsibility for others' happiness or permit others to take advantage of them due to a false sense of obligation may especially benefit from this intervention.

Additionally, *resocialization* helps women of all ages self-advocate and express their social identity. Empowerment and self-expression are crucial for middle-aged and older women, since societal pressures may push women to shame themselves for their older age. Instead of a push to "seem younger," resocialization and other techniques in FT can help a female client maintain self-acceptance, while also acknowledging the current systemic barriers she may be facing, such as ageism. With these techniques, as well as other FT-based interventions, feminist counselors continue to advocate for and encourage self-advocacy for all clients, especially middle-aged and older female clients in their current contexts.

In summary, RCT, CBT, and FT lenses are all contemporary and broadly used approaches that are efficacious with women today (Jones-Smith, 2016). These approaches and their various techniques, undergirded with genuine and accurate empathy and advocacy, are applicable to women of all ages. These techniques are not "problem-specific"; thus, they can be translated across clients who face unique intrapersonal and interpersonal issues. The contexts within which women

live, and learn to live, are also salient as practitioners determine the most effective approach for each client. In addition to individual interventions for middle
and older adult women, advocacy is another area in which practitioners can be of
significant assistance to all of their clients.

ADVOCACY AND SOCIAL JUSTICE CONSIDERATIONS FOR WOMEN

Beliefs from a generation ago regarding the experiences and expectations of
midlife women were considerably different than they are today. As the baby
boomer population has aged, the definitions of "midlife" and "old age" have shifted.
Earlier in this chapter, we referenced some of the shifts and role changes affecting both midlife and older adult women. It even may seem a bit ironic that the
women who once embraced the adage, "Don't trust anyone over 30," now claim
that "50 is the new 30." The generation that was apprehensive about the "over 30"
demographic sector is now well past their own 30th birthdays and most have
already doubled that age marker. In fact, the most recent and complete U.S. Census
data collected indicated that 20% of the female population is 60-years-old or older
(U.S. Census Bureau, 2012). Younger adults, often called the millennial generation, have overtaken the baby boomers in terms of number; thus, the needs of
middle and older adult women will be met by this younger aged cohort. For
helpers to consider being effective advocates, we need to understand the variety
of ways that contemporary women enact middle and older adulthood within our
changing society and its varied social norms.

As advocates, we can benefit by keeping in mind what Gould (1978) stated,
"People change with age because new priorities require new attitudes and new
behaviors" (p. 201). As we reflect on the efficacy of our work and our goals as
advocates, counselors, and other types of helpers, we must remain conscious and
aware of the age-related and gender-related experiences and influences that
women face. A woman's identity is not defined by a single demographic variable,
but by her multiple identities and her unique experiences as she moves through
life. Our clients are the product of both internal and external influences. To advocate and serve them, we must encourage them to acknowledge and share the
diverse collection of experiences that contribute to their unique identities.

To incorporate inclusivity in counseling practice requires that clinicians
embrace others' differences in both their professional and personal lives. For
example, as society changes and legislation and public opinion shift, so too do
the constellations of families and the shape of women's roles in and out of each
family shift. Women continue to face gendered, ethnic, sexual identity, and age-
related microaggressions and/or overt forms of discrimination (Sue & Sue, 2008).
Just by virtue of gendered and age-related appearance, women may be targets
of both individual and societal discrimination in a variety of forms. Even more
unfortunate is the occurrence of overt aggressions between women. Whether
it is fat shaming, beauty slamming, straight versus lesbian bashing, or women
demeaning, women harming other women is particularly heinous. Until all women
feel safe to embrace and take pride in their own unique identities, they cannot
easily embrace and accept all other women.

CONCLUSION

As we reflect on the layers of experience over the second half of a woman's life, it is essential that we bear in mind that every woman's story is just that, *her story*. To understand the experiences and realities of all individuals, we must be culturally sensitive and aware. We must be willing to continually reeducate ourselves about the latest research, studies, and real-life stories regarding women who embody a wide variety of diversities and cultural experiences. Awareness and advocacy are essential as the intersectionality and multiplicity of internal and external identity factors continuously evolve and influence our clients. Who a woman may be today is not necessarily who she will be tomorrow. To fully comprehend and effectively serve our middle and older adult clients, we must first learn about the factors that support their resilience and give shape to their complex identities and lives. Women continue to surpass men in longevity due to their ability to better react to life's stressors (National Center for Health Statistics, 2015). When working with maturing clients, share with them the value and positive health benefits of their help-seeking behaviors and provide them with a safe space to make sense of their own stories. Model advocacy and appreciation for each client's unique circumstances and identity. Your work may be instrumental in validating their stories and consolidating their legacies.

CALL TO ACTION

As advocates, counselors can volunteer to support women's rights in various ways. This may include participation in community rallies, legislative meetings, and in other public and private arenas (Foley, 2015; Matlin, 2008; Neukrug, 2011; Sue & Sue, 2008). Counselors should also voice their support for further equity for all people, including all women, by incorporating cultural sensitivity into the various roles in their own lives (Sue & Sue, 2015). In terms of communication, the power of the Internet is significant. It has been embraced by individuals across the life span and deep into older adulthood. In fact, women in this life stage also are becoming more reliant on social media sites and electronic communication. A recent report from the Pew Research Center (2013) noted that more than 45% of individuals 65 and older use social media sites. Due to this trend, as well as to the millennial generation's size and number, the Internet provides unparalleled opportunities for individuals to publicly express messages of advocacy as well as encourage grassroots involvement around the globe for women. As our means of global communication increase, advocacy messages for gender equity and justice should expand, and the efficacy of these messages should increase (Matlin, 2008; Sue & Sue, 2008; U.S. Census Bureau, 2012).

REFLECTION AND DISCUSSION QUESTIONS

1. Where do you believe efforts toward advocacy for middle and older adult women should begin? How do you see your role as an advocate in helping women of all ages?

2. What, if any, traditional gender stereotypes do you believe still inhibit women today? What, if any, traditional age-related stereotypes do you believe still inhibit or shape the lives of women today?

3. What personal experiences with ageism or sexism have you met with in your life? How do these experiences shape how you would work with a middle or older adult woman dealing with the psychological effects of ageism and/or sexism?

4. What societal elements do you believe present the greatest obstacles to the cultural shift toward truly equal and responsive treatment of women? How are these elements manifested through Western cultural norms and traditions?

HELPFUL RESOURCES

Books

- Ephron, N. (2008). *I feel bad about my neck: And other thoughts on being a woman.* New York, NY: Vintage.
- Northrup, C. (2010). *Women's bodies, women's wisdom: Creating physical and emotional health and healing.* New York, NY: Bantam Books.

Professional Websites and Organizations

- Association for Adult Development and Aging (AADA; www.aadaweb.org)—Provides resources and links related to counseling midlife and older adults
- Association for Humanistic Counseling (www.afhc.camp9.org)—Provides information relevant to counselors who would like to learn more about the infusion of humanistic principles into their work
- Healthy Women (www.healthywomen.org/ages-and-stages/midlife-and -beyond)—Provides resources for women at all stages of the life span including midlife and older adulthood
- Life Reimagined (www.lifereimagined.aarp.org)—AARP-sponsored website that provides online learning modules that are designed to help users reinvent and reinvigorate their lives
- Next Avenue (www.nextavenue.org)—PBS-sponsored website with the tagline "where grown-ups keep growing"

DEDICATION

We dedicate this chapter to the many women interviewed, including and especially, Ms. Terri Parker, the first author's mother. We deeply appreciate the interviewees' authentic responses and stories, which helped us personalize our chapter and realistically represent the diversity inherent in this population. Each and every woman has a unique and beautiful story.

In order to be effective advocates for women everywhere, we all must embrace our own identities, regardless of age, ethnicity, culture, or other differences.

REFERENCES

American Psychiatric Association. (2013). *Diagnostic and statistical manual of mental disorders* (5th ed.). Arlington, VA: American Psychiatric Publishing. doi:10.1176/appi.books .9780890425596.744053

Antonucci, T. C., Lansford, J. E., & Akiyama, H. (2001). Impact of positive and negative aspects of marital relationships and friendships on well-being of older adults. *Applied Developmental Science, 5,* 68–75. doi:10.1207/S1532480XADS0502_2

Arthur, M. B., & Rousseau, D. M. (1996). Introduction: The boundaryless career as a new employment principle. In M. B. Arthur & D. M. Rousseau (Eds.), *The boundaryless career* (pp. 3–20). New York, NY: Oxford University Press.

Borzumato-Gainey, C., Kennedy, A., McCabe, B., & Degges-White, S. (2009). Life satisfaction, self-esteem, and subjective age in women across the life span. *Adultspan, 8,* 29–42.

Brimrose, J., McMahon, M., & Watson, M. (2013). Career trajectories of older women: Implications for career guidance. *British Journal of Guidance and Counselling, 21,* 587–601. doi:10.1080/03069885.2013.779639

Butler, R. N. (1969). Age-ism: Another form of bigotry. *The Gerontologist, 9*(4, Pt. 1), 243–246.

Chrisler, J. C., Barney, A., & Palatino, B. (2016). Ageism can be hazardous to women's health: Ageism, sexism, and stereotypes of older women in the healthcare system. *Journal of Social Issues, 72,* 86–104. doi:10.1111/josi.12157

Chrisler, J. C., Golden, C., & Rozee, P. (2008). *Lectures on the psychology of women* (4th ed.). New York, NY: McGraw-Hill.

Crowder, R. (2016). Mindfulness based feminist therapy: The intermingling edges of self-compassion and social justice. *Journal of Religion & Spirituality in Social Work: Social Thought, 35*(1/2), 24–40. doi:10.1080/15426432.2015.1080605

Degges-White, S. (2001). Midlife transitions in women: Cultural and individual factors. *Adultspan Journal, 3,* 4–11. doi:10.1002/j.2161-0029.2001.tb00100.x

Degges-White, S., & Borzumato-Gainey, C. (2013). *Friends forever: How girls and women forge lasting relationships.* Lanham, MD: Rowman & Littlefield.

Degges-White, S., & Myers, J. (2006). Transitions, wellness, and life satisfaction: Implications for counseling midlife women. *Journal of Mental Health Counseling, 28,* 133–150. doi:10.17744/mehc.28.2.eaumlpbm0rxdrldk

Degges-White, S., & Van Tieghem, J. (2015). *Toxic friendships*. Lanham, MD: Rowman & Littlefield.

Donorfio, L. K. M., & Kellett, K. (2006). Filial responsibility and transitions involved: A qualitative exploration of caregiving daughters and frail mothers. *Journal of Adult Development, 13*, 158–167. doi:10.1007/s10804-007-9025-4

Duffey, T., & Somody, C. (2011). The role of relational-cultural theory in mental health counseling. *Journal of Mental Health Counseling, 33*(3), 223–242.

Erikson, E. H. (1959). *Identity and the life cycle: Selected papers, with a historical introduction by David Rapaport*. New York, NY: International University Press.

Ferraro, F. R., Muehlenkamp, J. J., Paintner, A., Wasson, K., Hager, T., & Hoverson, F. (2008). Aging, body image, and body shape. *Journal of General Psychology, 135*(4), 379–392. doi:10.3200/GENP.135.4.379–392

Foley, E. (2015, June 28). Same-sex marriage advocates still fighting to change opponents' minds. *Huffington Post*. Retrieved from http://www.huffingtonpost.com/2015/06/28/gay-marriage-opponents_n_7682086.html

Gagne, D. A., Von Holle, A., Brownley, K. A., Runfola, C. D., Hofmeier, S., Branch, K. E., & Bulik, C. M. (2007). Eating disorder symptoms and weight and shape concerns in a large web-based convenience sample of women ages 50 and above: Results of the gender and body image (GAB) study. *International Journal of Eating Disorders, 45*, 832–844. doi:10.1002/eat.22030

Gould, R. (1978). *Transformations: Growth and change in adult life*. New York, NY: Simon & Schuster.

Gurung, R. A. R., Taylor, S. E., & Seeman, T. E. (2003). Accounting for changes in social support among married older adults: Insights from the MacArthur Studies of Successful Aging. *Psychology and Aging, 18*, 487–496. doi:10.1037/0882-7974.18.3.487

Hammer, T., Crethar, H., & Cannon, K. (2016). Convergence of identities through the lens of relational-cultural theory. *Journal of Creativity in Mental Health, 11*(2), 126–141. doi:10.1080/15401383.2016.1181596

Harper, F. G. (2010). Relational-cultural therapy by Judith V. Jordan. *Journal of Creativity in Mental Health, 5*(1), 105–106.

Horton-Parker, R. J., & Brown, N. W. (2002). *The unfolding life: Counseling across the lifespan*. Westport, CT: Bergin & Garvey.

Jones-Smith, E. (2016). *Theories of counseling and psychotherapy: An integrative approach* (2nd ed.). Los Angeles, CA: Sage.

Jordan, J. V. (2010). *Relational cultural therapy*. Washington, DC: American Psychological Association.

Kohut, H. (1977). *The restoration of the self*. New York, NY: International Universities Press.

Koza, J. (2010). Women's responses to fashion media images: A study of female consumers aged 30–59. *International Journal of Consumer Studies, 34*, 272–278. doi:10.1111/j.1470-6431.2009.00854.x

Lai, Y., & Hynie, M. (2011). A tale of two standards: An examination of young adults' endorsement of gendered and ageist sexual double standards. *Sex Roles, 64*, 360–371. doi:10.1007/s11199-010-9896-x

Lewis, K. V., Harris, C., Morrison, R., & Ho, M. (2015). The entrepreneurship-motherhood nexus: A longitudinal investigation from a boundaryless career perspective. *The Career Development International, 20,* 21–37. doi:10.1108/cdi-07-2014-0090

Madnawat, A. V. S., & Kachhawa, P. S. (2007). Age, gender, and living circumstances: Discriminating older adults on death anxiety. *Death Studies, 31,* 763–769. doi:10.1080/07481180701490743

Matlin, M. (2008). *The psychology of women* (6th ed.). Belmont, CA: Thomson.

Morgan, L. K., & Kisley, M. A. (2014). The effects of facial attractiveness and perceiver's mate value on adaptive allocation of central processing resources. *Evolution and Human Behavior, 35,* 96–102. doi:10.1016/j.evolhumbehav.2013.11.002

Narayan, C. (2008). Is there a double standard of aging? Older men and women and ageism. *Educational Gerontology, 34,* 782–787. doi:10.1080/03601270802042123

National Center for Health Statistics. (2015). *Health, United States, 2014: With special feature on adults aged 55–64.* Hyattsville, MD: Author.

Neugarten, B. L. (1996). *The meanings of age.* Chicago, IL: University of Chicago Press.

Neugarten, B. L., Moore, J. W., & Lowe, J. C. (1965). Age norms, age constraints, and adult socialization. *American Journal of Sociology, 70,* 710–717. doi:10.1086/223965

Neukrug, E. S. (2011). *Counseling theory and practice.* Belmont, CA: Cengage.

Newton, N., & Stewart, A. (2010). The middle ages: Change in women's personalities and social roles. *Psychology of Women Quarterly, 34,* 74–84. doi:10.1111/j.1471-6402.2009.01543.x

Oakley, M. A., Addison, S. C., Piran, N., Johnston, G. J., Damianakis, M., Curry, J., & Weigeldt, A. (2013). Outcome study of brief relational-cultural therapy in a women's mental health center. *Psychotherapy Research, 23*(2), 137–151. doi:10.1080/10503307.2012.745956

Pew Research Center. (2013). Social networking fact sheet. Retrieved from http://www.pewinternet.org/fact-sheets/social-networking-fact-sheet

Quadagno, J. (2001). *Aging and the life course.* Boston, MA: McGraw-Hill.

Rogers, C. (1951). *Client-centered therapy: Its current practice, implications and theory.* London, UK: Constable.

Schlossberg, N. K. (1984). *Counseling adults in transition.* New York, NY: Springer Publishing Company.

Stuckey, H. L., & Nobel, J. (2010). The connection between art, healing, and public health: A review of current literature. *American Journal of Public Health, 100,* 254–263. doi:10.2105/ajph.2008.156497

Sue, D. W., & Sue, D. (2008). *Counseling the culturally diverse theory and practice* (5th ed.). Hoboken, NJ: Wiley.

Sue, D. W., & Sue, D. (2015). *Counseling the culturally diverse* (7th ed.). Hoboken, NJ: Wiley.

U.S. Census Bureau. (2012). Population estimates: Data for all geographies. Retrieved from http://www.census.gov/popest/data/datasets.html

Vandewater, E., & Stewart, A. (2006). Paths to midlife well-being for women and men: The importance of identity development and social role quality. *Journal of Adult Development, 13*, 76–86. doi:10.1007/s10804-006-9004-1

White, M., & Epston, D. (1990). *Narrative means to therapeutic ends*. New York, NY: W. W. Norton.

CHAPTER 9

Violence Against Women and Girls

Rebecca Vazquez and Atsuko Seto

"The ordinary response to atrocities is to banish them from consciousness. Certain violations of the social compact are too terrible to utter aloud: this is the meaning of the word unspeakable. Atrocities, however, refuse to be buried. Equally as powerful as the desire to deny atrocities is the conviction that denial does not work. . . . Remembering and telling the truth about terrible events are prerequisites both for the restoration of the social order and for the healing of individual victims."
—*Herman (1997, p. 1)*

LEARNING OBJECTIVES

After reading this chapter, you will be able to:

1. Understand the prevalence and forms of violence against women and the impact of such on their well-being as survivors.
2. Conceptualize the counseling process through an empowerment lens while recognizing the stages of prevention, intervention, and restoration.
3. Understand the definitions and distinctions of compassion fatigue, burnout, and vicarious trauma in order to learn how to implement wellness practice into clinical work.

As counselors and agents of change, we have a responsibility to confront violence against women and to understand this as a global occurrence instead of a localized issue. This chapter is dedicated to telling the truth about the atrocities that women of all ages have faced and continue to experience in today's world. As Judith Herman (1997), a renowned leader in the field of traumatic stress, expressed in the opening quote, vocalizing these atrocities is necessary for the restoration and healing process for survivors of violence. Although disturbing and difficult to grasp, we must open our eyes to perpetual issues of violence against women before we can help facilitate both individual and systemic restoration. The word "women" is used in this chapter to represent women of all ages unless a distinct separation needs to be made to address developmentally specific issues.

As you journey through this chapter, you may be learning about these atrocities for the first time. Some readers may be all too familiar with the information because it has profoundly affected them or someone they love. We encourage you to pay attention to your own reactions to the content presented and practice appropriate self-care strategies if you are overcome by intense emotions and thoughts.

This chapter includes brief historical, political, and cultural perspectives on violence against women as well as the current state of this issue. Following this overview, we discuss various forms of violence against women that impact their emotional, physical, and psychological well-being. Although the contents of this chapter are not exhaustive, our hope is to provide you with a fundamental knowledge of how violence against women has manifested throughout society. Clinical implications discussed in this chapter include an overview of the clinical foundation in working with survivors of violence and the three layers of the counseling process: prevention, intervention, and restoration. Finally, we discuss the impact of this work on the counselor, along with how to promote posttraumatic growth in clients.

HISTORICAL REFLECTION ON VIOLENCE AGAINST WOMEN

The United Nations (UN, 1993) defines violence against women as, ". . . any act of gender-based violence that results in, or is likely to result in, physical, sexual or psychological harm or suffering to women, including threats of such acts, coercion or arbitrary deprivation of liberty, whether occurring in public or in private life" (p. 3). This definition has been relevant throughout time and across cultures. According to Fox (2002), religious traditions, Greek philosophy, and legal systems have greatly influenced societal views of women and their treatment for centuries. The patriarchal nature of these social structures has led to an unequal power distribution and subsequent discrimination against women (Fox, 2002; UN, 2006). Fox (2002) specifically referred to this phenomenon as "patriarchal privilege" and noted how its presence led to historical formation of rigid, unbalanced gender roles within religious, philosophical, and legal traditions (p. 16).

One of the earliest recorded incidents of violence against women can be seen in the ancient Greek image illustrated in Figure 9.1, dated to around 450 BCE.[1] Experts describe the image as a drunken man, holding his own robe and walking stick, aggressively knocking on a bolted door. His presumed wife stands on the other side of the door with a timid stance and a lamp, suggesting that this incident took place in the middle of the night (Llewellyn-Jones, 2011). This scenario took place more than 2,000 years ago, yet today is still a familiar occurrence.

Social Inequality

History has illustrated contradictions between how women were portrayed and how they were actually treated in society. An example of this is found in the ancient African text, the Ifa. A poem within the Ifa reveres women with statements such as,

FIGURE 9.1 Line drawing of a red-figure *chous*. Metropolitan Museum of Art, 37.11.19; c. 450 BCE.

Source: Llewellyn-Jones (2011). Reprinted with permission from Dr. Lloyd Llewellyn-Jones and Anton Powell.

"Obarisa said that people should always respect women greatly. For if they respect women greatly, the world will be in right order" (Olatunji, 2013, p. 6). Despite this clear instruction from an influential social entity, women were often given a lower status than men in the name of tradition (Olatunji, 2013).

Legal systems in many parts of the world have perpetuated injustice and gender inequality. Lansing (2006) noted that rapes in England were common but convictions were rare. Often, cases were settled out of court by the provision of a dowry by the family, or by marrying the victim to her attacker in order to preserve the reputation of the victim and her family, which still occurs in modern-day society (Lansing, 2006). In Latin America during the 19th century, the legal system clearly favored men. According to the Colombian Criminal Code of 1873, men who battered or even killed their wives as a result of an "involuntary lapse of reason" or during "absolutely involuntary inebriation" were excused of any responsibility for their actions (Uribe-Urán, 2013, p. 57).

These social inequalities are not only found in a historical, global context, but also in a current context within the United States. A prime example of such inequalities is the income gap between men and women. According to the U.S. Department of Labor, Bureau of Labor Statistics (2011), women in the United States were earning around 81% of what their male counterparts did in 2010. Although the United States has taken strides to close the economic gap, as well as address other forms of gender inequality through various legislations, there is still much work to be done to ensure equality for women within the United States.

Wartime Violence Against Women

Wartime violence against women is another unfortunate historical reality. Across countries and conflicts, women have been seen as "an effective and inexpensive war tactic" (Munro, 2014, p. 50). Whether used as a way to obtain information or to instill fear in the community as a whole, wartime sexual violence has been documented in many parts of the world including, but not limited to, El Salvador, former Yugoslavia, Sierra Leone, Japan, Bangladesh, Iraq, and Colombia (Cohen, Green, & Wood, 2013). Although the international community has denounced the use of sexual violence in global conflicts, it is still considered a contemporary weapon that is systemically used to gain control and instill fear within a community. Specifically, wartime rape has been identified as a tool in genocide and ethnic cleansing (Munro, 2014).

Unfortunately, much of the information previously presented is not only historical fact, but also a current truth. In spite of notable strides that have been made to create safety and equity, various forms of violence are a daily reality for many women around the world today.

WHERE ARE WE NOW?

The movement toward ending violence against women has gained significant momentum since the end of the 20th and the beginning of the 21st centuries. With the advent of technology, public awareness campaigns have flourished, and international platforms have been established to support the efforts to confront violence against women. Both male and female celebrities have joined the cause of eradicating gender-based violence, drawing more resources and attention to the movement. Global organizations, such as the United Nations (UN) and the WHO, have developed declarations to denounce violence against women for moral, health, economic, and social justice reasons. More recent federal, state, and local statutes address issues that directly impact women who experience violence. For example, survivors of sex trafficking often have been arrested for prostitution and treated like criminals instead of victims, resulting in additional devastating effects on many aspects of their lives (Polaris Project, 2015a). In order to address this injustice, states across the union have begun to implement Safe Harbor laws, which recognize this damaging inconsistency within the legal system and seek to provide appropriate services to survivors of sex trafficking (Polaris Project, 2015a).

Despite these signs of progress, the prevalence of violence against women remains at a pandemic level. Worldwide, 35.5% of women have been subjected to sexual and/or physical violence, with the highest prevalence (45.6%) in African nations (WHO, 2013). Approximately half of women killed in 2012 were murdered by intimate partners or family members (United Nations Office on Drugs and Crime [UNODC], 2013). According to the International Labour Office (ILO, 2012), women and girls represent 55% of the estimated 20.9 million victims of forced labor trafficking and 98% of the estimated 4.5 million individuals forced into sex trafficking. More than 700 million women alive today were forced to marry before they were 18 years of age. More than one in three, or about 250 million women, were forced into marriage before the age of 15 years (United Nations Children's Fund [UNICEF], 2014a). With the prevalence of violence against women and girls still existing at staggering levels, counselors need a solid understanding of how to address these issues and support the survivors of violence. Regardless of clinical settings, most counselors will encounter female clients who have been victims of violence (Sawyer, Peters, & Willis, 2013). Therefore, understanding the magnitude of this issue and various forms of violence that impact women of all ages is crucial in counseling and advocating for this population.

POWER AND CONTROL

In order to grasp the complexity of violent relationships, we will begin with one of the most notably used tools in the field of trauma work. In 1984, advocates from the Domestic Abuse Intervention Program (DAIP) in Duluth, Minnesota, partnered with battered women to develop the Power and Control Wheel (Figure 9.2),[2] which is delineated as the following:

> The Power and Control Wheel is not a theory or conceptual framework and it does not attempt to give a broad understanding of all violence in the home or community but instead offers a more precise explanation of the tactics men use to batter women. Battering is one form of domestic or intimate partner violence. It is characterized by the pattern of actions that an individual uses to intentionally control or dominate his intimate partner. That is why the words "power and control" are in the center of the wheel. A batterer systematically uses threats, intimidation, and coercion to instill fear in his partner. These behaviors are the spokes of the wheel. (L. Stavnes, personal communication, December 19, 2016)

The image of the Power and Control Wheel has had a great impact on the understanding of battering around the world. Although it is commonly believed that violence occurs when men who batter lose control, it is clear through what women have shared about their experience that this is not the case. This visual representation of the lived experiences of battered women serves as a foundational tool in understanding violence against women.

The gender-neutral terms "perpetrator" or "abuser" are used throughout this chapter. Although the vast majority of perpetrators of violence against women are men, women have also been documented as perpetrators. The intention here is to acknowledge that although the majority of survivors are women, men are also victimized by violence (Thureau, Le Blanc-Louvry, Thureau, Gricourt, & Proust, 2015; UN, 1993). The word "survivor" is used to refer to women who have been victims of violence. Although the terms "victim" and "survivor" may be used interchangeably, in some settings "survivor" is often preferred and is typically viewed as empowering (Jordan, 2013). In working with individuals who

FIGURE 9.2 Power and Control Wheel developed by the Domestic Abuse Intervention Program (DAIP).

Source: Power and Control Wheel developed by the Domestic Abuse Intervention Program (DAIP), 202 East Superior St. Duluth, MN 55802, 218-722-2781. www.theduluthmodel.org. Reprinted with permission.

have experienced violence, counselors should be open to using each client's preferred term in order to promote client self-empowerment and establish a therapeutic working alliance.

Domestic Violence

What comes to your mind when you think of the term DV? Do you think of a woman with a black eye? Or, perhaps, a movie? A loved one? A celebrity scandal? DV is most often portrayed in heterosexual couples with the man being physically and emotionally violent toward the woman. However, DV can occur in any relationship including, but not limited to, same-sex, bisexual, and transgender couples, couples in which one partner has a disability, a female perpetrating against a male partner, and relationships in which no physical violence exists. Power and control exist essentially in all intimate relationships, but the function and distribution of power and control varies from couple to couple. DV occurs when the dynamic of power and control in a relationship is invasive, malicious, and/or oppressive (Coy, Scott, Tweedale, & Perks, 2015; Herman, 1997).

Emotional Abuse

The emotional effects of DV can have devastating impacts on survivors. Although physical violence is quite destructive, many survivors attest that emotional abuse including verbal insults, name-calling, psychological mind games, and humiliating the survivor in private or public tends to be harder to heal from than physical abuse. Common thoughts and beliefs held by survivors include: "It's my fault. I am to blame"; "I should have known better or tried harder"; "Love hurts"; "I gotta be tough and not let things bother me"; and "I can't trust anyone, not even myself" (Johnson, 2012, p. 377). These messages are instilled and reinforced by the perpetrator, resulting in survivors feeling guilty, ambivalent, and hopeless.

Physical Abuse

It is important to recognize that physical abuse within the context of a relationship can occur on a continuum. Physical abuse includes, but is not limited to, pushing, slapping, kicking, punching, broken bones, permanent injury, and use of weapons. Campbell et al. (2003) developed the *Danger Assessment* instrument, which is designed to assess the severity of violence and homicide risk in intimate relationships. According to Campbell et al. (2003), strangulation is considered of high lethality and should be assessed for whenever working with survivors of violence.

Financial Abuse

Although financial abuse may not automatically come to mind as a form of DV, it is a pervasive form of power and control. For many women living with DV, their options are contingent on their ability to provide for themselves and their children. This dynamic can be especially prevalent among survivors with disabilities or undocumented immigrants who may have to rely on their partners to access available resources (Kaltman, Hurtado de Mendoza, Gonzales, Serrano, & Guarnaccia, 2011; Nosek, Foley, Hughes, & Howland, 2001). Financial control can take many forms: (a) determining that the woman cannot work, (b) preventing her from keeping a job, (c) forcing her to work and bear financial burdens so that the perpetrator no longer has to, (d) forcing her to hand over her paycheck, (e) denying access to important household financial information, and (f) making her have sex for money to support children. Controlling money is one way to ostracize a survivor and isolate her from others. Without adequate financial resources, safety and stability can be difficult to achieve.

Sexual Violence

Although sexual violence is often present within DV, it also occurs outside of intimate relationships and is addressed separately in this chapter. Legally, sexual violence is often referred to as sexual assault or rape. Because local legislations may define these terms differently, counselors need to be aware of the relevant laws in the states where they practice. Regardless of the terminology, the feeling of shame often consumes survivors of sexual violence due to tremendous stigma and vulnerability that are associated with the act. As such, many incidents of sexual violence go unreported (U.S. Department of Justice, 2014). Despite the fact that many women choose not to disclose an incident of sexual assault, the number of reported cases of sexual violence against women is alarming. The National Sexual Violence Resource Center (2015) reports that one in five women in the United States will be raped at some point in their lives. As previously mentioned, sexual violence can be used to exert power and control in the context of war as well as in familial or intimate relationships.

Childhood Sexual Abuse

The impact of childhood sexual abuse (CSA) is difficult to fully comprehend. Perpetrators are often adults in a position of power and trust to the child. The child, who has yet to develop her sense of self, is likely to suffer immense confusion, and humiliation as a result. Vilenica, Shakespeare-Finch, and Obst (2013) poignantly note that sexual trauma during adulthood can shake the established foundations of an individual, whereas CSA plays a significant part in shaping children's foundational views of themselves, others, and the world. Many survivors of CSA report feeling "damaged" or inherently bad, largely due to the assumption that "good things happen to good people [and], bad things happen to those who deserve bad things" (Vilenica et al., 2013, p. 40). It is not uncommon for "survivor guilt" to plague survivors, in spite of their bravery and resourcefulness. The guilt can serve as a way of regaining a sense of power in the midst of a disaster. To imagine that there was something more that could have been done may be easier to face than the reality of helplessness (Herman, 1997). Sexual violence during the formative years of childhood can result in a wide range of reactions including, but not limited to, depression, sexual dysfunction, anxiety, suicidal ideation and attempts, strained interpersonal relationships, and poor sense of self (Foster & Hagedorn, 2014; Vilenica et al., 2013).

Incest

Incest, or sexual abuse within the family system, is considered a universal taboo (Atwood, 2007). Since it is hardly ever spoken of, one might think incest is a rare occurrence. However, Atwood suggests, "If there is a universal rule against something, then that something must be occurring universally. The incest itself is universal, not the absence of it" (p. 288). Survivors of incest are nearly always coerced into keeping the abuse secret. Depending on the age of the child, the offender may frame the abuse as a "game" or as "special time" that must remain secret between them (Ballantine, 2012). This dynamic often leads to a false sense of mutuality or complicity, which can result in immense feelings of guilt and shame (Ballantine, 2012). The perpetrator might also threaten them or other loved ones with harm or other forms of retribution. If the survivors disclose, they are often made to feel as if they are causing the trouble in the family, especially in family systems that are in denial of the abuse.

Date Rape

Date rape is defined as a type of sexual assault in which the survivor and the perpetrator are, or have been, in some form of personal relationship (Russo, 2000). Although not a legal term, date rape is often used to describe sexual violence among adolescent and college-age populations (Lanier & Green, 2006). According to the U.S. Department of Justice (2014), women between ages 18 and 24 years experience the highest rate of rape and sexual assault victimizations compared to their counterparts in all other age groups. Date rape is often associated with victim blaming, which can include labeling the victim as a "tease" if she changes her mind and using the victims' attire or behaviors (e.g., voluntary use of alcohol and/or drugs) as a justification of the assault (Lanier & Green, 2006). Ultimately, victim blaming shifts the responsibility away from the perpetrator and to the victim. Such attitudes still exist in our society and often contribute to survivors feeling culpable for the violence perpetrated against them.

Adolescent girls and young adult women are most vulnerable to drug-facilitated sexual assaults, which are commonly associated with date rape. According to the U.S. Department of Health and Human Services' Office on Women's Health (OWH, 2012), the three most common date rape drugs are rohypnol, gamma hydroxybutyric (GHB), and ketamine because these particular drugs are often odorless and colorless and do not have a distinctive taste, rendering them easy to slip into a victim's beverage. The effects of these drugs, including loss of consciousness, confusion, loss of muscle control, memory loss, nausea, distorted perceptions of sight and sound, and impaired motor function, often exacerbate the devastation of the assault (OWH, 2012). Survivors often report being unaware of the attack until hours after the incident, and many times have little or no recall of the assault, contributing to lower rates of arrest and subsequent prosecutions.

Human Trafficking

Issues regarding human trafficking, also referred to as modern-day slavery, have gained a great deal of attention in society and within the counseling profession. The U.S. Department of Health and Human Services' Office on Trafficking in Persons (2012) defines human trafficking by utilizing a three-pronged criteria involving force, fraud, or coercion. Force refers to beatings, sexual violence, or confinement used to control individuals, especially during earlier stages of victimization, to establish power and control (Stotts & Ramey, 2009). Fraud involves the manipulation used to entice victims. For example, a promise of employment is used to gain access to women in economic need. Coercion refers to threats and psychological manipulations to which trafficking survivors are often subjected.

Debt bondage and threats to the survivor or to her family members are frequently used by perpetrators to maintain their position of power and control (Stotts & Ramey, 2009). Ultimately, human trafficking is a crime of vulnerability. Whether economic, emotional, or physical in nature, traffickers aim to exploit any vulnerability in women for their personal gain.

Sex Trafficking

The commercial sex trade is one of the most widespread forms of trafficking around the world (Hossain, Zimmerman, Abas, Light, & Watts, 2010). Although this form of trafficking occurs across a variety of settings, residential brothels, online forums, street prostitution, massage parlors, and strip clubs are among the most common (Stotts & Ramey, 2009). It is important to note that sex trafficking and prostitution are not synonymous. One way to conceptualize the difference is to ask who is profiting from the commercial sex act. Survivors of sex trafficking have to give all or most of their earnings to their trafficker (also known as pimp or madam), whereas those who engage in prostitution are not forced by a third party and keep the money earned by performing sexual acts (Hyde & DeLamater, 2014). It is also important to note that the term "child prostitute" is not accurate because it implies that the minor has consented to engage in prostitution. According to federal statutes (e.g., Trafficking Victims Protection Act [TVPA] of 2000, Preventing Sex Trafficking Act and Strengthening Families Act of 2014, and the Justice for Victims Trafficking Act of 2015), minors cannot consent to being exploited and therefore are victims of sex trafficking, not prostitutes (U.S. Department of Health and Human Services' Office on Trafficking in Persons, 2016). It is also important to recognize that many adult women who are viewed as "prostitutes" were actually sexually exploited minors who are still in the commercial sex trade.

Labor Trafficking

This form of trafficking involves use of violence, threats, lies, debt bondage, or other forms of coercion to force people to work against their will (Polaris Project, 2015b). Individuals trafficked for labor are made to work long hours, often under inhumane conditions, for little or no pay. Like sex trafficking, there are various settings in which labor trafficking can occur. Domestic work, construction, factory, and agriculture are milieus where individuals can be enticed and exploited with the promises of financial stability for themselves and their families. Other trends of labor trafficking include door-to-door sales crews, carnivals, and health and beauty services (Polaris Project, 2015b). This form of trafficking is not mutually exclusive from sex trafficking and can be difficult to detect.

GLOBAL VIOLENCE AGAINST WOMEN

Although each of the aforementioned forms of violence occurs within a global context, there are also culturally bound practices that are more prevalent in specific regions of the world. As the world continues to become smaller through technology, migration, and globalization of certain industries, counselors are encouraged to develop a global understanding of these issues.

Acid Throwing

The practice of acid throwing, in which women and girls are targeted by men and boys for refusing their advances, has been documented in several parts of Asia, the Middle East, and Africa (Chowdhury, 2005). Bhullar (2013) defines *acid throwing* (otherwise known as acid attack or *vitriolage*) as the "act of throwing acid or similarly corrosive substance onto the body of another with the intention to disfigure, maim, torture, or kill" (p. 60). Physiological effects of the acid include a loss of vision, body disfigurement (mostly on the face), and, if left long enough, deterioration of the bone (Bhullar, 2013). Women disfigured by acid are often ostracized and forced to depend on others for survival, since their injuries make it difficult for them to find work (Bhullar, 2013).

Honor Killing

Collectivist cultures tend to value welfare of groups (e.g., community, family) over an individual's well-being. For some cultural and religious groups, honor killings represent a preservation of a family's honor, or "*izzat*," which is a multidimensional construct that refers to honor and reputation that guides relationships in Hindu and Persian cultures (Dorjee, Baig, & Ting-Toomey, 2013). With this in mind, *honor killings* are defined as the "premeditated murder of a relative (usually a young woman) who has allegedly impugned the honor of her family" (Chesler & Bloom, 2012, p. 43). Dorjee et al. (2013) explain that the honor of the males is considered "dynamic" and able to change within a collectivistic cultural context. Female honor, however, is viewed as "static" and cannot be redeemed, hence honor killings are often associated with females who have been divorced, suspected of adultery, victims of rape, or in a relationship with someone whom the family does not approve of. Therefore, women who are perceived to have brought shame to the family are viewed as causing irreparable damage to the *izzat*. Honor killings are often the extreme manifestations of families' attempts to redeem their social status within the community (Dorjee et al., 2013).

Female Genital Mutilation

The cutting of female genitalia has been practiced for centuries among groups in Africa, Asia, and the Middle East (UNICEF, 2014b). Its origins are deeply rooted in historical, cultural, and religious traditions that are highly contested today (Baron & Denmark, 2006). Tremendous strides have been made to reduce this practice because it has been recognized as a violation of human rights and gender inequality. Not only do girls who undergo female genital mutilation (FGM) experience excruciating pain, but they are also at a higher risk for infertility, complicated child birth, chronic kidney and urinary infections, HIV, and even death (Baron & Denmark, 2006; UNICEF, 2014b). According to Mulongo, McAndrew, and Hollins Martin (2014), survivors of FGM are susceptible to depression, anxiety, posttraumatic stress disorder (PTSD), and low self-esteem and are at a greater risk of a mental illness. Despite the intense emotional and physical consequences of FGM, research findings suggest that girls who are uncircumcised often fear a loss of cultural identity and exclusion from their community (Baron & Denmark, 2006; Mulongo et al., 2014).

CLINICAL FOUNDATION

"Being able to come here and trust [the counseling process], I was able to open up and bring down walls that I've had my entire life. . . . Because I made that connection and I felt I could trust, that meant that I could be safe. You're not going to laugh at me or tell people what goes on here. I didn't think I had to keep everything inside. I could let it out. And that was empowering—talking about my fears, my insecurities, all the different abuse I went through. Just letting it out. And knowing that you're here to listen."—A 29-year-old Caucasian female client

This section is dedicated to providing counselors with a helpful and practical clinical framework for working with survivors of violence. We begin this section by discussing the three main foundational concepts for creating a therapeutic alliance with clients: safety, empowerment, and advocacy. As articulated in the preceding quotation, establishing safety and trust in a counseling relationship is essential to working with survivors of violence and facilitating their healing.

Safety

According to the Merriam-Webster online thesaurus ("Safety," n.d.), the antonyms of safety are "danger, exposure, and jeopardy," which are precisely what many survivors of violence have faced in their lives. The counseling relationship should, therefore, be one of safety. This aligns with Maslow's (1943) Hierarchy of Needs, which places safety as a primary requirement for fostering one's well-being and as a prerequisite for achieving greater self-actualization. The need for both psychological and physical safety is something that can be taken for granted. Sadly, for many survivors, the very places (i.e., their bedrooms, homes, schools, and communities) that are supposed to offer them a sense of safety and support have been sources of danger.

In creating a safe space with clients, counselors can ask their clients directly if they have any safety concerns. Doing so conveys counselors' sensitivity and respect to clients and helps to strengthen therapeutic relationships. Although counselors may not be able to control what happens outside of the counseling room, they can help clients critically and creatively think through their own need for safety. This skill is called safety planning (Waugh & Bonner, 2002) and is discussed in detail later in the chapter. Safety is not only crucial in the physical sense but emotionally as well (Foster & Hagedorn, 2014). For example, clients may feel safe in the counseling process and even with their abuser(s), but they may feel unsafe when they are alone. Some may be overcome by intrusive thoughts, feelings, and memories subsequent to a traumatic event, which can contribute to residual feelings of danger and fear. Therefore, conceptualizing safety in a comprehensive manner with each client can assist with establishing rapport, extending empathy, and establishing trust in the counseling process.

Empowerment

Empowerment is conceptualized as a complex and multidimensional process, as opposed to a one-dimensional, linear process (Chamberlin & Schene, 1997). It has become a keyword in public awareness campaigns and in the literature; however, a clear definition has yet to be constructed and agreed upon. One definition that we find helpful in understanding empowerment within a counseling relationship is "the active, iterative process of self-directed and goal-oriented accrual of individual and social agency" (Jefferson & Harkins, 2011, p. 105). Agency, in this context, refers to persons' ability to actively make and enact choices regarding their lives (Hoener, Stiles, Luke, & Gordon, 2012). Empowerment is crucial to grasp and practice when serving women who have experienced violence in their lives.

As previously discussed in this chapter, acts of violence are tools used by perpetrators to gain power and control over their victims by purposefully taking away their choices. A crucial part of the healing process is working side by side with survivors to explore their options and helping them make their own decisions, even if those decisions are different from what others see as the correct decision. Oftentimes, with good intentions, counselors and concerned people in survivors' lives may impose their decisions on survivors (e.g., "You *have* to leave your abusive boyfriend" or "If you really love your kids, you *should* leave this relationship") without recognizing that it disempowers survivors by undermining their ability to make decisions for themselves. Counselors can work *with* clients on identifying potential dangers and assist them in learning how to trust their ability to direct their lives. There may be dangers that are unknown to the counselors, even after a thorough assessment. It is important that clients are encouraged to follow their instincts in making decisions as they are the experts in their lives and know the nuances of risk that are present.

The decision to leave a violent situation can place the survivor at a higher risk for violence as the perpetrator attempts to maintain control in the relationship. This is a primary reason why counselors should check the urge to give directional advice to the client. To support survivors in having a sense of control over their own lives, counselors should actively help them identify their options, provide them with useful information so that they can make informed decisions, and create an appropriate space that respects their dignity. The concept of empowerment may sound simple and ordinary to counselors. Practically speaking, however, empowerment can be challenging for counselors to practice since it requires relinquishing their own power and supporting the client's. In other words, despite their years of training and expertise, counselors must truly acknowledge that they are not an expert on the client's life. Only the client is the expert on her own life. The role of the counselor, therefore, is to come alongside survivors in their pursuit of safety and healing.

Advocacy

Advocacy has become an integral part of counselors' professional identity. The advocacy competencies developed by Lewis, Arnold, House, and Toporek (2002) encompass both the micro- and macro-levels of advocacy within multiple contexts. The domains of advocacy competencies also distinguish "acting with" from "acting on behalf" of the client. Counselors work *with* clients to identify their personal strengths and resources, help them advocate for themselves, and support them in carrying out their plans. In this process, counselors may become aware of external barriers that impede clients and act on their behalf to increase access to services. This is an important distinction for counselors working with women and girls who have been victimized because each clinical setting will call for counselors to interact with various systems (e.g., child welfare, legal system, social services) to help clients empower themselves. Understanding the difference between "acting with" and "acting on behalf" can help establish appropriate boundaries and avoid the common clinical extremes of doing too much for the client (which can be enabling or disempowering) or doing nothing at all.

UNDERSTANDING CONTEXTS THAT IMPACT SURVIVORS OF VIOLENCE

Now that a clinical foundation of safety, empowerment, and advocacy has been established, we explore some of the practical, systemic considerations of working with this population. Each of the following systems can serve to empower or disempower clients and, therefore, are important to consider in the counseling process.

Family and Culture

Counseling women who have experienced violence does not occur in a vacuum but, rather, within several contexts that impact survivors in various ways. Family is one of the most intimate systems that influences one's view of the world. Women receive both implicit and explicit messages from their family about gender roles, boundaries, safety, and self-worth (Agoff, Herrera, & Castro, 2007; Collins, 1998). Unhealthy family dynamics can perpetuate a cycle of violence by exploiting vulnerable members of the family, silencing their voices, and denying the realities of abuse (Jewkes, 2002). Additionally, it is important to understand cultural values and beliefs that influence the function of individuals and families (Agoff et al., 2007; Collins, 1998).

Legal System

Decisions made in legal milieus often have a direct impact on survivors of violence. For example, many states' laws and policies regarding DV emphasize family reunification. This emphasis can deter the courts from considering the physical and emotional safety of women and children and serve to perpetuate the problem (Coy et al., 2015). Because the legal system was not founded on trauma-informed principles, court decisions can inadvertently disempower women and children. When working with survivors of violence, it is important for counselors to assess for any legal involvement (e.g., restraining orders, criminal or civil charges) because survivors may be unaware of their legal rights and experience confusion and frustration during legal proceedings. Although counselors do not provide legal advice to their clients, they can help clients empower themselves through learning about their legal rights and how to effectively navigate the system.

Immigration System

Although considered a part of the broader legal system, the immigration system has distinct nuances that deeply affect women who face violence. Many women emigrate because of violence in their home countries; however, undocumented survivors of violence often avoid seeking help out of fear of deportation (Kaltman et al., 2011). Additionally, some experience significant loss of their support system and cultural identity, which increases the sense of alienation (Edelson, Hokoda, & Ramos-Lira, 2007). There are federal and state statutes that protect undocumented women and children who experience violence. The Violence Against Women Act (VAWA) and the TVPA are excellent examples of such legislations. Many states allow for undocumented survivors of DV to obtain restraining orders and file criminal charges against perpetrators without being subjected to deportation. Educating undocumented survivors of their rights and protections under the law can minimize their fear and potentially increase safety. Moreover, a thorough assessment of clients' experiences with violence in their home country, during the migration process, and in their current country of residence is important in understanding their circumstances and offering appropriate services.

CLINICAL IMPLICATIONS

Now that we have reviewed historical, systemic, and clinical foundations, this section focuses on the actual phases of counseling, including prevention, intervention, and restoration. It is important to recognize that counseling women who have experienced violence can look different based on when the violence occurred.

Prevention

Many of the efforts to thwart violence against women have focused on supporting survivors postviolence and holding perpetrators accountable. Sadly, the goal of preventing the actual occurrence of violence remains elusive (Keating, 2015; Wolfe & Jaffe, 1999). Some prevention strategies that target women (e.g., self-defense courses) have been criticized for their tendency to assume women's responsibility to prevent violence from occurring or blaming them for acts of violence. This approach to prevention has also been challenged since it perpetuates a one-dimensional solution to gender-based violence (Frazier & Falmagne, 2014). As such, there has been an increase in prevention strategies that challenge gender norms and notions of masculinity that normalize men's misuse of power in relationships (Frazier & Falmagne, 2014; Lapsansky & Chatterjee, 2013). Counselors can implement a variety of creative prevention strategies based on their clinical setting and the identified needs of clients and communities that they serve.

Intervention

A number of interventions can take place to effectively support survivors of violence. If the violence is recent or ongoing, safety becomes the primary clinical concern. Safety planning is an intervention often used in DV counseling to assess for risk and to plan for the individual's safety in case of future acts of violence (Waugh & Bonner, 2002). In this process, the client is considered the expert of his or her situation, and the clinician's role is to explore available options with the client, as well as provide unbiased support. A safety plan should be as comprehensive as possible, taking into account the survivor's physical, emotional, and financial safety (Waugh & Bonner, 2002).

In addition to developing an individualized safety plan, it is important for the counselor to assess for symptoms of trauma. In order to better understand the symptomology of trauma survivors, counselors are encouraged to refer to the fifth edition of the *Diagnostic and Statistical Manual of Mental Disorders (DSM-5)*, which contains revisions to stress-related diagnoses (American Psychiatric Association [APA], 2013). Common trauma symptoms include *intrusion symptoms* (e.g., nightmares, flashbacks), *avoidance symptoms* (e.g., persistent avoidance of trauma-related thoughts, feelings, or external reminders), *negative alterations in cognitions and mood* (e.g., inability to recall details related to trauma, negative beliefs about the self and the world), and *alterations in arousal and reactivity* (e.g., aggressive behavior, hypervigilance, exaggerated startle response, sleep disturbance; APA, 2013). Assessing for the presence, intensity, and frequency of these symptoms is a vital part of the counseling process. Throughout the assessment of safety and trauma symptoms, it is important to normalize survivors' experiences and provide psychoeducation. Many survivors often feel "crazy" and do not recognize that their symptoms are normal reactions to abnormal situations. Once a thorough assessment has been completed, there are a myriad of treatment approaches that are considered to be effective in working with survivors of trauma. The following options are not an exhaustive list, but are meant to provide a foundational understanding of what is recommended in the literature and used in clinical practice.

Animal-Assisted Therapy

The therapeutic use of the bond between humans and animals has been an effective approach in working with trauma survivors. Animal-assisted therapy relies on the nonjudgmental, reflective nature of animals to help clients reduce physiological stress and increase self-awareness (Geist, 2011). Experiencing gentle contact with animals promotes a sense of safety, trust, and acceptance within the therapeutic environment, which is conducive to working with trauma survivors (Dietz, Davis, & Pennings, 2012). The use of trained therapy animals, such as dogs and horses, is not viewed as a stand-alone treatment option but rather is used to bolster existing therapeutic approaches (Geist, 2011).

Eye Movement Desensitization and Reprocessing (EMDR)

Eye movement desensitization and reprocessing (EMDR) has gained momentum in recent years as an evidence-based treatment for survivors of trauma. According to Shapiro (1995), EMDR is "an interactive, intrapsychic, cognitive, behavioral, body-oriented therapy" that rapidly processes the trauma of the past (pp. 52–53). This approach consists of an eight-phase treatment approach coupled with protocols for specific issues, such as anxiety, pain, posttraumatic stress, and grief. The eight phases involve (a) obtaining a thorough client history and creation of treatment plan; (b) preparing the client for using EMDR; (c) assessing the target issue components to be addressed; (d) desensitizing the target material with eye movements or an alternate form of stimulation; (e) installing the desired positive cognition; (f) conducting a body scan to determine if any effects from the target issue remain; (g) closure; and (h) reevaluation (Shapiro, 1995). Although the atypical use of eye movement and claims of rapid improvement with trauma survivors has generated some controversy within the field, research suggests that EMDR could be a viable treatment option for female survivors of trauma (Diehle, Opmeer, Boer, Mannarino, & Lindauer, 2015; Edmond & Rubin, 2004).

Trauma-Focused Cognitive Behavioral Therapy (TF-CBT)

Trauma-focused cognitive behavioral therapy (TF-CBT) is one of the most researched therapeutic approaches (Diehle et al., 2015). This approach is commonly used with traumatized youth and consists of the three distinct phases: an initial coping skills-building phase (stabilization phase); a trauma narrative and processing phase; and a final phase of consolidation and closure (integration phase; Murray, Cohen, Ellis, & Mannarino, 2008). TF-CBT includes a wide range of practical strategies for regulating distress, including distraction, mindfulness, perceptual bias modification, self-awareness skills, and cognitive coping skills (Cohen, Mannarino, Kliethermes, & Murray, 2012). The therapeutic relationship plays a pivotal role throughout the treatment phases as it models to clients a predictable, consistent, and safe relationship that is essential to their healing and restoration.

Sensory Approaches and Mindfulness

When trauma occurs, it can cause a disconnection from oneself and normal bodily sensations and thoughts can become fragmented and distorted. As a result, there has been increased attention in the field on the use of sensory-based techniques, which provide practical and effective ways of self-regulating emotional and physiological arousal (Scanlan & Novak, 2015). Encouraging survivors to engage in soothing multisensory experiences (i.e., sight, smell, taste, touch, and hearing) has been highlighted as noninvasive, self-directed, and empowering (Scanlan & Novak, 2015). Likewise, mindfulness encourages clients to engage in nonjudgmental, present-moment awareness of their minds and bodies (Goodman & Calderon, 2012). By increasing their self-awareness, survivors can acquire a sense of control, develop internal resources for symptom reduction, and promote meaning making (Goodman & Calderon, 2012). Both sensory approaches and mindfulness techniques are geared toward maintaining the client in the present and should be used in conjunction with other treatment approaches.

It is important to reiterate that there are a myriad of clinical interventions that have not been detailed in this chapter. Counselors and counselors-in-training are encouraged to stay abreast of research pertaining to current, best-practice treatment approaches.

Restoration

Restoration refers to engaging in "reparative behaviors and a recommitment to the values damaged by the offense" (Cornish & Wade, 2015, p. 98). One way that the literature has conceptualized the restoration process is through *posttraumatic growth*. The concept of posttraumatic growth is one of hope for both the counselor and the client. Tedeschi and Calhoun (2004) define posttraumatic growth as the "positive psychological change that results from engaging in the struggle associated with traumatic or highly challenging circumstances" (p. 1). Tedeschi and Calhoun identify three areas of growth that survivors can experience in this phase of their healing: changes in self-perception, interpersonal relationships, and life philosophy. The restoration phase of the counseling process usually occurs when a client feels relatively safe, but is still struggling with the ongoing effects of the violence she experienced in her daily life. When survivors are able to achieve a sense of safety and stability, some may realize that the emotional impact of their trauma has yet to be processed. Survivors in this stage often express frustration saying things like, "I should be over this by now." Counselors can help to normalize such feelings and assess if clients are ready to delve into deeply seated emotions and thoughts related to the trauma. If the client is willing to do so, the restoration process can be likened to picking up the pieces of their shattered self. Although the restoration process can be complicated and expose a client's vulnerability, it is also rewarding for her as she begins to develop a positive sense of self.

COMPASSION FATIGUE, BURNOUT, AND VICARIOUS TRAUMA

The current American Counseling Association's *Code of Ethics* (ACA, 2014) specifies that counselors must ". . . monitor themselves for signs of impairment from their own physical, mental, or emotional problems and refrain from offering or providing professional services when impaired" (p. 9). Without precautions, counselors can be psychologically harmed by trauma work (Hernández, Engstrom, & Gangsei, 2010). As such, the literature concerning the impact of trauma on counselors is growing. Theoretical terms such as vicarious trauma, compassion fatigue, and professional burnout are often used interchangeably to describe how working with trauma survivors impacts counselors. However, each of these terms has distinctions that are important to recognize.

Vicarious trauma is defined as "the transformation that occurs within the therapist (or other trauma worker) as a result of empathic engagement with clients' trauma experiences and their sequelae" (Pearlman & Mac Ian, 1995, p. 558). This experience may mirror the client's responses to trauma and often can be characterized by feeling unsafe, a reduced sense of self, less interest in others, a negative worldview, and increased negative affect (Newell & MacNeil, 2010; Sansbury, Graves, & Scott, 2015). Although vicarious traumatization interferes with the counselor's emotions and cognitive schemas, memories, and/or sense of safety, it is important to note that these symptoms are not considered pathological in either the counselor or the client (Hernández et al., 2010) because they are understood as normal reactions to traumatic events.

Compassion fatigue differs from vicarious traumatization in that it more generally describes counselors' overall experience of their emotional and physical fatigue, resulting from the long-term use of empathy. It does not necessitate direct interactions with traumatized clients (Newell & MacNeil, 2010; Sansbury et al., 2015) and is often found in combination with many of the "bureaucratic hurdles," such as billing, administrative work, and other work-related stressors (Newell & MacNeil, 2010, p. 61). Compassion fatigue is not limited to counselors who do trauma work and takes into account other factors involved in the ongoing need to be empathetic (Hernández et al., 2010).

Professional burnout is defined as a "gradual and progressive process that occurs when work-related stress results in emotional exhaustion, an inability to depersonalize client experiences, and a decreased sense of accomplishment" (Sansbury et al., 2015, p. 115). Professional burnout is similar to compassion fatigue in that it does not require direct contact with clients; however, burnout develops over time, whereas compassion fatigue and vicarious traumatization can have a sudden onset.

Survivors' stories of violence can affect counselors deeply. There seems to be consensus among scholars that ongoing self-care is necessary for counselors to be effective and fully present to clients, to avoid professional impairment, and maintain professional boundaries (Wicks & Buck, 2014; Williams, Richardson, Moore, Gambrel, & Keeling, 2010). Some techniques suggested by the literature include engaging in alone time, exercise, mindfulness, meditation, autohypnosis, music, and spirituality (Wicks & Buck, 2014; Williams et al., 2010). Self-care in a professional context could include supervision, manageable client caseloads, peer consultation, and a supportive work environment. Although personal and professional self-care can be difficult to incorporate consistently, they are an integral part of maintaining balance, career longevity, and compassion.

Just as vicarious trauma can affect counselors negatively, the reverse is also possible. Vicarious posttraumatic growth, or vicarious resilience, posits that counselors can be positively affected by witnessing the trauma of their clients (Barrington & Shakespeare-Finch, 2013; Hernández et al., 2010). Counselors have reported gains in relationship skills, an appreciation for the resilience of people, satisfaction from observing growth and healing, and enriched self-understanding as a result of working with those who have experienced violence. The research on this phenomenon is limited but seems promising (Barrington & Shakespeare-Finch, 2013; Tedeschi & Calhoun, 2004). By implementing self-care strategies, counselors can help to facilitate their own vicarious posttraumatic growth and resilience.

VOICES FROM THE FRONTLINES

Throughout the chapter, we have noted how survivors should be considered the experts of their own lives. In closing, we thought it would be appropriate and helpful to conclude this chapter with the voices of women who have survived violence in their lives. Giving women a forum to voice their experiences is especially important as they have often been silenced, either by the perpetrator, the shame, the fear, or other causes. The first author obtained consent from several of her clients to share with readers their responses to the questions that follow. The women have each sought counseling for issues of domestic and/or sexual violence.

What Is One Thing That You Want a New Counselor to Know About Working With Survivors of Violence?

"The most important thing is to find a way to get them to tell their story. Gain that trust and tell their story. Because you bring it out of the dark and into light and that's what really changed everything for me. Once I told it in group, it just took so much of that power of the guilt, the shame, and the pain. And I think that's the most important thing—telling one's story. And in order to do that, there's got to be trust. Trust is taken away when one is sexually abused as a child. And then you just go through life not trusting for many reasons. But I was so ashamed and scared to tell that dirty little secret that I didn't trust anyone to believe me, to feel compassion. So once I gained trust with certain people I was able to finally tell my story."—A 29-year-old Caucasian female

How Has Culture Impacted Your Healing Process?

"The beliefs from my family that divorce is not an option. That was a big impact. And that we had to stick it out. They say work it out, but it really is stick it out. Because it's not workable, but you have to stay in the relationship, which is hard. But it's not only culturally, but because we are so religious, you know, time has changed, but their mentality and tradition haven't. So even though I made a decision to leave, I had to get permission from the priest to finalize it. That was something pushed on me by my parents. So basically, if I didn't get that permission, I would have had to go back again. It wasn't going to be acceptable. It has such an impact because it makes it harder to make a better decision at that point."—A 40-year-old Latina female

How Did You Know It Was Time to Begin the Counseling Process?

"Going through the same stages with different individuals. They had the same characteristics as my ex who I dated on and off for 16 years. And my friendships, everything. They all had abusive characteristics in them or everything that I did not want. Whether it was a friendship or a boyfriend, I just did not want any of that so I felt it was time to bring it all out in order to process it, get through it, and overcome it."—A 27-year-old African American female

All of these survivors experienced horrific acts of violence in their lives. Their stories are filled with violations of trust and boundaries that are difficult to grasp. Yet, each of these survivors represents hope, both for counselors and future clients. May their voices inform and inspire our work.

CALL TO ACTION

Although the extent to which people engage in advocacy and social justice work varies widely, each action taken individually and together can contribute to promoting stronger and more unified voices of women across the life span. Such efforts include but are not limited to: (a) educating the public on how violence affects girls and women (e.g., prevalence of various forms of violence, long-term effects of sexual abuse on girls, social media and its influence on gender-based violence); (b) working with local legislators to address systemic barriers that perpetuate a cycle of violence against women; (c) coordinating sexual assault prevention programs that encourage men to take a more active role in ending violence; and (d) creating a safe platform through which survivors can share their stories to connect with one another.

Several resources are provided at the end of this chapter to assist counselors in developing a specific plan of action to advocate for this population, including Polaris Project for survivors of human trafficking and National Network to End Domestic Violence (NNEDV), an organization that, among its various projects to empower survivors of DV, alerts advocates on relevant legislative actions. Additionally, we provided statements from a few survivors of violence to emphasize the importance of giving undivided attention to each woman's voice in her struggle and healing, which is the foundation to any clinical, social justice, and advocacy work.

REFLECTION AND DISCUSSION QUESTIONS

1. What assumptions do you have about survivors of violence? How might these assumptions nurture or hinder your work with this population?
2. Safety, empowerment, and advocacy were discussed as essential components of the clinical foundation that are helpful in working with this population. What are some ways that you would implement these concepts into your work with this population?
3. Processing traumatic incidents can be overwhelming for both the client and the counselor. Discuss your ideas for helping clients to effectively process their intense emotions and thoughts associated with trauma.
4. Working with this population can affect a counselor on multiple levels. Discuss in a small group what self-care strategies will help you manage the impact of this work.

HELPFUL RESOURCES

Books

- Courtois, C. A. (2014). *It's not you, it's what happened to you: Complex trauma and treatment.* Telemachus Press.
- Davis, L. (1990). *The courage to heal workbook: A guide for women and men survivors of child sexual abuse.* New York: HarperCollins.
- Dorkenoo, E. (1994). *Cutting the rose: Female genital mutilation: The practice and its prevention.* London, UK: Minority Rights Group.
- Herman, J. (1997). *Trauma and recovery: The aftermath of violence—from domestic abuse to political terror.* New York, NY: Basic Books.
- Herman, J. L., & Hirschman, L. (1981). *Father-daughter incest.* Cambridge, MA: Harvard University Press.
- Jones, A., & Schecter, S. (1992). *What to do when loves goes wrong: What to do when you can't do anything right: Strategies for women with controlling partners.* New York, NY: HarperCollins.
- Lloyd, R. (2011). *Girls like us: Fighting for a world where girls are not for sale, an activist finds her calling and heals herself.* New York, NY: HarperCollins.
- Van der Kolk, B. A. (2014). *The body keeps the score: Brain, mind, and body in the healing of trauma.* New York, NY: Viking.
- Zambrano, M. M. (1985). *Mejor sola que mal acompañada: Para la mujer golpeada.* Seattle, WA: Seal Press.

Professional Websites and Organizations

- Amnesty International USA | Protect Human Rights (www.amnestyusa.org)
- Futures Without Violence (www.futureswithoutviolence.org)
- GEMS (Girl Educational & Mentoring Services; www.gems-girls.org)
- National Network to End Domestic Violence (NNEDV; www.nnedv.org)
- Polaris Project (www.polarisproject.org)
- V-Day: A Global Movement to End Violence against Women and Girls (www.vday.org)

ENDNOTES

1. Line drawing of a red-figure *chous.* Metropolitan Museum of Art, 37.11.19; c. 450 BCE.

2. Domestic Abuse Intervention Project 202, East Superior Street Duluth, MN 55802, 218-722-2781 (www.theduluthmodel.org)

REFERENCES

Agoff, C., Herrera, C., & Castro, R. (2007). The weakness of family ties and their perpetu-ating effects on gender violence. *Violence Against Women, 13*(11), 1206–1220. doi: 10.1177/1077801207307800.

American Counseling Association. (2014). *ACA code of ethics.* Alexandria, VA: Author.

American Psychiatric Association. (2013). *Diagnostic and statistical manual of mental disor-ders* (5th ed.). Arlington, VA: American Psychiatric Publishing.

Atwood, J. D. (2007). When love hurts: Preadolescent girls' reports of incest. *American Jour-nal of Family Therapy, 35,* 287–313. doi:10.1080/01926180701389644

Ballantine, M. W. (2012). Sibling incest dynamics: Therapeutic themes and clinical chal-lenges. *Clinical Social Work, 40,* 56–65. doi:10.1007/s10615-011-0331-8

Baron, E. M., & Denmark, F. L. (2006). An exploration of female genital mutilation. *Annals of the New York Academy of Sciences, 1087*(1), 339–355. doi:10.1196/annals.1385.018

Barrington, A. J., & Shakespeare-Finch, J. (2013). Working with refugee survivors of tor-ture and trauma: An opportunity for vicarious post-traumatic growth. *Counselling Psychology Quarterly, 26,* 89–105. doi:10.1080/09515070.2012.727553

Bhullar, D. S. (2013). Acid throwing: A cause of concern. *Journal of Punjab Academy of Foren-sic Medicine and Toxicology, 13*(2), 60–62.

Campbell, J. C., Webster, D., Koziol-McLain, J., Block, C., Campbell, D., Curry, M. A., . . . Laughon, K. (2003). Risk factors for femicide in abusive relationships: Results from a multisite case control study. *American Journal of Public Health, 93,* 1089–1097. doi:10.2105/ ajph.93.7.1089

Chamberlin, J., & Schene, A. H. (1997). A working definition of empowerment. *Psychiatric Rehabilitation Journal, 20*(4), 43–46.

Chesler, P., & Bloom, N. (2012). Hindu vs. Muslim honor killings. *Middle East Quarterly, 19*(3), 43–52.

Chowdhury, E. H. (2005). Feminist negotiations: Contesting narratives of the campaign against acid violence in Bangladesh. *Meridians, 6*(1), 163–192. doi:10.2979/mer.2005.6 .1.163

Cohen, D. K., Green, A. H., & Wood, E. J. (2013). Special report: Wartime sexual violence: Misconceptions, implications, and ways forward. Retrieved from http://www.usip .org/sites/default/files/resources/SR323.pdf

Cohen, J. A., Mannarino, A. P., Kliethermes, M., & Murray, L. A. (2012). Trauma-focused CBT for youth with complex trauma. *Child Abuse and Neglect, 36*(6), 528–541. doi:10 .1016/j.chiabu.2012.03.007

Collins, P. H. (1998). It's all in the family: Intersections of gender, race, and nation. *Hypatia, 13,* 62–82. doi:10.1111/j.1527-2001.1998.tb01370.x

Cornish, M. A., & Wade, N. G. (2015). A therapeutic model of self-forgiveness with inter-vention strategies for counselors. *Journal of Counseling and Development, 93,* 96–104. doi:10.1002/j.1556-6676.2015.00185.x

Coy, M., Scott, E., Tweedale, R., & Perks, K. (2015). "It's like going through the abuse again": Domestic violence and women and children's (un)safety in private law contact proceedings. *Journal of Social Welfare and Family Law, 37,* 53–69. doi:10.1080/09649069.2 015.1004863

Diehle, J., Opmeer, B., Boer, F., Mannarino, A., & Lindauer, R. (2015). Trauma-focused cognitive behavioral therapy or eye movement desensitization and reprocessing: What works in children with posttraumatic stress symptoms? A randomized controlled trial. *European Child and Adolescent Psychiatry, 24,* 227–236. doi:10.1007/s00787-014-0572-5

Dietz, T. J., Davis, D., & Pennings, J. (2012). Evaluating animal-assisted therapy in group treatment for child sexual abuse. *Journal of Child Sexual Abuse, 21,* 665–683. doi:10.1080/ 10538712.2012.726700

Dorjee, T., Baig, N., & Ting-Toomey, S. (2013). A social ecological perspective on understanding "honor killing": An intercultural moral dilemma. *Journal of Intercultural Communication Research, 42*(1), 1–21. doi:10.1080/17475759.2012.723024

Edelson, M. G., Hokoda, A., & Ramos-Lira, L. (2007). Differences in effects of domestic violence between Latina and non-Latina women. *Journal of Family Violence, 22,* 1–10. doi:10.1007/s10896-006-9051-1

Edmond, T., & Rubin, A. (2004). Assessing the long-term effects of EMDR: Results from an 18-month follow-up study with adult female survivors of CSA. *Journal of Child Sexual Abuse, 13,* 69–86. doi:10.1300/j070v13n01_04

Foster, J. M., & Hagedorn, W. B. (2014). A qualitative exploration of fear and safety with child victims of sexual abuse. *Journal of Mental Health Counseling, 36,* 243–262. doi:10.17744/mehc.36.3.0160307501879217

Fox, V. C. (2002). Historical perspective on violence against women. *Journal of International Women's Studies, 4,* 15–34.

Frazier, K. E., & Falmagne, R. J. (2014). Empowered victims? Women's contradictory positions in the discourse of violence prevention. *Feminism and Psychology, 24,* 479–499. doi:10.1177/0959353514552036

Geist, T. (2011). Conceptual framework in animal assisted therapy. *Child and Adolescent Social Work Journal, 28,* 243–256. doi:10.1007/s10560-011-0231-3

Goodman, R. D., & Calderon, A. M. (2012). The use of mindfulness in trauma counseling. *Journal of Mental Health Counseling, 34,* 254–268. doi:10.17744/mehc.34.3.930020422 n168322

Herman, J. (1997). *Trauma and recovery: The aftermath of violence—from domestic abuse to political terror.* New York, NY: Basic Books.

Hernández, P., Engstrom, D., & Gangsei, D. (2010). Exploring the impact of trauma on therapists: Vicarious resilience and related concepts in training. *Journal of Systemic Therapies, 29,* 67–83. doi:10.1521/jsyt.2010.29.1.67

Hoener, C., Stiles, W. B., Luka, B. J., & Gordon, R. A. (2012). Client experiences of agency in therapy. *Person-Centered and Experiential Psychotherapies, 11,* 64–82. doi:10.1080/147797 57.2011.639460

Hossain, M., Zimmerman, C., Abas, M., Light, M., & Watts, C. (2010). The relationship of trauma to mental disorders among trafficked and sexually exploited girls and women. *American Journal of Public Health, 100,* 2442–2449. doi:10.2105/ajph.2009.173229

Hyde, J. S., & DeLamater, J. D. (2014). *Understanding human sexuality* (12th ed.). New York, NY: McGraw-Hill.

International Labour Office. (2012). ILO global estimate of forced labour: Results and methodology. Retrieved from http://apflnet.ilo.org/resources/ilo-global-estimate-of -forced-labour-2012-results-and-methodology/at_download/file1

Jefferson, D. J., & Harkins D. A. (2011). "Hey, I've got a voice too!" Narratives of adversity, growth and empowerment. *Journal for Social Action in Counseling and Psychology, 3*(2), 103–127. doi:10.1037/e506052012-287

Jewkes, R. (2002). Intimate partner violence: Causes and prevention. *Lancet, 359,* 1423–1429. doi:10.1016/s0140-6736(02)08357-5

Johnson, B. C. (2012). Aftercare for survivors of human trafficking. *Social Work and Christianity, 39*(4), 370–389.

Jordan, J. (2013). From victim to survivor—and from survivor to victim: Reconceptualizing the survivor journey. *Sexual Abuse in Australia and New Zealand, 5*(2), 48–56.

Kaltman, S., Hurtado de Mendoza, A., Gonzales, F. A., Serrano, A., & Guarnaccia, P. J. (2011). Contextualizing the trauma experiences of women immigrants from Central American, South America, and Mexico. *Journal of Traumatic Stress, 24*(6), 635–642. doi:10.1002/jts.20698

Keating, B. (2015). Violence against women: A disciplinary debate and challenge. *The Sociological Quarterly, 56,* 108–124. doi:10.1111/tsq.12075

Lanier, C. A., & Green, B. A. (2006). Principal component analysis of the College Date Rape Attitude Survey (CDRAS): An instrument for the evaluation of date rape prevention programs. *Journal of Aggression, Maltreatment and Trauma, 13,* 79–93. doi:10.1300/j146v 13n02_06

Lansing, C. (2006). Crime and criminals. In M. Schaus (Ed.), *Women and gender in medieval Europe: An encyclopedia* (Vol. 14, p. 180). New York, NY: Routledge.

Lapsansky, C., & Chatterjee, J. S. (2013). Masculinity matters: Using entertainment education to engage men in ending violence against women in India. *Critical Arts Projects, 27*(1), 36–55. doi:10.1080/02560046.2013.766972

Lewis, J. A., Arnold, M. S., House, R., & Toporek, R. L. (2002). ACA advocacy competencies. Retrieved from http://www.counseling.org/knowledge-center/competencies

Llewellyn-Jones, L. (2011). Domestic abuse and violence against women in ancient Greece. In S. Lambert (Ed.), *Sociable man: Essays on ancient Greek social behaviour in honour of Nick Fisher* (p. 231). Swansea, UK: Classical Press of Wales.

Maslow, A. H. (1943). A theory of human motivation. *Psychological Review, 50,* 370–396. doi:10.1037/11305-004

Mulongo, P., McAndrew, S., & Hollins Martin, C. (2014). Crossing borders: Discussing the evidence relating to the mental health needs of women exposed to female genital mutilation. *International Journal of Mental Health Nursing, 23,* 296–305. doi:10.1111/ inm.12060

Munro, P. (2014). Wartime rape: Waging wars through women's bodies. *Undercurrent, 10*(3), 50–52.

Murray, L. K., Cohen, J. A., Ellis, B. H., & Mannarino, A. (2008). Cognitive behavioral therapy for symptoms of trauma and traumatic grief in refugee youth. *Child and Adolescent Psychiatric Clinics of North America, 17,* 585–604. doi:10.1016/j.chc.2008.02.003

National Sexual Violence Resource Center. (2015). Statistics about sexual violence. Retrieved from http://www.nsvrc.org/sites/default/files/publications_nsvrc_factsheet_media -packet_statistics-about-sexual-violence_0.pdf

Newell, J. M., & MacNeil, G. A. (2010). Professional burnout, vicarious trauma, secondary trauma stress and compassion fatigue: A review of theoretical terms, risk factors, and preventative methods for clinicians and researchers. *Best Practices in Mental Health, 6*(2), 57–68.

Nosek, M. A., Foley, C. C., Hughes, R. B., & Howland, C. A. (2001). Vulnerabilities for abuse among women with disabilities. *Sexuality and Disability, 19*, 177–189.

Olatunji, C. P. (2013). An argument for gender equality in Africa. *CLCWeb: Comparative Literature and Culture, 15*(1), 1–8. doi:10.7771/1481-4374.2176

Pearlman, L. A., & Mac Ian, P. S. (1995). Vicarious traumatization: An empirical study of the effects of trauma work on trauma therapists. *Professional Psychology: Research and Practice, 26*, 558–565. doi:10.1037/0735-7028.26.6.558

Polaris Project. (2015a). Human trafficking issue brief: Safe harbor. Retrieved from https:// polarisproject.org/sites/default/files/2015%20Safe%20Harbor%20Issue%20Brief.pdf

Polaris Project. (2015b). Labor trafficking in the U.S. Retrieved from http://www.polaris project.org/human-trafficking/labor-trafficking-in-the-us

Russo, L. (2000). Date rape: A hidden crime. *Trends and Issues in Crime and Criminal Justice/ Australian Institute of Criminology, 157*, 1–6.

Safety [Def. 1]. (n.d.). In *Merriam-Webster's online thesaurus*. Retrieved from http://www .merriam-webster.com/thesaurus/safety

Sansbury, B. S., Graves, K., & Scott, W. (2015). Managing traumatic stress responses among clinicians: Individual and organizational tools for self-care. *Trauma, 17*, 114–122. doi:10.1177/1460408614551978

Sawyer, C., Peters, M. L., & Willis, J. (2013). Self-efficacy of beginning counselors to coun- sel clients in crisis. *Journal for Counselor Preparation and Supervision, 5*(2), 30–43. doi: 10.7729/52.1015

Scanlan, J. N., & Novak, T. (2015). Sensory approaches in mental health: A scoping review. *Australian Occupational Therapy Journal, 62*, 277–285. doi:10.1111/1440-1630.12224

Shapiro, F. (1995). *Eye movement desensitization and reprocessing: Basic principles, protocols, and procedures.* New York, NY: Guilford Press.

Stotts, E. L., & Ramey, L. (2009). Human trafficking: A call for counselor awareness and action. *Journal of Humanistic Counseling, Education and Development, 48*, 36–47. doi: 10.1002/j.2161-1939.2009.tb00066.x

Tedeschi, R. G., & Calhoun, L. G. (2004). Posttraumatic growth: Conceptual foundations and empirical evidence. *Psychological Inquiry, 15*, 1–18. doi:10.1207/s15327965pli1501_01

Thureau, S., Le Blanc-Louvry, I., Thureau, S., Gricourt, C., & Proust, B. (2015). Original communication: Conjugal violence: A comparison of violence against men by women and women by men. *Journal of Forensic and Legal Medicine, 31*, 42–46. doi:10.1016/j.jflm .2014.12.014

United Nations. (1993). Declaration on the elimination of violence against women. Retrieved from http://www.un.org/documents/ga/res/48/a48r104.htm

United Nations. (2006). Ending violence against women: From words to action. Study of the Secretary-General: Executive summary. Retrieved from http://www.un.org/womenwatch/daw/vaw/launch/english/v.a.w-exeE-use.pdf

United Nations Children's Fund. (2014a). *Ending child marriage: Progress and prospects.* New York, NY: Author.

United Nations Children's Fund. (2014b). *Female genital mutilation/cutting: What might the future hold?* New York, NY: Author.

United Nations Office on Drugs and Crime. (2013). Global study on homicide 2013: Trends, contexts, data. Retrieved from http://www.unodc.org/documents/gsh/pdfs/2014_GLOBAL_HOMICIDE_BOOK_web.pdf

Uribe-Urán, V. M. (2013). Physical violence against wives and the law in the Spanish American world, 1820s–2000s. *Bulletin of Latin American Research, 32,* 49–80. doi:10.1111/blar.12107

U.S. Department of Health and Human Services, Office on Trafficking in Persons. (2012). Fact sheet: Human trafficking. Retrieved from http://www.acf.hhs.gov/programs/endtrafficking/resource/fact-sheet-human-trafficking

U.S. Department of Health and Human Services, Office on Trafficking in Persons. (2016). Fact sheet: Assistance for child victims of human trafficking. Retrieved from http://www.acf.hhs.gov/endtrafficking/resource/eligibilityfs

U.S. Department of Health and Human Services, Office on Women's Health. (2012). Date rape drugs fact sheet. Retrieved from http://www.womenshealth.gov/publications/our-publications/fact-sheet/date-rape-drugs.html

U.S. Department of Justice. (2014). *Special report: Rape and sexual assault victimization among college-age females, 1995–2013.* Retrieved from http://www.bjs.gov/content/pub/pdf/rsavcaf9513.pdf

U.S. Department of Labor, Bureau of Labor Statistics. (2011). Women in the labor force: A databook. Retrieved from https://www.bls.gov/cps/wlf-databook-2011.pdf

Vilenica, S., Shakespeare-Finch, J., & Obst, P. (2013). Exploring the process of meaning making in healing and growth after childhood sexual assault: A case study approach. *Counselling Psychology Quarterly, 26,* 39–54. doi:10.1080/09515070.2012.728074

Waugh, F., & Bonner, M. (2002). Domestic violence and child protection: Issues in safety planning. *Child Abuse Review, 11,* 282–295. doi:10.1002/car.758

Wicks, R. J., & Buck, T. C. (2014). "Alonetime": Recovering a rich classical resource for counselor self-renewal. *Journal of Mental Health Counseling, 36,* 288–301. doi:10.17744/mehc.36.4.yj86250233132831

Williams, I. D., Richardson, T. A., Moore, D. D., Gambrel, L. E., & Keeling, M. L. (2010). Perspectives on self-care. *Journal of Creativity in Mental Health, 5,* 321–338. doi:10.1080/15401383.2010.507700

Wolfe, D. A., & Jaffe, P. G. (1999). Emerging strategies in the prevention of domestic violence. *The Future of Children, 9*(3), 133–144. doi:10.2307/1602787

World Health Organization. (2013). Global and regional estimates on violence against women: Prevalence and health effects of intimate partner violence and non-partner sexual violence. Retrieved from http://apps.who.int/iris/bitstream/10665/85239/1/9789241564625_eng.pdf

CHAPTER 10

Educational and Work Environments

Amy D. Zavadil

LEARNING OBJECTIVES

After reading this chapter, you will be able to:

1. Recognize U.S. civil rights legislation and regulations that encourage equity for women and girls.
2. Understand cultural and organizational factors that may influence risks, resilience, and progress.
3. Identify resources to assist individuals who experience harassment or discrimination in education or the workplace.

LEARNING AND WORKING ENVIRONMENTS

Civil rights laws (Title IX and Title VII, among others) in the United States have existed for decades to ensure girls and women can learn and work in environments free from discrimination and harassment. Yet persisting harassment in both school and work settings continues to create hostile environments. Empowering girls and women, and those who interact with them, to recognize and respond to behaviors and structures that contribute to the creation of hostile environments is essential to shifting cultural norms that permit or perpetuate harassment and discrimination. Though progress has been made, women's access to education and work remains as a human rights initiative globally (Bellitto, 2015; Goldin, 2006; Porter, 2016).

This chapter describes the prevalence of school and workplace harassment; provides a brief introduction to applicable law; highlights the impact of harassment on individuals; and introduces promising practices in counseling, prevention, and advocacy contributing to cultural shifts.

Prevalence of Sexual Harassment

Although there is a greater range of opportunities for women today, with some variation among cultures, women are socialized with inequities and power differentials that favor males over females, starting at a very young age. According to Hill and Silva (2005), two thirds of college students report that they and/or their friends have been sexually harassed on campus and at least half know someone who has been sexually assaulted. More than half of women indicate experiencing sexual harassment in the workplace (Holland & Cortina, 2016). Though this may vary depending upon the definitions and methodology used in research, it is frequently reported that approximately one in four women experience an attempted or completed sexual assault before graduating college (American Association of University Women [AAUW], 2001; Birdeau, Somers, & Lenihan, 2005; Bursik & Gefter, 2011; Fisher, Cullen, & Turner, 2000; Hill & Silva, 2005; White House Council on Women & Girls, 2014). Lesbian, gay, bisexual, and transgender (LGBT) students experience sexual or gender-based harassment at even higher rates than other students (Hill & Silva, 2005; Katz-Wise & Hyde, 2012; Krebs, Lindquist, Berzofsky, Shook-Sa, & Peterson, 2016; Rankin, Weber, Blumenfeld, & Frazer, 2010). LGBT students also have a greater likelihood of being the target of homophobic comments or derogatory remarks (D'Augelli, 1992; Rankin et al., 2010).

Research related to workplace sexual harassment in the 1980s and 1990s focused primarily on quid pro quo (this for that) harassment, such as promise of a pay increase in exchange for sex. Although this type of harassment still exists, since the 1990s the conceptualization of harassment has shifted to acknowledge structural and societal influences and behavior that create, what is considered in civil rights enforcement, a hostile environment. An early conceptualization of sexual harassment was Fitzgerald et al.'s (1988) three-part model of harassing categories that are distinct yet related. This includes gender harassment, including verbal or physical behaviors based on gender or gender stereotype; unwanted sexual attention, including unwelcome or inappropriate sexual advances (e.g., suggestive remarks, repeated attempts to date, unwanted touching); and sexual coercion, including subtle or explicit conditions tied to sexual behavior (Fitzgerald et al., 1988). From this model, the Sexual Experiences Questionnaire (SEQ; Fitzgerald et al., 1988) was developed and this three-part construction has been used extensively to measure and assess prevalence of sexual harassment in a variety of work and education settings.

Women, particularly of multiple marginalized identities, experience harassment in different ways. Women of color and LGBT women report intertwined experiences of harassment that may be difficult to identify whether the incident was sexist, racist, or homophobic in nature (Berdahl & Moore, 2006; Combs & Milosevic, 2016; Konik & Cortina, 2008; Pope et al., 2004; Yoon, Funk, & Kropf, 2010). This suggests the necessity of recognizing the intersectionality of experiences of sexual harassment; that is, women who also are sexual or racial minorities (or have a disability, or are of a religious minority) are likely experiencing multiple or compounded effects of harassment. One example of this is described in the following quotation (as published in Combs & Milosevic, 2016, p. 22):

"I take pride in being a Black woman. Sadly, others don't always understand or accept all that I bring to the workplace. . . . Unfortunately, I am treated sometimes in a manner that is inappropriate, but I am not able to pinpoint it to my gender or race."—A Black female professional

Though some research has begun to look at how women of color (Combs & Milosevic, 2016; Yoon et al., 2010), lesbian women (Tomlinson & Fassinger, 2003), and women of other marginalized identities experience harassment in different ways, there is need for continued work to better understand the impact of their experiences. Pope et al. (2004) expressed the importance of counselors recognizing that discrimination is "a fact of life in U.S. society" (p. 165). It is important that counselors explore with clients their individual experiences of harassment and recognize the potential for multiple or intertwined forms of oppression. It is necessary to understand that individuals are impacted not only by experiences of harassment or discrimination, but also by their perceived potential for discrimination in the school or workplace; these factors influence individuals' decision making and development as well as experience of climate or culture (ALGBTIC LGBQQIA Competencies Taskforce et al., 2013; Badgett, Sears, Lau, & Ho, 2009; Chung, 2003; Combs & Milosevic, 2016; D'Augelli, 1992; Katz-Wise & Hyde, 2012; Parnell, Lease, & Green, 2012; Pope et al., 2004; Sigal & Jacobsen, 1999; Tomlinson & Fassinger, 2003). Consider, for example, the complex relationship of developmental impacts. Where an individual is in her own identity formation can influence her experience or perception of harassment. A supportive climate, or absence of harassment, can support healthy development. Conversely, experiences of harassment and bullying can also influence future behavior as a perpetrator or victim of future harassment (Miller et al., 2013). This is an area ripe for further research to better understand how identity development, work or campus climate, and experience of harassment influence individuals at different ages and stages of life.

In schools, on campuses, and in the workplace, bullying, a form of interpersonal harassment that may or may not be gender motivated, is also prevalent. Bullying includes behaviors that demean or target an individual without targeting a particular characteristic (such as gender, sexual orientation, or other protected status). Increasingly, such behavior is prohibited by organizational policy even if not based on a civil rights-based protection, such as gender or racial discrimination and harassment. It is estimated that in the United States, 30% to 60% of employees experience some form of workplace bullying (Fitzpatrick et al., 2011). Almost a quarter of school- and college-age students report being bullied during the academic year (Lund & Ross, 2016; U.S. Department of Education, National Center for Education Statistics [NCES], 2015).

Impact of Harassment

There is not one explanation of how experiences of harassment, including sexual assault, impact an individual. There are a multitude of influences that can serve to exacerbate or minimize the adverse impact of harassment. Generally speaking, experiences of harassment tend to be underreported, can result in negative impact on work or academic performance and satisfaction, and may include adverse physical and mental health implications. The majority of individuals who experience sexual harassment in both work and educational settings report significant emotional distress as a result of the experience (Charney & Russell, 1994; Combs & Milosevic, 2016; Hill & Silva, 2005; Holland & Cortina, 2016; Katz-Wise & Hyde, 2012; Kitzrow, 2003; Yoon et al., 2010). Female students are more likely to experience disruption of education than male students (Hill & Silva, 2005). Similarly, workplace harassment can have economic impacts on the victim and organizations through absenteeism, employee turnover, and legal expenses (Campbell, Dworkin, & Cabral, 2009; Gutek & Koss, 1993; Neall & Tuckey, 2014; Yoon et al., 2010). Sexual and gender-based harassment and other bullying behaviors are not individual issues; they are experiences influenced by social and cultural interactions, can have cumulative effects of experience over time, and warrant a multifaceted response that attends to individual, institutional, and community factors.

Legislation and Policy

Understanding that there are laws and policies that exist to support women's equity can be empowering and can encourage advocacy and change. Since the Civil Rights Act of 1964 in the United States, there have been a growing number of federal legal protections enacted to address gender equity and sexual and gender-based harassment. It is also important to note that laws and regulations evolve over time and are open to interpretation, as they are influenced by case law. Today, women have increased access to education and work opportunities, yet still report experience of hostile environments and other harassment in schools and workplaces at greater rates than men (Boudet, Petesch, Turk, & Thumala, 2013; Goldin, 2006; National Coalition for Women and Girls in Education [NCWGE], 2012). Legislation and related regulations or guidance expect educational and work environments free from discrimination and harassment and require that workplaces and schools provide policy and procedure to address concerns of discrimination or harassment.

Workplace Civil Rights Legislation

In the 1970s, the federal court began to consider legal arguments related to sexual harassment in the workplace under sex discrimination or violation of Title VII of the Civil Rights Act of 1964 (Berring & Chan, 2014). This nondiscrimination legislation prohibits discrimination based on race, color, religion, sex, and national origin (Civil Rights Act, 1964). The interpretation and application of these protections, in practice, continue to evolve. In 1978, Title VII was amended to also prohibit discrimination based on pregnancy (Civil Rights Act, 1964). It took an additional decade for the court to recognize sexual harassment and unwanted sexual behavior in the workplace as creating a hostile environment in violation of Title VII. It was in 1986 that the U.S. Supreme Court, in *Meritor Savings Bank v. Vinson* (1986), found two types of sexual harassment prohibited by Title VII: "Harassment that involves the conditioning of concrete employment benefits on sexual favors, and harassment that, while not affecting economic benefits, creates a hostile or offensive working environment" (as quoted in Berring & Chan, 2014, p. 5). Thus began the distinction of quid pro quo (this for that) harassment and hostile environment harassment—both covered protections of Title VII. It took much effort, advocacy, and activism for the courts to recognize sexual harassment in the workplace as discriminatory and warranting legal protections (Holland & Cortina, 2016; Siegel, 2004).

In the 1980s, the shift toward recognizing hostile environment harassment began to be recognized by the law. This initiated a transition from recognizing harassment as only that which is sexual in nature, to acknowledging that behavior that is sexist, sexualized, or gendered in nature can be discriminatory and in violation of Title VII civil rights law (Holland & Cortina, 2016). Efforts to address sexual harassment and gender equity in the workplace and beyond are still ongoing. Counselors can assist a client who discloses experience of harassment or discrimination at work through exploring available response options within the workplace, such as locating procedures for reporting, discussing concerns, or seeking resolution. For some, seeing policies that state prohibited behavior can be validating to their experience and provide options to consider.

Organizational culture influences the policies and practices related to discrimination and the protections afforded in a given field of work or specific workplace. Workplace policies dictate organizational mechanisms that respond to allegations of harassment and typically include options to resolve matters through informal means prior to pursuing a disciplinary response. Although informal resolution may have benefits, it is also important to support informed decision making, particularly for those who may be unaware of their legal rights in regard to employer policy (Edelman, Erlanger, & Lande, 1993). Also, organizational norms and power differentials in the workplace can make it difficult for lower level employees to fully understand and act on their legal rights. Although the existence of workplace policies prohibiting sex or gender discrimination is widely recognized in workplaces as an obligation of the law, social or organizational norms may present a barrier to reporting violations. In addition, the civil legal process to hold an employer liable for workplace harassment, via U.S. Equal Employment Opportunity Commission enforcement (the government agency that enforces employment discrimination laws), indicates that employers are not held liable if they make effort to prevent or remediate harassment (e.g., have a procedure to address reports of harassment) and the target of harassment did not use corrective mechanisms, such as reporting through the available grievance procedures (Holland & Cortina, 2016). A client can benefit from a counselor's assistance in exploring the impact of harassing or discriminatory experience and the related decision making that is available, and may be otherwise overwhelming to navigate.

There are additional legal protections that can be helpful in addressing workplace concerns. Legislation (e.g., Americans with Disabilities Act of 1990) and guidance from the U.S. Equal Employment Opportunity Commission also provide protections from discrimination or harassment related to pregnancy and disabilities. Pregnant women, new parents, or individuals with recognized disabilities may be entitled to additional rights of approved leave afforded under the Family Medical Leave Act (FMLA). Being aware of rights can serve to empower an individual to recognize and seek out options to address problematic behavior in the workplace and to support access in the workplace. Organizations, however, may fail to promote these rights and workplace norms may discourage workers from claiming such rights (Albiston, 2005). Counselors can encourage a client to review his or her workplace policies and benefits as part of exploring options to address workplace challenges (Rostosky & Riggle, 2002). In the United States, societally structured meanings of "work" and "being a good worker" have had an impact on women as a gender in the workplace, as well as on men who wish to participate in family caregiving. Pressure to conform to traditional social and gender norms can come not only from employers and workplace policies but also from coworkers with fixed beliefs about work and gender roles (Albiston, 2005). This can be further complicated for those in same-sex relationships. Counselors can offer a confidential space in which clients can process concerns, fears, and questions that arise when navigating institutional structures and choosing to advocate for themselves or others.

Civil Rights in Education Settings

In educational settings in the United States, Title IX of the Education Amendments of 1972 (Title IX), which applies to all schools that receive federal funding, affords similar protections that Title VII offers in the workplace and prohibits discrimination based on sex in education and related programs. Title IX has evolved over more than four decades since it passed into law to ensure equal opportunity in education for all students. The NCWGE published a chronology of Title IX protections in celebration of 40 years since the passing of the law (NCWGE, 2012). It was emphasized that Title IX is not about entitlement for women, but rather is and has been about achieving gender equity in education. Title IX protects students against sex-based harassment and discrimination, including gender stereotyping; prohibits sex discrimination in employment and education programs; requires equity in school athletic opportunities; mandates equity in technical and career programs; promotes equity and access for women in science, technology, engineering, and math (STEM) education; provides protection for pregnant and parenting students; and requires schools to have a Title IX coordinator to oversee compliance and equitable campus procedures related to sexual and gender-based discrimination, including sexual violence (NCWGE, 2012).

In 2001, the U.S. Department of Education, Office for Civil Rights (OCR, the government agency that enforces Title IX compliance) issued a revised sexual harassment guide reviewing policy and response to sexual and gender-based harassment in school settings. This document outlined compliance expectations and provided a framework for evaluating hostile environment harassment. Guidance letters (legal regulation guidance referred to as Dear Colleague Letters or DCLs) from the OCR also outlined expectations of due process rights in public school disciplinary proceedings and clarified that Title IX protects against harassment, but does not impede First Amendment free speech protections (U.S. Department of Education, OCR, 2003). The OCR periodically releases and posts on the website of the U.S. Department of Education guidance documents, or DCLs, to respond to current issues of gender equity in education (www2.ed.gov/about/offices/list/ocr/frontpage/faq/rr/policyguidance/sex.html). In April 2011, the OCR issued a DCL that focused on campus sexual assault, prompting a flurry of response in the legal system, as well as institutional response and student activism over the years since its release. The 2011 DCL stated that sexual violence is a form of sex discrimination prohibited by Title IX and described specific obligations of an educational institution to respond to student-on-student sexual harassment, including sexual assault. Follow-up response included the January 2014 establishment of the White House Task Force to Protect Students from Sexual Assault (2014), which issued a report in April of 2014 summarizing the state of sexual violence on college campuses. This led to the creation of www.notalone.gov, a website designed to centralize access to information about campus sexual violence and provide resources to support schools' response to sexual violence. A question and answer document was released by the U.S. Department of Education, Office for Civil Rights in 2014 to further explain the protections of Title IX and related expectations of educational institutions (OCR, 2014). In May 2016, a DCL was issued to confirm that schools should "treat a student's gender identity as the student's sex" (OCR, 2016, p. 2) in application of Title IX. The numerous responses in recent years from the White House and U.S. Department of Education signal a growing understanding of the complexity of gender, the ongoing importance of attending to issues of harassment to achieve gender equity in education, as well as raising concerns about progress, or lack of progress, in this area. Counselors can support their clients who are students (and their parents, as applicable) in navigating options to address harassment that may be interfering with academic progress or other access to education programs. In many instances, a student can seek assistance from his or her school, such as extended deadlines or adjustments to his or her schedule, when an experience of sexual violence is interfering with access to education. Increasingly, students are aware of their rights, learning about advocacy and activism from social media (see www.knowyourix.org), and demanding attention to gender equity.

"I would like to see institutions admitting the issue exists, instead of increasing the silencing of survivors."—Sophomore undergraduate student activist

"We need to heal what's broken, and see systematic justice. . . . All of us being able to participate [in education] and feel safe."—Recent graduate, sexual assault survivor, anti-sexual violence activist

Legislation to Fight Violence Against Women

The Violence Against Women Act (VAWA, 2013), which has also evolved in the years since inception, has undertaken the enforcement of existing laws protecting women's right in the workplace and education, promoted education for police and other first responders, and improved services for victims of violence. Originally passed in 1994, VAWA has been reauthorized in 2000, 2005, and 2013, with each iteration building upon lessons learned through the work of support services afforded through VAWA funding. The Federal Office on Violence Against Women (OVW) was created in 1995 to oversee implementation of programs and funding, as well as compliance with the regulations of VAWA. Runge (2013) described the evolution of VAWA as a necessary response to women's experience of higher rates of criminal victimization, including sexual assault, domestic violence (DV), dating violence, and stalking. The progression of VAWA is a chronicle of the increasing attention to the impact of gender-based violence on women's access to education, work, and economic progress.

VAWA was the first major law to address sexual assault and DV specifically, while seeking to address training and response related to these crimes. Runge (2013) provided a clear explanation of the evolution of VAWA (detailed later), which was informed by field reports from responders who benefited from VAWA grant funding. The reauthorization of 2000 expanded the types of violations covered to include dating violence, elder abuse, and DV of people with disabilities. Following the first 5 years of VAWA, it was recognized that intimate partner violence occurred between individuals in dating relationships not covered by DV law. Next came increased support to rape crisis centers and recognition of special populations, such as elders and those with disabilities, as warranting additional understanding and specialized response. The reauthorization of 2005 expanded the training focus to include health care professionals who serve victims of violence. There was also an addition of housing assistance and nondiscrimination in housing practices, which were included to remove barriers many women faced in attempting to leave violent relationships. The reauthorization of 2013 recognized additional populations warranting attention, including immigrants, tribal populations (Indian/Alaskan Native tribes), and victims in higher education settings (campus sexual violence). Runge (2013) also noted the importance of ongoing assessment and advocacy for victims of all types of sexual violence. As the complex issue of sexual violence and traumatic response continues to be better understood, what is being learned by activists, counselors, and other helping professionals can inform the evolution of VAWA and other legislation, policy, and practices.

It is also noteworthy to consider the evolution of our understanding of the forms and impact of sexual violence in the 20 years since VAWA has been enacted. It took the passing of VAWA to gain federal recognition that sexual assault is not perpetrated solely by strangers. In fact, research indicates that the majority of sexual assaults are committed by someone known to the victim (Krebs, Lindquist, Warner, Fisher, & Martin, 2007; Runge, 2013). A federal definition of dating violence was not established until the 2000 reauthorization of VAWA. The criminal (Uniform Crime Reporting) definition of rape, which emphasized consent and omitted the need for force to be present to constitute rape, was not amended until 2012. Consent is now a key point of discussion in campus sexual violence education and response. There has been increasing understanding of sexual assault and related protections for women over time, yet much still remains to be done. Counselors can contribute to these efforts through support of their individual clients as well as seeking opportunities to contribute to the prevention efforts across all grades of school, encouraging the use of trauma-informed practices when working with individuals who experience harassment or assault and advocating for ongoing attention to creating communities that support civility and non-discrimination efforts.

In addition to federal legislation and guidance documents, most states and localities have human rights and civil rights legislation that supports or enhances protections against discrimination, such as organization-level policies that prohibit discrimination in education and in the workplace. Potential for growth remains, such as enhancing accessibility of public and private employers' non-discrimination policies and domestic partner benefits, as well as the continuing need for ongoing advocacy (Chung, 2003). Although legal protections are evolving and policies against discrimination and harassment are common and communicated in schools and workplaces, staff training regarding appropriate behavior is less consistent across settings. Even with well-known institutional policy in place, if coming forward is not encouraged, women tend to create plans to avoid or cope with existing harassment rather than use policy to seek support in addressing their concerns. In some cases, women even alter their career choices (Marshal, Dalyot, & Galloway, 2014). Counselors who are aware of or seek information about current legislation can offer support to clients who are making decisions, coping with harassment, and considering options for self-advocating. Counselors can also engage in advocacy more broadly, maintaining awareness of gender equity protections afforded at state and federal levels.

Additional Factors Influencing Gender Equity

Finally, it is important to consider other cultural beliefs, practices, and norms that influence women's experience of and response to sexual harassment and/or violence. Religious practices and beliefs may serve as empowerment and support for some individuals, but can also present significant barriers (Porter, 2016). Some interpretations of religious texts such as the Bible or the Qur'an have been used to reinforce gender-role norms or support violence (Fortune, Abugideiri, & Dratch, 2010). In the Orthodox Jewish faith, religious law has been used to reinforce power and control in DV, as a man must agree to grant his wife a "get" (divorce document in Jewish law) to permit her to divorce. Individuals of all religious faiths can be impacted by sexual and/or intimate partner violence; the traumatic experience is complex and one's faith can provide support or increase shame (Fortune et al., 2010; Jayasundara, Nedegaard, Sharma, & Flanagan, 2014). Many faith traditions include strongly held beliefs about the sanctity of marriage that can increase shame or doubt for victims of abuse, whether these beliefs are internalized or imposed. Fortunately, there is an increasing effort to address sexual and DV (e.g., FaithTrust Institute, a national, multifaith training and educational organization [www.faithtrustinstitute.org]), reduce the barriers to leaving abusive relationships, and increase the strength and support for victims within religious communities (Fortune et al., 2010). It is important that counselors remain open to how a client may speak about his or her religious or spiritual beliefs. Such beliefs may be useful resources; however, they should not serve as justification for violence.

GLOBAL PERSPECTIVES OF GENDER EQUITY

Outside the United States, women's rights continue to lag, as reported by the United Nations (Nmehielle & Madhava Menon, 2014) and the World Bank (Boudet et al., 2013). Around the world, the rights and status of women vary and gender gaps exist in the types of work and pay available to women. Legal and societal frameworks that deny rights based on gender, gender identity, and sexual orientation stigmatize individuals, create adverse impacts on health and well-being, and contribute to or create hostile environments (Holland & Cortina, 2016; Nmehielle & Madhava Menon, 2014; World Health Organization, 2013). Worldwide, approximately 35% of women experience sexual violence (World Health Organization, 2013).

Globally, access to education and employment remains a human right that is not consistently available to women and girls. The Millennium Development Goals of the World Bank have made progress in girls' access to education globally, but cultural norms and other social barriers make for ongoing power differentials for women worldwide (Bellitto, 2015). Laws prohibiting gender discrimination do exist outside the United States, but with only varying degrees of successful implementation. Although countries such as the United States and Norway have minimal gender gaps in education, in other parts of the world, girls and women have little or no access to education (Sen & Mukherjee, 2014). Cultural barriers and lack of monitoring or enforcement hinder progress (Bellitto, 2015; Boudet et al., 2013; Holland & Cortina, 2016; Nmehielle & Madhava Menon, 2014). In some Central and South American countries, for example, there has been success in providing incentives for families who allow access to secondary education to girls, though cultural barriers remain in those countries where social norms expect a girls' role to be marriage (Bellitto, 2015).

STRUCTURAL INTERVENTIONS

Legal policy is but one necessary contribution to addressing the complex process of achieving gender equity. Institutional and structural attentions are needed to support access to education and employment. These may include revising hiring practices, such as using "blind review" of applicant information to reduce bias, training and development for teachers and administrators, and ongoing assessment to monitor progress (Marshall et al., 2014; Porter, 2016; Wylie, Jakobsen, & Fosado, 2007). In the workplace and in school settings, there is a growing trend to create inclusive community climates by offering employee resource groups or affinity groups, gathering around a common interest, such as gender equity, or identity within an organization, so as to establish networks of support and belonging (Combs & Milosevic, 2016). Setting clear community expectations through easily accessible policies and providing training to community members in work and educational settings are essential to increasing understanding and creating a culture of equity.

PREVENTION EDUCATION

With the passing of the 2013 Violence Against Women Reauthorization Act (S.47, 2013, VAWA), colleges and universities are legally required to provide training related to sexual violence, including educating students to recognize adverse behaviors, raising awareness of policy and procedure, and training campus members in bystander intervention skills. Prevention education must explicitly discuss how women and men are socialized differently, with different knowledge, attitudes, and experiences that inform their beliefs (Banyard, 2014; Fonow, Richardson, & Wemmerus, 1992).

McMahon and Banyard (2012) provide a framework for prevention of sexual violence through bystander intervention—a promising community prevention practice. Bystander intervention is also useful for addressing bullying, hazing, and harm reduction related to alcohol and substance use. Based on prosocial behavior and encouraging community members to see their role in intervening to prevent or stop adverse behavior, bystander intervention research identifies five steps for effective bystanders. These are notice the event; interpret observed behavior as problematic; recognize personal responsibility to act; know what to do; and take action. Bystander intervention can be direct or indirect (Bell, 2008; McMahon & Banyard, 2012) and is useful in primary prevention (intervening at the harassment level), secondary prevention (interrupting sexual harassment or sexual violence), and tertiary prevention (stepping in to respond after harassment has occurred or upon receiving disclosure of sexual assault; McMahon & Banyard, 2012). Bystander intervention skills can be taught through group prevention education workshops as well as discussed one-on-one, whether in a counseling setting or when advising others who seek guidance regarding how to support a friend. Bystander intervention is a community approach to prevention that focuses on the adverse behavior, thus avoiding victim blaming. It empowers individuals to own a personal role in shifting culture regarding gender norms, empathy, and community expectations that do not condone sexually aggressive behavior (Lewis-Arévalo & Seto, 2014).

COUNSELING IMPLICATIONS

One third to one half of students report knowing someone who has experienced sexual harassment and/or assault (Hill & Silva, 2005; McMahon, 2010). A vast majority of students report some personal experience with harassing behaviors (Hill & Silva, 2005) and a majority of women indicate having experienced sexual harassment in the workplace (Holland & Cortina, 2016). Counselors and other helping professionals are in a position to assist persons navigating an experience of discrimination, harassment, and/or assault. When an individual discloses an experience of sexual assault, how the disclosure is received sends important messages to the individual and can influence future help seeking (Campbell et al., 2009; Harvey, 1996). Knowledge of protections of law, policy, and support services that exist in educational and work environments can empower clients who are beginning to process their experience of harassment and are considering how to respond. Counselors can support clients on their path to healing by supporting informed decision making, working together to identify the range of potential barriers to reporting and help seeking, as well as recognizing resilience and protective factors that are unique to each individual.

Exploring Options and Barriers

For clients who have experienced harassment in the past, counselors may wish to explore these experiences and review coping skills. Clients experiencing school or workplace harassment or discrimination may benefit from assistance in understanding reporting options, available resources, and deciding how to proceed. In educational settings, individuals who experience sex discrimination (including sexual violence) are due remedies (OCR, 2001), which may include academic accommodations, such as deadline extensions, or adjustments to campus-related housing or work. Campus or community advocates may be helpful in navigating available procedures for seeking accommodations to support continued access to education.

To provide sufficient support in career decision making and workplace discrimination, it is increasingly important for counselors to be familiar with concepts of workplace bullying. Such bullying may be related to discrimination or a protected status, but may also be mistreatment that cannot be clearly attributed to a specific motivation (Fitzpatrick et al., 2011). It is important to understand that when a person experiences harassment or discrimination, regardless of nature or intent, it can impact career and personal well-being. Acknowledging potential barriers, such as campus or workplace climate, bullying, harassment, or discrimination, is an essential step toward building confidence and self-efficacy to create opportunities rather than focusing on limitations (Lindley, 2005; McWhirter, 1997). It is important to validate a client's experience, to counteract the tendency to engage in self-blame, as well as the tendency of others and society to engage in blaming the victim (Campbell et al., 2009). Counselors may assist a client in processing his or her experience and in considering available response options. It is essential to recognize that although laws and procedures may be available, these processes can be time-consuming and emotionally taxing even when carried out effectively. Empowering a client to make informed choices and encouraging ongoing use of support and advocacy are critical.

Self-Care

Ethical feminist practice includes attention to self-care and seeking consultation (Enns, 1993). Literature related to the impact on counselors helping individuals who have experienced gender-based discrimination, including sexual violence, is growing. For example, there is potential for vicarious trauma or secondary traumatization for counselors working with issues of sexual violence (Killian, 2008; Trippany, Kress, & Wilcoxon, 2004; Way, VanDeusen, Martin, Applegate, & Jandle, 2004). Also impacted are those engaged in prevention education, advocacy, and activism and who are facilitating discussion of sexual harassment and violence. In addition, the potential for vicarious trauma may be greater for peers and peer facilitators who support or receive disclosure from sexual assault survivors (Branch & Richards, 2013) and who may not have developed the coping skills or self-awareness necessary to independently reduce adverse impact.

Anger arising from their work in sexual violence treatment and prevention can motivate counselors and counselors-in-training, advocates, and prevention educators to persevere in their efforts toward ending gender-based violence (Wasco & Campbell, 2002). Similarly, learning to verbalize anger and other emotions can help individuals develop coping skills, which are valuable both personally and professionally (Enns, 1993). For those who are engaged in advocacy, activism, and prevention, discussing the dissonance that is experienced when their own beliefs are challenged while they work to educate others and shift culture can aid in coping and solidifying personal meaning of and commitment to their efforts. Engaging in reflection and dialogue with others can empower individuals to develop and be true to their internal voice of self-authorship and to support personal development and healing (Pizzolato, Nguyen, Johnston, & Wang, 2012). Sharing with fellow advocates and educators the emotions related to the experience of working with survivors, and brainstorming skills and possible responses, can bring relief to those involved in this difficult work.

CONCLUSION

The legal landscape in the United States is constantly evolving, with much activity in recent years in the areas of gender-based and sexual harassment, particularly in the workplace and education settings. As demonstrated by the evolution of the VAWA, ongoing assessment of needs and practices is essential, along with continued education regarding gender inclusivity. Gender equity efforts are a part of the global human rights discussion. Access to education and employment has improved, yet much progress remains to be realized. Counselors and counselor educators can contribute to social change and cultural shift by continuing to educate ourselves and others, and advocating on personal and community levels.

CALL TO ACTION

The work toward gender equity worldwide in education and work settings is very much a work in progress. The World Bank (Bellitto, 2015; Boudet et al., 2013) and the United Nations (Sen & Mukherjee, 2014) make clear that gender equity and women's empowerment is an essential human right with wide ranging benefits to health and wellness. Counselor advocacy, at local, state, federal, and international levels, is critical to supporting gender equity efforts. It is incumbent upon each of us to continue to learn more about promoting gender equity in our own activities, within our immediate community, and abroad. Action can include self-awareness through ongoing education, showing up for others who host events to promote equity, and supporting and participating in professional organizations and associations that advocate for

(continued)

CALL TO ACTION (continued)

gender equity. Maintaining awareness of existing rights and advocating for accountability to supportive and inclusive law, policy, and practice are important to empowering women toward mental health, resilience, and personal and professional success.

REFLECTION AND DISCUSSION QUESTIONS

1. What surprised you about the law, policy, and legislative progress described in this chapter?
2. In what ways have you experienced work or campus climates that felt either empowering or discriminatory toward women?
3. How do you think experience of harassment might influence individuals' development or decision making at different ages and stages of life? In different settings?
4. What have you read about Title IX, campus, or workplace gender harassment in mass media or social media? Does the media portrayal align with your own experiences?

HELPFUL RESOURCES

Federal Legislation, Guidance, and Policy Information

- Clery Center for Security on Campus (www.clerycenter.org/current-legislation)
- National Women's Law Center (www.nwlc.org)
- U.S. Department of Education, Office for Civil Rights (OCR) know your rights (www2.ed.gov/about/offices/list/ocr/know.html)
- U.S. Department of Education, OCR policy publications (www2.ed.gov/about/offices/list/ocr/publications.html)
- U.S. Department of Justice, Civil Rights division (www.justice.gov/crt/publications)
- U.S. Department of Justice, Office on Violence Against Women (www.justice.gov/ovw/selected-publications)
- U.S. Equal Employment Opportunity Commission (www.eeoc.gov/laws/statutes/titlevii.cfm)
- U.S. Equal Employment Opportunity Commission, enforcement guidance (www.eeoc.gov/laws/guidance/enforcement_guidance.cfm)
- U.S. State Bullying Law & Policy (www.stopbullying.gov/laws)

- White House Council on Women and Girls (www.whitehouse.gov/administra tion/eop/cwg)
- White House Task Force, Not Alone (www.notalone.gov; www.whitehouse .gov/1is2many/notalone)

Global Initiatives

- The World Bank, Millennium Development Goals (www.worldbank.org/mdgs)
- United Nations Population Fund (www.unfpa.org/gender-equality)

Advocacy and Prevention

- Faith Trust Institute (www.faithtrustinstitute.org)
- National Resource Center on Domestic Violence (www.nrcdv.org)
- Rape, Abuse, and Incest National Network (RAINN; www.rainn.org)
- Stalking Resource Center (www.victimsofcrime.org/our-programs/stalking -resource-center)
- Zonta International, empowering women through service and advocacy (www .zonta.org)

REFERENCES

Albiston, C. (2005). Bargaining in the shadow of social institutions: Competing discourses and social change in workplace mobilization of civil rights. *Law & Society Review*, *39*(1), 11–50.

ALGBTIC LGBQQIA Competencies Taskforce, Harper, A., Finnerty, P., Martinez, M., Brace, A., Crethar, H., . . . Hammer, T. (2013). Association for Lesbian, Gay, Bisexual, and Transgender Issues in Counseling Competencies for Counseling with Lesbian, Gay, Bisexual, Queer, Questioning, Intersex, and Ally Individuals. *Journal of LGBT Issues in Counseling*, *7*, 1, 2–43. doi:10.1080/15538605.2013.755444

American Association of University Women. (2001). *Hostile hallways: The AAUW survey on sexual harassment in America's schools* (Research Report No. 923012). Washington, DC: Harris/Scholastic Research. Retrieved from http://files.eric.ed.gov/fulltext/ED4541 32.pdf

Badgett, M., Sears, B., Lau, H., & Ho, D. (2009). Bias in the workplace: Consistent evidence of sexual orientation and gender identity discrimination 1998–2008. *Chicago-Kent Law Review*, *84*, 559–595. Retrieved from https://escholarship.org/uc/item/5h3731xr

Banyard, V. (2014). Improving college campus–based prevention of violence against women: A strategic plan for research built on multipronged practices and policies. *Trauma, Violence, and Abuse*, *15*(4), 339–351. doi:10.1177/1524838014521027

Bell, B. (2008). *Step up! Be a leader, make a difference: Prosocial behavior/bystander intervention program for students, facilitator guide*. Tucson: University of Arizona.

Bellitto, M. (2015). The World Bank, capabilities, and human rights: A new vision for girls' education beyond 2015. *Florida Journal of International Law, 27*, 91–119.

Berdahl, J., & Moore, C. (2006). Workplace harassment: Double jeopardy for minority women. *Journal of Applied Psychology, 91*(2), 426–436. doi:10.1037/0021-9010.91.2.426

Berring, R., & Chan, A. (2014). *Women and sexual harassment: A practical guide to the legal protections of Title VII and the hostile environment claim.* Binghamton, NY: Routledge.

Birdeau, D. R., Somers, C. L., & Lenihan, G. O. (2005). Effects of educational strategies on college students' identification of sexual harassment. *Education, 125*(3), 496–510. Retrieved from https://www.questia.com/library/p5118/education

Boudet, A. M. M., Petesch, P., Turk, C., & Thumala, A. (2013). *On norms and agency: Conversations about gender equality with women and men in 20 countries.* Washington, DC: World Bank. doi:10.1596/978-0-8213-9862-3

Branch, K. A., & Richards, T. N. (2013). The effects of receiving a rape disclosure: College friends' stories. *Violence Against Women, 19*(5), 658–670.

Bursik, K., & Gefter, J. (2011). Still stable after all these years: Perceptions of sexual harassment in academic contexts. *Journal of Social Psychology, 151*(3), 331. doi:10.1080/00224 541003628081

Campbell, R., Dworkin, E., & Cabral, G. (2009). An ecological model of the impact of sexual assault on women's mental health. *Trauma, Violence, and Abuse, 10*(3), 225–246. doi:10.1177/1524838009334456

Charney, D., & Russell, R. (1994). An overview of sexual harassment. *American Journal of Psychiatry, 151*(1), 10–17. doi:10.1176/ajp.151.1.10

Chung, Y. B. (2003). Career counseling with lesbian, gay, bisexual, and transgendered persons: The next decade. *The Career Development Quarterly, 52*(1), 78–86. doi:10.1002/j.21610045.2003.tb00630.x

Civil Rights Act of 1964 § 7, 42 U.S.C. §2000e et seq. (1964). Retrieved from http://www.eeoc.gov/laws/statutes/titlevii.cfm

Combs, G. M., & Milosevic, I. (2016). Workplace discrimination and the wellbeing of minority women: Overview, prospects, and implications. In M. L. Connerley & J. Wu (Eds.), *Handbook on well-being of working women* (pp. 17–31). Dordrecht, The Netherlands: Springer. doi:10.1007/978-94-017-9897-6

D'Augelli, A. (1992). Lesbian and gay male undergraduates' experiences of harassment and fear on campus. *Journal of Interpersonal Violence, 7*(3), 383–395. doi:10.1177/0886260 92007003007

Edelman, L., Erlanger, H., & Lande, J. (1993). Internal dispute resolution: The transformation of civil rights in the workplace. *Law and Society Review, 27*, 497–534. doi:10.2307/3054103

Enns, C. Z. (1993). Twenty years of feminist counseling and therapy from naming biases to implementing multifaceted practice. *The Counseling Psychologist, 21*(1), 3–87. doi:10.1177/0011000093211001

Fisher, B., Cullen, F., & Turner, M. (2000). *The sexual victimization of college women.* Washington, DC: U.S. Dept. of Justice, Office of Justice Programs, National Institute of Justice. Retrieved from http://files.eric.ed.gov/fulltext/ED449712.pdf

Fitzgerald, L., Shullman, S., Bailey, N., Richards, M., Swecker, J., Gold, A., . . . Weitzman, L. (1988). The incidence and dimensions of sexual harassment in academia and the workplace. *Journal of Vocational Behavior, 32*(2), 152–175. doi:10.1016/00018791(88)90012-7

Fitzpatrick, M., Cotter, E., Bernfeld, S., Carter, L., Kies, A., & Fouad, N. (2011). The importance of workplace bullying to vocational psychology: Implications for research and practice. *Journal of Career Development, 38*(6), 479–499. doi:10.1177/0894845310390035

Fonow, M. M., Richardson, L., & Wemmerus, V. A. (1992). Feminist rape education: Does it work? *Gender and Society, 6*(1), 108–121. doi:10.1177/089124392006001007

Fortune, M., Abugideiri, S., & Dratch, M. (2010). A commentary on religion and domestic violence. *Domestic violence: Intersectionality and culturally competent practice.* New York, NY: Columbia University Press. Retrieved from http://www.faithtrustinstitute.org/resources/articles/Commentary.pdf

Goldin, C. (2006). *The quiet revolution that transformed women's employment, education, and family* (No. w11953). Cambridge, MA: National Bureau of Economic Research. doi:10.1257/000282806777212350

Gutek, B., & Koss, M. (1993). Changed women and changed organizations: Consequences of and coping with sexual harassment. *Journal of Vocational Behavior, 42*(1), 28–48. doi:10.1006/jvbe.1993.1003

Harvey, M. (1996). An ecological view of psychological trauma and trauma recovery. *Journal of Traumatic Stress, 9*(1), 3–23. doi:10.1002/jts.2490090103

Hill, C., & Silva, E. (2005). *Drawing the line: Sexual harassment on campus.* Washington, DC: AAUW Educational Foundation. Retrieved from http://files.eric.ed.gov/fulltext/ED489850.pdf

Holland, K., & Cortina, L. (2016). Sexual harassment: Undermining the wellbeing of working women. In M. L. Connerley & J. Wu (Eds.), *Handbook on well-being of working women* (pp. 83–101). Dordrecht, The Netherlands: Springer.

Jayasundara, D., Nedegaard, R., Sharma, B., & Flanagan, K. (2014). Intimate partner violence in Muslim communities. *Arts and Social Sciences Journal, 1,* 2. doi:10.4172/2151-6200.S1-003

Katz-Wise, S., & Hyde, J. (2012). Victimization experiences of lesbian, gay, and bisexual individuals: A meta-analysis. *Journal of Sex Research, 49*(2–3), 142–167. doi:10.1080/00224499.2011.63724

Killian, K. (2008). Helping till it hurts? A multimethod study of compassion fatigue, burnout, and self-care in clinicians working with trauma survivors. *Traumatology, 14*(2), 32–44. doi:10.1177/1534765608319083

Kitzrow, M. (2003). The mental health needs of today's college students: Challenges and recommendations. *NASPA Journal, 41*(1), 167–181. doi:10.2202/1949-6605.1310

Konik, J., & Cortina, L. (2008). Policing gender at work: Intersections of harassment based on sex and sexuality. *Social Justice Research, 21*(3), 313–337. doi:10.1007/s11211-008-0074-z

Krebs, C., Lindquist, C., Berzofsky, M, Shook-Sa, B., & Peterson, K. (2016). *Campus climate survey validation study.* Washington, DC: Bureau of Justice Statistics. Retrieved from http://www.bjs.gov/index.cfm?ty=pbdetail&iid=5540

Krebs, C., Lindquist, C., Warner, T., Fisher, B., & Martin, S. (2007). *The campus sexual assault (CSA) study*. Washington, DC: National Institute of Justice, U.S. Department of Justice. Retrieved from https://www.ncjrs.gov/pdffiles1/nij/grants/221153.pdf

Lewis-Arévalo, C., & Seto, A. (2014). Reducing campus sexual assaults through bystander intervention programs: How counselors can help. *Journal of Counselor Leadership and Advocacy, 1*(2), 128–139. doi:10.1080/2326716X.2014.902760

Lindley, L. D. (2005). Perceived barriers to career development in the context of social cognitive career theory. *Journal of Career Assessment, 13*(3), 271–287. doi:10.1177/10690727 05274953

Lund, E. M., & Ross, S. W. (2016). Bullying perpetration, victimization, and demographic differences in college students: A review of the literature. *Trauma, Violence, and Abuse, 17*(1). doi:10.1177/1524838015620818

Marshall, C., Dalyot, K., & Galloway, S. (2014). Sexual harassment in higher education: Re-framing the puzzle of its persistence. *Journal of Policy Practice, 13*(4), 276–299. doi:10 .1080/15588742.2014.929070

McMahon, S. (2010). Rape myth beliefs and bystander attitudes among incoming college students. *Journal of American College Health, 59*(1), 3–11. doi:10.1080/07448481.2010.483715

McMahon, S., & Banyard, V. L. (2012). When can I help? A conceptual framework for the prevention of sexual violence through bystander intervention. *Trauma, Violence, and Abuse, 13*(1), 3–14. doi:10.1177/1524838011426015

McWhirter, E. (1997). Perceived barriers to education and career: Ethnic and gender differences. *Journal of Vocational Behavior, 50*(1), 124–140. doi:10.1006/jvbe.1995.1536

Meritor Savings Bank v. Vinson, 477 U.S. 57 (1986).

Miller, S., Williams, J., Cutbush, S., Gibbs, D., Clinton-Sherrod, M., & Jones, S. (2013). Dating violence, bullying, and sexual harassment: Longitudinal profiles and transitions over time. *Journal of Youth and Adolescence, 42*(4), 607–618. doi:10.1007/s10964-013-9914-8

National Coalition for Women and Girls in Education. (2012). *Title IX at 40: Working to Ensure Gender Equity in Education*. Washington, DC: NCWGE. Retrieved from http:// www.ncwge.org/TitleIX40/TitleIX-print.pdf

Neall, A. M., & Tuckey, M. R. (2014). A methodological review of research on the antecedents and consequences of workplace harassment. *Journal of Occupational and Organizational Psychology, 87*(2), 225–257. doi:10.1111/joop.12059

Nmehielle, V. O., & Madhava Menon, N. R. (2014). Opportunity, inclusion, and equity as imperatives for meaningful law and justice-guided development. In H. Cissé, N. R. M. Menon, M.-C. C. Segger, & V. O. Nmehielle, *The World Bank Legal Review: Fostering Development through Opportunity, Inclusion, and Equity* (Vol. 5, pp. 3–20). Washington, DC: The World Bank. doi:10.1596/978-1-4648-0037-5

Parnell, M. K., Lease, S. H., & Green, M. L. (2012). Perceived career barriers for gay, lesbian, and bisexual individuals. *Journal of Career Development, 39*(3), 248–268. doi:10.1177/ 0894845310386730

Pizzolato, J., Nguyen, T., Johnston, M., & Wang, S. (2012). Understanding context: Cultural, relational, & psychological interactions in self-authorship development. *Journal of College Student Development, 53*(5), 656–679. doi:10.1353/csd.2012.0061

Pope, M., Barret, B., Szymanski, D. M., Chung, Y. B., Singaravelu, H., McLean, R., & Sanabria, S. (2004). Culturally appropriate career counseling with gay and lesbian clients. *The Career Development Quarterly*, *53*(2), 158–177. doi:10.1002/j.21610045.2004.tb00987.x

Porter, S. (2016). Girls' education, development and social change "Seeding, Strengthening and Linking" (Global Fund for Women). *Policy Futures in Education*, *14*(5), 517–538. doi:10.11771/1478210315625904

Rankin, S., Weber, G., Blumenfeld, W., & Frazer, S. (2010). 2010 State of Higher Education for Lesbian, Gay, Bisexual and Transgender People. Retrieved from http://www.campuspride.org/wpcontent/uploads/campuspride2010lgbtreportssummary.pdf

Rostosky, S., & Riggle, E. (2002). "Out" at work: The relation of actor and partner workplace policy and internalized homophobia to disclosure status. *Journal of Counseling Psychology*, *49*(4), 411. doi:10.1037/0022-0167.49.4.411

Runge, R. R. (2013). The evolution of a national response to violence against women. *Hastings Women's Law Journal*, *24*, 433–459.

Sen, G., & Mukherjee, A. (2014). No empowerment without rights, No rights without politics: Gender-equality, MDGs and the post-2015 development agenda. *Journal of Human Development and Capabilities*, *15*(2–3), 188–202. doi:10.1080/19452829.2014.884057

Siegel, R. B. (2004). A short history of sexual harassment. *Directions in Sexual Harassment Law*, *1*, 11–18.

Sigal, J., & Jacobsen, H. (1999). A cross-cultural exploration of factors affecting reactions to sexual harassment: Attitudes and policies. *Psychology, Public Policy, and Law*, *5*(3), 760. doi:10.1037/1076-8971.5.3.760

Tomlinson, M. J., & Fassinger, R. (2003). Career development, lesbian identity development, and campus climate among lesbian college students. *Journal of College Student Development*, *44*(6), 845–860. doi:10.1353/csd.2003.0078

Trippany, R., Kress, V., & Wilcoxon, S. (2004). Preventing vicarious trauma: What counselors should know when working with trauma survivors. *Journal of Counseling and Development*, *82*(1), 31–37.

U.S. Department of Education, National Center for Education Statistics. (2015). *Indicators of School Crime and Safety: 2014* (NCES 2015-072), Figure 11.1. Retrieved from https://nces.ed.gov/fastfacts/display.asp?id=719

U.S. Department of Education, Office for Civil Rights. (2001, January 19). *Revised Sexual Harassment Guidance: Harassment of students by school employees, other students, or third parties: Title IX*. Retrieved from http://www2.ed.gov/about/offices/list/ocr/docs/shguide.html

U.S. Department of Education, Office for Civil Rights. (2003, July 28). Dear Colleague Letter: First Amendment. Retrieved from http://www2.ed.gov/about/offices/list/ocr/firstamend.html

U.S. Department of Education, Office for Civil Rights. (2011, April 4). Dear Colleague Letter: Guidance on Addressing Sexual Harassment/Sexual Violence. Retrieved from http://www2.ed.gov/about/offices/list/ocr/letters/colleague-201104.html

U.S. Department of Education, Office for Civil Rights. (2014, April 29). *Questions and Answers on Title IX and Sexual Violence*. Retrieved from http://www2.ed.gov/about/offices/list/ocr/docs/qa-201404-title-ix.pdf

U.S. Department of Education, Office for Civil Rights. (2016, May 13). Dear Colleague Letter on Transgender Students: Notice of Language Assistance. Retrieved from http://www2.ed.gov/about/offices/list/ocr/letters/colleague-201605-title-ix-transgender.pdf

Violence Against Women Act Reauthorization of 2013, 42 U.S.C. § 16701. Retrieved from https://www.gpo.gov/fdsys/pkg/BILLS-113s47enr/pdf/BILLS-113s47enr.pdf

Wasco, S., & Campbell, R. (2002). Emotional reactions of rape victim advocates: A multiple case study of anger and fear. *Psychology of Women Quarterly, 26*(2), 120–130. doi: 10.1111/1471-6402.00050

Way, I., VanDeusen, K., Martin, G., Applegate, B., & Jandle, D. (2004). Vicarious trauma: A comparison of clinicians who treat survivors of sexual abuse and sexual offenders. *Journal of Interpersonal Violence, 19*(1), 49–71. doi:10.1177/0886260503259050

White House Council on Women and Girls. (2014). Rape and sexual assault: A renewed call to action. Retrieved from http://www.whitehouse.gov/sites/default/files/docs/sexual_assault_report_1-21-14.pdf

White House Task Force to Protect Students from Sexual Assault. (2014). *Not Alone: The First Report of the White House Task Force to Protect Students from Sexual Assault.* Retrieved from https://www.notalone.gov/assets/report.pdf

World Health Organization. (2013). Global and regional estimates of violence against women: Prevalence and health effects of intimate partner violence and non-partner sexual violence. Retrieved from http://apps.who.int/iris/bitstream/10665/85239/1/9789241564625_eng.pdf

Wylie, A., Jakobsen, J., & Fosado, G. (2007). Women, work, and the academy: Strategies for responding to "post-Civil Rights Era" gender discrimination. *Barnard Center for Research on Women, 2,* pp. 1–17. Retrieved from http://bcrw.barnard.edu/wp-content/nfs/reports/NFS2-Women_Work_and_the_Academy.pdf

Yoon, E., Funk, R., & Kropf, N. (2010). Sexual harassment experiences and their psychological correlates among a diverse sample of college women. *Journal of Women and Social Work, 25*(1), 8–18. doi:10.1177/0886109909354979

CHAPTER 11

Females and Their Bodies

Dana Heller Levitt and Connie S. Ducaine

LEARNING OBJECTIVES

After reading this chapter, you will be able to:

1. Define and explain the implications of lookism.
2. Discuss the differences between disordered eating and clinical eating disorders.
3. Recognize the factors that influence body image and disordered eating and the strategies counselors can use to detect and address them.
4. Develop and implement prevention efforts for promoting positive body image.
5. Engage in counseling and advocacy interventions regarding positive body image for girls and women.

Throughout their lives, girls and women receive messages about their bodies: how they should look, what they should be used for, and who has control over them. This chapter examines the culture of "lookism" and the toxic messages women and girls receive about their bodies and the subsequent impact of those messages on body image, eating disorders, self-mutilation, and other issues that disproportionately affect females. We address prevention and intervention efforts, global concerns related to body image, and outreach efforts in which counselors can engage with girls and women regarding this topic.

LOOKISM

The construct of lookism, or "discrimination in favor of people who are perceived as physically attractive and against people who are not physically attractive"

(Cavico, Muffler, & Mujtaba, 2013, p. 83), is not a new phenomenon, even though it has only recently appeared in the literature. The definition of beauty changes and is a product of a variety of factors (e.g., economy, culture, age, religion); however, some form of beauty bias permeates our culture at any point in time. Beauty ideals are constructed by both men and women and the messages about these potentially damaging ideals are disseminated by individuals and society as a whole. The messages regarding appearance are channeled by our culture (Santos & Updegraff, 2014), society, the media, TV programming (Eyal & Te'eni-Harari, 2013), and behaviors of family and friends (e.g., teasing and casual comments). Often, the perpetrators are unaware of the damage being done by their insensitivity. The implications of lookism (or beauty bias) can impact girls and, if the cycle is left unbroken, put them at risk of becoming perpetrators of the same bias. Understanding the implications of lookism across the female life span is important if we intend to help girls and women develop healthy self-esteem and positive body image, while preventing disordered eating and other damaging behaviors.

Research suggests that this form of discrimination can have long-term effects on females since it creates self-esteem issues that ultimately impact educational and career choices (Crosnoe, 2007). In some instances, appearance and weight-based teasing have a greater impact on self-esteem than the individual's actual weight (Keery, Butelle, van den Berg, & Thompson, 2005). The reality is that discrimination based on appearance starts early (Harriger, Calogero, Witherington, & Smith, 2010) and follows women throughout their lives (Little & Roberts, 2012; Toledano, 2013). The factors that perpetuate the problem are many, and even women themselves contribute to the focus on beauty. One researcher determined that more than 57% of the compliments women gave to other women were appearance related with only 26% related to performance (Reese-Miller, 2011).

Discrimination based on appearance can be triggered by facial appearance, body size or type, or any other physical attribute that does not meet another's perception of "beauty" (Little & Roberts, 2012). This type of discrimination is difficult to prove, but the impact on the victim's body image and self-esteem is significant. With little legal protection offered for individuals who are discriminated against based on appearance or size, those who perpetrate this type of bias, particularly in the employment arena, are often not held accountable for their actions (Gumin, 2012). "Weightism," or discrimination based on size, has the risk of becoming a pervasive issue in the United States, as many Americans are overweight or obese. This specific form of lookism appears to be particularly problematic for females who are plagued by weight discrimination in employment, education, and health care (Fikkan & Rothblum, 2012). For example, employers may generally select a candidate who is thinner, and by Western standards more attractive, than a candidate who is overweight or obese regardless of comparable qualifications.

Lookism is an issue of broad impact in a variety of settings, including school and work (Harris & Small, 2013). The negative implications of lookism have also been documented outside the United States (Harris & Small, 2013; O'Brien, Latner, Ebneter, & Hunter, 2013). Although different cultures have their own ideals of beauty, many women and girls are held to appearance metrics set by the dominant culture that leave them striving for a goal that is unsuitable and possibly unattainable.

DEFINING FACTORS RELATED TO BODY ISSUES

The deleterious effects of lookism are numerous and have affected females in Western cultures for decades, resulting in eating disorders and related issues such as body image disturbance. Self-mutilation, perhaps not directly related to lookism, but certainly relevant to females' body awareness, is also a significant issue for girls and women globally (Muehlenkamp, Claes, Havertape, & Plener, 2012). We provide brief definitions of these issues to create the context for understanding how we can adequately support women in body-related matters.

Body Image

"It's a sad situation when a 6-year-old girl says, 'I don't want to have a baby because I don't want to get fat.' Wherever that message is originating, we need to change it."—A counselor who is the mother of pre-teen daughter reflecting on her daughter's comments when she was in first grade

Body image is defined as attitudes toward one's body and actions to obtain what is perceived as ideal (Grosick, Talbert-Johnson, & Myers, 2013). Messages about the "thinness ideal" and negative perceptions of those larger than that idealized size can lead to body image disturbance among girls and women (Levitt, 2004). Sadly, girls as young as age 3 years have already started to embrace the thin ideal (Harriger et al., 2010). Body image disturbance is often characterized by a preoccupation with weight, appearance, and a general dissatisfaction with how one appears in comparison to others. This can be particularly challenging for adolescents who are developmentally inclined to base their self-esteem on their goodness of fit with peers and are particularly susceptible to external expectations of acceptable appearance (Levitt, 2016).

The National Eating Disorders Association (NEDA, 2015) classification of negative body image includes a distorted perception of one's shape, or perceiving one's body not as it actually exists. Someone with a negative body image might be convinced that her body shape indicates personal failure and become self-conscious or ashamed of her body. The media, particularly as it perpetuates lookism, is a significant contributor to this dissatisfaction (NEDA, 2015). Conversely, women with positive body image feel comfortable and confident in their bodies, regardless of their shape and appearance. The sense of pride and acceptance of one's unique appearance can contribute to a sense of appreciation of self and recognition that physical appearance exemplifies little about one's value and character (NEDA, 2015). Unfortunately, attaining a positive self-image is a challenging feat for many girls and women. Ideas to encourage positive body image through prevention and intervention efforts are discussed later in this chapter.

Eating Disorders

The term "eating disorders" is overused in Western culture to describe a plethora of issues related to body image and disordered eating. In their true form, eating disorders are clinical manifestations and encompass serious emotional and physical issues that can be life-threatening. Clinical eating disorders may have little to do with body image and may instead be a manifestation of issues such as loss of control, trauma response, or identity development. Three clinical eating disorders classified in the *Diagnostic and Statistical Manual for Mental Disorders-5* (*DSM-5*, American Psychiatric Association [APA], 2013) that may impact girls and women include anorexia nervosa, bulimia nervosa, and binge eating disorder. Each of these disorders is diagnosed based on distinct criteria outlined in the *DSM-5*. All have injurious effects on individuals and their support system. To support girls and women who may be impacted by a clinical eating disorder, counselors must be familiar with the information outlined in the *DSM-5*.

Disordered Eating

Women engaged in disordered eating may be inaccurately considered by peers and society to have an eating disorder. Disordered eating may include such behaviors as dieting, excessive exercise, undereating, nonclinical bingeing, and sporadic use of purging methods (Grosick et al., 2013). These behaviors can overtake the individual's attention and interfere with activities. Disordered eating behaviors can start at an early age, sometimes as early as 9 or 10 years (DeLeel, Hughes, Miller, Hipwell, & Theodore, 2009), and become a normative experience leading into adolescence and adulthood (Chao et al., 2008; Neumark-Sztainer, Wall, Story, & Sherwood, 2009; Pinhas, Morris, Crosby, & Katzman, 2011). Such behaviors can manifest into clinical eating disorders if protective factors are not in place (Grosick et al., 2013).

Self-Injurious Behavior

Self-mutilation and other nonsuicidal self-harm activity can be categorized under the umbrella classification of self-injurious behaviors (SIBs). This classification includes these and other behaviors by which girls and women express their physical or psychological discontent. Researchers have found that self-harm is on the rise and that young women with disordered eating patterns may be at an appreciable risk (Paul, Schroeter, Dahme, & Nutzinger, 2002; Ross, Heath, & Toste, 2009). The prevalence of SIB appears to be higher in older adolescent females with a greater likelihood of comorbidity for those with longer histories of binge eating and purging behaviors (Peebles, Wilson, & Lock, 2011). Claes, Soenens, Vansteenkiste, and Vandereycken (2012) reported that almost 40% of their study participants had engaged in at least one form of SIB and the actions appeared to be related to self-critical attitudes. These types of attitudes are inherent in perfectionism, which is associated with multiple mental health disorders, including eating disorders and self-harm (Claes et al., 2012; Egan, Wade, & Shafran, 2011). The relationship between an individual's inner voice, a quest for perfection, and the manifestation of self-harm suggests that women and girls (and those who support them) must be attuned to messages that are sent by society and take care not to reinforce messages that perpetuate their self-talk about body image.

Prevalence and Influences

Disordered eating and body image disturbances have become commonplace in Western society, but their exact prevalence rates are difficult to determine. Eating disorders occur primarily in females (APA, 2013) and in less than 5% of the general population. Many cases go undiagnosed due to lack of treatment seeking because of the shame and stigma associated with eating disorders (Pinhas et al., 2011). In their study of girls and boys aged 5 to 12 years in Canada who visited pediatricians, Pinhas and colleagues (2011) found that among their sample, 96.9% engaged in food avoidance and 82.6% reported preoccupation with food. In a study of overweight adolescents, 89% of females reported at least one extreme weight control behavior (Neumark-Sztainer et al., 2009). The complete cause of body image disturbance, disordered eating, and eating disorders has yet to be clearly determined; however, the general influences, described later, remain fairly constant over time and culture.

Social Influences

Body image preoccupation and discontent have become normative for many girls and women. With this in mind, it is not surprising that females are 10 times more likely than males to develop eating disorders (Mussell, Binford, & Fulkerson, 2000). Social pressure to meet a beauty ideal, discussions among girls and women, and external influences from boys and men (e.g., comments about other girls' and women's appearance) create an atmosphere ripe for a focus on appearance and comparison. Social networking also contributes to such pressure, particularly because people feel free to make statements that they would hesitate to say in person.

Social networks among children can also contribute to weight and body esteem issues and have the potential to become damaging as they get older. Children who experience teasing from peers about their weight and appearance learn early that there is a stigma associated with being overweight or unattractive (Lawrie, Sullivan, Davies, & Hill, 2006). This can lead children to develop negative self-concepts and adopt negative attitudes about their appearance and the appearances of others (Mussell et al., 2000). Weight-based teasing experienced as girls has been shown to impact behavior of young women as they age (Quick, McWilliams, & Byrd-Bredbenner, 2013). Peer approval is particularly important for children as they emerge toward adolescence when comments from peers, either directly related to appearance or other factors, carry greater weight than positive comments from family. Thus, negative peer appraisal can significantly contribute to a negative body image and reduced general self-esteem (Bailey & Ricciardelli, 2010).

Adolescent girls are susceptible to social influences that relate to negative body image, disordered eating, and clinical eating disorders. Girls and women tend to engage in "fat talk," which includes negative statements about others and themselves such as, "I'm so fat, I could never wear that" (Arroyo & Harwood, 2012). Fat talk contributes to negative body image and body dissatisfaction. It is also related to self-esteem, which can then influence body image. Furthermore, low self-esteem naturally follows related issues such as depression and pressures to be thin (Arroyo & Harwood, 2012; Corning, Bucchianeri, & Pick, 2014).

Poor self-esteem is related to the stressors of maintaining the body ideal and to stressors that can lead to disordered eating behaviors. Because disordered eating may be a means of exerting control or coping with negative feelings (NEDA, 2015), it seems logical that such behavior may follow in the context of the social acceptance of disordered eating. Salafia and Lemer (2012) found that characteristics and habits related to body image and eating disorders were related to social and even academic pressures for college women. For college women in particular, the path can lead from normative stress to body dissatisfaction, dieting, and ultimately bulimic symptoms (Salafia & Lemer, 2012).

Family Influences

"As a drug and alcohol counselor, I have had female clients that presented with substance abuse issues, only to discover there were also patterns of disordered eating. As these clients shared their narratives, many reported being teased about their size or shape by family members, and feeling as if they were failing because they were too large, too small, too short, too tall . . . never quite measuring up."
—A 50-something female counselor working in a community agency

Harmful behaviors related to social acceptance of body dissatisfaction do not emerge spontaneously. Researchers have determined that appearance-based teasing that originates in the home contributes to adolescent girls' body dissatisfaction (Schaefer & Blodgett Salafia, 2014). We approach this section cautiously and without blame of parents or caregivers. Much like social influences, actions such as teasing are often innocent in their intent yet have challenging and sometimes dangerous consequences.

Children are guided by what they hear and experience with their parents. The way a girl hears her mother speak about her body and appearance and her experiences of lookism are formative in young girls' development. Girls who hear their mothers engage in fat talk may be more likely to adopt such attitudes as they develop (Grosick et al., 2013). Teasing by family members about weight and appearance may likewise contribute to negative body image and reduced overall self-esteem in girls (Keery et al., 2005). Adolescent girls report that their mothers exert the strongest influence on their desire to lose weight through both indirect and overt messages (McCabe & Ricciardelli, 2005). Oswald, Franzoi, and Frost (2012) studied the relationship between young women's body esteem and parents' endorsements of sexist attitudes and beliefs. It is these attitudes toward sexism and the often-subtle objectification of women that demonstrate the strongest influence on a daughter's self-esteem and body image. Oswald et al.'s (2012) research found that fathers' endorsements of sexist beliefs were more significantly correlated with body esteem issues for their daughters.

Although teasing and parental modeling are directly related to weight and appearance issues for girls, other factors may influence the development of body image challenges. Girls lacking healthy coping skills may respond to stressful home situations with disordered eating and other unhealthy behaviors (Salafia & Lemer, 2012). Competitive or enmeshed family relationships may contribute to poor self-esteem and coping strategies, whereas more supportive environments offer protective factors that facilitate the development of healthy ideals and attitudes (Mussell et al., 2000). Stress can lead to negative body image and disordered eating habits (Choate, 2005, 2007), whereas healthy messages from families can offer protection. Therefore, the nature of the family environment, relationships, and attitudes toward food norms and restrictions seems particularly salient in preserving girls' developing self-image and coping strategies.

Media Influences

"The images displayed in the media do not reflect the true diversity that exists in our country. The body shapes depicted on TV and in print give us a false impression of what is the ideal or what is possible for most people. Women are made to feel bad about themselves rather than celebrated for their individual beauty."—A 30-something, transgender female counselor working with transgender clients

The thinness and perfectionism ideals crafted by digitally enhanced media portrayals of females have a tremendous impact on the attitudes of consumers across the life span (Grosick et al., 2013). The ideal slimmer body shape tends to follow fashion trends: to wear the most popular styles, one should aim for a slimmer size (Levitt, 2004). The thinness ideal is unattainable for most women, yet the media suggests this ideal is necessary to be successful socially, romantically, and professionally. Thinness ideals are particularly powerful in advertising and have been for generations (Kilbourne, 2010).

Girls and women are held to a standard introduced through life-long exposure to images in magazines, on television and in movies, and now through social media that reinforces the thinness ideal. Yet images they are fed are digitally altered; not even the models are able to achieve the established ideal. Still, adolescent girls are heavily influenced by media images of thinness and engage in behaviors to work toward the perceived perfect body (NEDA, 2015). Jean Kilbourne's (2010) revolutionary work in her *Killing Us Softly* series provides examples of how media images influence social perceptions and expectations about appearance. It is interesting to note that although the majority of her work focused on White women in U.S. culture, recent trends in body image disturbances suggest a more global reach and challenge for counselors.

Cultural Influences

> *"Unfortunately many women and girls are sent the message that there is something wrong with them if their size is not measured in a single digit. Sometimes the message is subtle while other times it is very pointed—a woman's worth is measured by the size of her body. It is also suggested that she must have a character defect if she cannot achieve or maintain a specific body shape. Not all cultures may share the same beauty ideals, but they do exist for females from all different backgrounds."*—A 30-something female counselor

Although most media images are related to Western ideals and consumerism, there is increasing attention to these influences globally and cross-culturally. Body image issues have become increasingly prevalent for women in developing countries who are exposed to Western media and tourism (Anderson-Fye, 2004; Crawford et al., 2009; Khan, Khalid, Khan, & Jabeen, 2011). Both men and women with Westernized perspectives who visit developing nations bring with them ideals of beauty. They may unintentionally share their attitudes and beliefs about appearance through their consumption of local food, clothing, and entertainment that can therefore have unintended negative consequences for the native persons' attitudes and beliefs about appearance. Women who come from regions of the world where body dissatisfaction is not an issue may become susceptible to these ideals when they are exposed to Western ideals through education, travel, and the media (Rikani et al., 2013). For example, a woman visiting the United States for the first time may be impacted by the ideals of beauty through glossy advertisements, smaller clothing sizes, and the attention one receives based on physical attractiveness. As a result of this exposure, this woman may begin to look at herself negatively.

The characterization of eating disorders as a White, upper middle class, adolescent issue is changing, in part due to the globalization from media exposure and consumption, as well as an increase in research with culturally diverse samples. Early research in eating disorders typically did not account for differences in socioeconomic status (SES) or racial diversity (DeLeel et al., 2009; Mussell et al., 2000). Some cultures are more accepting of larger body types, and, in fact, contradict images seen in the media and socially. Recently, researchers have found that Black and Hispanic women were more likely to speak more favorably about their bodies than White women (Fiery, Martz, Web, & Curtin, 2016). Women of color, despite these protective factors, are still susceptible to eating disorders and experience them more often than was previously thought. Research on gender roles, pioneered by Sandra Bem in the 1970s, likewise went through a similar transformation of understanding issues from a broader cultural context. Although perfectionism associated with weight and shape overvaluation seems to fall along gender lines (Siegling & Delaney, 2013), more recent research on eating disorders and body image in racially diverse populations is showing that expectations for women and girls are related to factors of bodily capacity. For example, the African American community historically places cultural emphasis on women's abilities to bear and carry children and this attitude may result in a more flexible concept of beauty (Chao et al., 2008). Counselors are encouraged to learn from their clients and through their own research how the female body is valued in an individual culture.

Such cultural ideals must be factored into our understanding of the etiology of body image, disordered eating, and eating disorders. Regardless of race or ethnicity, women around the world are impacted by messages connecting body size and shape to global self-esteem. Counselors should avoid making assumptions about influences and challenges impacting the young women they counsel. The manifestations may be as diverse as the populations who are influenced by these messages.

PREVENTION

Prevention efforts tend to focus on decreasing body dissatisfaction and curtailing the development of eating disorders. Education is a key component in addressing the social, media, and cultural messages that abound, as well as helping individuals and families understand the impact of their words and the influences that contribute to poor body image and eating disorders. There are few empirical studies to support psychoeducation, the primary form of prevention, as a means of teaching about and preventing body image disturbance and eventually eating disorders. As early as 2000, Mussell and colleagues advocated for a need to address systemic factors related to the onset and maintenance of the challenges that persist in counselors' work in this area today. More recently, researchers evaluated interventions that focused on health and issues related to body image rather than psychoeducational materials directly related to eating disorders. Findings demonstrated that the modified content in a positive frame did impact factors related to eating disorders (Wilksch et al., 2015).

Prevention efforts can take place in many settings, including home, school, and community. Educational workshops, a primary approach to prevention, can be effective when included within existing programs, such as orientations, sorority meetings, faith-based groups, and school-based assemblies (Choate & Schwitzer, 2009). Choate (2005) developed a body image resilience model that can be used to identify five protective factors against body image disturbance: family and peer support; gender-role satisfaction; global and physical self-esteem; coping strategies and critical thinking; and holistic wellness and balance. In this section, prevention efforts are organized according to these protective factors and examples are provided of actions that can be taken in family, peer, school, and sociocultural domains. This approach is consistent with a developmental and wellness perspective that is beneficial for counselors to employ in this area (Remley & Herlihy, 2016).

Family and Peer Support

We know that self-esteem can be drawn from familial relationships and that family relationships and self-esteem together can influence one's sense of body esteem. Neumark-Sztainer and colleagues (2009), therefore, recommend that a focus on strengthening family relationships be included in prevention efforts. Focusing on family interactions and communications can address self-esteem for all family members, thereby acting as a protective variable in the onset of clinical and nonclinical disorders. Since global self-esteem decreases for girls through adolescence, this approach not only addresses greater developmental issues, but also keeps a focus on positivity and makes the family a resource should girls begin to experience esteem challenges (Lawrie et al., 2006).

Parents can be included in prevention efforts that take place in the school setting. Educational programs for students can be extended to working with parents as well, providing them with information about the issues and preventive approaches they may engage in at home (Grosick et al., 2013). Educating parents about the effects of their attitudes about appearance, as well as warning signs in their children, may create a more collaborative approach between the school and home (Choate, 2007). Parent education is a frequent task and responsibility for school counselors.

Peer support is likewise protective against body issues and other factors impacting self-esteem. During adolescence in particular, girls seek acceptance from peers, which sometimes translates into a need to fit a certain physical mold. For adult women as well, having a supportive peer network can ameliorate such beliefs and provide a more nurturing environment to focus on women's strengths not related to their bodies. Counselors engaged in prevention should look for opportunities to help clients and students create strong social networks (Choate, 2007). For school-aged youth, this could include mentoring, social activities, and other structured opportunities for girls to interact with one another in a supportive environment. Small group counseling focused specifically on health and wellness may be introduced in the school to engage younger adolescents in activities that promote their own and others' well-being and self-esteem (Akos & Levitt, 2002).

For adult women, creating pathways to interaction that nurture one's mind and soul are equally important. Empowerment efforts are a good way to turn negative energy about shape and appearance into a constructive realm. Women may help to transform the culture of lookism through advocacy, such as teaching women to refuse to tolerate bias and jokes about weight and appearance (Choate & Schwitzer, 2009). A college-based program helped to raise awareness of body image and challenged women to not engage in fat talk (Arroyo & Harwood, 2012). In addition to teaching women strategies for reducing fat talk, we can likewise teach women to identify with other qualities not related to appearance and to nurture that in others. A part of this is teaching women and men how to compliment women's other qualities and actions, rather than focusing on appearance. These changes, although simplistic in nature, send strong messages to women about their value and worth (Choate, 2007).

Gender-Role Satisfaction

Bem's (1974) research addressed the socialization of males and females along a continuum of masculinity and femininity. The female gender role includes an expectation for women to be nurturing caretakers who are somewhat submissive and do not assert their intelligence, rights, or power. This includes a focus on finding a male life partner and serving his needs and those of the children she is expected to bear and raise. This characterization is found on the extreme feminine end of the continuum, yet it is still prevalent in some cultures. In the United States, this hyperfeminine perspective includes the social construct that women are expected to use their physical appearance as a means of attracting others (Choate, 2007).

A deeply ingrained sense of gender role is difficult to challenge. Feminist efforts since the 1960s have challenged women and girls to move beyond limited gender-role constraints, identify their strengths and talents, and seek fulfillment professionally, personally, and relationally. Prevention programming and outreach can educate girls and women about the history of women's empowerment and continue necessary efforts to strengthen their voices in society. They can thus explore gender roles and challenge what does not fit for them. Most importantly, counselors should encourage women to value the strengths that they see in themselves and other girls and women that are not affiliated with appearance.

It is beneficial for women to engage in dialogue about their strengths and contributions, including leadership roles that may encompass more androgynous characteristics (Bem, 1974). Exposure to female role models is especially important across the life span to challenge gender stereotypes (Choate, 2007). Female role models may exemplify gender roles across the continuum and can help girls and women see a more flexible model of leadership and success.

Online forums may be an optimal place to engage women in discussions, as they offer opportunities to communicate with a large audience of like-minded women. This would also facilitate international conversations and thus could include exploration of the different cultural emphases on body image ideals. For younger participants, open discussions about puberty and related bodily changes may provide perspectives on what they can expect developmentally when they approach emerging adulthood (Choate, 2007).

Whether in person or online, a counselor can moderate discussions focused on improving self-efficacy related to social pressures (Mussell et al., 2000), which might include assertiveness training or appropriate expression of emotions that are typically characterized as masculine traits, such as anger. Self-efficacy, a prominent construct in feminism, refers to the belief or confidence that one can successfully complete a task or behavior. A strong sense of self-efficacy has the potential to help females overcome the challenges presented by deeply entrenched gender roles and can facilitate the development of both a positive body image and healthy changes to eating behaviors (Kinsaul, Curtin, Bazzini, & Martz, 2014).

Global and Physical Self-Esteem

My preteen daughter's pediatrician recently discussed with me her body mass index (BMI) and the size that she would likely be throughout her development. She then discussed the importance of limiting junk food and continuing athletic activity. Wearing my counselor and parent identities, I was dismayed by the discussion. I encourage my daughter to have a balanced lifestyle, enjoy all foods in moderation, relish in her athleticism and physical accomplishments, and intentionally separate her self-worth from her physical appearance. What was most disturbing about this conversation was that it took place in front of an impressionable child who will face the physical changes of puberty in the next few years and already contends with social and peer messages about women's bodies.

I share this personal story to highlight the importance of prevention beyond the scope of girls and women and their families and peers. It is important to educate health professionals, teachers, and other significant adults about the messages they may unintentionally send about body image. McVey, Gusella, Tweed, and Ferrari (2009) developed a 10-week online educational program designed to help high school teachers promote healthy body image with adolescents. "The Student Body: Promoting Health at Any Size" was a case study-based program with six modules and suggestions for implementing a related classroom activity. After participating in the program, the participants in the study reported feeling better about their bodies. The healthy modeling that teachers learned to communicate to adolescents can be adapted for health professionals in other settings as well. Counselors can be key consultants with others in the community to create opportunities to enhance a positive physical and global self-esteem.

Higher self-esteem is a strong protective factor against negative body image and can be enhanced through prevention programming. There is a direct connection between global esteem (i.e., self-worth) and physical self-esteem (Lawrie et al., 2006; Neumark-Sztainer et al., 2009). Messages about body image can come from multiple sources and influence physical self-esteem both positively and negatively. School- and community-based mentoring programs may create another opportunity for the growing adolescent to strengthen global self-esteem and develop positive female friendships (Choate, 2007). School counselors can consult with physical education teachers, health staff, and other key personnel to raise awareness about body image messages being communicated through adult modeling and explore possible interventions in their individual areas of practice (Akos & Levitt, 2002). Strengthening family support should also be addressed given the importance of a validating home environment (Neumark-Sztainer et al., 2009).

Girls and women across the life span can benefit from considering the health benefits of exercise as distinct from the idea of weight loss, as an increasing number of girls and women around the globe view physical activity related to weight loss. Reframing exercise as health promoting and contributing to well-being is a positive step in increasing physical self-esteem. Exercise and activity programs held in gyms and community venues, as well as workshops about health and wellness, can help communicate this message. Physical activity for the sake of well-being, such as going for a walk with partners or families after a meal, can be encouraged by counselors, teachers, health professionals, and community advocates. Activities such as reading, art, music, or gaming can also elevate physical self-esteem (Choate, 2007). People who engage in nonappearance-based activities gain a sense of accomplishment and satisfaction that is equally valuable for global self-esteem.

Coping Strategies and Critical Thinking

Poor coping strategies have been associated with bulimia and other eating disorders (Salafia & Lemer, 2012), as well as SIBs. Therefore, emphasis needs to be placed on developing healthy and protective ways to cope with emotionally challenging situations. Protective factors may include teaching healthy emotion management and learning healthy ways to handle stress. Strong social networks can provide supportive structures of people to whom one can reach out in a time of crisis or difficulty (Choate, 2007). Teaching girls and women about how to cope with stress is an important part of prevention.

Psychoeducation should focus on systemic factors that affect girls and women (Mussell et al., 2000), such as the media, which may be the greatest factor influencing body image. Counselors and educators can introduce projects that expose media depictions that perpetuate harmful stereotypes and propose letter-writing campaigns to challenge these messages (Akos & Levitt, 2002). Education about media messages can include speakers who address the impact of media and help girls and women deconstruct these messages (Grosick et al., 2013). Girls and women can benefit from a supportive and nurturing environment such as a small group with other girls and women where they can promote the self-esteem of their peers (Akos & Levitt, 2002). In an age of technology and media consumption beyond magazines and television, this approach seems particularly salient as a preventive factor.

Holistic Wellness and Balance

Wellness encompasses five dimensions: spirituality, self-direction, work and leisure, friendship, and love (Myers, Sweeney, & Witmer, 2000). Spirituality may contribute to centering and self-affirmation. Friendship and love may help to create a sense of purpose and connectedness. Choate (2007) emphasizes a broad holistic focus in her recommendations for school counselors, including an emphasis on global self-esteem as a protective factor. Wellness-based prevention may include a focus on nutrition and sleep for healthy development (Choate & Schwitzer, 2009). We recommend developing networks with allied health professionals to collaborate on an approach that promotes general health and wellness in place of a focus on appearance and weight.

INTERVENTION

Counseling approaches are as varied as the counselors providing these services. There are evidence-based practices regarding the treatment of eating disorders, such as cognitive behavioral therapy (CBT). Other approaches may take a more spiritual or holistic approach, such as existential theory. Feminist theory stands apart given its emphasis on empowerment of girls and women in the presence of societal challenges. Many of the prevention efforts discussed in the previous section may be incorporated into individual, family, or group counseling interventions. In one study, 79% of seventh- and eighth-grade students turned to their families for support and advice regarding health and appearance (Grosick et al., 2013). It seems fitting, then, to consider treatment in the family context as well as individual- and peer-based experiences. Family counseling provides an opportunity for the family unit to discuss body image messages and the need for family support and development together. It is important for the family counselor to work with the family as a unit instead of identifying the issues as resting solely within the child or adolescent. Many of the preventive factors discussed in the previous section can be turned into opportunities to openly dialogue and create family togetherness, in addition to strategies that can work in individual and group counseling contexts.

In this section, we provide a brief outline of counseling emphases in individual and group counseling. We focus on emphases rather than techniques to provide the reader with a beginning framework for interventions that may be tailored to the individual counselor's approach to counseling.

Individual Counseling

A primary goal for counseling, aside from the unique goals specific to the client, is to foster healthy self-esteem. Feminist therapy is an effective approach to counseling girls and women when addressing issues of body image and body esteem. Feminist therapy applies the political principles of the feminist movement to therapy (Evans, Kincade, & Seem, 2011) with the goal of empowering women and overcoming barriers related to social roles and constructs. Feminist therapy can aid in understanding the impact of gender stereotypes and helping to redefine the roles and expectations of women in society. Within feminist therapy, there is consciousness raising through various techniques, including gender-role analysis, in which clients are encouraged to identify how culture has influenced their own beliefs, attitudes, and gender-role behaviors (Enns, 2014). The body image difficulties that girls and women face can be acknowledged and challenged in feminist counseling and can contribute to healthier body image and self-esteem.

CBT, the most empirically validated treatment for eating disorders, is also often used with presenting issues that are less clinically diagnosable, including SIBs. CBT has a concrete focus that is particularly effective with adolescents who are in treatment for a range of issues (Hogue, Henderson, Ozechowski, & Robbins, 2014; Vuthiarpa, Sethabouppha, Soivong, & Williams, 2012). Counselors can use CBT to challenge deleterious behaviors before they become problematic or after they are already affecting the individual's well-being. Counselors might work with their clients to address the short- and long-term consequences of their behaviors through the use of reflection and open-ended questions, along with homework assignments to be completed between sessions. With adolescents and adults, a focus on motivation and changing maladaptive behaviors and concerns about weight and appearance can prevent further issues from developing (Choate & Schwitzer, 2009).

A related theoretical approach, dialectical behavior therapy (DBT), employs a longer treatment period incorporating mindfulness practices with behavior modification. DBT counselors working with individuals with body dissatisfaction address their concerns through the use of mindfulness and emotion regulation as well as teaching distress tolerance and interpersonal effectiveness skills (Choate & Schwitzer, 2009). Interpersonal effectiveness training can help girls and women articulate their concerns and needs, including identifying when one is hurt or offended by appearance-related comments. There is demonstrated effectiveness in working with individuals with eating disorders that can be adapted as a preventive form of counseling for less clinical manifestations (Lenz, Taylor, Fleming, & Serman, 2014).

Interpersonal therapy (IPT) takes a different approach. It focuses on the relational component of body image dissatisfaction and connects girls and women with one another as protective supports. In IPT, the counselor works with the individual through three stages of counseling: (a) identifying the problem as one of grief, role transition, role dispute (i.e., different expectations of someone else for one's role), or interpersonal deficits; (b) brainstorming options to make positive changes in relationships; and (c) reviewing progress and processing feelings regarding termination of the counseling relationship (Choate & Schwitzer, 2009). This approach is wellness oriented, individualized, short in duration, and teaches protective skills that clients can take with them upon termination.

Group Counseling

Group counseling is a well-regarded approach to counseling given the social support that it provides (Akos & Levitt, 2002; Choate & Schwitzer, 2009). In fact, group therapy is the preferred approach for counseling around body image because of social support and connectedness (Grosick et al., 2013; Mussell et al., 2000). This form of counseling can focus on promoting healthy body image and interpersonal connectedness and, as a result, contribute to an individual's wellness (Gladding, 2012).

The approach to group counseling may differ depending upon the client's developmental stage. For all groups, it may be more effective for recruitment and screening to advertise as body acceptance or connectedness rather than eating disorders prevention or body image (Levitt, 2004). When the group is school based, activities within the sessions that teach about sociocultural pressures, the media, and realistic attainment of beauty standards are particularly helpful (Choate & Schwitzer, 2009). Group counselors can be active and creative in their approaches. NEDA suggests activities such as body tracings filled with written strengths that do not pertain to appearance, media literacy campaigns, or creating collages of both unrealistic and realistic portrayals of women. Careful screening for group composition is important considering the susceptibility to hearing others' unhealthy practices (Levitt, 2004).

With college-aged and older women, counseling approaches that focus on interpersonal discussion can be successful given these women's developmental capacities to engage in insight and connection (Gladding, 2012). Teaching strategies to reduce fat talk and discussing the impact of peers and society on body acceptance can be facilitated through supportive, discussion-focused environments (Arroyo & Harwood, 2012; Gladding, 2012). Social, familial, cultural, and media influences can be discussed openly in supportive group environments, which can normalize the experience for women.

CALL TO ACTION

As members of a helping profession, counselors have an obligation to advocate on behalf of our clients and others who have been marginalized. There are several steps clinicians can take to honor their responsibility to engage in advocacy and social change related to lookism and body image. These include (a) understanding the nature and scope of the problem; (b) increasing self-awareness and addressing any personal biases; (c) creating an environment where those who are impacted are safe to express themselves; and (d) seeking opportunities to advocate.

Addressing the first step requires counselors to elevate their awareness and to understand the depth of the problem created by anti-fat bias and weight stigmatization. We must be mindful of the discrepancy between the images that we are bombarded with in the media and reality. The anecdotal and research evidence that many adults in the United States have a weight "problem" informs us that a significant portion of our clients will be facing this issue. As counselors we need to acknowledge that anti-fat bias may be an issue in our clients' lives.

In addition to understanding the issue, we must evaluate our perceptions and values as they relate to our biases. The Implicit Association Test (IAT), which "measures attitudes and beliefs that people may be unwilling or unable to report" (Project Implicit, 2013), provides an avenue for counselors to test their preferences for thin body types. This self-examination offers counselors the opportunity to explore these issues and enhance connections with clients.

As counselors we can advocate by being mindful of what we say, read, and watch, and by speaking up. As counselors we should remind others (and ourselves) that thin does not necessarily equal healthy, nor does a high BMI necessarily indicate unhealthy. Acknowledging that the human body comes in different shapes and sizes is a good starting point, as is monitoring our "fat talk." As professionals, we should take every opportunity to shine the spotlight on the negative impact of lookism and related body image issues. Through active advocacy efforts or individual conversations, counselors can be agents of change through their prevention and intervention efforts.

REFLECTION AND DISCUSSION QUESTIONS

1. How does body image differ for girls and women in the United States relative to non-Westernized countries? What influence do you think counselors can exert, both domestically and globally, to begin to advocate for change?

2. Boys and men are influences on girls' and women's sense of body esteem. We often look at these as negative forces. What are some of the positive ways that boys and men can influence body image? How might counselors encourage this positive approach?

(continued)

REFLECTION AND DISCUSSION QUESTIONS (*continued*)

3. As a counselor, you may find yourself addressing body image and social influences of such even when these are not presenting issues for counseling. How do you think body image can permeate individuals' lives, and how will you address these factors in counseling?

4. Review the suggested methods for addressing body image in counseling. As you consider your proposed setting for counseling work, which seem most salient and applicable?

HELPFUL RESOURCES

- Academy for Eating Disorders (AED; www.aedweb.org)—Offers information related to eating disorders research, education, treatment, and prevention
- Binge Eating Disorder Association (BEDA; www.anad.org/get-information/about-eating-disorders/eating-disorders-statistics)—Offers an overview of binge eating disorder; causes and risk; and questions to ask treatment providers
- *International Journal of Eating Disorders* (onlinelibrary.wiley.com/journal/10.1002/%28ISSN%291098-108X)—Features research intended to advance the scientific knowledge needed for understanding, treating, and preventing eating disorders
- *Journal of Eating Disorders* (www.jeatdisord.com)—Publishes research on the science and clinical practices of the treatment of eating disorders
- National Association for Anorexia Nervosa and Associated Disorders (ANAD; www.anad.org/get-information/about-eating-disorders/eating-disorders-statistics)—Detailed statistics by population, including mortality information
- National Eating Disorders Association (NEDA; www.nationaleatingdisorders.org/general-information)—General information regarding eating disorders including types, symptoms, and statistics
- Operation Beautiful (www.operationbeautiful.com)—A website focused on ending negative self-talk and "fat talk"
- The Cornell University Research Program on Self-Injury and Recovery (www.selfinjury.bctr.cornell.edu/resources.html)—Provides resources related to self-injury with detailed information on myths and facts; information is also available regarding the relationship between eating disorders and nonsuicidal self-injury

REFERENCES

Akos, P., & Levitt, D. (2002). Promoting healthy body image in middle school students. *Professional School Counseling, 6*, 138–144.

American Psychiatric Association. (2013). *Diagnostic and statistical manual of mental disorders* (5th ed.). Arlington, VA: American Psychiatric Publishing.

Anderson-Fye, E. P. (2004). A "Coca-Cola" shape: Cultural change, body image, and eating disorders in San Andrés, Belize. *Culture, Medicine, and Psychiatry, 28,* 561–595. doi:10.1007/s11013-004-1068-4

Arroyo, A., & Harwood, J. (2012). Exploring the causes and consequences of engaging in fat talk. *Journal of Applied Communication Research, 40,* 167–187. doi:10.1080/00909882.2012.654500

Bailey, S. D., & Ricciardelli, L. A. (2010). Social comparisons, appearance related comments, contingent self-esteem and their relationships with body dissatisfaction and eating disturbance among women. *Eating Behaviors, 11,* 107–112. doi:10.1016/j.eatbeh.2009.12.001

Bem, S. L. (1974). The measurement of psychological androgyny. *Journal of Consulting and Clinical Psychology, 42,* 155–162.

Cavico, F. J., Muffler, S. C., & Mujtaba, B. G. (2013). Appearance discrimination in employment. *Equality, Diversity and Inclusion: An International Journal, 32*(1), 83–119. doi:10.1108/02610151311305632

Chao, Y. M., Pisetsky, E. M., Direker, L. C., Dohm, F. Rosselli, F., May, A. M., & Striegel-Moore, R. H. (2008). Ethnic differences in weight control practices among U.S. adolescents from 1995 to 2005. *International Journal of Eating Disorders, 41,* 124–133. doi:10.1002/eat.20479

Choate, L. H. (2005). Toward a theoretical model of women's body image resilience. *Journal of Counseling and Development, 83,* 320–323.

Choate, L. H. (2007). Counseling adolescent girls for body image resilience: Strategies for school counselors. *Professional School Counseling, 10,* 317–326.

Choate, L. H., & Schwitzer, A. M. (2009). Mental health counseling responses to eating-related concerns in young adult women: A prevention and treatment continuum. *Journal of Mental Health Counseling, 31,* 164–183.

Claes, L., Soenens, B., Vansteenkiste, M., & Vandereycken, W. (2012). The scars of the inner critic: Perfectionism and nonsuicidal self-injury in eating disorders. *European Eating Disorders Review, 20*(3), 196–202. doi:10.1002/erv.1158

Corning, A. F., Bucchianeri, M. M., & Pick, C. M. (2014). Thin or overweight women's fat talk: Which is worse for other women's body satisfaction? *Eating Disorders, 22,* 121–135. doi:10.1080/10640266.2013.860850

Crawford, M., Lee, I., Portnoy, G., Gurung, A., Khati, D., Jha, P., & Regmi, A. (2009). Objectified body consciousness in a developing country: A comparison of mothers and daughters in the U.S. and Nepal. *Sex Roles, 60,* 174–185. doi:10.1007/s11199-0008-9521-4

Crosnoe, R. (2007). Gender, obesity, and education. *Sociology of Education, 80*(3), 241–260.

DeLeel, M. L., Hughes, T. L., Miller, J. A., Hipwell, A. L., & Theodore, L. A. (2009). Prevalence of eating disturbance and body image dissatisfaction in young girls: An examination of the variance across racial and socioeconomic groups. *Psychology in the Schools, 46,* 767–775.

Egan, S. J., Wade, T. D., & Shafran, R. (2011). Perfectionism as a transdiagnostic process: A clinical review. *Clinical Psychology Review, 31*(2), 203–212. doi:10.1016/j.cpr.2010.04.009

Enns, C. Z. (2014). Feminist psychotherapy. In P. Moglia (Ed.), *Salem health: Psychology and behavioral health* (4th ed., pp. 772–774). Oceanside, NY: Salem Press.

Evans, K. M., Kincade, E. A., & Seem, S. R. (2011). *Introduction to feminist therapy: Strategies for social and individual change.* Thousand Oaks, CA: Sage.

Eyal, K., & Te'eni-Harari, T. (2013). Explaining the relationship between media exposure and early adolescents' body image perceptions: The role of favorite characters. *Journal of Media Psychology: Theories, Methods, and Applications, 25*(3), 129–141. doi:10.1027/1864-1105/a000094

Fiery, M. F., Martz, D. M., Webb, R. M., & Curtin, L. (2016). A preliminary investigation of racial differences in body talk in age-diverse U.S. adults. *Eating Behaviors, 21,* 232–235. doi:10.1016/j.eatbeh.2016.03.004

Fikkan, J., & Rothblum, E. (2012). Is fat a feminist issue? Exploring the gendered nature of weight bias. *Sex Roles, 66*(9/10), 575–592. doi:10.1007/s11199-011-0022-5

Gladding, S. T. (2012). *Groups: A counseling specialty* (6th ed.). Upper Saddle River, NJ: Pearson.

Grosick, T. L., Talbert-Johnson, C., & Myers, M. J. (2013). Assessing the landscape: Body image values and attitudes among middle school boys and girls. *American Journal of Health Education, 44,* 41–52. doi:10.1080/19325037.2012.749682

Gumin, M. (2012). Ugly on the inside: An argument for a narrow interpretation of employer defenses to appearance discrimination. *Minnesota Law Review, 96,* 1769–1794.

Harriger, J. A., Calogero, R. M., Witherington, D. C., & Smith, J. E. (2010). Body size stereotyping and internalization of the thin ideal in preschool girls. *Sex Roles: A Journal of Research, 63*(9–10), 609–620. doi:10.1007/s11199-010-9868-1

Harris, C., & Small, J. (2013). Obesity and hotel staffing: Are hotels guilty of "lookism?" *Hospitality and Society, 3*(2), 111–127. doi:10.1386/hosp.3.2.111_1

Hogue, A., Henderson, C. E., Ozechowski, T. J., & Robbins, M. S. (2014). Evidence base on outpatient behavioral treatments for adolescent substance use: Updates and recommendations 2007–2013. *Journal of Clinical Child and Adolescent Psychology, 43*(5), 695–720. doi:10.1080/15374416.2014.915550

Keery, H., Butelle, K., van den Berg, P., & Thompson, J. K. (2005). The impact of appearance-related teasing by family members. *Journal of Adolescent Health, 37,* 120–127. doi:10.1016/j.jadohealth.2004.08.015

Khan, A., Khalid, S., Khan, H. I., & Jabeen, M. (2011). Impact of today's media on university student's body image in Pakistan: A conservative, developing country's perspective. *BMC Public Health, 11,* 379–386. doi:10.1186/1471-2458-11-379

Kilbourne, J. (2010). *Killing us softly 4* [DVD]. Northampton, MA: Media Education Foundation.

Kinsaul, J. A., Curtin, L., Bazzini, D., & Martz, D. (2014). Empowerment, feminism, and self-efficacy: Relationships to body image and disordered eating. *Body Image, 11*(1), 63–67. doi:10.1016/j.bodyim.2013.08.001

Lawrie, Z., Sullivan, E. A., Davies, P. S. W., & Hill, R. J. (2006). Media influence on the body image of children and adolescents. *Eating Disorders, 14,* 355–364. doi:10.1080/10640260600952506

Lenz, S. A., Taylor, R., Fleming, M., & Serman, N. (2014). Effectiveness of dialectical behavior therapy for treating eating disorders. *Journal of Counseling and Development, 92,* 26–35. doi:10.1002/j.1556-6676.2014.00127.x

Levitt, D. H. (2004). Drive for thinness and fear of fat among college women: Implications for practice and assessment. *Journal of College Counseling, 7*, 109–117.

Levitt, D. H. (2016). Helping students with eating disorders and body image concerns. In B. T. Erford (Ed.), *Professional school counseling: A handbook of theories, programs, and practices* (3rd ed., pp. 469–480). Austin, TX: Pro-Ed.

Little, A. C., & Roberts, S. C. (2012). Evolution, appearance, and occupational success. *Evolutionary Psychology, 10*(5), 782–801. doi:10.1177/147470491201000503

McCabe, M. P., & Ricciardelli, L. A. (2005). A prospective study of pressures from parents, peers, and the media on extreme weight change behaviors among adolescent boys and girls. *Behaviour Research and Therapy, 43*, 1–17. doi:10.1016/j.brat.2004.05.004

McVey, G., Gusella, J., Tweed, S., & Ferrari, M. (2009). A controlled evaluation of web-based training for teachers and public health practitioners on the prevention of eating disorders. *Eating Disorders, 17*, 1–26. doi:10.1080/10640260802570064

Muehlenkamp, J. J., Claes, L., Havertape, L., & Plener, P. L. (2012). International prevalence of adolescent non-suicidal self-injury and deliberate self-harm. *Child and Adolescent Psychiatry and Mental Health, 6*(1), 10–18. doi:10.1186/1753-2000-6-10

Mussell, M. P., Binford, R. B., & Fulkerson, J. A. (2000). Eating disorders: Summary of risk factors, prevention programming, and prevention research. *The Counseling Psychologist, 28*, 764–796. doi:10.1177/0011000000286002

Myers, J. E., Sweeney, T. J., & Witmer, J. M. (2000). The wheel of wellness counseling for wellness: A holistic model for treatment planning. *Journal of Counseling and Development, 78*, 251–266.

National Eating Disorders Association. (2015). Learn. Retrieved from http://www.national eatingdisorders.org/learn

Neumark-Sztainer, D., Wall, M., Story, M., & Sherwood, N. E. (2009). Five-year longitudinal predictive factors for disordered eating in a population-based sample of overweight adolescents: Implications for prevention and treatment. *International Journal of Eating Disorders, 42*, 664–672. doi:10.1002/eat.20733

O'Brien, K. S., Latner, J. D., Ebneter, D., & Hunter, J. A. (2013). Obesity discrimination: The role of physical appearance, personal ideology, and anti-fat prejudice. *International Journal of Obesity, 37*(3), 455–460. doi:10.1038/ijo.2012.52

Oswald, D. L., Franzoi, S. L., & Frost, K. A. (2012). Experiencing sexism and young women's body esteem. *Journal of Social Clinical Psychology, 31*, 1112–1137. doi:10.1521/jscp.2012.31.10.1112

Paul, T., Schroeter, K., Dahme, B., & Nutzinger, D. O. (2002). Self-injurious behavior in women with eating disorders. *American Journal of Psychiatry, 159*, 408–411.

Peebles, R., Wilson, J. L., & Lock, J. D. (2011). Self-injury in adolescents with eating disorders: Correlates and provider bias. *Journal of Adolescent Health, 48*(3), 310–313. doi:10.1016/j.jadohealth.2010.06.017

Pinhas, L., Morris, A., Crosby, R. D., & Katzman, D. K. (2011). Incidence and age-specific presentation of restrictive eating disorders in children: A Canadian pediatric surveillance program study. *Archives of Pediatrics and Adolescent Medicine, 165*, 895–899. doi:10.1001/archpediatrics.2011.145

Project Implicit. (2013). About the IAT. Retrieved from https://implicit.harvard.edu/implicit/iatdetails.html

Quick, V. M., McWilliams, R., & Byrd-Bredbenner, C. (2013). Fatty, fatty, two-by-four: Weight-teasing history and disturbed eating in young adult women. *American Journal of Public Health, 103*, 508–515. doi:10.2105/AJPH.2012.300898

Reese-Miller, J. (2011). Compliments revisited: Contemporary compliments and gender. *Journal of Pragmatics, 43*, 2673–2688. doi:10.1016/j.pragma.2011.04.14

Remley, T. P., & Herlihy, B. P. (2016). *Ethical, legal, and professional issues in counseling* (5th ed.). Upper Saddle River, NJ: Pearson.

Rikani, A. A., Choudhry, Z., Choudhry, A. M., Ikram, H., Ashgar, M. W., Kajal, D., . . . Mobassarah, N. J. (2013). A critique of the literature on etiology of eating disorders. *Annals of Neurosciences, 20*, 157–161. doi:10.5214/ans.0972.7531.200409

Ross, S., Heath, N. L., & Toste, J. R. (2009). Non-suicidal self-injury and eating pathology in high school students. *American Journal of Orthopsychiatry, 79*, 83–92. doi:10/1037/a0014826

Salafia, E. H. B., & Lemer, J. (2012). Associations between multiple types of stress and disordered eating among girls and boys in middle school. *Journal of Child and Family Studies, 21*, 148–157. doi:10.1007/s10826-011-9458-z

Santos, C. E., & Updegraff, K. A. (2014). Feeling typical, looking typical: Physical appearance and ethnic identity among Mexican-origin youth. *Journal of Latina/o Psychology, 2*(4), 187–199. doi:10.1037/lat0000023

Schaefer, M. K., & Blodgett Salafia, E. H. (2014). The connection of teasing by parents, siblings, and peers with girls' body dissatisfaction and boys' drive for muscularity: The role of social comparison as a mediator. *Eating Behaviors, 15*, 599–608. doi:10.1016/j.eatbeh.2014.08.018

Siegling, A. B., & Delaney, M. A. (2013). Toward understanding body image importance: Individual differences in a Canadian sample of undergraduate students. *Eating Disorders, 21*, 117–129. doi:10.1080/10640266.2013.761083

Toledano, E. (2013). The looking-glass ceiling: Appearance-based discrimination in the workplace. *Cardozo Journal of Law and Gender, 19*, 683–714.

Vuthiarpa, S., Sethabouppha, H., Soivong, P., & Williams, R. (2012). Effectiveness of a school-based cognitive behavioral therapy program for Thai adolescents with depressive symptoms. *Pacific Rim International Journal of Nursing Research, 16*(3), 206–221.

Wilksch, S. M., Paxton, S. J., Byrne, S. M., Austin, S. B., McLean, S. A., Thompson, K. M., . . . & Wade, T. D. (2015). Prevention Across the Spectrum: A randomized controlled trial of three programs to reduce risk factors for both eating disorders and obesity. *Psychological Medicine, 45*(9), 1811–1823. doi:10.1017/S003329171400289X

CHAPTER 12

Men as Allies

Christopher Kilmartin

LEARNING OBJECTIVES

After reading this chapter, you will be able to:

1. Understand the forces that facilitate and inhibit men's participation as social justice allies to women.
2. Appreciate the process of development in the knowledge, skills, and attitudes necessary to be effective male allies.
3. Identify organized male ally efforts.

Members of privileged groups have important roles to play in social justice efforts. Because they have social advantages and greater access to resources, they are in unique positions to address issues in ways that are more difficult for those with disadvantages, as they are somewhat protected from the negative outcomes of doing so. Thus, White people can work to reduce racism, wealthy people economic inequality, heterosexual people homophobia, and so forth. In this chapter, I highlight how the participation of those in privileged groups is essential to the success of social movements.

Note that I use the plural first person "we" in speaking about men because I identify as a man and am perceived as one. I want the reader to understand that I am writing from a particular point of view. It may also be important to recognize some other forms of identity/roles I occupy: I am cisgendered, heterosexual, White (appearing; actually I am part Asian but do not look like it), able-bodied, middle-aged, and a retired psychology professor.

I have been working most of my career to reduce sexism and its most toxic by-product, gender-based violence. This type of work disrupts the narrative of male dominance, so I occasionally receive "hate mail" from (mainly) men who are uncomfortable with what I do or say. Personally, this experience highlights the relative protection of being a man in this social movement because these messages have always taken the form of antifeminine shaming such as the accusation that I am a "male-basher" (when in reality, I have great faith in men and believe that we can do better, as opposed to the real male-bashers who believe that men are simple and aggressive by nature) and antifeminine name-calling such as "mangina." But in contrast to the experience of women who write feminist blogs, nobody has ever threatened to kill or rape me. Thus, my experience has been one of irritation, inconvenience, and sometimes even amusement, in contrast to fearing for my safety.

Men have long been involved as allies to women, albeit in a small minority. In their 1992 book, *Against the Tide: Pro-feminist Men in the United States, 1776–1990*, Michael Kimmel and Thomas Mosmiller chronicle the history of male political allies to women in the efforts to win the right to vote, have legal recourse as survivors of gender-based violence, gain access to higher education, and receive equal pay for equal work. More recently, men have been active in organized efforts as allies especially in addressing the scourge of sexual violence in organizations, such as Men Can Stop Rape, One in Four, and Promundo. There are forces that both facilitate and produce barriers to challenging the status quo of men's dominance, and so those who do so must take advantage of the facilitators and overcome the barriers.

FACILITATING FORCES

Perhaps the most important motivators for men to participate in antisexism efforts are a sense of fairness and an awareness that we have an important role to play that is, at times, different from the roles that women occupy in the movement. Men have an opportunity to influence other men who may be dismissive of women, to model healthier forms of masculinity, and to educate other men. We can use our positions of privilege to create leverage in social systems.

A "tempered radical" is a person who is willing to work from within a given social structure or institution as an organizational catalyst for change (Meyerson & Tompkins, 2007). The radicalism of these individuals arises from their being at odds with the dominant culture of a group (such as a military unit, company, academic department, and so forth) and yet they are dedicated to the success of the group. They engage in divergent thinking because they are not fully embedded in the group culture and thus are able to view it critically. As such, tempered radicals often make others uncomfortable with their willingness to challenge the accepted assumptions of the group. Examples of tempered radicals would include an athlete willing to interrupt stereotypical antifeminine talk in the locker room or a fraternity president willing to bring in an expert on the prevention of gender-based violence and use his position to influence the fraternity members. Tempered radicals are willing to speak up about injustices despite the enormous social pressure to conform. As advocates and examples to others, they promote change. They are willing to seize teachable moments and engage in deeper conversations than more embedded cultural natives (i.e., those who are less aware of alternatives to the values and practices of their organizations; Meyerson & Tompkins, 2007). Because masculinity is culturally defined as antifemininity, which is used to pressure men to conform to disrespectful attitudes about women (Kilmartin & Smiler, 2015), male profeminist allies to women must adopt the tempered radical identity.

Other facilitators to becoming an ally include being asked and being supported for our participation, both by women and other men. Most men are fair-minded; they like women, are friends with women, and are offended by sexism (Kilmartin & Berkowitz, 2005). However, they overestimate other men's sexism (Kilmartin et al., 2008). When progressive men and women let them know that they are not alone in their egalitarian yearnings and invite them to join in antisexism efforts, many men respond in a positive way. Yet this work is difficult and is sometimes met with hostility from retrogressive others (including some women) so it is vital for men to have support systems available to them. Some of these support systems are informal, such as everyday conversations that acknowledge and affirm their work and experiences as allies. Others may be more structured, such as weekly meetings for peer educators in which a facilitator helps them process the events connected with their efforts. For example, in the peer facilitator training for sexual harassment and assault prevention that I led at the U.S. Naval Academy with colleagues Gail Stern and John Foubert, each facilitator was required, as his or her "homework" every evening of the 6-day course, to have a conversation with someone not in the program about his or her work. This assignment served two functions. First, it required facilitators to practice having deeper and more difficult conversations about highly sensitive subjects. Second, we learned, through debriefing sessions, that it allowed for a level of support as the peer facilitators understood that they were together in becoming agents of change. We emphasized that their work was not only important in the programming that they were being trained to deliver, but also in the everyday conversations they would have with their fellow midshipmen (which, somewhat ironically, is still used as a term to describe both male and female academy students).

The Nature of Sexism and the Willingness to Intervene

Sexism is a form of prejudice, and it is important to have a clear understanding of how it works. Many people in dominant groups define prejudice in individualistic terms, as a consciously held attitude (Whitely & Kite, 2009). From this point of view, people believe that they have no work to do as long as they think that people should be treated fairly. However, prejudice cuts deeper than individuals in that it systemically disadvantages subordinate group members and creates an inequality of outcome. For example, 80% of the U.S. Congress and 95% of Fortune 500 chief executive officers (CEOs) are male (Bump, 2015). One who views prejudice in individualistic terms can deny that sexism exists because there are individual women in positions of power (e.g., female legislators and business executives) and men who are disadvantaged (e.g., the more than 2 million incarcerated men in the United States). But dominance and subordination have never applied to all members of groups in equal measure. The effect of sexism is to place women-as-a-group in a state of relative "un-freedom" compared with men-as-a-group (Lerner, 1986), as they have more constraints on their behavior, such as institutional barriers to some areas of employment, a greater likelihood to be sexually harassed in the workplace or in public, and poorer pay than men for equal work. Identifying as a male ally means growing beyond the understanding of sexism as simply what an individual believes about women, to an understanding of how it operates within social systems.

To participate in a social movement, one must believe that the current system is both unfair and unstable, as well as changeable. An understanding of the systemic nature of inequality, combined with a sense of fairness and a belief that we, as men, can do better and make a change in the world, is critical to men's participation as allies.

Diffusion of responsibility is one of the most important social psychological phenomena discovered in the history of the science. We know from both laboratory studies and naturalistic observations that people are less likely to intervene as bystanders when they are in larger groups, and that if they do intervene, it takes longer for them to do so (Latané & Darley, 1968). To take action, one must progress through a series of cognitive steps: (a) notice the event; (b) define it as a problem; (c) take responsibility for intervening; (d) decide on a course of action; and (e) implement the intervention (Latané & Darley, 1968). The third step is inhibited in large groups through diffusion of responsibility. If there are only two people present when a problem arises, theoretically, each has 50% of the responsibility to do something about it. When there are 50 people present, each only shoulders 2% of the responsibility, which is often not enough to motivate the person to undergo the transition from the second step ("*Someone* ought to do something.") to the third step ("*I* need to do something."). However, knowledge about the phenomenon helps one overcome it and take action. If we teach men about how they are affected by diffusion of responsibility, we help put them into a position to progress through the five cognitive steps and take action.

Taking action also requires that the person has confidence that his or her behavior will make a difference. Therefore, training in which men learn the various skills they can use to be effective allies is an essential facilitator. To parallel: An emergency medical technician (EMT) who sees a person clutch his or her chest and fall to the ground can progress through the five cognitive steps in less than a second because he or she has practiced doing so and has developed the skills to help. Likewise, well-trained male allies can become confident in their abilities to make a difference by intervening in dangerous situations such as those in which another man is attempting to take a drunk person to an isolated room or challenging a hateful statement about women by another person.

To practice, they can role-play confronting other men who behave in sexist ways or who are exhibiting behaviors associated with increased risk of committing a sexual assault. Preliminary evidence indicates that engaging in this type of practice may have the result of effecting a measureable decrease in their own sexism (Kilmartin, Semelsberger, Dye, Boggs, & Kolar, 2015). It is well known that people look to their attitudes to shape their behaviors, but what is less obvious is that our attitudes may undergo change from the process of self-observation—an "outside-in" change (Aronson, 2012). If men practice the behavior of being allies, even in an artificial situation like role playing, they may become more sympathetic to the plight of women in the world. For example, a male athlete who is asked by his coach to volunteer to box "care packages" for rape survivors who report to an emergency room (which include, among other things, sweatpants and t-shirts for rape survivors to wear home, as their clothes are taken as evidence) may take steps to increase his own commitment to working as an agent of change. The exception to this process is that participation in the activity cannot be accompanied by a sizeable reward, as then the person would attribute his or her participation to the reward. If in the example the athlete was given $50 to do this work for an hour, it would be unlikely to result in any attitudinal movement.

Men who may be further along in the process of their work can play an important role in developing others through modeling and mentoring. There is a growing critical mass of men who are involved in various ally activities and can inspire younger men who have egalitarian yearnings. Organizations such as Men Can Stop Rape and the international organization Promundo are promoting healthier versions of masculinity and helping men engage in this work. The resources section at the end of this chapter includes more information about these organizations.

Enlightened Self-Interest as an Entry Point to Ally Development

Men's participation as allies does not have to be totally altruistic. They may be motivated to participate if they believe that doing so will result in advantages for them. In fact, men who become allies to women may accrue a variety of benefits such as gaining closer relationships with both men and women, as well as a heightened awareness of self and greater freedom in self-expression. In the occupational world, ally development can also move one forward in his career. For example, a man who participates in a peer education group will develop communication skills that may be useful in his job.

> "I have a zero tolerance on the use of nicknames. It's important to address female co-workers by their chosen name, and zero tolerance on 'ranking.' No conversations about who is hottest, cutest, etc. Maintain respectful boundaries such as business appropriate conversations, no overly friendly greetings such as hugging (which is culturally not accepted here) and no touching. I guess to sum it up, for myself and the people that I work with I expect respect without prejudice."—A male filmmaker in his 50s, China

Men in leadership positions can greatly benefit from understanding how they can establish a climate of respect for women in their organizations and its implications for their work performance, as an organizational climate of respect and inclusion creates the condition for optimal individual and group functioning. I ask business people I train, "How does sexual harassment affect your bottom line?" Their first response is, "There could be a lawsuit." This is certainly the most obvious answer, but lawsuits are relatively rare and represent only the tip of the iceberg. My follow-up questions are: "How many of you have ever had a job that you hated?" Only the lucky few have not. "How did it affect your behavior? Did you not go that 'extra mile'? Did you call in sick when you weren't sick? Did you quit just as soon as you could find another job?" Poor psychological conditions in the workplace cause problems that go well beyond legal action.

Sexual harassment in the workplace has enormous human and financial costs. It is associated with greater use of health insurance and sick leave; lowered morale and productivity; and greater turnover (Willness, Steel, & Lee, 2007). All of these factors decrease profits and result in a toxic environment. When productive female employees leave because they feel unwelcome and the company gets such a reputation, their pool of potential hires shrinks. This is a condition referred to as "talent bleed." Moreover, the negative atmosphere created by sexual harassment does not only affect the person who is victimized; it also affects those who witness the harassment. As I often tell corporate audiences, sensitivity is good business. It is not something you do only because you are a fair-minded person. It is inextricably interwoven with your performance as a manager in a mixed-sex environment, which characterizes virtually every workplace. Learning to be an effective ally to women and set a climate of inclusion is critical to organizational and leadership goals.

In the military, the goal is to accomplish whatever mission to which the unit is assigned. Doing so requires team members to work together in an atmosphere of shared purpose. Mission readiness is severely compromised by having team members disrespected, or especially, traumatized. The scourges of sexual assault and sexual harassment of soldiers by other soldiers therefore creates a serious problem. Sadler, Booth, Cook, and Doebbeling (2003) found that in units where a military commander participates in and/or condones a hostile work environment, women are at a 600% increased risk for sexual assault. And since most of these commanders are men, being an effective ally to women is crucial to their performance as a military officer and the success of their unit.

Military leaders are often trained to avoid the "slippery slope" of lax order and discipline. For instance, allowing minor uniform violations may lead to more serious infractions. Women in the service tell stories of how their underwear is stolen when they send it to the military laundry facility, how their pictures are removed from the wall or defaced, and how they are subject to routine instances of sexism. A commander who allows these behaviors to take place without investigating and holding offenders accountable condones the hostile environment and contributes to poor morale and unit cohesion.

All of this work hinges critically on an understanding of one's masculine socialization and cultural conformity pressure. Men Can Stop Rape has instituted "Men of Strength" clubs, an after-school program for high school boys in which they discuss with one another what it means to be a man in the modern world. Thus, they provide a unique space to talk with boys in radically different ways such as describing how they are emotionally affected by their relationships with one another, girls, and their parents, and to undercut the myths that males are unfeeling, simple creatures who only care about sports and sex. They help them understand that men are complex and dignified beings who are capable of working for social change. Many believe that high school boys would not be interested in such conversations, but that is anything but the case. In every school where they have instituted the program, they have a waiting list of interested boys (P. Lemmon, personal communication, May 15, 2007). It is obvious that men and boys are hungry to learn about this very important essence known as masculinity. If we provide a space where they are comfortable in learning about it, the response can be transformative.

Barriers

If there were no barriers to men's participation, the majority of us would be allies. So any analysis to male ally development must include an investigation into what keeps men away from this work. Unfortunately, many of these obstacles are significant.

Perhaps the most overarching barrier is the social construction of masculinity as antifemininity. Boys are often socialized to believe that the worst thing they can possibly do is to run, look, throw, or act like a girl. So they learn to watch what girls and women do and avoid those behaviors. Due to the fact that we live in a male-dominated culture, femininity is often defined as being less valued than masculinity and boys and men can learn that they lose social status by aligning themselves with girls and women.

Linguistic structures reflect and reinforce this social construction. Male and female are often referred to as the opposite sexes despite the fact that the sexes are not opposites. I often challenge students and audiences to tell me a way in which the sexes are opposite. The response is either that they draw a blank or say that male and female genitalia are opposite. But then I say, "Would you consider a nut to be the opposite of a bolt or a sleeve to be the opposite of an arm?" Another apt analogy references a comparison of PC and Mac computers. They are somewhat different, but also do a lot of the same things. Nobody would answer the question, "Do you have a Mac?" with "No, I have the opposite computer." In actuality, as neuroscientist Lise Eliot (2009) points out, the Y chromosome is by far the smallest of the 46 chromosomes, containing only about 60 genes of the more than 25,000 in the total human genome. Therefore, men and women share 99.8% of our genetic material.

The use of the term "battle of the sexes" is even more problematic than the "opposite sex," as it pits men and women against one another even more explicitly. This is the most curious battle in the history of humankind, in which 90% of the combatants are supposedly in love with and having children with the enemy. Moreover, many people feel quite comfortable reinforcing these sexist beliefs. For instance, there is a board game called "Battle of the Sexes." Few people would consider a board game entitled "Battle of the Races" or "Jews vs. Christians" to be acceptable. Sexism is often seen as an appropriate social activity.

Men who uncritically accept these ideologies are prone to adopt adversarial sexual beliefs in which they see men and women in competition, and zero-sum sexual beliefs, in which they view women's progress as hurting men. In fact, in the extreme, both of these ideologies are associated with the risk of committing gender-based violence and are at the base of the considerable hostility directed toward feminist women. An extreme example of this antifeminine aggression can be seen in "men's rights activists" who propose that women routinely lie about being sexually assaulted when in actuality false accusations are quite rare, probably close to 2% and certainly no higher than 8% of reports (Lisak, Gardenier, Niksa, & Cote, 2010), and promote retrogressive gender relations emphasizing men's dominance. The group "Return of Kings" even directly advocates for men raping women.

The mantra of many of my presentations is that it is very difficult to resist a pressure that one cannot name. Because many men do not learn about masculinity or male privilege, they have difficulty in resisting this social pressure. This is true even when masculine conformity creates conflicts with an individual's important life goals, such as achieving intimacy in relationships; when conformity hurts another person, such as engaging in physical aggression to demonstrate one's masculinity; or when it can affect one's own health, such as when men refuse to seek medical or psychological services because they consider it unmanly to ask for help. When we help men understand how masculinity or privilege operate, we free them for the next steps in becoming allies: first, deciding if they are motivated to put forth the effort to challenge hegemonic masculinity, and second, to undertake the process of learning how to do so.

Most men who behave in sexist ways do so to win the approval of other men, and many men who hold more favorable views of women do not challenge other men's sexism because they fear their disapproval. At the interpersonal level, sexism will not stop until men lose social status with their peers for engaging in it. At the societal level, it will not stop until the social-structural inequalities between men-as-a-group and women-as-a-group are eradicated through women's full participation in economies and governments.

Men's fears of other men's disapproval are based in distorted social norm beliefs. When men make sexist jokes or refer to women by animal names or the names of their genitals, most men are offended (Berkowitz, 1994). But they tend to overestimate other men's acceptance of these attitudes (Kilmartin et al., 2008). The analogy is laughing at a joke that you do not think is funny. If others observe your laughing at the joke, they would think that you found it to be funny because you did not let them in on your private reaction. Men routinely are bothered by other men's sexism but believe that they are unusual in this reaction because they are comparing their inner experience with other men's appearances. The men who are behaving badly believe that their attitudes are normative when in fact they are not. This is a phenomenon known as false consensus. Men who are offended by sexism believe that they are in the minority when in fact they are not. This is another phenomenon known as pluralistic ignorance. For example, a man suggests that a bachelor party include an outing to a strip club. The four men who want to go think they are in the majority (false consensus), whereas the eight who do not believe that they are in the minority (pluralistic ignorance).

Social psychologists have long known that the appearance of unanimity is a strong barrier to intervention. When the group opinion appears to be held by everyone except the person who is privately in the minority, conformity is commonplace unless the person with the minority opinion has very high status in the group. However, when even one person in the group voices a minority opinion, conformity drops sharply (Asch, 1965). In other words, there is a meaningful difference between being one voice against nine and being two voices against eight. Therefore, one ally who speaks up against sexism can embolden other like-minded men to stand with him. Later in this chapter, I provide examples of how this process can work to overcome this considerable barrier.

Amplifying Facilitators and Overcoming Barriers

To develop men as allies, it is necessary to create the conditions for transformation. Men who are potential participants will have to learn about the issues. They must also become aware of their socialization to eschew the feminine and dominate women as well as the social pressures of the moment that may inhibit them from taking action. Then they need help to acquire the abilities to be effective. The processes include education, introspection, attitude change, support, and skill development.

> "Sexism is seductive. Men are constantly invited into forms of domination over women. Either we resist because we live habitually gender-just lives in which we see such behaviors as unthinkable or even incomprehensible, or we resist because we recognize that here is a moment when we can choose sexist inequality or justice, and we choose justice."—A male activist and professor, Australia

Since most males grow up in societies that are prejudiced against women, it is necessary to engage them in the awareness of and reduction of that prejudice. There are several processes that are known to contribute to bias reduction. First is the attainment of a critical mass in the subordinated group. Even if there is an imbalance of power in the social setting, when the less powerful group reaches a point where they are 25% to 30% of the total population, they can bring enough pressure to bear on the dominant group to begin to effect change (Langelan, 1993). For example, a business executive notices that female employees are much more likely to resign or request transfers when they work for a certain male manager. The executive also notices the negative effect of staff instability on the unit's performance and either removes the manager or allows him to undergo a process to correct his behavior. Perhaps the executive then decides to hire diversity and inclusion consultants to train all managers. In this case, even if there is no official complaint of this manager's treatment of women, the critical mass of women in the unit has had an effect.

Fortunately, the development of critical masses of women in many settings is inevitable in the long run. Most U.S. corporations already have achieved it, and in many militaries throughout the world, a critical mass of women has either been achieved or is slowly getting closer. Women are 57% of college students in the United States and are now a majority of graduate medical students (Kilmartin & Smiler, 2015). When critical mass is reached, people in the dominant group are more likely to respond to minority group members as individuals rather than representatives of their group. However, some groups remain largely segregated, such as fraternities, athletic teams, and some military units, and these homosocial enclaves require special attention in sexism reduction efforts.

It is important to think about gender, as well as other forms of identity, in both the processes of continuity (ongoing disadvantages for women) and change (progress in the struggle for equality). For example, the U.S. Congress that took its seats in 2015 was 80% male, 80% White, and 92% Christian. It was the most diverse Congress in the history of the United States (Bump, 2015). Thus, there is continuity in that many groups are underrepresented, and there is also change in that progress (albeit in slow increments) is ongoing in the increase in the ratio of underrepresented groups.

Dovetailing on critical mass theory is reliable evidence that prejudice is reduced through meaningful, pleasant, cooperative, interdependent, and equal status contact with other groups. Eliot Aronson (2012) and colleagues demonstrated this phenomenon through the "jigsaw classroom" technique in elementary schools whereby children did work in heterogeneous groups, learning lessons together and depending on others for their scholastic performance. This technique resulted in fewer instances of conflict among racial groups. In contrast, the failed school busing social experiment of the 1960s resulted in greater levels of racial prejudice and conflict because contact is a necessary, but not sufficient, process for change. Because students from different backgrounds were merely thrown together without any superordinate goals, they were able to segregate and failed to develop relationships with one another.

This prejudice reduction process occurs when men and women must work together in concert for mutually shared purposes (Brewer & Brown, 1998). The vast majority of colleges and universities are mixed-sex environments where men and women work together, thus creating the necessary interdependence. This interdependence is often found in corporate cultures as well. Theoretically, any time one can develop a situation in which men and women rely on one another to get the job done, there will be a reduction in sexism, especially if it is accompanied by gender education.

I witnessed the processes of interdependence and dominance simultaneously in my year as visiting professor at the U.S. Air Force Academy in 2013–2014. As with all of the service academies, the summer before the fall semester of the first year for cadets involves several weeks of military basic training. I arrived in July and observed this process. Small groups of cadets, none of which were all male despite men being 78% of the academy population, worked together to complete challenging obstacle courses. On the positive side, men and women were interdependent in that the performance of the squad depended on all its members because they had to help one another on group tasks, such as helping other squad members to scale walls. On the other hand, those who were tall and those with better upper body strength were at a significant advantage because of the design of the course, and thus men, both because of their predominance within the population and their physical advantage (on average), tended to assume the leadership positions within the groups. In the classroom, I saw numerous examples of men and women in effective working groups, which also facilitated the development of nonsexual cross-sex friendships.

These social/structural factors in prejudice reduction such as increased critical mass of women and the integration of the sexes in cooperative and equal status tasks mean that there will be, and is, an inevitable reduction of sexism as time goes on, especially in postmodern economies where the gendered division of labor is increasingly a nondivision of labor. There is virtually no work that men can do that women cannot do. Most couples need two full-time incomes and have access to reproductive technologies that allow for control of the size and timing of families. Women and men are increasingly finding themselves cooperating in both domestic and paid labor and so stereotypes are slowly breaking down. I am not so naive to believe that sexism will be over in my lifetime or even that of my students (after all, it took us 6,000 years to get here). I do think that even though resistance and setbacks always accompany change, we are headed in the right direction.

Many college men whom I encounter seem to believe that they will be able to use their fathers' and grandfathers' formulas to get along in the world, but, especially in modern economies, it is not their fathers' or their grandfathers' worlds. They also tend to believe that they will get along by treating women as objects and refusing to do "women's work," which could result in their being left behind in modern cultures (which is why I call masculinity education my "no man left behind" program). For instance, men in leadership positions in mixed-sex groups compromise the groups' effectiveness by not encouraging a culture of acceptance and inclusion, and as a result they may not advance in their careers. Military groups are less "mission ready" and the leaders of those units are seen as less fit for promotion than the leaders of better functioning groups. Men who see their parental roles as limited to those of provider and disciplinarian may pay a price in emotional distance from their children. Those who suppress vulnerable emotions over time lose their abilities to experience a high level of positive emotions. Men who refuse to ask for help suffer in silence, with negative effects on their physical and emotional health.

Everyday Allies

"Everyday allies" are men who practice supportive behaviors whenever they encounter the opportunity. One of the most important of these behaviors is to challenge men who behave in sexist ways. Those who tell derogatory jokes about women or refer to them by animal names or the names of their genitals expect that other men will go along with the joke and give them other forms of social approval. They are often surprised when they lose social status for engaging in disrespect toward women when allies criticize their sexist behavior or distance themselves interpersonally. I always tell men that there is no need to "get out your flip chart" and do a 30-minute lecture. Sometimes a few words indicating one's disapproval can be very powerful.

> "One of my greatest accomplishments is having learned to intervene successfully in situations where another person or group is being demeaned or discriminated against and to teach others to do the same. I find that it is only a first step to be aware of my dominant identities and privileges. The next step is to be an active, engaged ally who is working to end them."—A male consultant, educator, and trainer in his 60s

A middle-aged man named Dave related one illustration of this process to me. When he was in college, he and two friends went to a restaurant for lunch.

A young woman came in, and Dave and one of his friends began to make loud comments about her attractiveness. She looked over at them at one point, and Dave explained to me that, in retrospect, he realized that she appeared uncomfortable. After several comments, the third friend, who had been silent up until this point, turned to Dave and their other friend and simply said, "Shut up." Dave was overcome with a sense of shame and spent a good deal of time soul searching in the aftermath of that incident. Now in his mid-40s, Dave told me that his friend's lesson has stayed with him his entire life, and he never again harassed a woman in public. Two simple words changed him forever.

Aspiring allies need to know that rarely are the men whom they challenge going to respond with heartfelt thanks for the enlightenment. Although Dave later thanked his friend, that event is probably more the exception than the rule. Men who challenge other men's sexism may not be able to tell whether they are being influential. Therefore, they engage in the behaviors as a leap of faith, planting seeds that they may never see grow.

In the 1990s, I brought Canada's White Ribbon campaign to my campus and helped other universities adopt it as well. This weeklong event, begun on the first anniversary of the "Montreal Massacre" (a gender-based crime that resulted in the deaths of 14 women), is an effort to get men involved in working to end violence against women. During our local campaign, an editorial appeared in the campus newspaper criticizing it as nothing more than an effort to "get in good with women so they will sleep with you." The editor conveniently ignored that an essential part of the campaign was to raise money for organizations that deal directly with gender-based violence, which is a very tangible contribution. I sent a letter in response (to which the editor reacted), and we had a very public exchange in the newspaper for several weeks. At that time, I thought the debate was "more heat than light," that the dialogue was little more than an angry exchange that did little to influence him or the readers. However, he e-mailed me several years later to apologize for his disrespect and to thank me for helping him see the value of these efforts, despite the fact that it took him several years to "get it."

He was kind enough to let me know that I had helped, but again, this gratitude is not often forthcoming. Men need to engage in these behaviors, which often result in unpleasant exchanges, simply because it is the right thing to do. We cannot wait until we are comfortable with confronting other men's sexism. We must learn to do it despite our discomfort, and over time, we will gain confidence in our ability and thus become more comfortable and skilled. We invest time and effort in learning a skill when we value the outcome, and many men are committed to this work because they understand its importance.

Specifically, there are some everyday ally phrases that men can use to challenge other men. Oftentimes, men will make sexist comments in a very off-the-cuff fashion, and it can be remarkably effective to just ask the person to repeat the comment: "I'm sorry. What did you say?" At that point, he is forced to reflect on his actions and even if he repeats the phrase, he may experience some degree of remorse. Other possibilities include, "Wow. I didn't know anybody thought that anymore" or "I think you might be making her uncomfortable," or simply, "Stop harassing women."

Langelan (1993, p. 336) produces a pad of paper and says: "That's very interesting. You have just harassed a woman . . . [I am] conducting a research project on sexual harassment, and I want to include you in the survey. I want to take just a few minutes to ask you a few questions. This is important research." She then goes on to ask questions such as, "How do you feel when you say or do this kind of thing?," "In general, why would you say you do this?," "Do you do this to all women or do you pick out certain kinds?," and "Are there any types of women that you never harass? Who?" Some harassers will actually stand there and be interviewed and they are no doubt changed by the process in that they are forced to reflect on their practices rather than merely enacting them without consequence or accountability.

The way in which an ally engages in this disruption of sexism depends largely on his individual style. Most of us have been in situations where we were so surprised at an offensive behavior that we were unable to respond in the moment. Then, later we think "I wish I would have said . . . [some great phrase that was thought of later]." When this happens, I always advise people to take that phrase and "put it in your pocket" so you are ready to use it.

Men in leadership positions are in an especially good position to be influential allies. In 2013, an Air Force base in England featured a stand-up comedy show to entertain the troops. In the course of the performance, one of the comedians told rape jokes. The General in charge of the base was offended and walked out. It did not take him long to realize that he could have done more, and so the following morning he sent an e-mail to all troops apologizing for failing them as a leader. He had the authority to shut down the show and should have done so. Unfortunately, he was unable to process the situation and act at the time. He did do the next best thing though and seized a teachable moment to let his charges know that he was serious about condemning these kinds of actions.

"Many men come into this field wanting to be a knight in shining armor fighting for the cause of women's empowerment. While there is a time and a place for heroics—probably in ways that you never imagined—often the best thing you can do to help women is to sit down, shut up and listen to what they have to say without interrupting."—A male international project officer in his 30s, Switzerland

"I believe that it is important for allies to criticize themselves constantly, listen to and remain humble about feedback from the disadvantaged, and use their privilege to achieve gender equity. Being an ally can be difficult, but it is essential to realizing equality."—A male specialist in programming for men, USA

Once men decide that they would like to work on developing as allies, they need strategies for undertaking this process. Following are several suggestions:

• Listen to women's voices. Reflect on what it is like to be a woman in a sexist society. Read important feminist works. Perhaps even take a women's studies course.

- Learn about your own socialization as a man and how it involved antifemininity and privilege.

- Accept constructive feedback about their work nondefensively. For example, they may exhibit protective attitudes toward women or fail to reflect on their male privilege. Good intentions do less to translate into progress when people are defensive about their behaviors.

- Resist the impulse to respond with, "Men have it hard too." We do, but you are changing the subject.

- Engage in "snowballing." Talk to like-minded others and build a critical mass of peers who are willing to engage in organized action.

- Take sexism as seriously as racism, religious intolerance, or any other form of prejudice.

- Work toward understanding the distinction between mere chivalry and true respect. Chivalry involves following rules such as opening doors for women and refraining from coarse language in their presence. These behaviors are trivial and are based on the mistaken assumption that all women are alike and all want the same things. Respect involves listening to a person, developing a relationship, and taking the person's needs and desires into account. It requires considerably more effort than opening a door for someone.

- Understand how microaggressions, such as calling adult women "girls," telling someone that they are being oversensitive, or sexualizing women's bodies, have a cumulative negative effect on women's lives.

There are many more suggestions online in an article entitled "Everyday Ways for Men to Be Allies to Women" (Binning, 2013).

ORGANIZED EFFORTS

After engaging in some of the everyday ally development I described, men are in a position to take a larger role in changing the world through engaging in many of the organized efforts for gendered social equality. To describe all of them is beyond the scope of this chapter but a few are as follows:

- Men Can Stop Rape is a nonprofit agency based in Washington, DC. It provides campus and military presentations on the prevention of sexual violence; provides technical assistance; and recently published a document on best practices in engaging men on campus (Men Can Stop Rape, 2016). Its Men of Strength clubs are after-school programs in which high school boys can explore what it means to be a man in the modern world.

- Promundo is an international organization based in Brazil. Noting that gender-based violence is negatively correlated with men's family involvement across cultures (Coltrane, 1998), Promundo leads international efforts to strengthen men's ties with their families and communities (such as the African Fathers Initiative). It also provides technical assistance and research, in addition to collaborating with organizations with similar missions (International Center for Research on Women and Promundo, Heilman, Hebert, & Paul-Gera, 2014).

Similarly, the Pixel Project is an international effort focused on reducing gender-based violence by encouraging fathers to connect with their children and with one another.

- Mentors in Violence Prevention (MVP) is a U.S.-based organization that provides a "playbook" of scenarios for discussions of gender-based violence with athletes and military. It also provides train-the-trainers events and organizes a network of local chapters.

- The Men's Program is a sexual assault prevention, peer education presentation, which has an evidence base for its effectiveness, as does its risk reduction counterpart, the Women's Program (Foubert, 2011).

- Democratic Control of the Armed Forces (DCAF) is an international organization based in Geneva, Switzerland. Among other efforts, it organized a handbook on teaching gender in the military in the service of promoting equal rights for women internationally, aiding in recruitment and retention of women in the armed services, and promoting the operational capability of military units through inclusive climates (Balon et al., 2016).

- A Call to Men is a New York-based organization seeking to empower young men to redefine masculinity and develop as allies. It provides inspirational lectures, trainings for young men, coaches, and community organizers, and a curriculum for helping middle school and high school boys to examine their attitudes toward masculinity.

I have often said that sending people out into the world without gender awareness is like sending them out without computer skills, as the changing landscape of the world means that both will only become more important as time goes on. As the social and physical separation of the sexes slowly breaks down in postindustrial economies, gender is, and will continue to become, less of an organizing principle both in paid labor and domestic work. Women and men will have more in common than ever. Therefore, men who ally themselves with women and act as agents of change will find themselves "ahead of the curve" and, although they will experience resistance to evolving gender relations, they will reap the benefits of the transformation and progress in virtually all aspects of their lives.

CALL TO ACTION

Join a men's advocacy group in your community. If you cannot find one, begin the process of organizing one by setting specific goals and recruiting interested men. A good technique is to "snowball." Approach men who seem like they might be interested and if they are, ask them if there are other men they know who might also want to join in the effort. Sometimes it is also helpful to ask community leaders to identify men whom they think would be interested and send formal requests to them. For example, on a college campus, you could ask faculty, especially those who teach in gender studies, to suggest male faculty, staff, and students who could participate.

(continued)

CALL TO ACTION (*continued*)

It is important to think developmentally. These kinds of efforts evolve over time. For example, the U.S. Naval Academy Sexual Harassment and Assault Prevention Education (SHAPE) program began as a lecture and performance series in which experts visited the campus a few times throughout the year. From there, funds were accessed to bring in a team of consultants to write curriculum and train peer educators. Then, staff members were hired to run the program, which was financed by operating funds rather than special grants. Thus, a program that began as a series of one-shot presentations became institutionalized, and now all students receive 20 hours of training during their 4 years at the Academy. On my last visit there in 2016, the program coordinators said that SHAPE now "runs itself."

REFLECTION AND DISCUSSION QUESTIONS

Men:
1. Are there times when you act as an ally? What is happening at those times that encourages you to be an ally?
2. How do you act as an ally? In what situations are you most and least likely to act?
3. What rewards do you receive for doing it? What barriers prevent you from doing it?
4. What would help free you to do it more often?

Women:
1. What kinds of behaviors/activities of men would you like to see change?
2. What kinds of behaviors of men would you find helpful in your daily life?

HELPFUL RESOURCES

- A Call to Men (www.acalltomen.org)—Promoting healthy, nonviolent masculinity with a focus on young men and boys
- Men Can Stop Rape (www.mencanstoprape.org)—A U.S.-based education and advocacy organization focused on the prevention of sexual violence
- National Organization for Men Against Sexism (www.nomas.org)—The oldest organized men's profeminist group
- One in Four—U.S.-founded organization that has spread to other parts of the world. Countries maintain separate websites

- Promundo Global (www.promundoglobal.org)—An international organization promoting gender-based violence prevention through education and local community programming
- White Ribbon (www.whiteribbon.ca)—Canadian-based organization of men working to end men's violence against women

REFERENCES

Aronson, E. (2012). *The social animal* (11th ed.). New York, NY: Worth.

Asch, S. E. (1965). Effects of group pressure upon the modification and distortion of judgments. In H. Proshansky & B. Seidenberg (Eds.), *Basic studies in social psychology*. New York, NY: Holt, Rinehart, and Winston.

Balon, B., Björsson, A., Geiss, T., Holvikivi, A., Kadar, A., Lysychkina, I., & Watson, C. (Eds.). (2016). *Teaching gender in the military: A handbook*. Geneva, Switzerland: DCAF and PfPC.

Berkowitz, A. D. (1994). *Men and rape: Theory, research, and prevention programs in higher education*. San Francisco, CA: Jossey-Bass.

Brewer, M. B., & Brown, R. J. (1998). Intergroup relations. In D. T. Gilbert, S. T. Fiske, & G. Lindzey (Eds.), *The handbook of social psychology* (Vols. 1 and 2, 4th ed., pp. 554–594). New York, NY: McGraw-Hill.

Binning, M. A. (2013). 101 everyday ways for men to be allies to women. Retrieved from https://www.facebook.com/notes/margaret-a-binning/101-everyday-ways-for-men-to-be-allies-to-women/681659385195553

Bump, P. (2015, January 5). The new congress is 80 percent white, 80 percent male, and 92 percent Christian. Retrieved from https://www.washingtonpost.com/news/the-fix/wp/2015/01/05/the-new-congress-is-80-percent-white-80-percent-male-and-92-percent-christian

Coltrane, S. (1998). Theorizing masculinities in contemporary social science. In D. L. Anselmi & A. L. Law (Eds.), *Questions of gender: Perspectives and paradoxes* (pp. 76–88). Boston, MA: McGraw-Hill.

Eliot, L. (2009). *Pink brain, blue brain: How small differences grow into troublesome gaps and what we can do about it*. New York, NY: Houghton Mifflin Harcourt.

Foubert, J. D. (2011). *The men's and women's programs: Ending rape through peer education*. New York, NY: Routledge.

Heilman, B., Hebert, L., & Paul-Gera, N. (2014). *The making of sexual violence: How does a boy grow up to commit rape? Evidence from five IMAGES countries*. Washington, DC: International Center for Research on Women and Promundo.

Kilmartin, C. T., & Berkowitz, A. D. (2005). *Sexual assault in context: Teaching college men about gender*. Mahwah, NJ: Lawrence Erlbaum.

Kilmartin, C. T., Semelsberger, R., Dye, S., Boggs, E., & Kolar, D. W. (2015). A behavior intervention to reduce sexism in college men. *Gender Issues, 32*, 97–110.

Kilmartin, C., & Smiler, A. P. (2015). *The masculine self* (5th ed.). Cornwall-on-Hudson, NY: Sloan.

Kilmartin, C., Smith, T., Green, A., Kuchler, M., Heinzen, H., & Kolar, D. (2008). A real time social norms intervention to reduce male sexism. *Sex Roles: A Journal of Research, 59*, 264–273.

Kimmel, M. S., & Mosmiller, T. E. (1992). *Against the tide: Pro-feminist men in the United States, 1776–1990*. Boston, MA: Beacon.

Langelan, M. J. (1993). *Back off! How to confront and stop sexual harassment and harassers*. New York, NY: Simon and Schuster.

Latané, B., & Darley, J. M. (1968). Group inhibition of bystander intervention in emergencies. *Journal of Personality and Social Psychology, 10*(3), 215–221. doi:10.1037/h0026570

Lerner, G. (1986). *The creation of patriarchy*. New York, NY: Oxford University Press.

Lisak, D., Gardenier, L., Niksa, S. C., & Cote, A. M. (2010). False allegations of sexual assault: An analysis of ten years of reported cases. *Violence Against Women, 16*, 1318–1334.

Men Can Stop Rape. (2016). *Current practices and challenges with engaging men on campus*. Washington, DC: The Department of Justice Office on Violence Against Women.

Meyerson, D., & Tompkins, M. (2007). Tempered radicals as institutional change agents: The case of advancing gender equity at the University of Michigan. *Harvard Journal of Law and Gender, 30*(2), 303–322.

Sadler, A. G., Booth, B. M., Cook, B. L., & Doebbeling, B. N. (2003). Factors associated with women's risk of rape in the military environment. *American Journal of Industrial Medicine, 43*, 262–273.

Whitely, B. E., Jr., & Kite, M. E. (2009). *The psychology of prejudice and discrimination*. Belmont, CA: Wadsworth/Cengage.

Willness, C. R., Steel, P., & Lee, K. (2007). A meta-analysis of the antecedents and consequences of workplace sexual harassment. *Personnel Psychology, 60*(1), 127–162. doi: 10.1111/j.1744-6570.2007.00067.x

Index

CPSIA information can be obtained
at www.ICGtesting.com
Printed in the USA
BVHW020028300623
666605BV00003B/15

9 780826 129161